Arthur Thurlow Cunynghame

My Command in South Africa, 1874-1878

Comprising Experiences of Travel in the Colonies of South Africa and the

Independent States

Arthur Thurlow Cunynghame

My Command in South Africa, 1874-1878

Comprising Experiences of Travel in the Colonies of South Africa and the Independent States

ISBN/EAN: 9783744756075

Printed in Europe, USA, Canada, Australia, Japan

Cover: Foto ©Andreas Hilbeck / pixelio.de

More available books at **www.hansebooks.com**

MY COMMAND

IN

SOUTH AFRICA.

1874–1878.

COMPRISING

EXPERIENCES OF TRAVEL
IN THE COLONIES OF SOUTH AFRICA AND THE
INDEPENDENT STATES.

BY

GENERAL SIR ARTHUR THURLOW CUNYNGHAME, G.C.B.

THEN LIEUTENANT GOVERNOR AND COMMANDER OF THE
FORCES IN SOUTH AFRICA.

WITH MAPS.

SECOND EDITION, WITH A NEW PREFACE.

London:
MACMILLAN AND CO.
1880.

[Right of Translation and Reproduction reserved.]

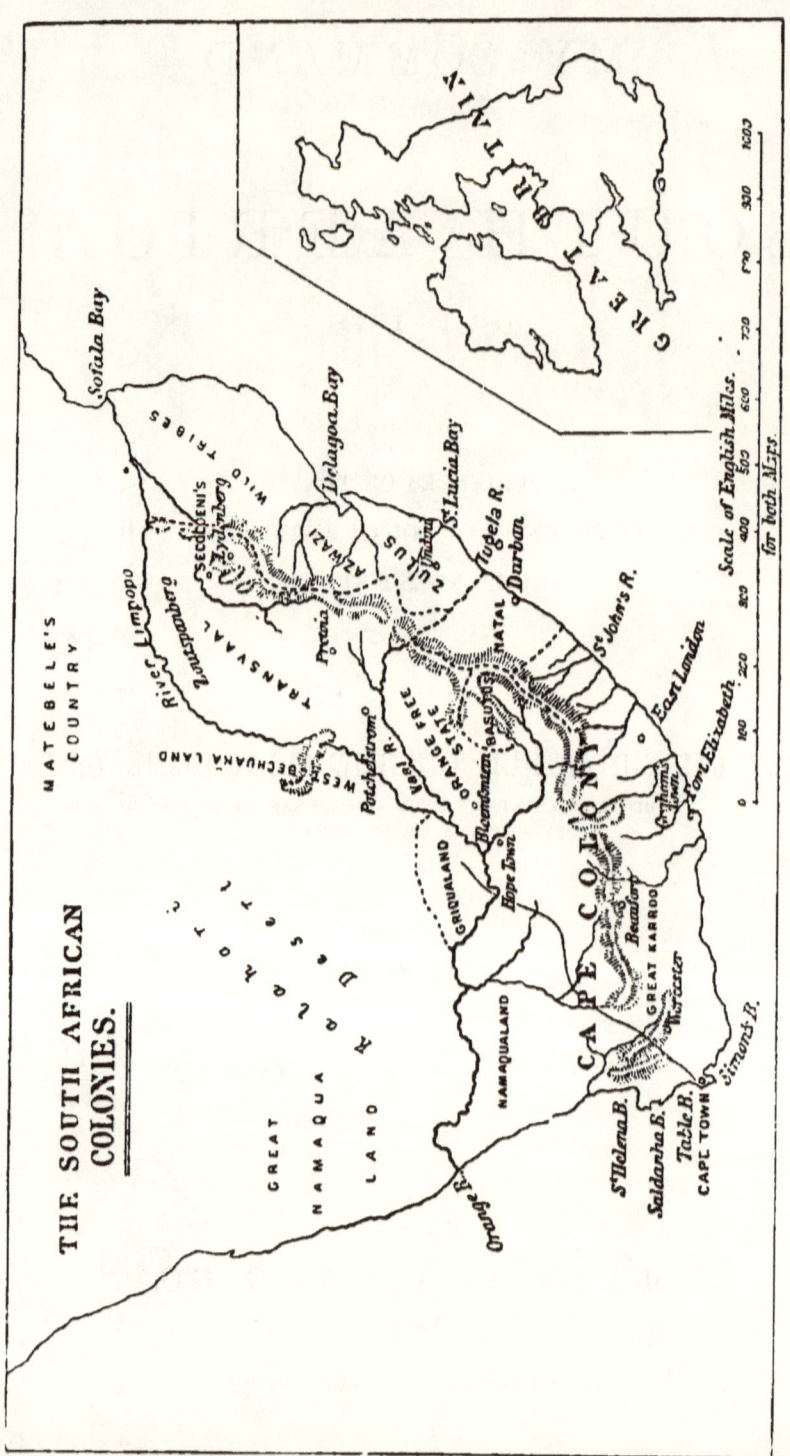

PREFACE

TO THE SECOND EDITION.

THE noble efforts to found colonies which have been made by England have been rewarded by results unequalled either in ancient or modern times. Many problems have yet to be solved. One of the most important of these is, how to preserve the independence of the colonies without causing them to lose their filial affection for their mother country.

Some of the difficulties of this problem will be illustrated in the following pages. They contain descriptions of the country and anecdotes of its inhabitants. The Book is divided into five parts. Chapters I. to XI. contain an account of a journey from Cape Town to the Eastern Frontier, the Free States, and Basuto land. Chapters XII. to XVIII. describe my visit to Pondo land and Natal. In Chapters XIX. to XXII. I give an account of the threatened rebellion in the Diamond Fields, and the expedition sent to check it. Chapters XXIII. to XXX. deal with the annexation of the Transvaal; and Chapters XXXI. to XLI. are devoted to a description of the war on the eastern frontier of the Cape Colony. In these pages I shall often have the pleasure of praising the conduct of my own officers and others; sometimes I shall be obliged to speak severely of men from whose policy I differed, but I am sure that I have not put down anything in malice, and I take this opportunity of thanking those of my friends in South Africa whose kindness so greatly contributed to the pleasure of my stay.

By far the greater part of the information in this volume is derived from personal observation, but many interesting facts have been gathered from articles written in the colonial newspapers by gentlemen of knowledge and ability, to whom, as a body, I wish to acknowledge my gratitude for their valuable assistance.

The colonies of South Africa, taken all together, are in area about 450,000 square miles, or equal in size to United Germany, France, Belgium, and Holland; and nearly five times as large as Great Britain. The total population is rather more than two and a half millions, of which about 440,000 persons are white.

There are only five principal ports in South Africa; Cape Town, Port Elizabeth, East London, Durban, and Delagoa Bay. With the exception of the last named, none of them possess very great natural advantages, and some are mere roadsteads. The coast is rocky. The rivers run between high banks, and are torrents in winter, and streams in summer. The coldest time of the year is in our summer, but the climate is delightful, and excellent for pulmonary complaints. The country is very varied, containing mountain chains, deserts, scanty forests, and boundless plains, once swarming with game, which have been destroyed in enormous quantities. Copper, coal, gold and diamonds form the chief mineral wealth of the country, but almost every species of metal exists. The chief pursuit is cattle-grazing, and the chief export is wool. Fruit-trees grow well all over the colony, and naartjes (Tangerine oranges) cost, in the season, a penny for twelve. In Natal, pine-apples grow by the wayside. The vine, apricot, apple, pear, loquot, and cherry, all thrive there. Fish are plentiful, and you can live well on that food for 6d. a-day; but they are not of so good a kind as those in the northern seas. Housekeeping at Cape Town costs on the average much the same as in England. While fruit and fish are cheap, and meat not so dear as at home, butter is very expensive. European luxuries cost about one-fourth more than at home, and clothes perhaps one and a half times the price here. This is due to the difficulty of finding good workmen in Cape Town to cut them out and make them.

Repairs of all sorts are very expensive, particularly if they require any degree of skill. The arts do not flourish at the Cape. You might try every shop in Capetown and not be able to buy an oil canvas or colours, but music is cultivated, and many pianos come over from England. Reading is practised to a limited extent only, and even the barristers, whom one would expect to find provided with good libraries, seem to rely in argument rather upon readiness and elocution than upon an extensive reference to authorities. The chief amusements of all classes are riding, driving, shooting, and billiards; and unfortunately there is too great a tendency on all sides, from the highest to the lowest, to "take a glass with a friend" at all hours of the day, a practice which, to say the least of it, involves a considerable waste of time and money. Life proceeds at the colony at rather a slower pace than in England—there is more breathing-time, and the happy faces and jovial manners of the inhabitants suggest the idea of a people accustomed to a rude plenty, and not harassed to death by constant worries.

Trade morality, I fear, does not rise to a very high level at the Cape. I dare say it is not worse than in other lands, and, being a soldier, I am not, perhaps, very well qualified to express an opinion. I can only go by what I have heard, but I certainly recommend any young gentleman who lands in Cape Town with money in his pocket to look well to the bargains he makes, and, above all, to be careful of the speculations in which he embarks.

I now propose to give a short sketch of the history of the various colonies in South Africa.

1. THE CAPE COLONY.—Area, 220,000 square miles; population, 235,000 white, 820,000 black.

This colony was first formed by the Dutch as an invalid station for persons on their way to India. The Dutch garrison was small, and when the first importation of slaves took place from the Guinea coast, they outnumbered the whites. In its early days the colony never flourished very brilliantly. Its first encounter with savages was with the Hottentots. These people and the Bushmen may be looked upon as the aborigines of South Africa. An earlier race is believed to have preceded them, so barbarous in character as almost to furnish an example of the "missing link" between man and the ape. The Hottentots are a yellowish-coloured African race, not of a very warlike disposition, and capable of being civilised. They are, however, now so mixed with Kafirs and other races, that it is doubtful whether any men of pure blood remain. The Bushmen are diminutive savages, who present an example of the lowest known form of human life. Almost impossible to tame, active as animals, and quick-sighted as birds, they seem incapable of understanding what it is to live in peace with their neighbours. When hunted in their rocks they retire, and never surrendering, fire poisoned arrows at the invaders. They do not seem to understand that their opponents can have any other wish than to destroy them, so that, like wild animals, they fight to the last. They have been hunted like game by the Kafirs, and I regret to say that on some occasions white men have been guilty of very great cruelties towards them.

In 1795 the English first appeared in the colony. They did so under authority of, and in trust for, the Prince of Orange, the last Stadtholder of the Dutch Republic, who was then a refugee in England. In 1806, however, the English took the colony for themselves. This step was little noticed at home, for at that time all England was ringing with the news of the battle of Trafalgar.

During the time that the whites—the Dutch first, and the English afterwards—were effecting a lodgment on the western side of the peninsula, another race was advancing round it from the north-east. These were the Kafirs. By the word Kafir we designate all who belong to any one of five or six great tribes or families of barbarians who have come down from some unknown region in the centre of the continent. Savage in war, idle in peace, of predatory habits, uncivilised, and incapable of acquiring civilisation, they broke the power of all nations that opposed them; and, had they not met white races more determined still, they would undoubtedly have swept over the whole of South Africa. Then ensued a series of collisions. The first of any importance was in the year 1811, and is known as the first Kafir war. After this other Kafir wars took place, of which that in 1835 was the most sanguinary. In most of them the whites were unprepared; in all of them, after temporary reverses, they were successful. The arms of the Kafirs then consisted almost entirely of assegais, with which they could do but little damage to regular troops, and the Boers never found any difficulty in conquering, killing, and enslaving natives armed only with such weapons.

But not only were there wars with the natives. Intestine troubles succeeded. The Boers rebelled in 1815, and it was necessary to shoot some of them.

Meanwhile the boundaries of the colony were being pushed further and further eastward. In 1834 a measure of great importance was passed—the slaves were manumitted. Compensation was ordered to be made, but an unfortunate delay took place in the payment of the money, so that the Dutch slave-owners, in despair at no longer having absolute control over their farm-servants, and of ever receiving the promised equivalent, sold their rights to Jews and middlemen for a trifle, and "trekked" far out of the country into the districts now known as Griqualand, the Orange Free State, and the

Transvaal. The question of slavery has ever been a sore one with the Dutch. They are so attached to that institution that they will not readily consent to live in any country where it is abolished; and it is to the desire of the Boers each to "whop his own nigger" in peace, that we may trace the opposition which has been experienced in our endeavours to bring the Transvaal and the Orange Free State under English rule.

The colony still continued extending its boundaries, occasionally fighting, and ever growing more populous till the year 1872, when a responsible government was granted it, with a Legislative Council and House of Assembly, composed of members elected by various constituencies. As regards national feelings the colony may be roughly divided into east and west. In the west the old Dutch element is in the ascendant, in the east the English prevail. Although the Dutch community is well united in opinion, Englishmen of the east are divided into two groups, corresponding to the two ports of Elizabeth and East London, between which ports there is considerable commercial jealousy. A government which rests mainly on the support of the Dutch is thus able by playing off one section of the English against the other to create sufficient dissension amongst the members of the opposition to give it a majority, and this I believe has been the practice of governments hitherto.

In 1867 the first diamond was found, and there soon flowed into the colony a tide of wealth as welcome as it was unexpected. Railroads were commenced on a scale I think rather too extended at the commencement. To facilitate the making of these railways immense gangs of natives were employed, and by permission of their chiefs they were allowed to leave their own localities far away in Kafir land. To make them work only one inducement was effectual—the permission to purchase fire-arms. There was a law in the colony forbidding the acquisition of arms by natives without a special permit, to be given in those cases only in which the magistrate empowered to do so was personally acquainted with the character of the applicant. Unfortunately this salutary provision was not attended to, and permits were given with a laxity quite alarming. Companies of natives marched home, each bearing his musket over his shoulder. Instances occurred in which justices of the peace granted permits to natives in reckless profusion in order to curry favour with traders. The government set the example, and for a while, blinded by a desire to secure cheap labour, the colonists allowed the natives to arm, until at least 400,000 muskets and rifles, some of them breech-loaders, had been acquired. This was not done without protest. Warnings appeared in the newspapers, and the older colonists, who knew the Kafirs, were uneasy. I need hardly say that I fulfilled my duty by repeatedly pointing out to the Ministry the danger they were incurring. The circumstances which attended the sixth and last of our Kafir wars will be found stated in the last part of this work up to the time when my command ceased, at which period I consider that the first part of the war was virtually at an end. The late war against the Zulus may be regarded as the second part of the sixth Kafir war.

2. KAFFRARIA.—Area, 10,000 square miles; population, 450,000 blacks.

The district lying to the east of the Cape Colony is called Kaffraria. It is occupied chiefly by Kafir tribes. Amongst these are the Fingoes and Gaikas, who occupy part of British Kaffraria, sometimes called the Cis-Kei and the Galekas, Fingoes, Pondos, Pondomise, Tambookies, and Griquas, who occupy Kaffraria proper, or the Transkei. (See the map of Kaffraria, page 316.) These tribes have the same language, and are undoubtedly derived from the same stock. Amongst them the Fingoes, whose name signifies "dogs," and who have been persecuted almost to extinction by the others, are our only firm friends. Under British rule, though at first cowardly, they have developed fighting powers, and always joined our side. They have lived peacefully in their locations, and are by far the richest in cattle.

The whole of the Transkei is now under British protection, and in a short time we may expect that the barbarous customs which have hitherto prevailed there will be forcibly put an end to. The disarmament of all the natives has been decreed, and it is to be hoped that it will be vigorously carried out. No one will, I presume, object to depriving the Kafir of his gun, on the pseudo-philanthropic principle that it is like depriving a child of its toy.

3. BASUTO LAND contains a population of about 150,000 of contented natives, easy to govern. They were reduced to a miserable state by the wars of Chaka (the Zulu). The battle of Berea was fought in 1852 between them and the English, and peace established. In 1869, after continued war with the Free State, the boundaries were established, and the Basutos placed themselves under British protection.

4. NATAL.—Area, 18,700 square miles; population, 19,000 white, 300,000 black.

Natal was thickly populated by black races in the commencement of this century. In 1820 it suffered the first incursion of the Zulus. These formidable people inhabit the country to the north of Natal, and their renown is due to Chaka. He organised a military system so complete that the Zulus, since his time, may be considered the Prussians of South Africa. In the year above mentioned he desolated Natal, murdering men, women, and children; and laid it so completely waste that it became a desert. This he did, not that he wanted territory, but as an amusement. From the year 1825 to 1834, a body of English settlers occupied Natal. In the meantime Chaka was murdered by his brother Dingaan, a monster, whose deeds of cruelty filled all Zulu land with blood.

About the year 1834, the Dutch Boers made their first appearance in Natal, under the leadership of Pieter Retief, who, however, having been decoyed to a conference, was treacherously murdered with all his followers by Dingaan in 1837. Ten thousand Zulus then marched on Natal, which they almost succeeded in surprising. As it was, they murdered about 600 persons, besides Retief's party.

An attempt was made to avenge this by the advance of a body of men, mostly Kafirs under white leaders, styling themselves "the grand army of Natal." But the Zulus, after a desperate battle, completely destroyed it. In 1838 General Pretorius, the first president of the Transvaal, marched from thence with about 460 men, supported by a smaller force. Being attacked by about 10,000 Zulus, they killed 3000 of them with a loss of only four men killed, advanced into Zulu land and seized the capital. This was followed by a revolution in Zulu land, and a battle between Dingaan and Panda, his brother, by whom Dingaan was defeated and deposed.

In 1834 Natal was seized by the British, in whose possession it has remained. Since that time it has steadily increased in prosperity.

When Panda died, his son Cetewayo succeeded him. The martial system of Chaka has been steadily kept up since his time with but few relaxations.

5. THE ORANGE FREE STATE.—Area, 37,000 square miles; population, 30,000 white, 15,000 black.

The Free State was colonised chiefly by those Boers who left the colony in disgust at the emancipation of the slaves. In 1848 it was declared British territory, and after a fight with the English at Boomplaats the Dutch submitted. But in 1854 an unwise dread of expenditure caused the British Government to abandon the colony; and it became a republic, with a representative government and a president.

6. THE DIAMOND FIELDS, or GRIQUALAND WEST.—Area,

15,500 square miles; permanent population, 1000 white, 4000 blacks; fluctuating population of diggers, 40,000.

This tract of country, lying to the west of the Orange Free State, had originally been occupied by the Griquas, a mixed race of Dutch and Hottentots under Waterboer, Cornelius Kok, and Adam Kok. It was for a time nominally governed by the Orange Free State. Adam Kok, son of the above named Adam Kok, made an exodus with his people from Griqualand West in 1861 into a country north of Kaffraria, which, having been visited by the Zulus, had acquired the significant title of No Man's land. Here his tribe now reside. It is called Griqua land East. In 1867 the first diamond was found; and in 1869 a rush took place to the Diamond Fields, and in a short time a very large European community was established. In 1871 Mr. Campbell was sent to the Diamond Fields to act as magistrate. This was done by virtue of an Act of Parliament (of Great Britain), which provides for the trial in a colonial court of any persons not under the jurisdiction of a civilised community who shall commit a crime in any place on the globe south of the 22nd S. parallel of latitude. But as it was considered that this Act did not give Mr. Campbell full powers, a commission was obtained for him from Waterboer, the Griqua. Then occurred the rush to Kimberley, or "the New Rush Mine," the richest deposit of all.

In 1873 the country was declared a Crown Colony, the rights of the Orange Free State being abandoned on consideration of a payment of about £100,000.

7. THE TRANSVAAL.—Area, 120,000 square miles; population, 40,000 white, 250,000 black. The boundaries of the Transvaal towards the north-east and west have been always vague. The land is very fine and well watered, and the pasturage rich. There are fine forests, abundance of minerals and grain, fruits and all vegetables grow luxuriantly. A great future may be expected from it.

When the emigration of the Boers from Natal took place, the Republic was under the rule of a chief named Msilikazi. After several encounters, the Boers defeated him and drove him out of the country. After the battle of Boomplaats, the unsuccessful Boers retired from the Orange State and joined those who had established themselves in the Transvaal. General Pretorius was invested with the chief military command, a man whose honesty, moderation and talent, both as a general and statesman, entitle him to the highest praise.

The same timidity which caused the British Government in 1852 to abandon the Orange Free State caused them also in 1854 to abandon the Transvaal, and in that year it was erected into a Republic under the presidentship of Pretorius. For many years the country was almost unknown. During this period the Boers appear to have enjoyed the greatest happiness. Few in number and owning enormous tracts of country, they lived free from any rule except their own pleasure. Not that they indulged in deeds of violence, for they are not a violent or cruel race, but each was lord of his own family, and absolute in his own dominions. There were no school boards or inspectors, or commissioners or police to trouble them. Undisturbed even by the semblance of parental government, the thing they most detest, they led pastoral lives, varied only by the excitement of hunting and of an occasional skirmish with the natives. It is only fair to say that on such occasions they inflicted terrible vengeance whenever they had the power to do so, and when they had killed the men they made slaves of all the children.

But with the election of President Burgers the system was altered. A party which may be described as the progressionist got the upper hand, and liberal improvement became the order of the day. But progress requires great skill in its conduct, and President Burgers was too rapid for his times. His improvements and projects split the inhabitants of the

Transvaal into two parties, the Conservative and the Progressionist. Nevertheless the movement went on, and it was not until he had rendered the state almost bankrupt, and provoked the native tribes all round him by confiscating their land, that the English Government thought it time to intervene.

It is at present a disputed question whether our annexation of the Transvaal has been popular or not with the Boers. For my part I believe that, on the whole, it has. But whether popular or not I feel convinced that it will ultimately tend to the good of the country and ensure its progress. It is, however, to be hoped that we shall not this time commit the imprudence of giving a responsible government to the Transvaal too early. The history of the Colonies has shown that a country must be well advanced before it is fit for a responsible government. For a responsible government requires constant watching, and much pressure from the outside to prevent it from becoming a nest of incompetency, jobbery and corruption, and this supervision cannot be properly exercised unless the press and the people have considerable political education. At present the internal difficulties of the Transvaal are being settled by the strong hand of Sir Garnet Wolseley. Although there is some show of resistance at present I do not think it will be permanent.

8. ZULU LAND.—Area, about 10,000 square miles; population 250,000 (black). This country is inhabited by the most warlike of all the Kafir tribes. Cetewayo, the present king, almost rivals his uncle Dingaan in cruelty, and his uncle Chaka in military talent. After a sanguinary battle with his brothers, in which he was victorious, he was crowned by Sir Theophilus (then Mr.) Shepstone, secretary for native affairs at Natal. During the Presidentship of Mr. Burgers, disputes arose between the Transvaal and Cetewayo, principally in consequence of grants of Zulu land having been made without right by the

Transvaal Government. In these disputes, Mr. Shepstone acted as mediator, upholding Cetewayo against the Boers. But as soon as the Transvaal had been annexed by the English, and Mr. Shepstone made Governor, Cetewayo perceived that times had changed. Upon this his demeanour grew steadily more and more warlike, and in 1878 his attitude became so threatening, that the safety of the colonies of Natal and the Transvaal was seriously threatened. This induced Sir Bartle Frere to bring matters to a head, and last year an ultimatum was sent to him, requiring that the warlike customs of his tribe should be abandoned, and that he should give certain guarantees for keeping the peace. In the meantime the boundary dispute between him and the Transvaal had been made the subject of arbitration, and an award given, which, while it gave most of the land to Cetewayo, guaranteed the rights of the private persons who had settled thereon under authority from the Boers. Cetewayo considered this not a bonâ-fide restoration of the land.

The ultimatum of the English Government having been virtually rejected, and a delay demanded, which is well-known to be the natives' mode of refusal, an attack on the country was made by Lord Chelmsford, whose forces advanced from three points over the Tugela and Buffalo rivers.

The invading forces were thus disposed. The first column, under Colonel Pearson, prepared to advance into Zululand at the south-east angle, near the mouth of the river Tugela; the second and third columns, under Lord Chelmsford, prepared to cross at Rorke's Drift, about the centre of the south border of Zululand; and the fourth column, under Colonel Wood, was intended to operate from the north-west. The first to cross was Colonel Pearson, who engaged the enemy at Inyasani. After this he advanced to Ekowe, where he entrenched. His object was to detach, if possible, a portion of the Zulu army, and thus weaken the defence of the Zulu capital.

b

Meanwhile Lord Chelmsford, having crossed the Tugela at Rorke's Drift, marched straight towards the centre of Zululand, his object being to destroy the king's great kraals at Ulundi. The unfortunate reverse which the British then suffered needs no recapitulation. It is enough to say that the two centre columns were completely disorganised, and had to fall back on Natal. Lord Chelmsford returned to Pietermaritzburg to take steps for the public safety. On hearing of the disaster, Colonel Pearson sent his mounted men back into Natal, and prepared to stand a sort of siege. Colonel Wood fell back on Utrecht, for it was at first feared that the Zulu army, flushed with success, would turn its whole strength against him. About two months were thus spent in forced inactivity, while the arrival of troops, which had been immediately telegraphed for, was expected. No incident of any note occurred, except a minor casualty to Major Moriarty at Intombi, who was killed while superintending the convoy of some waggons to Luneberg in the Transvaal, where a detachment was stationed under Major Tucker. As soon as the reinforcements arrived, which was about seven weeks after the fight at Insandula, Lord Chelmsford's first care was to relieve Ekowe. For this purpose he organised a strong force under his personal command, with which, having crossed the Tugela, he fought the battle of Gingelovoo, in which he defeated the Zulus, and after which he relieved Ekowe and returned to Natal.

Meanwhile Colonel Wood, in order to create a diversion, made a raid into Zululand, in the course of which Colonel Buller's troops, which had been separated, were caught at Zlobane and seventy men killed. But the next day Colonel Wood avenged the disaster at Kambula, where, after four hours' hard fighting, the Zulu corps, which Wood's movement had the intended effect of diverting, was defeated with considerable slaughter.

General Crealock then took command of the lower column, and remained on the south side of the Tugela near the mouth; and Lord Chelmsford, having organised a fresh invading column under General Newdegate, took up his headquarters at Utrecht, so as to be near both Newdegate and Wood, and prepared a second time to invade Zululand. He did not cross again at Rorke's Drift. The reason of this was that the surveys made before the battle of Insandula had led to the belief that no practicable road existed from thence to Ulundi. It was therefore resolved to make a detour. Colonel Wood's column having moved down to join General Newdegate, the two columns advanced, leaving posts to protect their communications as they proceeded.

It was about this time, and while Lord Chelmsford's headquarters were still at Utrecht, that the Prince Imperial joined the army, and soon afterwards met with his death at the Isipisi mountain, about thirty miles within the frontier of Zululand. Lord Chelmsford's force then advanced on Ulundi, where a battle took place.

The following account of this important victory is extracted from an account given by a staff-officer who was present on the occasion:—

"The night before the battle of Ulundi will be long remembered by all ranks present. Late at night we were awoke by the war-song of the Zulus, a large force had come down to the river, and had been met by a regiment that came from a distant kraal to congratulate them on their supposed victory over the white man during the reconnaissance of the morning, and to talk to Panda's snake. The moon was full, and some of the Basutos, who knew the war-song, believed that it preceded an attack, so as quietly as possible the horses which were outside the laager were brought in. Once a stray shot from the outpost roused the picquet on the east of the laager. But soon the Zulu chant died away, as they retired to their kraals, and no further alarm roused us during the night. At daylight the whole force was under arms, and a hasty breakfast was made under the waggons. By 6 A.M. the Flying Column and 2nd Division had fallen in, and very shortly after, led by Lord Chelmsford, marched down to the Umvolosi river; this took only half an hour to cross. Just the other side was a very nasty bit of bush, but Buller was well in front covering the ground with his mounted infantry, and we knew he would give us ample warning of an attack. Still it was an anxious time, and glad we were when the rear of the column had cleared the bush. Buller, who by his gallant reconnaissance of the day before, had discovered the best position for the action, was covering the front and left, the Lancers under Colonel Drury Lowe in the rear, and Captain Shepstone on the right with his mounted Basutos. The conduct of this officer was a sufficient answer to the abuse which has been in some quarters bestowed on the Colonists. As soon as the column emerged from the bush, the Zulus were seen in great force descending the hill; we knew Cetewayo had 20,000 men, while our column consisted of less than 4000. But now that we had cleared the bush there could be no fear as to the result; a large square was formed, the front and rear face marching in four deep, the two sides in fours right and left, guns at the angles, carts (ambulance and ammunition) in the centre, with the Natal Native Contingent, and the square was advancing in the following order:—in front the 80th Regiment with 2 guns, commanded by Colonel Harness; in the centre, on the left flank, the 13th and 94th; on the right flank, the 90th and 58th, each flank having in the centre a detachment of the Royal Artillery with 9-pounder guns; the rear face of the square was formed by the 21st; behind the front face were companies of the Mounted Irregulars and Mounted Basutos, with the Dragoons; in advance of the rear ranks were the 17th Lancers and Mounted Irregulars; Gattlings were posted at each corner of the front face, and another company of the Royal Artillery with 9-pounders, was in the centre of the rear face. All arrangements were made under the personal superintendence of Lord Chelmsford. As the square moved on, the different regiments of Zulus formed for the attack on every side of the square. On the right, near the Nodwengu kraal, was the Nkobamakosi regiment. These men had fought at Isandlwana, and had suffered heavily there. Soon the reports of rifles told us that Colonel Buller and Captain Shepstone were engaged, and we could see the Zulus in clouds advancing rapidly, and the mounted infantry and Basutos steadily retiring. Just before we came to the position where the square was halted to repel the attack, we found the bodies of three men killed during Colonel Buller's reconnaissance; one was so frightfully mutilated that the square was for a moment halted, while a party of the Royal Engineers buried him, a chaplain reading a short service. The square was then halted, and at about 9 A.M. the Zulus had advanced near enough for the 9-pounders to come into action. They made some excellent practice, the shells bursting among the advancing hordes, who, however, did not hesitate, but came boldly on, driving our mounted men into the square. As soon as our front was clear, the infantry opened fire, firing volleys by sections, half companies, and battalions. The action now became general, and as the firing of the infantry was steady (there being no independent firing) the aim of the men was not much impeded by the smoke. Our men now began dropping, but the rear ranks took their place ; and an incident occurred here which is worthy of mention. Two men of the 90th Regiment fell back, one dead, the other wounded ; their places were immediately taken by two Basutos, who remained firing away with their white brethren till the end of the action. The Zulus were now within about 200 yards and were still advancing. Their firing was (luckily for us) bad, and very high ; but on the rear face, a large body came with a rush up to within about sixty yards of the square; such a withering volley was, however, poured in by the 21st that they were stopped. The guns now plied them with ease, and volley after volley was poured in. No troops could have advanced under such a fire, and they turned and fled. As they turned, the men of the 21st Fusiliers who formed the rear face of the square, cheered, and this seemed to frighten the Zulus on the other flanks, who got up out of the grass and retired sullenly. They were plied for a time with shot and shell, and when sufficiently broken the rear face of the square opened out, and amidst the deafening cheers of the whole force—the Lancers and Dragoons rode out, followed by Col. Buller's Mounted Infantry and Shepstone's Mounted Natives. The lances went crashing through the Zulu shields, and in a very few minutes had accounted for 150 of the enemy. Colonel Buller, after inflicting great loss on the retreating body, now rode for the Ulundi kraal—Lord William Beresford racing for the lead and getting first into the kraal. Cetewayo's house was almost empty, but a little ivory and a few curiosities were secured, and then it was set on fire; and also the great kraal with its 2000 huts, and soon from all the great military kraals volumes of smoke arose, which proclaimed to the furthest parts of Zululand the victory of Lord Chelmsford. The scene on the field was curious—within 60 yards of the square, at the rear face, lay a black heap of Zulus; they had fallen in all sorts of fantastic attitudes, some with their shields still raised in their stiffening hands—others still clenching their assegais. One man lay only 28 yards from the square, and many within 40 and 50. A great many wore belts and pouches, taken from the dead at Isandlwana. The dead of the different regiments could be distinguished by their shield and head-dresses, and it was found that nearly every regiment was represented. Four hundred men lay close round the square. But it has been ascertained that 1500 men were lost to the Zulus that day.

Our losses were 115 killed and wounded, and 19 officers wounded. Three officers were killed, Capt. Wyatt Edgell, of the 17th Lancers; Hon. W. Drummond and Lieut. Pardoe, of the 13th Regiment.

Submission now came in on every side. Lord Chelmsford resigned, and Sir Garnet Wolseley, having pacified Natal, proceeded to the Transvaal to settle the difficulties created by the discontented Boers. Zululand was divided into a number of tribal sovereignties, liberty given to the inhabitants to marry, the importation of arms forbidden, and the military system put down. With the capture of Cetewayo, which was soon afterwards effected, all show of resistance ceased, and the second part of the Zulu war came to an end.

9. ASWASI LAND.—This country lies to the north of Zululand. The Aswasis are probably as brave as the Zulus, but have not the same military discipline. They are hereditary enemies of the Zulus, and if backed by Europeans would probably fight against them. They assisted the Boers in their attack on Secocoeni's country, in the north of the Transvaal, and fought whilst the Dutch ran away.

10. The settlement of Lorenzo Marques (Delagoa Bay) is Portuguese. It has been from this port that the Zulus have obtained most of their arms; and it is much to be wished that it should be acquired by the English. It will probably be the port of the future for the Transvaal. Since the war with the Zulus some English ships have gone there to stop the supply of muskets and ammunition to the Zulus.

The question of Federation and the native questions are discussed in the following pages. I wish merely to add to what I have said there, that I think one of the great defects in the administration of native affairs, is the want of an efficient secret native police service. It happened repeatedly when I was in command that it was impossible to discover the motives and intentions of the various chiefs. Their characters could only be guessed at, and native councils of war often took place within two or three miles of our towns, within the colony, without the magistrates having the least idea of what had been said. Our secret information was derived from precarious rumours, and though the magistrates at various posts did far more in this respect than could have been expected of them, and frequently sent in admirable reports, neither means nor money were placed at their disposal sufficient to enable them to do what they might have done.

The spelling of South African names is rather a difficult matter, and depends much on "the taste and fancy of the speller." I have adopted the spelling as I found it. To those however who wish for accuracy in this respect as well as a concise and excellent history of the Cape, I recommend Theal's 'History of South Africa,' a work printed by natives at the Lovedale Institute near Alice.

The statistics above given are the best I could procure. I cannot vouch for their accuracy, as Government returns have as yet only been given for part of the colonies. The unfortunate issue of the first engagement, if compared with the battle fought between the Zulus and General Pretorius, will show the danger of arming savages with rifles. It is with the greatest pain that I have seen in the melancholy list of the killed in that action the names of many of my intimate friends and comrades.

Although South Africa is a rising colony, I hardly think it offers to the emigrant the chances which he would obtain in Australia or New Zealand. South Africa is not a very rich country, labour is hard to obtain, and it will be years before irrigation can be carried on on a sufficient scale to make agriculture a brilliant success. Nevertheless, land is so abundant, that the energetic colonist is sure at least to make a living, and provided he does not drink, has a good chance of becoming a rich man. The most valuable emigrant is the man who, having a strong bodily frame and knowing a trade, can turn his hand to anything. A blacksmith for instance, who is something of a hand at carpentering, and on occasion can mend a lamp or a clock, or do a little simple builder's and architect's work, is sure to command an excellent position in the Transvaal, especially if he has a portable forge, some tools, and a small lathe with him. He would commence as a smith; but in a very few years I believe he would become a landowner. On the other hand, it must not be imagined that the Transvaal is a paradise of wealth. Large portions of it, especially the Lowveldt, are very unhealthy during a portion of the year. Although there are minerals, they do not exist in very plentiful quantities, and although there is land well adapted for corn-growing, it is limited in amount. I shall often have to speak of the large farms owned by the Transvaal settlers, but it must be remembered that these huge areas are often arid and profitless, and only in part fit to use as grazing land. Hence let intending settlers remember, if they go to South Africa, that they cannot make certain of getting more than a comfortable independence, free from care, in a good climate, and with plenty of food for themselves and their families. But let them not look forward to returning as "nabobs" to England. Fortunes are sometimes made, but it is the exception, not the rule. Besides, the native question in the Transvaal is in some confusion, and the mere defeat of the Zulus which has taken place will by no means settle the matter. There are conflicting native and white interests in the Transvaal to an extent which an Englishman can hardly imagine, and which will I believe for years impede a thorough settlement of the country.

The chief political questions affecting the colonies are federation, the disarmament of the natives, the formation of a force for colonial defence, and the reformation of the law. The first three will be discussed in the following pages. The state of the law in South Africa offers a most interesting spectacle to the jurist. Ostensibly Dutch, it is really English, so that instead of consisting of a series of English statutes grafted on a Dutch root, the text-books of the famous Dutch jurists are either treated as obsolete, or else as mere ordinances; the spirit of the law being entirely English. A short time ago the free disposition of property by will was introduced. This change is sure to come about when a foreign system of laws is for a long time administered by English judges. Unfortunately the law remains very technical, and it is greatly to be wished that Consolidation Acts should be passed resembling those which have done so much to render litigation simpler and less costly in England.

London, Nov. 10th, 1879.

CONTENTS.

BOOK I.—THE CAPE COLONY. THE ORANGE FREE STATE.

CHAP.	PAGE
I. CAPE TOWN	1
II. OSTRICH-FARMING	11
III. WINE-GROWING	20
IV. SWELLENDAM	30
V. BOUND FOR THE EASTERN FRONTIER	39
VI. VOLUNTEER CAVALRY	52
VII. OUTSPAN—LOCUSTS	62
VIII. DUTCH CHARACTERISTICS—SPORT	75
IX. BASUTO LAND	82
X. BACK TO PORT ELIZABETH	96
XI. FEDERATION AND COLONIAL DEFENCE	100

BOOK II.—KAFFRARIA AND NATAL.

XII. THE KOMGHA	108
XIII. GANGALESWE	119
XIV. WITCHCRAFT	125
XV. UMTHONTHLO	139
XVI. JOJO—GRIQUALAND EAST	145
XVII. PIETERMARITZBURG	157
XVIII. THE TUGELA	164

BOOK III.—THE DIAMOND FIELDS.

XIX. GRIQUALAND WEST—THE DIAMOND FIELDS	171
XX. START FOR THE DIAMOND FIELDS	177
XXI. THE KIMBERLEY DIAMOND MINE	194
XXII. THE LOVEDALE INSTITUTE	215

BOOK IV.—THE TRANSVAAL.

CHAP.		PAGE
XXIII. THE ANNEXATION OF THE TRANSVAAL	.. .. ..	218
XXIV. TOUR TO THE TRANSVAAL	.. .. ..	238
XXV. BOTSE BELLO	.. ..	246
XXVI. LEYDENBURG	.. ..	253
XXVII. PILGRIMS' REST	.. ..	260
XXVIII. START FOR THE RETURN JOURNEY	.. .. ..	268
XXIX. POTCHEFSTROM	.. ..	274
XXX. THE TRANSVAAL FARMING—SPORT	.. .. ..	281

BOOK V.—THE SIXTH KAFIR WAR.

XXXI. "THE FRONTIER SCARE"—WAR	.. ..	296
XXXII. STATE OF THE FORCES	.. ..	306
XXXIII. THE FIRST PART OF THE WAR—GRIFFITHS DRIVES THE GALEKAS OVER THE BASHEE	.. ..	316
XXXIV. STUTTERHEIM	.. ..	323
XXXV. FURTHER SPREAD OF DISAFFECTION — THE FIGHT AT UMZITZANI	.. ..	327
XXXVI. MARCH OF THE BRITISH TROOPS OVER THE KEI	..	338
XXXVII. ATTACK BY THE KAFIRS UPON THE MAILS BETWEEN THE CIS- AND THE TRANSKEI	.. ..	343
XXXVIII. THE OPERATIONS OF THE BRITISH TROOPS IN THE TRANSKEI	351
XXXIX. USE OF THE TELEGRAPH IN THE WAR	.. .. ..	357
XL. DISMISSAL OF THE MINISTRY	.. ..	368
XLI. THE FIGHT AT QUINTANA	.. ..	372

MAPS.

THE SOUTH AFRICAN COLONIES	.. .. ..	*Frontispiece.*
KAFFRARIA	.. ..	*to face* 316
PLAN OF THE FIGHT AT QUINTANA	.. .. ..	,, 372

MY COMMAND IN SOUTH AFRICA.

BOOK I.—THE CAPE COLONY.

CHAPTER I.

CAPE TOWN.

IN the summer of the year 1873 I made an excursion to the north of Europe, travelling through Norway, Sweden, Finland, and Russia, and found myself at Moscow in the month of August. Whilst at Moscow I received by telegram an intimation that it was her Majesty's intention to entrust to me the command of the forces in South Africa; so, relinquishing the remainder of my tour, I lost no time in returning to London. At the commencement of October I sailed with my family and my personal staff in the Union Company's steamship *Teuton* for the Cape of Good Hope.

I need not allude to the incidents of the outward voyage, as they differed little from those which have been so often told in voyages across the line.

The *Teuton* was then a vessel of about 1500 tons, but, by the ingenuity of mechanics, she was subsequently increased by another thousand tons, introduced amidships, which in no way appeared to interfere with her speed, while it very much improved her capacity and comfort.

In our voyage out we touched at Madeira and at St. Helena.

On the 15th of November we steamed into Table Bay, Cape Town.

Hardly had the anchor dropped than we received news of an outbreak of one or more of the Kafir tribes, in the Crown Colony of Natal, which was also under my military command.

This news was conveyed to us by the Harbour-master, and corroborated by a letter from the Governor handed to me by an aide-de-camp, together with a newspaper article, from which the following is an extract:—

Natal, November 1st, 1873.—This morning's post brought intelligence that thirty Carabineers under Major Durnford had occupied a pass unsupported for some time; and being almost devoid of food they were obliged to catch a beast, kill it, and eat it raw.

A strong body of Kafirs came up the pass with a large number of cattle; there was an encounter, with the following casualties: Privates Erskine (son of the Hon. Mr. Erskine, the Colonial Secretary), Potterill, and Bond, and three native auxiliaries, killed. A letter from Colonel Milles, 75th Regiment, commanding her Majesty's troops, to the Hon. Mr. Erskine, says, "Your son behaved gallantly, and but for his saddle turning round would have returned safe." Langalebalele has escaped; his camp was found quite empty.

The following letter has come to hand from Drill-instructor Clarke: "The facts are these; we arrived at the top of the Bushman's Pass just as the Kafirs were taking their cattle up. We stopped them, when Major Durnford was himself attacked, and but for his shooting both his assailants, would have been killed; he was wounded, and Captain Boyes had a narrow escape. Elijah the interpreter had been stabbed before he fell, but was shot through the head as he lay. When young Erskine fell, owing to his saddle turning, he was instantly surrounded and stabbed to death.

"The encounter took place not far from headquarters. Langalebalele's people came on, sharpening their assegais, and taunting the Carabineers, who had orders not to commence hostilities. Mr. Shepstone was twenty or thirty miles distant, stationing guards at the different passes, but was immediately sent for. The Carabineers undertook their own commissariat arrangements. The troops are in pursuit of the rebels."

Another letter said :

" We were three days on the top of the berg, without food for either horse or man ; we were in the saddle on Sunday evening and Monday morning for eighteen hours, and twenty-one hours from Tuesday to last night. The Kafirs are well armed and drilled."

These extracts were sufficient to show me the military errors of this expedition. In the first place it was evident that the conduct of it was not intrusted to a military man, and indeed it would seem that four different authorities were in command, each exceedingly anxious to use his best endeavours, but all acting without cohesion or combination. Sir Benjamin Pine, the Governor himself, took the field, thereby ignoring the position of Colonel Milles. Mr. Shepstone commanded the native auxiliaries, and the volunteers were placed under Colonel Durnford. Due regard was not paid to transport or supplies, the volunteers making their own feeble and spasmodic arrangements for their rations.

Her Majesty's troops acted as a reserve, and their military arrangements were satisfactorily secured. One fatal error had been committed. Orders had been given that the troops were to withhold their fire until they were attacked, thereby giving the enemy an undue advantage, of which they showed that they were well able to avail themselves.

The result of these errors was confusion, valuable lives uselessly expended, the advance of the enemy, the retreat of the European colonial forces, and a general mismanagement and collapse, ending in violent recrimination. Precisely the same thing occurred four years later in the Cape Colony, from the same causes. Many weeks had been expended in Pietermaritzburg in making arrangements for the attack upon Langalobalele. His tribe inhabited a district on the borders of Basuto land, a country which was in charge of a British Resident Commissioner from the Cape Colony; and yet no intimation of the intention to attack this chief was made either to the Governor of the Cape, the Commander of the Forces, or even to the Resident in Basuto land. This omission was never explained. In the sequel it did not prove as disastrous as it might easily have done, but it demonstrated clearly the want of combination in South Africa, and gave me the first intimation of the benefit which would arise from Federation. Nothing could convince the public generally on that subject, until the lamentable war of 1877-78 threw a new light upon it.

On hearing of the rebellion of Langalebalele, and that his warriors had escaped over the Drakensberg Mountains into Basuto land, no time was lost in directing a force of the Frontier armed police to march from King William's Town through Tembu and Pondo lands and the lower spurs of the Drakensberg, if possible to intercept them, and to prevent the seeds of rebellion being sown in other provinces. The march of this force was conducted with great vigour and celerity, and it was mainly owing to their exertions on their arrival in Basuto land, directed by the Commissioner, C. Griffiths, that the rebellion was so quickly brought to an end. I regret to say that the exertions and privations which the police underwent in the most inclement season of the year were rewarded by the Colonial Government with merely a military record of praise.

The large prize in cattle captured in Basuto land was given over to the Natal Government, which, though profiting by their exertions, refused, as far as I could learn, to distribute any part of it to the Cape Colonial Police.

All these matters gave me cause for serious reflections, as I saw what difficulties must be encountered should war or rebellion occur in South Africa, and they induced me to make representations upon the subject. The answer I received was, that there was no occasion to contemplate a state of things which would be never likely to occur, such as a "Kafir war" or a "Kafir insurrection." These were the arguments used by the Colonial Ministry even up to the moment when, in 1877, the Frontier settlers were being murdered and their homesteads burned.

The rebellion of Langalebalele was soon quelled. He was not supported by the neighbouring chiefs; the possession of firearms had not as yet become general, and the want of success which attended this first demonstration boded ill for the natives. Cetewayo (pronounced Ketchwyo), the Zulu King, was on good terms with the English, having been lately crowned in Zulu land by Mr. Shepstone, the Natal Minister for Native Affairs. Langalebalele was confined first in Robben Island, near Cape Town, and afterwards by a sort of ticket-of-leave on a farm on the Flats near Cape Town. His treatment called forth a deal of acrimonious feeling. Bishop Colenso of Natal visited London for the express purpose of interceding in favour of Langalebalele, in which he was most successful.

The trial of this chief having been conducted in an irregular manner, an indemnity was directed to be paid to the neighbouring tribes whose property had been confiscated. The wives and children belonging to them were apprenticed to the Natal farmers, while the husbands became daily labourers in the colony. Thus ended the Kafir chief's dream of independence, and of setting the white man at naught; Langalebalele, with three of his wives and his son, now smoke the calumet of peace in his little farm near Cape Town, complaining more of his scanty ration of tobacco than of the loss of his kingdom. This rebellion being, in fact, extinguished as rapidly as it had come into existence, there was no need for my immediate presence in Natal.

The first necessity of my household was that of being properly lodged. The increasing wealth at the Cape, in consequence of the sudden augmentation of trade caused by the discovery of diamonds, had changed as it were by a magic wand the value of everything except the fixed incomes of British officers. Meat—which a few years since had been about 2d. per lb.—had now risen to 9d. A sheep could be purchased not many years ago for 3s. 6d., and now 5s. or 6s. is charged for the tail alone. The tails are of immense size; they weigh from five to six pounds, and are used instead of butter. Herodotus tells us about sheep whose tails were so long that the shepherds had to make them little carts, so that they might move about "carrying their tails behind them." The story has been often laughed at, and cited as a proof of his credulity; but from what I have seen of the Cape sheep, I could believe that it might have been quite true. A horse which could have been bought a few years ago for 10l. or 12l., now costs 50l.; and house-rent has risen in the same proportion. Servants are scarcely obtainable, the most unsatisfactory natives averaging 5s. or 6s. per diem.

After a short visit to the Governor and before we obtained a house, we stayed for a few days at the Royal Hotel. The pet companions of the lady and gentleman late arrivals from Natal, who had rooms next to ours, were a chameleon and a cobra. The first was interesting and harmless; but as the second was of a different character, and lived in a box on the verandah outside our sitting-room, we were reluctantly compelled, although the weather was very hot, to keep the window constantly closed.

The "liveliness" of our lodgings could not be adequately appreciated unless by personal experience; nothing of a defensive character proved of any avail, although we expended whole jugs of water on our floors, and prepared our beds with "Keating's powder." It was an early sample of the slovenly habits of the Africander, of which we subsequently had many a night's painful experience.

This discomfort, and the inviting appearance of the old Dutch rooms in the fort in Cape Town, made me determine to put them into order, and to inhabit the spacious saloons in which the Governors of the Dutch East Indian Colonies once reigned. I had never any cause to repent this decision. After a few weeks' labour, we were finally settled in our Southern home, surrounded by the comforts which, in a soldier's wandering career, I had been able to secure.

The season was becoming very hot and the town unhealthy, tempered, however, by the wind, without which Cape Town, unhealthy as it is, would have been wellnigh unbearable. This blustering gale, which drives all before it, is called "the Doctor." Report says that it is so violent that cabs are upset in the ranks, and people seen by the dozen clinging to the lamp-posts, whilst those who attempt to walk do nothing but mark time. I have myself seen it raise pebbles from the ground and dash them with great force against the windows, but I cannot say that I can quite answer for these "flying rumours, that gather as they roll"! Singularly enough, six miles distant on the other side of the mountain no one is inconvenienced by the wind, for while it is blowing a hurricane at Cape Town, a delicious calm pervades the beautiful valleys of Wynberg.

The first excursion which I made from Cape Town was to Stellenbosh. I was most kindly received there by Sir Christopher Brand, a gentleman of the old school. He had been for very many years Speaker of the House of Assembly, and was the father of Mr. Brand, the President of the Free States.

He drove us to his handsome Dutch house, containing some grand rooms. The owner is farming ostriches to a very considerable extent. He commenced by purchasing a pair for 55*l*., and having placed fences in judicious positions, has formed various parks and paddocks. In the second year, 1874, he sold some young birds, but again bred from the original pair. At the termination of this year he had repaid all his outlay, nearly 1000*l*., and still retained some twenty birds. An ostrich will lay about fifty eggs in one year. Should forty birds be reared, and each be sold at one month old for 10*l*., a very handsome profit can be made from the investment. Nor is this industry likely to fail for many years to come. At present the greater the supply, the greater apparently is the demand, and ostrich feathers appear never to have been more in vogue than at present. Ladies generally say that it is impossible they should ever get out of fashion, as they are so becoming, and there is no substitute for them; and as, unlike diamonds, they soon wear out.

In 1875 the price of a pair of ostriches went as high as 500*l*. Even then they may have proved a profitable investment, especially as feathers were selling at from 30*l*. to 40*l*. the pound weight.

Small ostrich farmers commence by enclosing three or four paddocks with a wire or other fence. They purchase one cock and two hens, for which they probably have to pay 400*l*. sterling. Each hen may lay fifty eggs in the season. The cock assists in the hatching, sitting even longer than the hen bird.

There are many other countries besides South Africa where I am convinced that the ostrich in a tame state might be most profitably reared. Amongst them I may name Scinde in the Bombay Presidency, the neighbourhood of Gibraltar in Spain, and Egypt. In these countries neither food nor labour is so expensive as in South Africa. I hear that this industry is already carried on in Australia, and in parts of America. An attempt is at present being made to breed ostriches in England, but with what success I have not learned.

Regarding the profits to be derived from ostrich farming, I will here quote a few words from the 'Graaff Reinet Herald.' Many of my readers will think that it is no wonder farmers should relinquish the cultivation of their lands, when so large a profit is to be obtained from rearing these birds:

OSTRICH FARMING.—The total value of ostrich feathers exported from the colony in 1874 is returned as 205,540*l*., including, we presume, wild and tame feathers. The value in 1865 was 65,662*l*., almost entirely wild. The increase, however, has been more in value than in quantity. Notwithstanding the number of domesticated birds has increased in that time from a thousand or so up to thirty thousand, the export of tame feathers has not increased in anything like that ratio, and probably the supply of wild feathers has even decreased. Notwithstanding these anomalous results, ostrich farming is at present one of the most profitable occupations on the face of the globe. A pair of full-grown birds may still be bought for 300*l*. or 400*l*. On a hundred acres or so of ground as many pairs as you require may be kept. From each pair, with fair luck, some twenty young birds per annum may be looked for, worth 15*l*. The young birds increase in value at the rate of between 2*l*. and 3*l*. per month. The feathers of a full-grown bird fetch about 10*l*. or 12*l*. per annum. From ten pair of full-grown ostriches, a number which a farmer could easily attend to without even the assistance of a servant, an income of 3000*l*. per annum ought to result. If, however, we say 2000*l*., to allow for contingencies, still it is hard to think of any occupation which pays so handsomely with so little trouble.

That a farmer should give up the cultivation of his land for ostrich-farming is only too natural. How much labour, how much anxiety, how much difficulty and trouble of every kind would be required before an equal income could be made by agriculture! If, however, we conclude that the occupation of ostrich-farming is a paying one for the colony, we may be greatly mistaken. We are exporting some 180,000*l.* worth, say, of tame feathers, and are importing a great deal more than that value of breadstuffs. So far as the colony is concerned, ostrich-farming is very like the tulip mania of Holland; immense sums of money are changing hands, on the speculation of great returns some day, but the whole occupation is at present more of the nature of commercial gambling; it is buying and selling for a rise. At present also the breeding of young birds is so profitable that the feathers are hardly attended to, and it is well known to farmers that both cannot be attended to with equal profit at the same time; brooding destroys the feathers, and plucking disturbs the birds and hinders them from laying. As the number of tame birds must be at least doubling, if not quadrupling, every year, and as wild birds are still being captured and domesticated, we shall in a few years come to a crisis. There will be a sudden fall in the price of young birds; farmers will begin to turn their attention to feathers instead of breeding; the supply of feathers will increase suddenly, and their value will necessarily fall. Those who have sold out before the fall will be rich men. Those who have held on, and have mortgaged their farms and run into debt to speculate in ostriches, will be ruined; and, what is worse, the minds of a large number of our farmers will have been diverted from habits of wholesome industry and directed to merely speculative plans for becoming rich. We are afraid that we shall see this crisis before we see the railway to Graaff Reinet. If the colony was in want of money, a tax of 1*l.* per annum on every ostrich would bring in a splendid revenue, and only act as a wholesome restraint on speculation.

CHAPTER II.

OSTRICH-FARMING.

THE subject is so interesting, that I shall not apologise for now inserting a few remarks on this strange bird, taken from Mr. De Mosenthal's excellent work, which I have every reason to believe to be in all respects truthful.

It is a joint work in which one writer exhibits a good deal of research, while the other details the result of his practical observation at the Cape of Good Hope. No pains have been spared by Mr. Harting in consulting all the authorities who have treated of the ostrich, from Xenophon and the Old Testament down to Professor Huxley and Mr. Blyth. Mr. De Mosenthal writes from all that fulness of knowledge with which a Consul-General and a Member of a Legislative Council in South Africa may reasonably be credited. It seems that the spectacle of a complete assortment of ostrich feathers at the late Vienna Exhibition gave rise to many inquiries; and the object of this volume is to respond to those calls by compiling a natural history of the ostrich family, and by showing how far it may be possible to increase and develop the traffic in the feathers, which are staple objects of commerce. Whether young ostriches can be turned out like hand-bred pheasants, or whether it will pay to set apart whole tracts of land in Europe for the rearing of these birds, is a question which must remain doubtful. Possibly some additional experience may enable an adventurous young Englishman, with 3000*l*. or 4000*l*. of his own, to set up an ostrich-farm at the Cape, just as he would start a coffee-plantation at Ceylon, or a tea-garden at Darjeeling or Cachar.

Mr. Harting is at some pains to remove any misconception as to the domicile of origin of these birds. He shows that they are mentioned in the Bible, in classical authors, and by ancient and modern travellers in Arabia and Mesopotamia; and that even to this day they are not extinct in the neighbourhood of Damascus. Xenophon, in the 'Anabasis,' several times writes of these "big sparrows," as some Greeks called them. The equivalent for ostrich in modern Persian is "shutur-murgh," or the "camel fowl." This is very like the Greek στρουθοκάμηλος. Other Greek writers mention these birds as κατάγαιοι or χερσαῖοι—that is, land-birds, or those that do not fly. It seems clear that the bird has at no time been indigenous to India, though the author correctly relies on the authority of Mr. Blyth for the fact that ostriches are frequently offered for sale at Calcutta, and are now and then purchased by native magnates like the Maharaja of Burdwan many years ago. The late Mr. Charles Prinsep, some time Advocate-General of Bengal, had a pair of ostriches in his garden at Belvedere, Alipore, once the residence of Warren Hastings, and now that of the Lieutenant-Governor of Bengal. The natives nicknamed them "big peacocks." There is no physical reason that I know of why the bird should not flourish in the sands and heat of Upper India. But there is the undoubted fact that neither the eggs nor the skeletons of the ostrich have been discovered there by inquiring naturalists. Everybody has heard of the speed at which it can run, its inability to raise itself off the ground, its amazing powers of digestion, its wariness, and the extreme inconvenience which may result to any incautious hunter who, after running it to a standstill, comes within the reach of its vigorous kick. De Mosenthal's book dwells on a number of other minute and less known particulars regarding its habits and powers.

It can travel immense distances, though its range of feeding is ordinarily limited to a space of twenty or thirty miles from its headquarters. It can run at the rate of twenty-six miles in the hour, the average rate of a Parliamentary train. It can dispense with water, though fond of bathing. Nothing comes amiss to it in the shape of food—"seeds, berries, fruit, grass, leaves, beetles, locusts, small birds and animals, lizards and snakes;" the process of trituration and digestion being aided by "sand, stones, grit, bones, and even pieces of metal." The male is polygamous, but takes his turn at incubation with the hen. The eggs make very fair omelettes, though apparently coarse in flavour, and the meat is highly prized; but, the author is careful to add, by natives. A French author describes the flesh of young ostriches as "assez bonne, quoique d'un goût très-prononcé," and that of adults as "très-désagréable"; and he adds that dogs will not touch it. To run down or capture the ostrich various methods are employed. Owing to the speed and endurance of the bird, several horsemen must hunt together on a concerted plan. One follows it at a hand gallop, and the others leisurely take another direction at right angles to its course, and come in like second horses with the Quorn or Pytchley, just when the first pursuer is blown.

Even then the ostrich has a trick of crouching in scrub or rocks, allowing the hunt to pass by, and so evading pursuit altogether. Bushmen and natives are guilty of more unsportsmanlike modes of compassing their object. One man discovers the nest, removes the eggs, and, putting himself in their place, awaits the return of the parent and assassinates her with a poisoned arrow. In Arabia the Bedouin steals up to the nest at the most anxious period of incubation and kills the female, following this up by the death of the male, when he returns unsuspectingly to roost at sunset. Some stalk the birds by means of a screen or imitation of the living ostrich. Others drive them, like deer in the Highlands, to a pass, or surround a vast plain by a cordon of hunters, who gradually contract their sphere of operations, and bewilder the unlucky birds by yelling and shouting and allowing them no rest. It is no wonder if the breed diminishes under so systematic a persecution, which spares neither sex nor age, and laughs at close-time. In South America it is stated that the return of slain or captured birds has averaged 400,000 per annum, so that a man may now ride hundreds of leagues from Buenos Ayres without seeing one. Mr. Harting has judiciously included in his book some account of other members of the great struthious family, including the Cassowary and the Emu, and he prominently notices the fact that while the South African Ostrich has two toes, the Rhea and the Cassowary have three. The Emu, which differs from the Cassowary in the head, beak, and wings, resembles beefsteak in flavour, and yields six or seven quarts of oil, well adapted either for burning or embrocation. It is difficult for those who have not varied a meal of damper in the Bush in Australia by such game as they can kill, to form a correct idea of the relative merits of the flesh of the Kangaroo and the Emu; but a writer on Australian sport gives the preference to the latter.

Mr. De Mosenthal's book is not merely a contribution to natural history: it aims at a distinctly practical object. There is a good deal of information to show how the trade in feathers may be stimulated, and it is hinted that the high price of beef and mutton might be kept down by a judicious investment in live emus, in addition to our present list of domesticated animals fitted for food. We are bound, however, to say that the authors seem to us to take a somewhat sanguine view of the adaptability of our climate to this object; and the experiences of a worthy gentleman in Surrey are quoted at some length, apparently without the smallest appreciation of the ludicrous shifts to which he was put in his heroic ardour to shine as a naturalist and the producer of a new stock.

In the year 1860, a pair of emus were landed from Sydney in the *Duncan Dunbar*. A series of experiments were tried and the results noted with as much minuteness as if the narrator had discovered a cure for cholera or an infallible specific for dealing with quiet drunkards. The emus were let loose in a large paddock enclosed by iron-hurdles and protected from the river, because, though very fond of water, they did not know how to manage themselves when out of their depth. Instead of waiting for the return of spring, the female perversely laid an egg in the second week of February, which, when discovered in a heap of litter, the writer thought "the most wonderful production I had ever seen." This was nothing to what followed; for the bird went on laying, in spite of cold weather and snow, until it had brought forth thirteen eggs in about the space of six weeks. One of the pair proceeded to sit on the eggs; the keeper of the Zoological Gardens was extremely dissatisfied because the writer naturally imagined the sitting bird to be of the female instead of, as it turned out, of the male sex; this tiresome creature created a scandal by going off one day while the family were at church, leaving the eggs to the chances of hot water and a sand bath, extemporised in a saucepan; the amateur telegraphed to the Zoological Gardens, and sat up himself all night regulating the temperature and turning the eggs, which were eventually sent up to town in hot bran, folds of flannel, and a tin case. All this resulted in the production of four young emus, as may be learnt in detail in Chapter XV. The truant emus returned to their home in Surrey, the author's scepticism as to the sexes was cleared away, and the sagacity of the keeper vindicated, when the larger bird one day dropped an egg on the ground, and its smaller mate turned it over and finally took on itself the entire duties of the mother. This process, or something like it, was repeated, till the nest was filled with sixteen eggs. We have several pages filled with the author's parental anxieties, his despondency, his moods of melancholy, and the tremendous reaction of joy when the striped body of a young emu was seen nestling close to its parent. "He hardly knew how to break the news indoors." I regret to add that the relations between the male and female emu are by no means of a peaceful character, though it may gratify the advocates of women's rights to know that in conjugal disputes the female has far the best of the battle, strikes the male, tears his feathers, causes him loss of blood, and remains for a time at least complete mistress of the situation.

In a subsequent season the experiment of incubation was resumed. Two young emus, not those sent to the Zoological Gardens, were so indisposed that they had to be attended by a local medical practitioner, and dosed with calomel pills, which, strange to say, brought them both round after they had been given over. Nothing was added to the stock of emus by the older birds, although one laid the enormous quantity of twenty-eight eggs. A lady and a gentleman in a pleasure-boat thoughtlessly frightened the mother off its nest and spoiled the hopes of the season. We are happy to say that, subsequently, a period of agonizing hopes and fears was exchanged for one of rejoicing when ten young emus were hatched, of which seven grew up to form a "lively and interesting family." It must not, however, be supposed that the book contains nothing but the touching expressions of a naturalist's affection for his chickens, or his heartrending lamentations over their infantile diseases and their untimely fate. The possibility of stocking a farm with ostriches is discussed in some forty pages, which form Part II. of Mr. De Mosenthal's volume.

Attempts have been made with some success to rear ostriches at Florence, Marseilles and Madrid for the sake of their produce. But it is tolerably clear that the Cape of Good Hope is far better fitted for this scheme than even Southern Europe. The climate is natural to the ostrich. Space is more available, and suitable food can be more easily supplied.

It is not yet quite settled what number one acre can bear, but it is evident that the birds require a good deal of space, strong fences, sheds for shelter, and houses for incubation. One gentleman sowed lucerne on 8 acres for 30 birds. Another allotted 500 acres to 23. A third stocked 1000 acres with 90, which raises a doubt in my mind whether his speculation could be made to pay. The land, it is affirmed by competent authorities, should be sandy, or at any rate should have sandy patches. Timber is said not to be necessary. The question of food is not free from difficulty. Naturally the ostrich feeds on sweet grass in the Karoo, or desert lands of the interior. Occasionally it resorts to the coast, where it will eat sour grass, which gives it lime and salt. Alkalies it must have in one shape or another, and ostrich-feeders are recommended to give Indian corn, locally termed "mealies," green-meat, and crushed bones. The latter supply the phosphate of lime, which seems to produce something of the effect ascribed by Mr. Squeers to pastry for schoolboys. Some breeders give lucerne in large quantities.

The ostrich flock is liable to be thinned. The birds fight and kill each other; they fall into holes when young; and they are killed by natives, or die of diphtheria, cold or wet. Crows maliciously destroy their eggs. Thunderstorms have an injurious effect on them, and too great or too little heat may prove fatal during incubation. Now and then a cock becomes troublesome and pugnacious, and an instance is given of one that attacked a rider and kicked his horse on the chest, though the animal soon showed that two could play at the game. Opinions seem to differ as to the proper time for plucking. The feathers are in prime condition at the period of incubation, which is precisely when the birds must be left alone. One fancier hit on the device of penning the birds, cutting off the best feathers with a sharp knife instead of plucking them out, and leaving the stumps to fall out or to be removed afterwards. The writer of this part of the book seems to incline to the opinion that the chickens have the best chance of life with an artificial machine, and that they do better when put into warm cribs and under blankets in their infancy than consigned to the natural heat of their parents. An amusing episode in their life is, that they now and then favour their owners with a dance, and spin round not ungracefully, like dancing dervishes.

Calculations differ as to the return in money which the trade yields. One gentleman estimates that one bird gives 8*l*. a-year. Another says that a full-grown male yields a pound of first-class feathers, worth at Cape Town between 40*l*. and 50*l*., but this must have been in the early days of farming, for an increase in the yield has been followed by a decrease in price. In 1868–69 it sunk to 2*l*. and 3*l*. per pound; but, "picked white," always commanded a high market. Six years afterwards, or in 1874, the price had again risen to 5*l*., and even to 8*l*., at Natal.

The total value of the exports has increased enormously. In 1854 the feathers exported from Cape Colony and from Natal together amounted to little more than 13,000*l*. In 1874 the value was more than 200,000*l*. By far the greater part of this was supplied by the Cape.

In 1865 the number of tame birds at the Cape was only 80. In 1875 it had swelled to 32,000. At the Cape, too, an Englishman is under constitutional government, and enjoys one of the finest climates in the world; and though he may not make a vast fortune, yet with prudence, attention, and a fair amount of capital, he may achieve a comfortable independence, and live a life preferable to farming sheep on the plateaux of hot Queensland, or losing them in snowstorms at some isolated station in the wilds of New Zealand.

There is a singular circumstance in respect to which the ostrich feather differs from that of all other birds. The quill, which in other birds is always unequally divided, is in the middle of the feather plume. It is said that this equal balance was probably the origin of the hieroglyphic of the Egyptians, which represented Justice by an ostrich feather.

CHAPTER III.

WINE-GROWING.

Although the chief industry at the Paarl and at Stellenbosh is the culture of the vine, yet the wine, far from improving, has for many years rather fallen off in its quality. This may be owing to many causes. The first, no doubt, is the high price of labour. The second may be the great expense of sending the wine to market at the Diamond Fields and other places in the interior of the colony. To these causes may be added the high duty charged by the colony of Natal upon the wines of the Cape, ignorance of proper methods of preparing them, and the difficulty arising from a want of sufficient capital to store them until they have become properly fit for use.

There can be no doubt that at present Cape wines deservedly stand low in public estimation. There may be many reasons for this. The quality of the earth appears to produce in the grape an earthy matter, which may affect the wine, making it resemble an inferior Madeira. From this flavour the most carefully prepared kinds are not free. The taste of the consumers generally is so undefined that they have not yet learned to distinguish the value of good Spanish wine, principally because they never see it. Lastly, perhaps, it may be more profitable to make the juice of the grape into brandy; for where carriage to a distant market is so expensive —such as sixpence or more per pound weight, or sixpence per pint, to the Diamond Fields—it acts as a great inducement to make an article with the greatest possible strength in proportion to its bulk.

Only a very small proportion of the brandy has any pretension even to imitate the Cognac of France, the larger proportion being manufactured into "Cape Smoke," a most disagreeable spirit, commonly used throughout the colony, and, indeed, throughout South Africa.

An association has lately been organised with a view of improving the wine in the Cape Colony, and as it is under the auspices of influential persons, and already possesses a very considerable capital, it has every chance of proving successful.

The general principle upon which it proposes to act is to improve the manufacture and pay attention to the keeping of the wine, and especial regard to the "madre," upon which all palatable sherries so largely depend. These objects require capital and great attention, and no success in wine can be obtained unless both are steadily kept in view.

I quote a few lines from the prospectus of "The South African Wine-Growers' Association":—

> The manufacture of Cape wine admittedly has not kept pace with the productions of other countries. The farmers have been wedded to obsolete habits, such as forcing the yield of the wine by excessive irrigation, picking the grapes without sufficient care, and improperly stopping fermentation by the introduction of bad spirit; while the merchants have given an almost uniform price for all wines, mixing them indiscriminately in large vats, and finally, by obnoxious compounds, forcing the apparent maturity, and imparting a debased flavour. These practices are obviously capable of easy and complete extinction. As wine-farming is one of the most important industries in South Africa, and capable of almost unlimited development, the matter was seriously

taken up rather more than a year since by a number of gentlemen with a view of remedying these evils by the introduction of skilled experts in wine-making, and by the application of sufficient capital to allow the wines properly to mature.

This project was welcomed by the farmers, whose individual means were unequal to the effort, and nearly eight hundred and fifty farmers have become shareholders. The value and importance of the undertaking has been fully recognised by his Excellency Sir Bartle Frere, Governor of the Colony, who has become patron of the Association.

One of the first acts of the Association, when duly registered, was to engage a skilled wine maker from Xeres, who gives it as his unhesitating opinion that, with the splendid soil and climate of South Africa, and the wonderful advantages of its hills and slopes, as fine wine can be produced there as in any country in the world.

The Paarl is a pretty town; the streets are lined with oak-trees which, being dwarfed when young, become very shady. There also are vineyards in a high state of cultivation and production. The valley of the Drokensfeldt, about ten miles above the town, is very beautiful, a fine old Dutch house and estate commanding the entrance.

Not many miles from the Paarl is the residence of Mr. H., a genuine type of the Africander; energetic, of so hard a constitution that no privation, no fatigue can overcome him; and generous in his hospitality, which is of a most varied kind, as I learned from the officer of my staff, who stayed with him. On three successive days his table groaned under luxuries, amongst which were joints of the ant-eating bear, the porcupine, and the ostrich, and other singular meats, which he had carefully obtained to surprise and please his English guests. He is like the hare with many friends.

As a rule, young ladies at the Cape are not supposed or expected to bring fortunes to their husbands. When they are sensible, and well instructed in the management of a house, they are considered a fortune in themselves.

Stellenbosh is a charming old Dutch town. The houses are very quaint, each with a gable end facing the road. Rows of stunted oaks line each street, through which flows a rill of clear water. It was with regret that I observed that the old Courthouse had been converted into a school, but the Government was in such difficulties prior to the discovery of the Diamond Fields, that public buildings had to be sold in all directions.

A very extensive fire had recently destroyed many of the old houses at Stellenbosh, nor is it likely that any great increase to the town will now take place. Speculation and investment are taking a wider range towards the east, hundreds of miles from Cape Town, where much greater profits can be realised.

It is much to be regretted that Stellenbosh does not possess any house worthy of being called an hotel in the humblest sense. Many of the country people drive to this town, but it is their invariable habit to visit their friends.

On leaving Stellenbosh I visited the Paarl, where there is a mountain of granite, the sun striking upon which heats the atmosphere unpleasantly.

From the Paarl we went on to Wellington, which was then the terminus of the only railroad in this colony, distant about seventy miles from Cape Town. In the next compartment to us were two Africander youths; one country, and the other town-bred; the former dressed in loose white coat, slouched hat, thick seal-skin vest and stout corduroy brown cords; the latter with smart blue necktie, soft black hat and tweed coat. They were happy over their bottle of Boer brandy and their banjo. They had an altercation at Wellington with the driver of the post-cart, as they desired him not to allow two native blacks to enter their carriage. The driver said he did not mind humouring these aristocratic proclivities, provided they would pay the fare for the places the natives would have occupied. They would not agree to this. Finally we saw them drive off, the four seated in the same vehicle, the pride of the white men giving way to this financial argument, and their annoyance forming a comical contrast to the broad grin of the Africans.

From Wellington we proceeded in the Diamond Field waggon through Baine's Kloof, a pass which was made by military labour in the first range of mountains which shuts in the lower districts round about Cape Town. This road is very narrow, but well made; the pass is high, and from its summit is seen a wide range of country laid out like a map beneath.

On the rocks in Baine's Kloof are carvings and paintings delineating the ostrich, the chamois, and other animals, executed no doubt by the Bushmen, who probably inhabited these rugged fastnesses at some former time.

After descending the mountain we crossed a river, the road being so narrow at one place that we were detained for a considerable time, a waggon having broken down exactly at the most inconvenient spot.

Here the railway works were progressing, many hundreds of natives from different parts of Africa being employed upon them. The daily fights amongst these people (who were overpaid, and, though new to spirits, drank them with avidity) were represented as so fearful that no European dared to interfere. Their heads are so hard that they are said to show but small signs of uneasiness when belaboured by the stoutest of cudgels. One of our English navvies said to me, " Lor, sir ! you may thrash them for a week and they don't mind it; they will come on and galox you, and worry you like a mastiff; your only chance is to have Dick Stivets (or iron-shod boots), they mind them, I warrant." These blacks are the amiable, enlightened youths that the Cape Colonial Government permitted to return to their native pastures, each carrying a rifle or a gun, saying that they could not even imagine harm, and much less would they use their weapons against the white man.

We now ascended by the pass to the village of Ceres. Here and there a stately secretary bird was walking, casting its eyes on either side, looking for the snakes, upon which it feeds. Very properly a penalty is imposed upon people who kill these destroyers of noxious animals.

We saw hundreds of natives, almost every one with his bottle of "Cape Smoke," and no wonder, as these savages earn from 4s. to 6s. per day.

The village of Ceres is prettily situated at the summit of the kloof, on the road leading into the Karoo. As it was the period of the Nacht Mael (or Holy Sacrament) the town was thronged with visitors, who came to attend the festival, a religious ceremony which takes place at each quarter of the year, and is seldom neglected.

Returning from Ceres down through the valley, we took the road to Worcester, and came across a herd of Racterick, which were not so wild as I had expected. Towards evening we entered Worcester. It is a rising town, exceedingly well watered, and reminded me much of an American city.

Mr. Cox, the Commissioner, received us with much kindness and attention; he was residing in a large house, the property of the Government, which had been built by Lord Charles Somerset, when Governor of the colony. It is said to have cost 38,000*l.*, and even that sum did not finish it; but this was before the days of legislative assemblies.

Strictures are made with regard to the extravagance of the government of Lord Charles Somerset. Some of these may be true, but few Governors of the colony can lay claim to having bestowed upon it greater benefits. To him is due the introduction into the country of some of the blood of the English racing stables, so that the Cape horse is now looked upon as one of the best in the world.

I saw a very old woman working in the garden, and was informed that she was the person who, when a girl, had given information to the Government concerning an outbreak among the natives. Upon that occasion many white people were killed, whilst many blacks afterwards suffered the extreme penalties of the law. She was very old—nearly a hundred—it was said, but she was still employed in the garden, drying peaches and plums.

Property at Worcester has very much increased in value, a natural consequence of opening up the country by the railroad.

During the first years of my residence at the Cape, few if any sanitary precautions were observed, and my utmost exertions with the Colonial Government or the City Commissioners failed to have any effect. In my four years of command I only succeeded in causing one drain to be covered in near the Castle, and this was in exchange for a permission highly advantageous to the Railway Company. On the arrival, however, of his Excellency Sir Bartle Frere, energetic steps were taken for the improvement of the drainage of the city. Very little pains had been taken about the supply of water, though the town possesses facilities for this purpose scarcely known in any part of the world. New tanks are now in progress, and if they are sufficiently capacious, they will prove invaluable; water can be readily stored and easily supplied to any part or to any building, however lofty. The reason of this carelessness is that the merchants, who have no thought for the improvement of the community at large, reside at a distance from the town. Their families, therefore, do not suffer from these inconveniences, and the shopkeepers, as a rule, retain too much of the old Dutch lethargy and economy to take any step which would cause increased taxation; even though it might add to the health and wellbeing of themselves and their children. Some years since whole families were poisoned by the lead of the water-pipes from the tanks, yet, at this moment, the same old lead pipes are used in many places to conduct the water through the city.

Although the Malay can live inexpensively upon fish, a large snook of 5 lb. or 6 lb. weight, the common article of their diet, costing only a penny or at most twopence, they have many expenses to meet. Every man who is above the extremest poverty indulges in the luxury of at least two wives, each of whom keeps her own establishment. These wives enjoy their holidays, are very fond of dress, and frequently insist upon picnic parties, which entails the necessity of hiring carriages for the country trip.

I was amused on one occasion by observing a Malay with his two wives choosing dresses. He placed himself between them, and, selecting the handsomest fabric for the younger and prettier, he put the other off with a less enticing and much cheaper article. Wives, however, are of considerable value. As a rule, they are not only required to keep themselves, but frequently to give a handsome sum of money weekly to their husbands. A washerwoman whom we employed gave up 1*l*. per week to her husband, and they are expected occasionally to pay all the expenses of the picnics, in which most of their earnings are spent.

On our arrival at the Cape the grape season had just commenced. Very fine grapes, apparently Black Hambro', were to be purchased at one penny per pound. These were sent in large quantities up the coast to Port Elizabeth and Natal, as, singularly enough, the change in the climate between the eastern and western portions of the colony is so great, that in the former the vine will not flourish.

Fish also was very plentiful, so much so that a Cape salmon of 10 lb. or 12 lb. weight could be purchased for 6*d*. or 8*d*., and other fish at a proportionately low price. Crayfish, which weigh 4 lb. or 5 lb. each, and which, when in season, are nearly as good as lobsters, are usually sold for a halfpenny a-piece.

It is said that crayfish are not good to eat when the moon is full. I endeavoured to find out the reason of this, but failed to do so, though I imagine it may be because they feed at spring-tides upon mussels and other fish, which, when thrown on the beach, are exposed to the sun, and soon become decayed.

I am bound to say, however, that the fish of the southern are most inferior to those of the northern hemisphere; and some of the mussels are very poisonous. On one occasion five warehousemen died through eating them, the effect being almost as rapid as that of prussic acid.

The cheapness of fish is one of the great reasons of the independence of the labour market. While the colony is prospering and labour is in request, the Malays, who at Cape Town are the principal source from which it is drawn, can buy their daily food in plenty for 4*d*. or 5*d*.; and as they love ease better than work, they keep up the rate of wages to 4*s*. and 5*s*. a day. The Legislature firmly set their face against the importation of coolies from China, the reason they give being that it would demoralise the community in general. The advocates for its introduction cannot obtain a voice in the House of Assembly. To breathe a syllable in its favour is sufficient utterly to defeat the chance of any candidate for parliamentary favour in Cape Town, where elections are determined to a great degree by the Malay element.

Household servants, of the most ignorant class, are not to be obtained much under 4*l*. per month, in addition to their food, and women for not less than 3*l*. These are the vilest of coolies, the most slovenly and dirty of servants, and their immorality is a blot to civilisation. My experience of the Chinese has proved them to be as clean and intelligent as any servants in the world. They combine the good qualities of the natives of Hindostan with the quickness of the Yankee.

All sorts of absurd stories were afloat about Cape Town

concerning the Celestials, which were greedily devoured by the unenlightened Dutch community. Amongst them was one that caused a great sensation. It was said that some Chinamen who arrived at San Francisco started a shop with a sausage-making machine, but lacking capital to carry on the concern, two of them agreed to murder the third, and turn him into sausages. This was the beginning of their success in business. The story was implicitly believed by many persons, who naturally desired that so hideous a tragedy should not be repeated at the Cape, and denounced the idea of allowing emigrant Chinese to enter the colony.

CHAPTER IV.

SWELLENDAM.

THE next part of the country in the neighbourhood of Cape Town which I visited, was Swellendam. We left the Wellington line of railway at D—— road, and after having passed through the pretty village of Somerset West, we ascended the mountains by Sir Lowry's Pass. The road is a great work, and one of immense utility; it is almost incredible that any waggon could have mounted the side of the range of hills before it was constructed. But a South African waggon, with a team of thirty-two bullocks, can accomplish almost anything. We stopped the first night at the house of Mr. Linden, the proprietor of 20,000 acres of land. He could not speak a word of English, so that our evening was naturally not a lively one. He was the happy possessor of 13,000 sheep, and as their value had risen in a few years from 2s. 6d. each to 1l., his wealth had increased very rapidly.

I saw large flocks of his sheep returning from pasturage, each led by a fine white goat. Mr. Linden was happy and content in his retired life, and though the town of Worcester was situated only a few miles distant, he never had visited it. Why should he? he had no business there, and why should he take the trouble to go? His farm was a fine one; it contained the grasses of the three veldts; sweet, sour, and mixed, or dry, wet, and equable, so that he had pastures for all seasons.

At Caledon we reached the mineral springs, where two boiling fountains were issuing from the rock.

These mineral springs would make the fortune of their owner in Europe, and may do so some day in Africa. Near them lay a piece of ground well adapted for the cultivation of tea. The warm ferruginous water could be brought to the soil, and would conduce to the development of the plant.

At Swellendam we were hospitably received by Mr. Barry, who has a large property both in the town and neighbourhood. He recommended me to proceed further into the country, and to mount the passes into the Karoo. I was very ready to do so, but I doubted its being feasible, as every one told me we should find neither lodging nor supplies. He assured me we should find both.

On leaving Swellendam we took an easterly course under the mountain range which separated us from the Karoo or Bock Veldt. As we were driving out of the town, we met a waggon with a team of ten horses, which a Dutch farmer (his nose surmounted by a huge pair of green goggles) was conducting with perfect ease. This ten-in-hand passed us at a rapid rate. He was assisted by a Hottentot, who sat beside him on the box, with a whip resembling a 17-feet salmon-rod, which he wielded with the utmost dexterity, touching-up any horse that his master ordered him, exactly on the part that he considered advisable.

A drive of about twenty miles brought us to the foot of the Southey Kop. There we found a well-furnished, comfortable hotel, where we breakfasted, and shortly after, ascending the mountain, reached the far-famed Karoo.

The road is a fine one. It was executed under the auspices of Mr. Santhey, late Colonial Secretary, and does credit both to him and to the colony. Prison labour constructed it; an excellent way of employing the services of those who would otherwise have been a burden on the Cape community.

We passed the afternoon buck-hunting on the hillside, shooting a great many buck. At night we slept at a farmhouse on the Slopes.

On the following day we were fortunate enough to see a few of the long-snouted baboons that inhabit these mountains, and are said to be very wicked and voracious. They worry dogs whenever occasion offers, and it is said that they will even attack a man. In the evening we were comfortably lodged and well treated; and the next day, when I made inquiries for the landlord and the bill, I discovered that the house, usually empty, had been furnished on the previous night; everything it contained having been sent in a waggon by Mr. Barry, whose hospitality we were still enjoying.

A number of the neighbouring proprietors, all Dutch, met us on the hill, each armed with his long gun, which his father may possibly have carried against the natives in the days of the Commandos. Our hunt was, however, very unfortunate. Dogs of all breeds, from the pure wolf to the lapdog, assisted in the amusement, covering the hillside, and yelping for pure spite. The deer, many miles distant, took the alarm, and, beyond an occasional glimpse, were never to be seen again. A dinner finished up the day, every kindness being shown to us by Mr. Moodie and his sister. On the following day we returned to Cape Town.

A subject of great magnitude and interest which attracted my attention was the defence of the Imperial harbours in South Africa. Should any accident occur to the Suez Canal, should it be destroyed or even rendered temporarily impassable in time of war, trade with our immense possessions in the East would be disturbed. It would be requisite, then, that our ships should adopt the alternative route by the Cape of Good Hope; thus returning to the line which was interrupted by the successful efforts of Mons. Lesseps.

There are three possible positions for harbours of defence for the British navy, Simon's Bay, Saldanha Bay, and Cape Town. I visited each of them, in order to study their relative advantages.

A careful inspection of Saldanha Bay leaves but little doubt that it does not possess the advantages of Simon's Bay. A crippled vessel would have the greatest difficulty in making the harbour with a foul wind, as it could not then get in without the assistance of a tug. The same objection applies to Cape Town; but an entrance into the inner bay at Simon's Town can be effected during all winds. In a fair wind the vessel, with her yards squared, runs directly from her moorings. In a foul wind, she makes the coast on one tack, and is then sure to find a wind off-shore which will bring her to her berth. There is a want of fresh water at Saldanha Bay, which it would be difficult to remedy, and in my opinion it is best adapted for its present use, viz. a quarantine station.

Assisted by the superior officer of the Royal Engineers and Artillery, and under instructions from home, a board was convened, and after an exhaustive inquiry plans were submitted for the improvement of the various town defences. These have received the approval of the authorities, and, if executed, they will defend our shipping in a very satisfactory manner.

When we reflect upon the enormous amount of British commerce which is carried on with India, China, and Australia, and with many other British possessions, it would be madness to leave to chance the defence of one of the great resting-places on the alternative route to the East.

Berg Island, which lies opposite to Saldanha Bay, is inhabited chiefly by rabbits, sea-birds, and enormous locusts. The ground is thickly strewn with the eggs of gulls and penguins, and the right of collecting which is leased for 25*l.* per annum. There are many guano islands off the coast, and as the rainfall is slight on the western seaboard, guano is abundant. The proprietor of one of them is said to realise profit from 800*l.* to 10,000*l.* a-year. He received this important right in exchange for some land at Cape Town, at a time when the Cape Government was poor and unable to pay cash.

On my return from Saldanha Bay I visited a large Dutch farmhouse, near the Berg river, with extensive out-buildings, the property of Mr. Kotsee. He received us with the greatest hospitality, ejecting most of his own family from their rooms to find us accommodation.

In the evening every inmate of the house joined at the supper table. The master and mistress, with their guests, sat above the salt. The junior members of the family and the Dutch servants sat below it. Good wines and choice meats were served to those in the former position; while those in the latter were helped afterwards, and contented themselves with the rough wines of the country.

At a short distance from the house ran the Berg river, navigable even beyond Mr. Kotsee's property. We were interested by his account of the last sea-cow which he had shot in the river. For some years it had been respected as a curiosity, but at last it became so ferocious that it attacked and killed two men. A hue and cry was then raised and it was ultimately killed. We saw the enormous teeth of the monster, and could readily imagine what a formidable brute it must have been.

On the following morning our host prepared for buck shooting. The Dutch are first-class hands at this sport, which is always carried on on horseback, and their horses by constant practice become perfectly trained. Mr. Kotsee mounted me upon his favourite mare. Good as she was, she managed, however, to tumble into a deep sand-hole, and sent me flying over her head, gun and all. But the sand was so soft and yielding, that in one minute I was again in the saddle, unhurt, and ready as ever for the sport.

The Dutch generally use a very long smooth-bore gun which we should regard as unwieldy and difficult to shoot with. Considerable practice is required to handle it, but it has this advantage, that, being long, it is impossible to fire into your own horse's head, as has occasionally happened with the short English double-barrelled weapon. They load these guns with swan-shot or very small pistol bullets, the charge weighing about one ounce.

The sportsmen proceed in line, one flank slightly in advance. The instant the buck, generally a Diker, starts out of the bush, the well-trained horse stops perfectly still, thus giving an opportunity to the rider for a shot, which with these Dutchmen generally takes effect, as they are almost daily accustomed to this sport from their youth upwards.

The day was so hot, it being in the middle of December, the hottest month in the year, that I did not remain many hours on the veldt, but before quitting the party we had killed about a dozen deer.

During the day we saw some wild ostriches. A heavy fine is set upon their destruction. In the breeding season their nests are sought out and carefully watched night and day by Hottentots until the young ones are hatched, when they are immediately caught, and brought up under turkeys or tame ostriches. I saw a curious instance of this at Swellendam, where an ostrich, three weeks old, and twice the size of its foster-parent, was carefully tended by an old turkey hen.

Leopards, which formerly were very numerous, are not unfrequently met with on these dry plains. They are destroyed by poisoned meat. An officer of the garrison purchased a pair, and requested permission to bring them into his quarters in the castle; but, as there were many young children of the Royal Artillery in the barrack, he was refused. He therefore left them in charge of a Malay in the neighbourhood. On going to claim them the Malay said, much to the owner's consternation, "There are the pair, but one has eaten the other!"

Mr. Kotsee employed a good many men on his farm, all natives. Their wages were 2s. 6d. a man per day, in addition to a cottage and two pints of wine, with full rations of meat and flour. Think of that, ye labourers of Great Britain!

Mr. Kotsee very naturally regretted the olden days when each farmer possessed his slaves. It was by them that the fine old farmhouses with their ample out-buildings were erected, and by their labour that the old Dutch proprietor cultivated his wines, and bred his sheep and his horses. He might then, indeed, consider himself lord of all he surveyed.

The fishing station at the mouth of the Berg river on St. Helen's Bay is of considerable importance, employing 800 men. Mr. Kotsee's brother caught 30,000 fish there in a few days, and sold them for 10s. per hundred. The number of crayfish caught on this coast is perfectly surprising; they average 5 lbs. weight, and are generally sold in Cape Town for 1d. each.

There are large farms in this district for horse breeding. Mr. Melkes pays great attention to the subject; he owns about 300 mares, and has imported some first-rate blood-horses from England. Of late years the wear and tear of horses at the Cape has been enormous.

On the discovery of the Diamond Fields a rush was made to them from all parts of the colony. Animals of two years old even were pressed into the service, and scenes of the greatest cruelty took place. The poor beasts, driven for hours and deprived of food and water, sunk by scores upon the roads running through the wild Karoo. But horses were then cheap and the reward at the fields very great, and the cry was, "Perish all, but let us snatch the prize before it is too late." This wholesale destruction, and the necessity of replacing those used-up, made horses reach fabulous prices; so that for a team of four, which I could certainly have purchased for 20*l.* a piece on my first visit to the Cape in 1842, 80*l.* each was now demanded. Such high prices naturally produced a desire on the part of the farmers to increase their stock, which requires time. I have no doubt, however, that breeding will be profitable, and that ere long a considerable importation will take place of Cape horses into England. It is calculated that horses can be bred in South Africa, and raised to the age of four years old at a cost of about 4*l.* each. Taking into account the expense of sending them home, the death of some, and other casualties, they certainly can be landed in London at about 20*l.* per head. They would fetch on an average 40*l.* or perhaps 60*l.* a piece, and a considerable profit would remain to the breeder or importer.

Formerly there was a large exportation of horses to India, and inquiries from that country have been lately made on the subject, the demand being for the purpose of remounting cavalry, but the Cape cannot now supply them. There has been a murrain or horse sickness, which has proved fatal, especially in the large horse-breeding districts in the north of the colony and the Transvaal.

There was a report that her Majesty's cavalry were to be mounted under an arrangement different from the old system, by which each commanding officer was to be charged with providing the horses for his regiment, and that in future the whole were to be selected under a general officer specially charged with this duty. Steps might certainly be taken for forming a dépôt in South Africa at which horses could be collected, and a certain number embarked by every mail steamer. I see no reason why excellent animals, with strength, breeding, and every requisite qualification, should not be supplied to our troops at home at an average price, including every expense, of 30*l.* or 33*l.* per horse. When this becomes known there is little doubt but that successful speculations will be made for the supply of the London market.

When I commanded a division of the Bombay army in Scinde, my best batteries were horsed with Cape horses, brought over under an arrangement made by the Governor of Bombay,

Sir George Clark, who, having been Commissioner on the settlement of the Orange Free State boundary, and being himself a first-rate horseman, wisely took measures to import these excellent animals into India. Many of the Dutch farmers near Cape Town have a great dislike to sell their horses. It frequently happens that a farmer possesses a far larger number than he can possibly require and yet nothing can induce him to part with one. He looks upon it as a sort of degradation; he is proud of possessing them and of showing them, but he will not hear of selling them. The boys of South Africa are lamentably deficient in truth-telling: I saw many instances of this. A lad who was driving my waggon, told me with pride how he had cheated a horsedealer by tying a cord round a horse's leg, so as to produce artificial lameness. I remember that on one occasion great offence was given by a sermon preached upon the subject of lying, by the Dean of Cape Town. I fear that the anger it occasioned was greatly increased by the consciousness that it was deserved.

One of the amusements most enjoyed in the cool season at Cape Town was hunting with fox-hounds, the property of the 24th Regiment.

There were plenty of foxes in the low-lands between Table and False Bays. The hounds were often taken to a greater distance, the dogs, horses, and horsemen, remaining at the house of some hospitable farmer. These hospitalities were returned by the officers, who at the termination of the season gave a grand entertainment to the farmers, which was very much appreciated. They showed much amazement at the mess dinner and plate. On one occasion a farmer whose plate had been changed more than once could contain his surprise no longer, and exclaimed, "What another clean plate! why, I have had six already and is there another still?"

CHAPTER V.

BOUND FOR THE EASTERN FRONTIER.

In the spring of 1874 I made my first tour of inspection into the interior of South Africa, and these tours eventually extended to many thousands of miles. They were most interesting and professionally valuable to myself, but the knowledge which I obtained was in the sequel, not very advantageous, as my experiences caused me to differ widely from the responsible advisers of the Cape Colonial Government. What I learned made me draw certain conclusions, which were too frequently verified, but the fact of my honestly avowing them was so distasteful that it procured me enemies, whose animosity grew more bitter when it became apparent that my forecasts had been correct.

On the 6th of May, I left Table Bay in the Union Company's steamer *Syria*, with my military secretary and one aide-de-camp.

One of our passengers was part owner of the new Rush Diamond Mine at Kimberley, and had visited Cape Town for the purpose of selling it. He had made the purchase two years previously from a Dutch farmer, at the fabulous sum, as it then appeared to the Dutchman, of 6000*l*. The price he now asked was 120,000*l*. In the following year 100,000*l*. was actually paid to the owners, and at that price it was, in my opinion, a most judicious purchase.

About 6 P.M. we passed Robben Island. This small tract of land has been devoted to many useful purposes by the Government. Political prisoners have there usually found their compulsory home. Many of the Kafir chiefs who rebelled in the war of 1846 were kept in durance there, and some who are now at large, and were foremost in the late rebellion spent years there.

Robben Island is also the abode of the lunatics of the Cape Colony. They are represented as seldom violent or intractable. Indeed one of them was especially useful to the sportsmen who went over periodically to shoot rabbits and quails. His services were always employed, for he possessed the qualities of the most sensitive of pointers. He was able to distinguish, with wonderful perception, the exact hiding-place of the quail, which he carefully approached and indicated to the sportsman, as well as the best trained sporting dog could have done. If, however, two or three birds were missed, he would return to his home disgusted with the sportsman's incapacity, and nothing could induce him to give further assistance. But if he found that he was attending upon a proficient in the art he would willingly hunt the whole day.

Robben Island is turned to a third purpose, that of sheltering lepers, wretched outcasts, cursed with the most hideous form of disease that mankind can bear. This island cannot therefore be looked upon as a paradise.

A magnificent view of Table Mountain is obtained from the sea, and as the evening sun lit up the distant landscape with its rays the bold outline of that celebrated plateau loomed grandly from the closing shades. The lights of receding Cape Town danced gaily on the rising surf, and an ominous whistling through the rigging gave promise of a rough reception off the Cape of Good Hope, known of old as the "Cape of Storms."

On the evening of the 7th we landed at Port Elizabeth, and were hospitably received by Colonel Wyld. There is no harbour here, only an open roadstead, but Sir John Coode, in his able report, has recommended that a breakwater or protector, after the plan of the one at Plymouth, should be placed in front of the town. I have seen it stated that the requisite expense, which would not exceed 900,000*l.*, has been voted to meet it, at a meeting of the Chamber of Commerce. Already the commerce of Algoa Bay far exceeds that of Cape Town, and as the merchants are more energetic and advanced Port Elizabeth will probably become the foremost harbour in South Africa.

As we expected an invitation to shoot bushbuck at Bushey Park, we did not now tarry in the town, but proceeded to the mansion of its warm-hearted proprietor, about eight miles distant from Port Elizabeth. The country through which we passed was quite open, but was said to have been one immense forest eighty years ago.

The owner of Bushey is a son of a settler of 1820, at which time the Government took energetic steps to send emigrants to Africa. They landed on the eastern portion of the colony, and this is the reason why so many English families are located near Algoa Bay. There can be no doubt that in this forest of the past there roamed large herds of elephants, as the bones of these animals are being continually found in the kloofs and watercourses.

We managed to kill six or eight bushbuck, and ate an excellent lunch of venison, under a thick bush in the valley. On our way back to the city we called at the house of Mr. Stewart, Consul-General for the Mexican Republic. Here we met Mr. Garland, who had just returned with two waggons containing the produce of his successful hunting on the Zambesi, on which expedition he had been absent for two years. He had started with these two waggons and forty oxen. The fitting out of his expedition must have cost him a considerable sum of money, but he was well repaid, for he told me he had killed every species of wild animal known in South Africa except the lion, which he kept clear of. One hundred and fifty elephants had fallen to the rifles of himself and friend. In one district alone in which he shot, five hundred elephants had last year been killed, and he felt sure that now that the Kafirs were being so largely armed, not one single elephant would be found on this side of the Zambesi in ten years time. To cross this river would appear to be most difficult, as the natives will not permit sportsmen to do so. It is said that when Livingstone first crossed he knelt down and publicly prayed. The Kafirs construed this into the act of taking possession of the country, and became so alarmed that they have now entirely closed this part of the river against the white man. A few natives of the Zambesi accompanied Mr. Garland to Port Elizabeth. Their astonishment at seeing the ocean was not to be described, and it was not less at the big ships they saw upon it.

Speaking of sporting, it is a singular fact that it is next to impossible to breed dogs in this country. Nineteen out of twenty die at an early age, and this becomes so disheartening that few persons now attempt it. One dreadful malady, however, to which dogs in Europe are subjected, is unknown in South Africa. It is stated, upon the best authority, that no instance of hydrophobia has ever appeared, which is the more singular as the arid influences to which portions of this continent is subjected are proverbial.

At Port Elizabeth the rate of labour was often higher than at Cape Town, no less than 7s. a day, or even more, being paid to the native Kafir for unloading lighters. Here was a contrast which afforded me an opportunity for some professional reflections. The subaltern officers under my own command, many of whom had paid nearly five hundred pounds for their commission, exclusive of their education and other expenses, were receiving from the State only 5s. 3d. daily pay; and a Suffolk labourer would be locked out for dreaming of asking more than 13s. a week. These natives have learnt to be very clever and cunning. It is stated that when the florin first came into use, a Scotchman of Port Elizabeth paid his Kafirs in florins instead of half-crowns. The natives were not long in finding out the trick, and now the florin is universally known amongst them as the "Scotchman." The wages of native servants are so high, and they are so independent, that I heard it was sometimes difficult to get a washerwoman even at 5s. a day.

I had made inquiries as to the best means of proceeding to Grahamstown, eighty miles distant. No less than 40*l*. was asked for the hire of a carriage to convey myself and staff this short distance. I had therefore taken the precaution of directing commissariat carts and mules from King William's Town to meet us. On the following morning, as we were leaving, we observed the milk-boy going his rounds. His manner of carrying the milk deserves mention. Over his head he placed a sack with a hole for his head, and one for each arm. At both front and rear were seen rows of pockets, in each of which he had placed a bottle of milk—milk at the Cape being invariably sold by the bottle.

The Cape Cart is an institution in South Africa. It is perfectly astonishing what it will hold and over what roads it will travel. Ours was a cart on two wheels with two seats—it was drawn by six mules, excellent animals. In addition to myself and two officers, it carried the driver, a large amount of baggage, three rifles, two fowling-pieces, and a plentiful supply of ammunition. In the second cart we placed our tent and various boxes of preserved meats. These provisions are absolutely essential in South Africa, whenever a journey is to be undertaken, if the slightest deviation is to be made from the high road, or beyond the immediate vicinity of the large towns. We thus travelled more comfortably and less expensively, though scarcely in so expeditious a manner as we might have done in the regular stage-coach.

The conveyance is fitted with a strong pole, and harnessed

like a curricle, a carriage which used to be very fashionable in England sixty or seventy years ago.

Some of the mules were old, but very good. Before I left South Africa many of them were changed, but I believe that I sat behind one of them in my different journeys in this country for more than eight thousand miles.

The next day we drove about forty miles. On the road we met at least one hundred and fifty large waggons, each drawn by a "span" of sixteen pairs of oxen abreast, thirty-two in all, loaded with twenty-two bales of wool. On a rough calculation the value of each load was about 70*l*. Thus we met upwards of 100,000*l*. worth of wool in the day on its way to Port Elizabeth. Most extraordinary sounds proceeded from the drivers of these waggons.

On the plains by the side of the road we saw a few bustards, and the blue Kafir crane, as well as many of those beautiful birds, the Kafir finch. They are black, and brilliantly coloured crimson or gold on the breast and under the wings, with an extremely long tail of but two feathers. Each male of the species is accompanied by two females, small insignificant creatures, not unlike the English wren. Thus, although they are polygamists after the manner of the country, they are not unreasonable in their indulgence.

We saw many beautiful blue and other parti-coloured birds, and met many Kafirs. I particularly remarked one good-looking girl with a bundle on her back. On nearer approach we discovered it to contain a baby, who was taking his nourishment, which was easily and readily supplied, over his mother's shoulder, during the march.

When halfway to Grahamstown we were overtaken by Cobb's coach. These carriages are of American build, and under the management of an American firm. They are very suitable to the wants of the colony in its present state and are well filled by passengers. I should imagine that the line must be profitable, as the fare from Port Elizabeth to Kimberley, a distance of about four hundred and fifty miles, is charged at the rate of 18*l.* for the single journey, with 1*s.* 6*d.* per pound for all luggage in excess of forty pounds. These coaches perform the journeys in about five and a half or six days, and when all circumstances are taken into consideration, the badness of the roads, the price of forage, the wear and tear of horses, &c., the charge, which would appear excessive in Europe, cannot be looked upon as out of the way in South Africa.

We met a well-laden waggon. The "forelooper," a boy attending to the leading oxen, neglecting his duty, the bullocks dashed off the road, and the ponderous machine went crashing down the steep banks. We could not, however, wait to see what injury had occurred. The proprietor of the hotel at Nazor had just returned from the Diamond Fields. Getting tired of his non-success there, he had sold his claim for 15*l.*, from which the new owner had obtained 300*l.* worth of diamonds on the morning after his departure, and in a very short time afterwards thousands of pounds more.

I had been led to believe that the Africanders were early risers, but on this and on many subsequent occasions I found it just the reverse. It was with much difficulty we could get the servants up in the morning to produce the requisite cup of coffee.

Early ablutions are not in high favour in South Africa. Indeed we were strongly advised against such proceedings. One colonial gentleman, who was thoroughly accustomed to travelling in this country, said to me, "General, be careful on your journeys very seldom to wash your face, for there is nothing which will cost you more annoyance or ultimate discomfort." The natives seldom indulge in what we are pleased to consider a necessity, but they frequently substitute for it a dust or sand bath.

It was here that a lady who had somewhat passed her

'*première jeunesse*,' begged to be allowed to occupy a seat in our second cart. Knowing the expense and difficulty of finding any conveyance in this country, I had not the heart to refuse. About seven miles from Grahamstown, Judge D—— with his six-in-hand, met us at the foot of the mountain. This he did to bring us into the city in finer style. He handled his ribbands artistically, and had promised himself a very flourishing entry. Judge of his dismay as he observed this elderly female, whom he took to be one of our party, and whom he recognised as the '*sage femme*' of the city. The Judge not only handled his reins like a practised whip but played on the bugle like a cavalry trumpeter. He is as good a soldier as he is a judge, and has edited several military books for the militia, which are professionally very valuable.

If any town on the east of the Cape Colony can be called old Grahamstown may lay claim to this distinction. It is certainly the handsomest that has yet been built in that country. The most dangerous moment for Grahamstown was when it was attacked by Kafirs, about forty years ago.

It possibly might have been plundered and burnt, but for the assistance of some hunters, who arrived by chance, and helped the small garrison with their heavy rifles. It was satisfactory to see the great progress which had been made with the railway. In a few years it will be completed as far as to the town.

The distance from Grahamstown to the port at the Kowie is not more than thirty-five miles. A good deal of money has been expended in the endeavour to create a harbour at Port Alfred, but the water is so shallow for a considerable distance from the shore that a really good and safe anchorage will probably never be made for any but the smallest vessels.

I had wonderful accounts of the quail shooting near the coast, which was stated to be then at its prime, so that a good shot could easily kill from fifty to sixty brace of quail in a day.

Good Sport.—A Journal has the following:—

A city sportsman—perhaps we should term him a semi-citizen—was successful in bagging no less than one hundred and a-half brace of quail on Saturday last. The birds were found on the Barville Park lands, near Port Alfred. The same sportsman was nearly as successful some three seasons ago, when he bagged ninety brace in one day. On five consecutive occasions on Saturday, his shot-pouch returned him twenty-five birds. Considering that the day's programme included nearly fifty miles of travelling, the above is perhaps an unprecedented feat in this colony.

At Grahamstown I had the pleasure of making the acquaintance of the Dean, a man of great ability, who has done much service to the colony by his energy and his writings. His advocacy of Federation, and of a provincial division of the country, has induced people to look narrowly into the subject. He has shown the colonists the benefits which would result to South Africa by such measures. It was said that he is looked upon by the Kafirs as a powerful rain-doctor. After a very long drought, he caused special prayers for rain to be said in the cathedral. Hardly had the congregation left the church when plentiful showers set in, which the Kafirs at once set down to magic.

Those who have been accustomed to move in railways in Europe can scarcely realise the tedium of travelling in South Africa. We were fortunate in being able to traverse the eighty miles from Port Elizabeth in two days. Again, the distances between military posts are little known at home. A story is often told of a War Office official who desired to know the reason why the chaplain at Grahamstown could not perform his evening service at King William's Town, being entirely ignorant of the fact that the two cities are ninety miles asunder.

We passed by scenes historical in the old war, and which have again become so in the recent one.

The kloofs and gorges in the mountains and forests remain unaltered, and demonstrate the perplexities of attack, and the facilities of defence. The attack, more especially, is increased in difficulty now that the Kafir is armed with a long shooting weapon in lieu of the assegai, which though deadly at short distances is ineffective beyond thirty or forty yards.

We forded the Great Fish river. It was stated to be low and therefore not dangerous, but our mules were immersed up to their shoulders, and our tent, which was strapped on behind the cart, was soaked in water. I was not sorry when we arrived at its eastern bank. When crossing this stream my predecessor in command remarked to the ferryman upon the danger incurred in passing it. The man answered that it only required a bishop or a general to be drowned, to cause a good bridge to be built. Before I left the colony a fine bridge had been erected.

In the recesses of the forest we came upon a party of young natives, who had been temporarily banished from their kraals, and said to reside in the woods for the purpose of undergoing the rites of circumcision. These youths appeared to be about fourteen years old. Their faces and bodies were smeared with whitewash. The heads of some of them were bound up in faggots of straw. Otherwise they were perfectly naked. The full time of probation, during which they are compelled to live in seclusion, is about five or six weeks. It is a custom obligatory on the Kafir, and it is a point of honour with him to show that he can bear the suffering without evincing fear, otherwise he is branded as a coward.

At Debe Neck, near the south-west of the Amatola Mountains, there is a singular feature to be observed in the excavations of the "Commitjee"—a curious small worm, something of the white-ant species. Many millions of these creatures are at work continuously, and succeed in forming large circular holes on either side of the road, extending for several square miles. They are generally about eight or ten feet in diameter, and four feet deep.

By a handsome approach over the Buffalo river we entered King William's Town.

On the following morning my review parade was augmented both by the mounted police and the volunteers, who turned out in some numbers to assist in the military manœuvres.

The Frontier Armed and Mounted Police, as they are distinctively called, are a special body, which was originally formed by Sir George Cathcart, when Governor of the Cape, at the termination of the war in 1852. It was found, and very naturally, that however valuable the services of the Burghers might be, they were too irregular to be really useful, so that it was absolutely requisite that the civil magistrates should possess a force immediately available at all times to repress disorders. The police force was in a great measure composed of farmers' sons, as the pay and allowances which were granted were considered at that time to be very handsome. A good horse could then be purchased for 10*l.*, meat was not more than 2*d.* per lb., and everything else was in proportion. As years rolled on, the Africander farmers' sons would no longer enter the service. Other fields of labour presented themselves, of a much more lucrative character ; such as diamond and gold digging, and transport riding (which means accompanying waggons to distant parts of the colony with merchants' goods). It became requisite to obtain young men from England. The selection was left to the Colonial Agent, possibly a clever man for civil duties, but not at all acquainted with military ones, having no special knowledge of our profession. He appears to have represented that the lowest standard of pay in this force was from five to six

E

shillings a-day per man, so that he had no difficulty in obtaining recruits. The men, however, found on their arrival that deductions from this pay were made for the purchase of horses, accoutrements, their own keep, that of their horses, and other extraneous expenses. They came to the conclusion, therefore, that they had been deceived, and said (with truth) that they were infinitely worse off than the British soldier, for whom all these extras were provided by Government.

A general discontent therefore pervaded the force, more especially as it required two years in most cases before the men could rid themselves of debt. Added to this, many of the officers had grown old in the service, and were without much hope of promotion. Although well acquainted with the country, they had not been brought up to military habits. They could command the quiet Dutch Boer, but when this horde of young Londoners were thrust upon them, with their knowing ways and clever tactics, these 'civil officers were quite disconcerted. There was scarcely more than one person in the Civil Government who was well acquainted with the manner of governing soldiers, and he was in a position far removed from detailed interference, being the Under-Secretary of the Government. It was impossible that the Under-Colonial Secretary should be able to lend his own skill to those in whose hands the force was placed, and the Government, who had lately accepted the responsibility of it, were far too jealous of their power to allow any military commander to supervise, much less to command, the Frontier Armed and Mounted Police.

The utmost they did was to request my inspection of the force. I found it composed of a fine set of young men, physically strong and robust. Three-fourths of their number appeared to be altogether ignorant of the very rudiments of discipline, and, with some notable exceptions, neither the officers nor the non-commissioned officers had any influence over the men.

I found the force, as a rule, miserably mounted, very indifferently clothed, wretchedly armed and equipped, and wanting in all the accessories necessary for taking the field. Upon all these points I reported to the Colonial Government in 1874. A few reforms were made subsequently; improvements took place in the horses, and in the equipment and clothing; but the command of the force, in my opinion, was not administered in such a way as to produce the success which might naturally have been expected. Unfortunately my fears were but too well verified. When the war and rebellion of 1877 and 1878 broke out, the force was so utterly disorganised, that the Colonial Minister of War, who at the time charged himself with its supervision, informed me that, although he was assisted by one of the cleverest military officers attached, he was positively unable, after two months' hard work, to discover the duties or even the whereabouts of fully 200 men out of a force of 1100.

This was the only cavalry force at my command wherewith to commence the war with Kreli, the Galeka chief, in a country which is specially adapted for the employment of cavalry.

I had however, a small body of artillery, under an officer in her Majesty's service; but the guns were inadequately horsed, and the carriages, which were constructed in the colony, broke down on the first occasion on which they were used.

CHAPTER VI.

VOLUNTEER CAVALRY.

ALL the Volunteer Cavalry paraded on the occasion of my inspection at King William's Town. I formed a high estimate of them. Many of the farmers had been non-commissioned officers in our cavalry regiments, and I clearly saw that their influence over the rest would be exercised for good if they were called upon for active service, and that, if only they would pay deference to authority, they would be valuable in war.

The Infantry Volunteers, composed of the young men of business in the city, would doubtless defend it with determination; but their services need not be relied upon for any concentrated operations at a distance, as they cannot leave their homes. The corps that eventually did valuable service in the Galeka Land Campaign were principally recruited in the large cities, but they were not composed of those members who had formerly been enrolled in the Volunteer ranks, or of the young well-to-do shopmen.

It became apparent that in case of need the colony lacked a force upon which it could rely to put down incipient rebellion. I forcibly represented this to the Government. I recommended a militia upon the Canadian model, as a ready and inexpensive method for meeting any difficulties that might arise. Already the frontier settlers were becoming uneasy, as from the manners of the natives they foresaw the coming struggle.

A very large sale of firearms, with but slender restrictions, had been going on; the black man was arming—for what purpose it was scarcely difficult to divine. There was but little or no game in the country, the reckless and wasteful habits of the savage having destroyed it. My warnings, which were yearly repeated, were however little heeded, being met with repeated assurances that there never would be another Kafir war; and as to arms, that the assegai was far more dangerous in the hands of the native than a musket.

How sadly the reverse has been proved in the late war, which has destroyed many a happy homestead! How few have fallen or been injured by the assegai! how many brave men have been shot down by the musket!

Early on the following morning the hounds met within a few miles of King William's Town. We had an excellent run of an hour and a half, killing one buck. Believing in the value of field sports to military men, I have always done my utmost to encourage them. They strengthen the nerves, evoke courage, give effect to natural intelligence, and are much better than loitering round the billiard table, or lounging on the parades or streets of a town. It is most satisfactory to see the general acceptation of these sentiments throughout England. Some are even in favour of giving marks to physical excellence in competitive examinations, and not treating mental acquirements as the only tests of fitness for military service.

Towards the end of the week, under the auspices of the Civil Commissioner, Mr. Rose Innes, an interesting and, to me, novel event took place. A native buck hunt was organised in the Perie Bush, an outlying portion of the Amatola range, rendered memorable by its military and historical recollections.

The magistrate gave permission to certain chiefs to assemble their men for the purpose of beating the bush for bucks. Two thousand Kafirs joined in the hunt. The arrangement was that they should drive the forest for three days—encompassing a large extent of country, so that on the third day, when the game was supposed to be driven to a centre, the English officers and other invited guests being posted in advantageous positions might have a good chance of killing them.

The produce of the three days' chase was about a hundred and twenty head of different species, but only two or three of these fell to the guns of the English sportsmen. The manner in which the natives hunted them was this: No sooner was a buck discovered in the bush than the Kafirs quickly formed a ring round it, gradually tightening the cordon so as to mob the animal in the centre. As they were dexterous with the assegai and knobkerrie at short distances, it was easily despatched. They immediately lighted a fire and, after a very superficial cooking, they ate the game then and there. This will account for the very short range of ground that was got over during the day, as parties of natives were killing, cooking, and eating the product of the chase in turn, and little was brought out of the forest but the skins and horns.

When the hunt was concluded, these savages treated us to a war-dance. Their heated bodies, begrimed with blood, added in no small degree to the diabolical picture in this deep-wooded glen, which became the scene of much bloodshed towards the termination of the war.

It is difficult for one who has not visited South Africa to realise the labour of threading one's way through its thorny jungles, but this became better understood when the Kafirs, under Sandilli, subsequently ensconced themselves in these fastnesses.

On my way home I was struck by the want of costume of the natives. The men were ploughing and cultivating their fields entirely in a state of nature. The women were simply attired in a tiny apron, rather prettily adorned with beads. The weather was hot, and no doubt long habit had caused them to consider this garb as suitable as well as pleasant.

Before leaving King William's Town I had ample opportunities of conversing with those who were well acquainted with the natives both within the colony and in the semi-independent states beyond. The general impression was that the natives would not settle down without at least one more trial of their strength, that the last war was only remembered by the old men, and that the young chiefs now growing into manhood felt themselves quite equal to the white man. An opinion prevailed that we were afraid of them, and desired to court and conciliate them. Otherwise why did we allow them to extort such enormous wages for working on the railroad, two and sixpence and three shillings a day, when the current rate throughout the frontier, previous to these Government works, had not been more than one shilling? And why did we allow to purchase arms and ammunition?

This was an exceedingly dangerous state of things, and there were few on the frontier who did not feel anxiety. Men of experience and in high position all stated their conviction that mischief was brewing.

Generally the Government policy of allowing the natives to buy guns promiscuously was condemned by those resident on the frontier. But a sort of infatuation possessed the people in the West and the Colonial Ministry. The Prime Minister stated in his speech at Sir John Coode's public entertainment that "the frontier newspapers made these assertions as attacks against the Ministry, and that the farmers on the frontier had grown to be cowards!"

Restrictions against the possession of arms were enacted, but they were so defective as not to be capable of explanation by the highest law officers of the colony. In the opinion of some, it was even lawful to kill a native who, being armed and carrying no licence, attempted to resist disarmament; but others contended that this offence could only be dealt with by a lengthened process of law, and punished with a very small fine. The law was carried out in so lax a manner that Kafirs on all sides (whether by permission or not) obtained arms, and it was scarcely necessary that muskets should be sold by traders under fictitious names, like that by which they were known to the Kafirs, " Baboons' thighs."

On Friday, the 22nd of May, we left King William's Town.

At Fort Cunynghame and Greytown we came upon a large number of Gaika Kafirs, who had come from their location to enjoy themselves with Cape brandy, at the canteen or shop. Numbers of them were lying on the ground, each with his bottle beside him.

The facility with which these untamed savages can obtain any amount of villainous drink is one of the most fruitful sources of danger. Some of the chiefs, being aware of the evil, forbid canteens in their locations; and have repeatedly requested that the same prohibition should be extended among the adjoining districts. The answer of authority has always been "that the natives should place a *moral* restraint upon themselves, and not imbibe more than is beneficial; and that trade cannot be impeded simply because it may engender evil consequences amongst the natives."

At the Dohne tollbar, some few miles beyond Greytown, the Chief Sandilli met me by invitation. He was a tall, good-looking man, and it is surprising how young he seemed for his age, more especially as he is reputed to be continually under the influence of liquor. He was delighted with the present I made him of a large tartan rug, but he begged for some spirits; and he asked for sixpence from each of my staff. I cannot believe that the request for so trifling a sum was made solely with the object of obtaining means for the temporary enjoyment of a bottle of "Cape Smoke." I imagine it was as a sort of recognition of his superiority before the bar of native opinion, so that those about should see that he received a sort of tribute even from the officers of the white men in the colony.

The next time I met Sandilli was at Greytown, where he was enjoying himself at the canteen with a circle of friends. My son took a very good likeness of him there. I have never seen him since, although I frequently hoped to have done so as a prisoner in Robben Island. His acts of rebellion justly entitled him to be lodged there. Towards the end of the war this wretched chief was shot in his retreat at the Perie Bush.

On the borders of Sandilli's location there were five canteens in about thirty-five miles of road. The sale of spirits in these houses in the aggregate was considered to amount to about two hundred and fifty gallons in the week, and it was stated that at least 2000l. passed over each small bar in the course of the year.

We here first came upon the genuine Gaika Kafirs. They do not now generally use the karofs, or prepared skins of the tiger, wild deer, or fox, but adopt our blankets. They manipulate them in their own special way by mixing a quantity of red clay with grease, with which they thickly smear the blanket. By this process it acquires some of the properties of the skin karofses which it has replaced. It keeps out the cold, renders the covering almost waterproof, and makes it last very much longer. The red clay is also stated to have the effect of protecting the persons of the wearers from vermin, and the ochre colour has not an unpleasant appearance, particularly on the women, whose bodies resemble a well-cleaned copper kettle. Many of the latter, however, now partially adopt our ladies' dress. A storekeeper at Peeltown told me that he excited the cupidity of a Kafir by telling him, that if he refused to purchase a lady's bodice at 1l. 17s. he would give it to his own wife. Upon this the native said "No; it having been offered to him he had a right to buy it," paid the money at once and took it away to his own location.

The Bontebok flats consist of excellent agricultural lands, but they are not now tilled, or very partially so.

Some years since a Company was started for the purpose of establishing farming and horse-breeding on them. The finest of mangels and turnips were grown, and excellent horses of first-class English blood were bred; but all enterprise in the Cape Colony was then stagnant, the Diamond Fields had not been discovered, there was no call for horses, no war to require them in India or Europe, and but little demand for fat mutton. Thus the enterprise fell through, involving its originators in a very considerable loss.

We stopped for the night at Pusey's Hotel, immediately over the Kei river. Here we met with some gold diggers returning from Pilgrims' Rest in the Transvaal. They showed us some nuggets, each three or four ounces in weight, averaging in value about 4*l.* sterling per ounce; but they all seemed to agree that the labour of extracting them was out of all proportion to their value. In this opinion a subsequent visit that I made to these far distant gold regions induced me to concur.

All the ground we were now traversing became the arena of constant contention during the war of 1878. We were on the borders of the Amatolas, to the kloofs and forests of which the Kafirs are sure to retire in the event of being pressed.

A few miles beyond Tylden, and near a station which was occupied for their young recruits by the mounted police, we came to the Kranz or rocky defiles, renowned for the drawings of the Bushmen.

These diminutive people have long since retired from this portion of the country or have been exterminated. Their hand was against every one. They appear to have been irreclaimable, and the hand of every one was against them. These pigmy savages never erected houses or kraals wherein to shelter themselves, but made use of caves in the sides of the mountains. They held ready near the mouth of these holes a bush, which they dragged after them when they entered; peering through the intervening spaces from behind, they readily fired their small poisoned arrows at any one who might be passing, with deadly effect; nor was it often easy to discover whence these arrows came.

As long as the Bushmen (Bosjesmans, as they were called by the Dutch) were in this country it is said that no man could travel with safety. They stealthily approached when least expected and, with murderous aim, shot an arrow into their victim. When they could not steal or carry off his horse, they shot at the animal, which at first showed no signs of injury, but ultimately, with fatal certainty, it had to be left on the Veldt to perish. When the traveller left, the horse was eaten by these incarnate savages, while the flesh was yet warm and quivering.

Very few are now to be met with in the colony, as nearly the last of them were said to have been destroyed about the year 1871 by an expeditionary force under Malappa, a son of Moshesh, the Basuto, in the lower spurs of the Drakensberg.

The men would not surrender, and were killed.

Some of the women were caught and sent into the colony, where they were apprenticed to farmers.

How strange it is that these creatures, so low in the social scale, should have possessed artistic skill superior to most savages! They have portrayed on the rough rocks scenes of the chase and of native customs with such vigour, with a few colours of so permanent a character, that the spectator might take them for rough first sketches by some untrained artist, executed only a short while since.

Each animal is characteristically rendered, and the manner of chasing and securing it, with the figures of those who assisted in running it down, are faithfully shown.

Possessing such admirable talents in so high a degree, these people were yet incapable of attempting the erection of any description of house, but sheltered themselves in such caverns and rocky niches as nature happened to provide.

Some of these drawings include forty or fifty figures, correctly representing the chase of the lion, the eland, the rhinoceros, the gnu, the blesbok, and many other wild animals, all vigorously drawn and coloured in a species of distemper.

These little people are described as wonderful hunters, their sense of sight being scarcely surpassed by that of the eagle, or their sense of hearing by that of the wolf. Their hardihood and endurance far surpassed that of any animal of the field, while their cunning and adroitness was only equalled by the fox.

Queenstown is a pleasant town. It was originally laid out hexagonally, somewhat in the form of an American House of Correction, so that every approach could be readily observed, and a cannon so placed that it could be turned on any avenue of attack. This plan was abandoned as the town increased, so that a fire can now be readily directed upon the market-place, the central point, from the houses which have been built outside it.

As a stronghold it is badly situated, being built immediately below a commanding line of hills. It seems to be progressing in wealth, and the railway, which will reach it in a few years, will cause it to develop rapidly, especially if the harbour at East London should prove a success. In that case the line will probably be extended to the Free State by way of Aliwal; though if it were made to pass by Bergersdorp, the necessity of constructing a bridge over the Caledon river would be avoided.

It was with some anxiety that I called for the account at the hotel at Queenstown; but I was reassured when I found that only 5*l*. was asked for myself and staff for the night, more especially as I had been told that no less than 105*l*. had been charged to the Duke of Edinburgh for one night's lodging, with entertainment for himself and staff.

It is frequently supposed by hotel keepers that the expenses of all officers and Government servants are met by the Government, and in all newly-settled colonies the Government is universally regarded as a tree from which everybody is entitled to pluck fruit.

The charges at Queenstown are known to be exorbitant, but I do not think that they are generally so on the eastern side of the colony. On the western, amongst the Dutch, they are so, for the English officer is specially looked upon there as fair game, whom it is right to spoil as far as possible.

It is reported that a late Governor, when travelling in the west, was charged 20*l*. for a common breakfast at an hotel; he remarked to the landlord that eggs must be very scarce and dear in those parts. The answer was, "No, but Governors are both scarce and dear, and it is a pity that they are not more frequently to be met with!"

Loyalty to her Majesty is proverbial throughout the colony. In Queenstown the respect for our Queen was so great that the barber refused to desecrate her birthday by cutting my hair.

CHAPTER VII.

OUTSPAN—LOCUSTS.

EARLY on the morning of the 24th of May we left Queenstown, and outspanned upon the Veldt.

To outspan is a very expressive Africander phrase, and is continually in the mouth of all travellers. Should the day's drive be over forty miles of road, and if this is to go on for some hundreds of miles, it is indispensable to be most watchful of your cattle. It is, therefore, advisable to start always, even in the winter season, by 6 A.M. A regular breakfast must not be thought of, but a cup of coffee, which there is sometimes a difficulty in obtaining at that early hour, must content the traveller. After having driven rather slowly for two hours, some convenient place should be selected near a river for the Outspan, or taking out the mules from the carriage.

No sooner are the animals released, than each selects a soft part in the sandy road and proceeds to have a roll; nor is the driver perfectly satisfied unless they severally turn themselves right over, and roll on both sides. Persons experienced in African travelling look upon this roll as even more valuable than food, and if the beast omits it, he is considered to show signs of not being up to his work.

There is one point which requires especial attention in South Africa. Both horses and mules, but especially the former, are subject to looseness, which, if neglected, is almost sure to lead immediately to the most serious consequences. It is requisite, therefore, to be provided with medicine against this common trouble. Some prefer a mixture of two ounces of opium with one of cutcha; this is placed in a soda-water bottle, half a bottle being given when the horse is affected. Others provide themselves with Brown's chlorodyne, and give as a dose half a small bottle, mixed with brandy.

While the horses are being taken care of by the drivers, a certain duty is allotted to each of the party. Some, with small hunting-axes, cut wood, if there be any, and if there be not, they collect in sacks the dry, hard manure, plenty of which is sure to be at hand: others make the fire; while the cook, who is indispensable in all such expeditions, cuts up the meat, prepares the pots, boils the water, and makes the soup or curry.

The whole of this, from the moment of halting to that of the sharp crack of the thong whip, the signal of departure, may be got through completely in two hours, but no idleness must be shown by any one.

The horses or mules being refreshed will travel even better than before, and three more hours can be run without another halt. Thus thirty miles may probably have been accomplished, when it will be wise to outspan a second time; a piece of bread and cheese may be taken, and after a delay of three-quarters of an hour, the second inspan should take place, after which the remaining ten miles can be readily and easily accomplished before nightfall.

For very long journeys it is my opinion that mules are to be preferred to horses; they certainly do not travel so rapidly, but they are much hardier and not so liable to sickness. They can more readily stand deprivation of food and water, and they bear cold infinitely better. It is frequently necessary to tie them to the cart at night, with no shelter, but slight covering and scanty food; as the weight and space taken up by their clothing and forage will scarcely allow more than one sheet for each mule and one good feed.

The mule is of a much less excitable temperament than the horse. He is usually ready to eat as soon as he is outspanned and has had his roll. This is by no means the case with all horses, as a nervous animal will decline food perhaps for hours, so that he soon loses condition and succumbs to fatigue.

During this day's trek we encountered an enormous flight of locusts; they were smaller in size than those I had seen in India, but, like their Hindoo cousins, they cause frightful destruction. Each flight was not more than eighty yards continuously, but always in the same direction; the swarm alighting for a minute or so probably to take a bite of grass, and then recommencing its journey eastwards.

The natives in the neighbouring country of Basuto land catch locusts in large numbers. They cook and pound them into powder, which, when well dried, will keep a considerable time. It is looked upon as excellent eating, and very much relished; I confess I thought it bitter, resembling very old caviare of the *mullet*, but not sturgeon caviare.

We now gained the foot of the Stormberg range of mountains. The cold was piercing, ice being about three-quarters of an inch thick upon all the pools of water. It is frequently imagined by those at home that South Africa is one continuous sandy plain. There can be no greater mistake. Probably there is no country in the world which is more diversified than South Africa. Mountains of stupendous height rise above plains of great extent. There are sterile tracts of sandy country, fertile slopes of great richness and beauty, forests, rivers, and waterfalls, and, in short, every description of scenery.

In all the small South African inns the coffee is most execrable, butter quite unknown, preserved milk invariably used, beef-steaks like leather, and the "bradie" the universal resource. "Bradie" would appear to contain every conceivable edible, chopped up fine and baked into a sort of forced-meat pudding.

It is to be regretted that our Cape colonies are so backward in conveniences for travelling, particularly in rest-houses and in means of movement. In the most distant parts of India the Government charge themselves with erecting rest-houses, where the traveller is sure to find a clean room, a bedstead, a table, and a sofa, and care is taken that fire and a supply of water for tea should be provided at small expense. At the larger and more frequented stages, fowls, bread, and other food can be obtained at fixed prices.

On the following day we saw a good many sand whirlwinds, or "dirt devils." In the southern hemisphere these are stated always to circle from left to right, whereas in the northern their course is from right to left. As far as I could see, this statement was verified on every occasion.

On the 27th of May we left again early, encountering droves of oxen coming from the Orange Free State. All of them were in very poor condition, lung sickness, it was said, having made great havoc amongst the cattle. It was reported that red water, a disease which had first shown itself in Natal, and had been so fatal there as almost to destroy transport traffic, had broken out on the northern side of the Caledon River. The only cure appears to be to inoculate the tail of the animal with the virus of the disease. This causes the greater part of the appendage to drop off, but it saves the beast, and tailless oxen are consequently everywhere to be met with. Some of the Kafirs are so proud of the oxen that they would prefer to see them die rather than they should lose their tails. Hence the difficulty of stamping out the disorder.

Aliwal is certainly a rising town, and the bridge which is now being constructed over the Orange River will add very much to its importance and wealth, as a large portion of the trade with the Free State now passes through the place.

It derived its name from the victory of Sir Harry Smith, who was Governor of the Cape, and had previously commanded a division of the army on the Sutlej, defeating the Sikhs at the battle of Aliwal.

Having been told of the natural warm spring running into a tepid lake near the town, I determined to visit it. After about two miles drive we reached this curious lake. There were two or three basins of water, the largest of which appeared to be about fifty yards across. In its centre there was a floating bath-house. The water in these basins was perfectly clear, so that the minutest grain of sand was readily discernible at the bottom. Its temperature was, as well as I could judge, about 90 degrees Fahrenheit, a most agreeable warmth for a bath. The depth of these pools I should judge to be about fifteen feet. We bathed, my staff officers jumping in and swimming about in the clear water. The hot sulphurous vapours were, however, somewhat overpowering, and I found I could not remain in it very long. The after effect to us all was a severe headache.

These baths will no doubt some day be much frequented. Since our visit I have been told that bath-houses and lodging-houses have been erected, and are now occupied.

There was a grand cricket match going on at Aliwal North. The young men from distant places were assembled, and a musical entertainment was held in the evening.

There is a very extensive native settlement of Tamboukies to the east, which is called Herschell, to which I shall again allude when I describe our return from the Free State to Port Elizabeth.

On the following day we crossed the river by the pont, which is placed somewhat lower down than the ford or drift at which the waggons cross. It took us a considerable time to embark our carts and mules and reach the opposite bank. A waggon that was fording the river lower down was halted midstream, and could not move, although thirty-two bullocks were attached to it.

We were now in the Orange Free State, a country noted for its flatness, and towards evening we arrived at the Caledon River, about thirty-two miles distant from Aliwal. Here we found a small hotel kept by an Englishman, who had come to the Free State for his health. He had brought his young wife, and, as he was delighted at meeting people from the old country, he was most anxious to oblige us. He much regretted that he could not make us more comfortable, as his furniture had not yet arrived, and all that he could offer us for supper was a few tins of salmon and some black bread. His wife appeared to be very much above her position, and talked very feelingly of her home in London, which she seemed deeply to regret ever having quitted. She said she had come against her parents' wishes but cared for nothing but to tend her husband, and to let him try the air of the Free State in the neighbourhood of Bloemfontein, so highly recommended for pulmonary complaints.

The next day we crossed the Caledon river by a punt, but had not left it more than a mile when the pole of our cart gave a growl, then smashed, and in an instant, falling backward, our feet were in the air.

The mules did not regard this as at all unusual or out of the way. They stood passively, cocking their ears and wagging their tails, not objecting to their temporary respite from labour. Crawling out we soon found ourselves in the road; but here was a predicament—a broken pole, the widespread veldt, and no house near. A little consideration decided me to attach the broken cart in rear of the sound one, so as to form a sort of four-wheeled spider. The plan was quite successful. Six mules were thus compelled to draw the two carts, while four mules ran loose. Every thoughtful and experienced driver in South Africa is careful at the commencement of his journey to be supplied with rims, or strong leather thongs. These are narrow strips of untanned leather, cut from the hides of bullocks. They are extremely tough, and much more durable than rope. We were well supplied with these useful articles, which enabled us once more to take the road. Fortunately a farmer passed us. His spring cart only contained his boy and himself. On seeing our difficulty he kindly offered me a seat to Smithfield, which was about ten miles distant.

My first care on arrival was to see the wheelwright, and get him to form a new pole as soon as possible from a stout tree of assegai wood. By the time the carts had arrived, very considerable progress had been made towards our refit. This wheelwright and blacksmith was the only workman at these trades in Smithfield. He had arrived on the previous day from the town of George in the "old colony" (as the colony of the Cape of Good Hope is familiarly called). He said that his brother had made him a present of a sufficient sum of money to find his way up, and that now he should soon be a made man. His brother had arrived in the colony only a few years since and had "gone in," as he expressed it, "for ostrich farming." He had been fortunate, and was now the owner of about 200 birds, the aggregate value of which could not be less than 2000l. This man made a new pole in a few hours, and although it was not quite so smart looking as the one made in King William's Town, it served every purpose. It was very rough but strong. In fact it was little more than a young tree fitted to the socket in the cart. For this we were required to pay 3l., and we considered ourselves fortunate in getting this rough stick even for that sum.

The wages of artisans of very common abilities are very high in the Free State. The daily rate of carpenters and bricklayers was 1l.; blacksmiths about the same price. The sum demanded for shoeing a horse was 1l., while the price of living, taking it all round, was about the same as it is at home. Thus, if a man is sober and industrious, he is sure to succeed very quickly in the Free State.

We spent the next night in the open veldt, lying on the

ground under our little tent. It was bitterly cold. The water in our tent froze, and there was no means of making a fire. The country is entirely devoid of wood; not one single tree did we meet with during the whole day's journey, and we could obtain no kraal dung. Wood for building purposes is at a fabulous price, and no one could be induced to commit such a sacrilege as to burn a log. All fires are made of cow-dung, which is an excellent substitute for coal, provided it can be obtained in sufficient quantities. We were glad to inspan on the 30th and be off. Shortly after we passed the farm of Jacob Tolyards, where we purchased a loaf of bread for 2s. 6d.

It is singular how phlegmatic the Dutch farmers are. It might be thought that men so far removed from the world would be glad to have a word with a stranger, but they do not wish to move ten miles from their own door, nor to see one who comes from ten miles beyond it.

The country in the Orange Free State consists chiefly of wide open plains. Rifles are now so common in the colony that the deer have no rest within a considerable range of the roads. The game, however, is so far privileged, because the black man is seldom allowed to carry arms. We did not meet with a single native kraal or village, for the Boers forcibly drove out all the aborigines when they took possession.

BLOEMFONTEIN.

On entering the city of Bloemfontein, we saw on our right a handsome monument dedicated to those who fell in the Basuto war. It is conspicuously placed on rising ground above the town in the immediate neighbourhood of the fort.

A lightning conductor was attached to every building. The storms in summer are both frequent and dangerous, the hailstones being stated to be of immense size, frequently penetrating even the corrugated iron roofs of the buildings, and beating down sheep in large numbers when in the open without shelter. We were directed by the officer who met us to drive to the Free State Hotel, where we were most comfortably lodged.

After breakfast we attended at the Church of England Cathedral, a very handsome building, to which is attached a comfortable roomy house for the Bishop of Bloemfontein. The service was conducted on the High Church system, the vestments of the clergy being handsomely decorated, and astonishing the simple Lutherans or Presbyterians, who from curiosity witnessed the service.

Mr. Brand, the President, received me with great kindness. He expressed himself courteously, but firmly, as regards the British Government on the subject of our annexation of the Diamond Fields. There is but little doubt that we were obliged to take that step. On the first discovery of these rich deposits, people from England, America, and the colonies of the Cape of Good Hope and Natal, at once flocked to them in large numbers. These wild lands were at that time very thinly inhabited by stolid Dutch Boers, who received the interlopers with fear and dislike.

It would cause too long a digression to enter upon the merits of the controversy whether these farms belonged by right to the Free State or to Great Britain. Circumstances compelled the Governor of Cape Colony to take them under his rule, otherwise perfect anarchy and riot must have reigned. The Dutch had not the power of controlling the inhabitants, and had we not stepped in, not only would the Free State Government have been defied by these temporary visitors from the four quarters of the world, but the Republic itself would have been annexed *by them*. Thus a difficulty on the borders of the Cape Colony had arisen which it would have been most dangerous to have permitted to continue. A settlement of this much-vexed question has, however, now been arrived at, in a most satisfactory manner, a payment of more than 100,000*l.* having been made to the Free State in compensation for any supposed claims they might have had in respect to Griqualand. This sum is in addition to another 100,000*l.* paid by our Government to the persons who first purchased the farm upon which the New Rush Mine at Kimberley now is.

Mr. Brand, the President, is the son of Sir Christopher Brand, the late Speaker of the House of Assembly at Cape Town. He is much liked and highly respected throughout the Free State and in the colony. In the afternoon we visited the castle. It is somewhat rude in structure, apparently very little having been done to it since it was originally built by the English. From the castle there is a fine view of Taba-Unchu, a mountain about forty miles distant, the intervening country being a perfect plain. This mountain stands boldly out, a very prominent feature and noted landmark for miles round.

It is from this direction that the attacks were made upon the settlers in Bloemfontein during their war with the Basutos, and many an anxious gaze was then directed from the castle to see if the enemy were advancing to endeavour to destroy the city.

When they read accounts of the prosperity which settlers enjoy, those who reside in quiet England scarcely bear in mind the anxieties which they must face. Too frequently their prosperity is only to be obtained by many a sleepless hour of watching the movements of a savage foe, whose discordant yells may suddenly wake them from dream-land, in the quiet hours of the night, to see their houses and homesteads in flames, their cattle driven off. They are fortunate if they are not left lifeless corpses on their own freeholds.

The fort contains some very useful Whitworth breech-loading cannon, which are stated to have proved most effectual in the Basuto campaign.

On the following morning I attended the President to the House of Assembly, where a debate upon education was proceeding. It was conducted in the Dutch language. I was informed that it terminated by a vote of a very large sum towards the advancement of schools throughout the State. A liberal grant was also made this year towards the construction of public buildings in Bloemfontein. Handsome structures are very numerous in the city. Amongst these, schools for all denominations and for both sexes predominate, but banks and private residences are progressing with great rapidity, and my subsequent visits assured me of the future prosperity of the place, from the immense advantages which had accrued to it during the great and increasing development of trade, and the benefits it derived from the Diamond Fields. So great has been the advance of the Free State in late years, that one pound bank notes, there called "blue books," which are now at par, in 1872 were selling at 11s. 6d. each.

After the country was annexed by Sir Harry Smith, the value of property increased, but when it was again relinquished, on orders from home, its prosperity was grievously retarded.

The climate of Bloemfontein is especially noted as being highly beneficial in pulmonary complaints, and the best physicians in Europe speak in glowing terms of its restorative powers. Most remarkable instances are quoted in which patients, who, on their arrival, were hardly able to crawl about, have, after a residence of a few months, been completely restored. Each year the number who seek this dry atmosphere is increasing. It has been found requisite to build lodgings and to make arrangements upon a European model for the convenience of visitors. The difficulties to be overcome are the distance from England to South Africa, the remoteness of Bloemfontein from Cape Town, Port Elizabeth, and Natal, the desperately bad roads to be traversed, the primitive nature of the conveyances, and the great expense of the journey.

One disadvantage to a temporary residence is the extravagant price of everything. This can be readily understood with European articles, especially as the charge for carriage from Cape Town amounts at least to 6d. the pound weight, and the customs duty (which goes to the benefit of the Cape Colonial Government) is equal to about 12 per cent. on each article *ad valorem*. This will not account, however, for the high prices of the commonest necessaries of life. Meat, though of very inferior quality, costs as much as in England, while bread is double the price, and butter from 5s. to 6s. per pound. Vegetables are so scarce that 2s. 6d. is generally asked for a cabbage, potatoes cost about 4d. to 6d. a pound, and eggs are not unfrequently 6d. each. I was told that a gentleman of this city, who understood gardening, gained at least 300l. a year from the sale of vegetables from a garden not more than one acre in extent.

What is the reason for such high prices where land is of unlimited extent, and boundless acres of pasturage are to be seen on all sides? It is owing to the general apathy of the Boers, and the lack of energetic European settlers. The Dutch themselves are perfectly contented to live on coarse meal dampers; and buck venison, shot on the veldt, serves in place of beef or mutton.

The markets are generally very distant from their homesteads, and the sale of everything which costs them trouble to produce is somewhat uncertain. Heretofore they have not been accustomed to be paid in coin for what they have to sell. Added to this, the price of garden seed is very high, the cost of all utensils used in manufacturing equally so, and the more pressing claims of their farms, such as banking rivers and herding sheep, leave them no opportunity for a more advantageous outlay of their time and capital.

In 1851 about 50 bales of wool left Bloemfontein for the southern markets. In 1874 10,000 bales were sent south. The imports of that year into the Free State were valued at 500,000*l.*; the exports 600,000*l*. The custom duties on all these imports went to the advantage of the Cape Colony and Natal.

CHAPTER VIII.

DUTCH CHARACTERISTICS—SPORT.

THE Orange Free State contains a large Dutch population, and in its wilder parts may be found true specimens of the Dutch Boer.

The habits of the Boer are very primitive. I visited the farm of a Dutchman called Petrus Lombard, who when young had trecked with his family from the colony. Old Lombard must have weighed at least twenty-five stone, and appeared to be in the last stage of dropsy.

The house, far from a large one, was crammed with women and children of all ages and colours, and in every stage of nudity. What clothes they possessed were of the old Dutch kind of cloth or greasy sheep-skin.

Such shouting, squalling, and holloing I think I never heard. Every now and then the voice of old Lombard rose above the din, calling for brandy. We supped upon our own provisions, and were lodged for the night in an outhouse, where the skins of lately killed buck, beans, corn, and bacon were stored, and where what sleep we could get was disturbed by the host's voice calling, "Sarah, bring water."

I ought here, once for all, to acknowledge the civility of the gentlemen of the Orange Free State. On many occasions they sent their carriages with beautiful horses for miles to meet us, and on our arrival at their farms they spared no pains to make our stay pleasant.

Next perhaps to the minister, whose position, both in the western part of the Colony and in the Free State, is quite supreme, the district surgeon is the man of greatest importance. There is nothing which a Dutchman looks upon as so requisite as physic. He will send hundreds of miles to procure it, and although extremely penurious in all other ways, niggardly, in fact, to the last penny, he will not scruple at the slightest symptom of illness to send for the doctor. Should a surgeon once obtain repute, deservedly or otherwise, his fortune is certainly made. The most ridiculous circumstances often ensure to him this good luck, and the amount of money he receives yearly is sometimes very surprising.

I was told that a medical practitioner lost his credit by simply prescribing the use of liberal ablutions to an elderly lady. Her husband was dreadfully angry, making his remonstrance in the following terms:

Young man, you are a stranger in this country, and recommend new customs, which are contrary to usages which we know to be the true rules for health. I have been now married to my 'vrow' for thirty-five years, during which time water has scarce touched her body. It is not, sir, by your persuasion that such inroads can be made into our manners; you are ignorant of our mode of life and do not understand our wants.

About four years ago a storekeeper received some glass balls about the size of eggs amongst his fancy goods from England. Soon after, a rather tiresome woman, the wife of a Dutch farmer came to his store. To get rid of her he gave her one of these cut balls, telling her that he had found it on her husband's farm. The old woman took it to her lord and master, who at once felt persuaded it was a diamond, and that he was possessed of great riches, as he knew from the size and brilliancy of the stone, that it must be enormously valuable. He was ill for three days with delight, and then drove over to Wynberg to dispose of it, enhancing its value to the storekeeper there by showing him that it was found already cut. No persuasion could convince him that he had been made the victim of a hoax.

There can be no doubt, however, that stray diamonds are occasionally found. Mr. Harker told us that he had purchased one of five carats weight, which he had every reason to believe was found on the veldt, not far from his own house.

Some little time before our arrival a German conjuror had visited this distant little village, when the Doppers were so alarmed at his tricks that they left the room in which he was exhibiting, and assembling in prayer, entreated to be relieved of the devil who had come amongst them.

In the neighbourhood of Lady Brand (the name of a township) there is an extensive cave in which the mission resided for some years before the church and station were built. The labours of the missionaries were the more admired by the natives on account of their devotion to their duties, and the acceptance of much privation.

It may interest my readers if I describe a day's shooting in the Orange Free State which I enjoyed at Mr. Wessel's farm, about sixteen miles from Wynberg.

We formed a line, and about twelve in number we rode up a gentle rise in the plain, passing over a low range of hills. In a few minutes we were within sight of a herd of game. It was the first time that I had seen blesbok or wildebeest in any number. The scene filled me with surprise and anxiety. Quietly feeding at a distance of 800 yards there were at least 500 of these two kinds of large deer.

I endeavoured to profit by the instruction I had received both as to the manner of approaching them, and as to the particular time for firing at them. But I own that excitement made me rather a bad pupil.

Starting then at a gallop we rode for the herd, which at first, confused by our sudden approach, stood still and stared, giving us an opportunity of getting still nearer to them. Selecting their leader, they sprang into motion. It was impossible to believe that they were going at a more rapid rate than a canter, so unwieldy did the stride of the wildebeest appear, and so ungainly that of the blesbok. In reality they were fast making away from us, when, at a word from Wessel, everyone jumped off his horse, and selecting his beast, fired. Loading again as rapidly as possible, we galloped after them at full speed.

A considerable number of blesbok came across me. Forgetful of my lesson to allow them to pass so as to enable me to fire at them from behind, I shot at their flank, when to my surprise, although they were not more than 200 yards distant not one fell. I reloaded and fired four or five shots before they were out of range, but with the same effect. Springing on my horse, I again followed in pursuit. What was my astonishment, in galloping over the ground in precisely the direction which my ball had taken, to see a brawny black fellow spring out of the low bush, armed with a long "brown Bess." He had been hidden, and was waiting in hope that the herd would pass close to his lair. He made spasmodic signs to me to show that my bullets had gone on either side of him and within a few inches of his head. I believe that had they even struck him they would have had little more effect than they had upon the wildebeest, for his head looked stronger than that of an ox.

His dogs were covered with blood. No doubt they had seized one of our wounded bucks, and brought it down, and their master had concealed it in the bush until we should be gone. The Kafir had been hidden from my view by the immense herd of game through which I had fired, and which was running between us; but he was a brave fellow, and by his grins one might have imagined that he enjoyed the share I gave him of the sport as much as I did the portion which fell to me.

How little did I then understand the method of stalking these animals! Further practice and a knowledge of their habits rendered it so familiar to me, that I could select to a perfect certainty the exact spot in the plain which the herd were sure to pass, and which, riding at a gallop, I could reach before their arrival.

At this time my aide-de-camp killed a blesbok, and, as he was going to despatch it, a deadly snake, called here the "shop-stricker," or sheep-hitter, struck at him and then glided into the bush. Had it not been for the high riding boots which he wore, it would have wounded him, perhaps mortally.

My want of success at the first gallop proved to me that I ought to have attended better to the advice of the Boers, not to fire until I got to the rear of the animals. Although you may lose a little in actual distance, the chances of killing them are thus immensely increased; for the bullet thus entering from the rear has less difficulty in reaching the heart. But the wildebest is a tough animal, and I consider that the express bullet of 450 (the military gauge) is too small generally to bring him down. I should much prefer the 500. Subsequently, I killed many of these animals, but when wounded they generally gave me a run of two or three miles before I could ride them down. I seldom had one skinned that I did not find one old bullet in him, and frequently two and even three.

I am convinced that the express bullet with a hollow point is not the bullet to obtain the game which is hit. The bullet expands and makes a wide wound, but in my opinion it is not heavy enough to bring down an animal larger than the small antelope. It wounds the larger ones and they no doubt eventually die, but they are able to run for such a distance after they are struck as to render the pursuit long and arduous, and wooded countries deprive the sportsman of his chances of recovering them.

Every day while we were hunting, our driver was employed in making "Beltong." This he did by cutting the meat of the blesbok and springbok into long slices and rubbing it with salt, then festooning it on a rim placed between the two carts and allowed it to dry in the sun and the cold dry wind.

Beltong, when carefully made, is most excellent, especially that of the tender springbok. It is universally used on all journeys in South Africa, and when the wild deer cannot be procured, it is made of strips of beef, which I found quite as good. The Boers are also extremely clever at making a species of rusk, excellent in taste, which will keep for weeks.

For an emigrant with some capital there is no part of South Africa which I think would be better than Wynberg. A very fine farm of about 6000 acres with some buildings on it could be purchased for about 2000*l.*; to stock it might cost perhaps 1000*l.* more; say 500*l.* for horses, carts, &c., and 500*l.* in hand.

Thus a young man with a fortune of 4000*l.* who possessed prudence and activity would be quite sure of a successful career if he undertook to settle in this part of the Free State. If fond of sport he could enjoy it to his heart's content. It would, however, be prudent for him to forego speculation until he had become well acquainted with the Dutch language, and the manners and customs of the people he is among.

The settler must not expect an immediate return for his exertions in money, but he will secure a freedom from those cares and anxieties which encompass a parent whose increasing family and responsibilities bid him look to the future of those he holds most dear.

Few people can imagine the quantity of antelopes which inhabit these plains, though no doubt they are rapidly diminishing. Mr. Adler told me that he had purchased more than 70,000 skins during the last year alone, and he was but a single merchant. The aggregate exportation of skins amounts to nearly one million in the year. These come generally now from the neighbourhood of Kronstadt or from eighty to a hundred miles north of Bloemfontein. The Westley Richard, and now the Martini-Henry, rifle are very busily at work. Possibly within the next ten years not a single head of game will exist on this side of the Vaal river. Everywhere we went we found the plains strewed with the skulls of blesbok and wildebeest, showing the thousands which must be destroyed yearly.

CHAPTER IX.

BASUTO LAND.

AFTER leaving the Orange Free State we went to Basuto land.

The Basutos are an interesting race of people and appear more advanced than the Kafir generally. Their late chief Moshesh, "the Shaver," so called because he not only symbolically but frequently in real fact shaved off the heads of his enemies, was a man of very considerable ability, and was considered a rare diplomatist.

Like Ranjeed Sing, he stuck firmly by the English, and the deepest regret he ever expressed was about his war (in which he was anything but conquered) with Sir George Cathcart.

On approaching Thaba Bosigo we were met by Masupa, the son of Letsi, the son of Moshesh. He was presented to me by Mr. Griffith, and he was at the head of 300 mounted men. They wore a sort of Dutch uniform, with a wide-awake hat in which was stuck a handsome ostrich feather; many of his followers were dressed in blue cloth, with hats similarly adorned. These dresses they wear on rare occasions, but no Kafir feels really at home or comfortable unless he is robed in his kaross or blanket. Those whom circumstances have for years compelled continually to use European clothes return with eager haste to their blanket whenever it is possible to adopt it.

At Thaba Bosigo we were kindly received at the French Protestant Mission Station. Their very comfortable house had been entirely gutted and destroyed by the Basutos during the war with the Free State Republic, but it had now been rebuilt and freshly furnished.

A considerable number of pupils attended the school, principally females, but I failed to discover that they had any other employment than reading and singing psalms. No useful trade was taught them, so that in my opinion a civilising influence was wanting here. At the Catholic station on the other side of the mountain, instruction was given in weaving, cloth-making, and certain trades which could not fail to prove useful.

The access to the mountain of Thaba Bosigo, the stronghold of Moshesh, is steep and difficult, and bade defiance to the attack of the Boers, though many brave attempts were made to take it by assault. The buildings upon it are now in ruins

The Cape House of Assembly has passed a resolution with regard to Basuto land to the following effect :

It is the opinion of this House that there should be established in Basuto land an industrial training school for the education of the Basutos and other natives in trades, handicrafts, and other occupations, upon the system as far as possible of that adopted at the Lovedale Institution, and further, that while the surplus revenues of Basuto land justify a sufficient provision therefrom in aid of this establishment every effort should be made to secure that the Institution should in the future be self-supporting.

In this the Lovedale Institution at Alice has been the chief example and now it is beginning to be recognised that the true way to tame a savage is to make him a useful artisan. .

We had come from Mapasa, and from the drift in the Caledon river by the same road which had been taken by Sir George Cathcart when he made his attack upon Moshesh in 1853.

The mountain, upon which the Kafirs attacked the 12th Lancers, lay on our left hand. Had the Kafirs then been armed with rifles, Sir George would have had a very difficult task to have occupied the position by the road which he took, presenting as it did defensible points at every thousand yards.

Sir George Cathcart had a noble mind and a courageous heart; but his career and his subsequent death point to a want of prudence, which certainly was exemplified on the occasion. He allowed his cavalry to become separated and disorganised in pursuit of cattle, and they drove the herds towards the river, until a portion of the troopers, getting entrapped in the ravines, were cut off by a very large mounted body of the enemy. Nothing remained but to cut their way through the Kafirs. This they gallantly did, but only to find that they were obliged to descend precipices or be sacrificed. Some succeeded in doing so, while others perished, and to this day the arms and dresses of some of those lancers who fell may be seen. The Kafirs, encouraged by success, then attacked the main body under the General himself, making repeated charges even up to the very muzzles of the two six-pounder guns, which he placed in a most excellent position to resist them. The steadiness of the infantry soldier now displayed itself, as he beat off their repeated assaults, and destroyed with grape the brave natives, who met their death with courage. At length they listened to the voice of their chief Moshesh and retired from the encounter.

On the following day terms were arranged with Moshesh, who paid a fine which had been awarded against him by the Governor, and the army retraced its steps, the General being much pleased to get out of the valley.

This is an oft-told tale of mountain warfare, where the defenders have so vast an advantage over the attack. Caution is required in the advance. Bull-dog courage is not sufficient to ensure success in such a position as that into which Cathcart thrust himself and his troops. He afterwards died a glorious death at Inkermann, when the army was crowning its victory.

I subsequently received from a friend a very interesting account of this action, in the following terms:—

The day after we entered the country of Moshesh by garrison orders our game-shooting (it was stated " with great regret ") must be stopped. On the second day we reached Platberg, the old Bastard location. Mr. Giddy, the missionary, was at his post, though the Bastards had fled before the wrath of the great Basuto.

On the 13th we made a camp, a meeting was convened, but none of the chiefs thought the day convenient. On the 14th the sons of the chiefs, besides many black princes and kings, called at our lines; but the Governor put forth an advertisement that he wanted the great chief, and declared that until it was answered he would not see any of the smaller black ones.

Owen, therefore, rode to Moshesh. He delivered this message, and on the 15th Moshesh turned up. He was very neatly attired in a new dark suit of clothing, and met everybody with a dignified and affable politeness, which extended to the lancer orderlies, whose hands he shook with fervour,' and also to Morocco, his neighbour (a pigeon he had often plucked). Having been admitted to the hospital marquee in front of His Excellency's tent, he was introduced to the General (Inkose Inkulu). The General, to cut a dash, was dressed in a glittering costume. He thought he had it all his own way, and came down on " old Mo " pretty stiflly. He desired him to pay 10,000 head of cattle and 1000 horses within three days, or be exterminated.

Poor Mo answered and said: " Oh, chief, live for ever! The Basutos are dogs, and I, O Inkose Inkulu, am but a son of them. Take my cattle, take my lambs, take my people, do as you please with them—thy servant can do no more; but," added the old cove, "I cannot send you the cattle in three days, being only a Kafir or a dog, and must take a dog's time to do my work."

The General, overjoyed at his knuckling down so quickly, said: "Be off, Mo; and if every cow be not in by the third day the Inkose will come and take all your cattle; but, if your people submit without a shot, he will not hunt them." Whereupon Mo observed, "that if you trod upon the pet corn of a cur he would very likely turn and bite." He then bowed and retired. In ten minutes he was on his way to the mountain, and the Governor telling every one he was sure of his cattle.

Three days were nearly spent before any kine appeared, and then at sundown 3400 lean and lazy beasts came in with an escort of 600 mounted Basutos.

When Nehemiah appeared it was thought that the whole fine had arrived, and the General observed to him that he was glad to see that he had brought the cattle and said, "Oh, I am glad to see that you have paid the fine, you've a great many huts on the road to Thaba Bosigo and I should be sorry to burn them." When the counters reported that the thousand horses and six thousand five hundred cows were short of the fine, Nehemiah was told that he need not dine with his Excellency, but to go home and tell his papa that the Inkose was coming.

Next day about two-thirds of the force went to the Caledon river, where they encamped and constructed a pont. This was about nine miles from Thaba Bosigo.

Orders were given to march at four next morning with three days' provisions, the infantry to cross by the pont, the cavalry by the ford.

The cavalry brigade was broken up, two hundred sabres were placed under the command of Napier, who went with his little force round to the left quite out of reach, and without support. Colonel Eyre advanced with 700 foot and 40 mounted Fingoes from the centre; and the General, with 200 foot, 2 guns, with an escort of 40 Lancers, 25 Cape Mounted Rifles, and his Fingo guard, took to the right.

We, the cavalry, got well out of sight, and before we were halfway to Thaba Bosigo, saw nothing but cattle all over the hills Munro and Carey with their troops pushed on and received a volley while getting over a stone wall; they charged, killing with lance, carbine, or sabre, some twelve or thirteen Basutos. Carey drove his sword right through a savage, and, after a better opposition than we expected, the Basutos dispersed and fled. They then pushed on, we closely following until we came suddenly upon a magnificent herd of cattle. After a hard gallop a few of us managed to head the herd and turn them back to Napier, though not without danger of being hurled over a krantz. I cannot describe to you the force of the stream of cattle which would have escaped, had we not luckily shot an ox or two in a narrow opening between two stones, the only outlet: this stopped the torrent rushing forward.

We got back, having ridden between several Kafirs whom I could easily have stabbed, but refrained. After getting the cattle back we were obliged to let them run to the flats as we could not keep them quiet.

Meanwhile Carey and Munro had parted company, the latter having returned to us, while Oakes, Somerset, and Warren had joined Carey with a few men, and pushed on to near Thaba Bosigo. The Basutos now assembled in our rear, and Tottenham with twenty-five men drew out to front them and support Somerset. Their numbers exceeded all estimate we had formed of them, and while all our reserve under Napier had gone down to the flats except a few stragglers, we thus had to bear up against a dense mass of disciplined horsemen on the hill, one mile and a half from our friends.

We did our best, we drove one squadron in, and then another at our best pace, and then confronted their main body more than 800 strong. We now re-dressed our line at 300 yards from their centre, which was three deep, their flanks advanced in an attitude to surround us. At these odds we charged and received at 70 yards' distance a concentric fire from the whole line, after which the semicircle closed its horns upon us, and we were surrounded and cut off. We were therefore compelled to dash back and re-form close to them, but their regular and overwhelming advance pushed us on and we were obliged at last to gallop for our lives.

Our retreat was headlong, for the enemy had headed us and pursued us with good speed. With difficulty any lived to tell the tale. Tottenham behaved like a hero; the last to turn, he remained almost the last in the retreat, and by cool courage and good riding managed to save a sergeant-major by shooting a Basuto while just about to stab him. After a mile we were pulled up by a stone wall, and here many fell. I had to run home my spurs and leap it as a last chance. Just before a Basuto had ridden between me and it, I cut him across the shoulder with my sword and saw no more of him. Tottenham got over the wall and saved one of his men.

At length some Cape Mounted Riflemen came back to our support, and their carbine shots checked our pursuers. We were still followed, however, and the enemy fired smartly wounding a man of the rear guard whom Tottenham brought off on his own horse.

Our captured cattle were now driven on as fast as possible, and though Kafirs collected on our flank, yet they would not face Tottenham's little rear guard commanded by himself on foot, and hampered with a wounded man upon his horse. The fighting now came to an end.

I then went to the camp and got some men to cover the passage of the cattle over the river. Somerset's party had had a narrow squeak but managed to prevent being run into by steady courage and good skirmishing. They reached camp in a sorry plight just when we did, but with a consciousness of having done their best, which repays any man for the greatest risks. Somerset brought in a soldier behind him. Simpkin just got in his wounded horse before it fell dead. They were fortunate to get off at all being surrounded by a force so great as to drive them over a krantz. Such was the cavalry fight, which, but for the isolation of our force at so remote a position, must have been a brilliant affair. As it was we held our prize, and bore off four thousand head of cattle to our camp. Of Tottenham's small rear guard twenty fell. Eyre and the Governor fired away till dark. The latter riding forward alone to parley was nearly shot, despite his white flag.

Moshesh fortunately sent in for peace. Every one wanted their revenge, and desired to attack the Basutos again, but the Governor refused, not liking to enter the hills again.

In the year following my visit to Basuto land two sons of Letsi, and grandsons of Moshesh, came down to Cape Town, when I was requested by the Governor to show them some small attention. After visiting the fort, and being much astonished at the "great mothers," the parents, as they expressed it, of rifles and muskets, I took them to the shooting grounds at Wynberg, and placing rifles in their hands requested them to compete with ourselves. We were all astonished at their success. The eldest beat all but two of their competitors, at a range of 500 yards.

The Catholic bishop had instructed Nehemiah, a very clever son of Moshesh, in the French language, which he spoke and read with ease. Thus, it was said, he had the advantage of amusing himself with all the recent French novels of the day, the contents of which he greedily devoured.

In 1876 Nehemiah passed over the lower Drakensberg, and settled in the neighbourhood of Adam Kok's Country in Griqualand East. Here he appears to have borne a part in resisting the Queen's Government. He was arrested and charged with rebellion. The report says that—

After the most patient and careful investigation it became obviously apparent to the whole assembly that the rebels were acting not only upon a carefully preconcerted plan of action, but also that they were acting under the orders of some head or chief, and it soon became apparent that that head was Nehemiah Moshesh, as two of the principal rebels stated that they were his men, and acting under his orders. Nehemiah was asked repeatedly and most distinctly to clear himself, and has hitherto failed to do so most signally. He was accordingly arrested by order of the chief magistrate, and is now in custody of the Frontier Armed and Mounted Police pending his trial. I am also glad to tell you that the whole meeting unanimously concurred in this course, and universally agreed in the opinion that a most serious crisis had been averted, and that Nehemiah's capture had prevented something like another Langalebalele affair.

It is now difficult to say in how far Nehemiah was really involved. He was brought down to King William's Town for trial, but the whole case was at once quashed for want of jurisdiction because the crime had been committed in a country which was not part of the Cape Colony.

It is surprising that this should not have been foreseen before he was brought to trial, though, as his offence was treason, it is difficult to see why he might not have been indicted.

The war of the Free State against the Basutos was a feud

lasting over two years, but in the end the Boers annexed a fine country.

They are however accused of some cruelty in carrying out the war. It is said that, advancing on to the Kafir villages at the moment of daylight, they would fire their cannon on the kraals, and having prepared their mounted men, so soon as the Kafirs started out of their huts, they would dash at them and cut them down to a man.

The necessities of the war and the urgent danger to the colony may palliate, if they do not excuse, such severities.

On reaching the lower end of the valley we were told that we were in the neighbourhood of the dwelling of Letsi, the eldest son of Moshesh, now the paramount chief of Basuto land.

I was anxious to see him, and for this purpose rode down to his village, in the midst of which was a square-built stone cottage resembling the meanest of the Boers' farmhouses. In the yard was a waggon which must have cost at least 150*l*.

This was utterly neglected, and from exposure and want of care was being allowed rapidly to fall to pieces; it was probably the gift of some Governor, in the hope that this chief might have been induced by its possession to cause his people to improve in the art of building.

Letsi came out to meet me, and ushered myself and staff into his sitting room.

He was a bulky man, dressed in a suit of corduroy, and appeared very intelligent. He expressed his great desire to follow in the steps of his father, and support our Government, to which he has faithfully adhered.

After some delay a repast was brought in, consisting of salmon from the everlasting English tins, black cakes, and coffee. Of these we were bound to partake much against our inclination, and after a few more compliments we took our leave. Mr. Griffith spoke well of Letsi; he seemed to consider him worthy of trust. At the termination of the interview the chief expressed his wish to present me with a pretty little white pony, which I afterwards rode many hundreds of miles in Pondo land. In return I requested his acceptance of an English saddle and bridle, with military appurtenances, which I sent him from Cape Town. Such interchanges of civilities are in my opinion conducive to friendly feelings, and are hardly sufficiently practised at the Cape.

On the following day we arrived at Madame Rowland's at Mafuten. She was a most charming person, well versed in the current literature of the day, with a pleasing family, among whom were two charming boys, who both rode wonderfully well, though they were little more than children.

Mr. Rowland gave us some interesting anecdotes of the Basutos:—

In illustration of the industry of the people, out of about 20,000 able-bodied labourers, 15,000 annually receive passes to go to work in the Free State, Colony, and Diamond Fields, while those who remain at home raise 30 to 40 bags of grain per household. He referred to the hysterical mania which has become epidemic in many of the villages. He compares the phenomena to those of spiritualism, especially in the silliness of the messages purporting to come from the unseen world. The minutes of the annual meeting, or " Pitso," are most interesting. Mr. Rowland suggested the restoration of " Kibakile." " Your sons," said he, " refuse to obey and to work, because you have left off thrashing them. When I was a boy in the large village of Beersheba there used to be, at about sunset, a great outcry in every direction after the cattle came home. Boys crying out 'Kibakile! Kibakile!' (I repent, or won't do so any more.) They were getting whipped for the misdeeds of the day. This Kibakile (*i.e.* the rod) was a great chief. Since ' Senckal's ' war he is dead: at least I never hear any one calling out his name

as formerly. That is why your herds are so negligent, and your children so disobedient. Now if you wish to help yourself, what you ought to do is to revive this great chief. Bring him to life again. He will put an end to all the disobedience and quarrels and expense of damages."
This remark was hailed with loud cries of "Let Kibakile rise again," and some gentlemen were so ungallant as to exclaim, "Our wives need him badly, too." Several of the speakers echoed this latter sentiment. One chief said, "Wives should also be corrected; they are also children and in the same position. But we are frightened of getting the cats if we beat them. If we may not beat them, then let us bring them here, and let them also receive the cats." Another gentleman's whole speech consisted of the curt observation, "Thanks; women should be flogged as well as men for insubordination." The chief Masopha complained bitterly of the treatment of Basutos, in the Free State. "They have," he said, "their guns taken from them, and are imprisoned and flogged; all under the Queen's pass."

We here saw a Basuto basket, made from palm leaves, and almost similar to those made in Morocco by the Moors of Barbary.

We saw a considerable number of ducks and many partridges, and the quail in August are said to be innumerable.

This country produces a large amount of maize and Kafir corn; and indeed Basuto land supplies the greater part of the bread-stuffs that are sent to the Diamond Fields.

We passed the stations of two or three successful traders, where it is said large fortunes are being made, much pains being taken to suit the taste of the native, in regard to the goods which are imported. The ladies are as particular in the selection of their beads as a Parisienne in her toilet. While I was there the only colour they would look at was a violet mauve, and a trader must take care to suit their fancies, or they will desert his store.

All that I saw in Basuto land made me believe that its inhabitants are more capable of advancement than any tribe I saw in South Africa, and are more ready to cast off their old habits and usages.

As an instance of this I will quote a few lines from the 'Little Light,' a very clever journal published in Basuto land.

All the young men of the Marija Institution, Basuto land, who last September obtained Government certificates, are now hard at work, and several of them have commenced new schools; several old ones have been reorganised, and there is a very fair increase in the number of scholars. At the out-station of Koloyana, in the Leribe district, the schoolmaster asked the neighbouring petty chiefs to send the children to school.

We learn from the 'Little Light,' that one of them, Mapeshoane, said, " that though he would like his boys to be circumcised, he would ask them which they would prefer, the school or circumcision." He explained the matter very fully to them, and the result was that they chose school. Accordingly to school they went. But their elders who had been circumcised gave them no rest, abused them by calling them names, until they ran away from school to go and be circumcised at a neighbouring village. It appears that the father of these children, hearing of this, went to the village, and on their arrival hunted them out from among the other boys, and gave one a sound thrashing. These boys, instead of returning home, hid themselves in the mountain, hoping that the father would go home and they could be circumcised. The father knowing this, gave special warning to the master of these abominable rites that if he dared to administer circumcision to his boys, he would try what the law would do to punish him. This settled the difficulty, the boys returned home and went to school. We congratulate Mapeshoane on account of his firmness shown in keeping these boys to their original choice, though we are sorry that he is one of the few chiefs who still upholds circumcision.

Many of the Mosaic customs are prevalent in this country; for instance, that of marrying a deceased brother's, or even father's, wife, by which means a provision is insured to her.

CHAPTER X.

BACK TO PORT ELIZABETH.

We now left Basuto land and returned to the colony.

Not long after crossing the Orange river we came upon a neat Fingo location. Their huts were much smarter than any I had previously seen, most of the small domiciles being gaily painted near the doors with curious coloured designs. They were surrounded by small courtyards, which underwent a perpetual course of brushing. The Government agent met us with a very large retinue of his people, probably a thousand in number. These men were all attired in their former war dress, with shield and assegai, feathers, paint, armlet, and war charms. Their salutation was most striking, a low moan like the roar of the sea or distant thunder.

At the command of their head men they formed into semi-circular bands, and commenced their war exercises, alternately advancing and retiring, attacking a supposed enemy and then drawing him on by a feigned retreat. These men were handsome specimens of the natives of South Africa, and are described as obedient and good subjects.

Under the energetic supervision of Mr. Halse their lands are being rapidly brought under cultivation, they are purchasing ploughs, and many of them own waggons and teams of oxen. As an instance of their independence I was told, that a few days before, a farmer from Aliwal North had come to the native village to endeavour to hire waggoners, offering to pay one shilling per diem wages. A native answered him saying that he would be quite ready himself to engage double the number of men the farmer required, and be willing to pay them at double the sum offered.

The war dances or exercises being over, we accompanied Mr. Halse to his house, where we received much kind hospitality; his handsome family doing their utmost to entertain us. The young ladies possessed a grand piano, and sang charmingly, a pleasing return to social amenities which for some weeks past we had not had an opportunity of enjoying.

Mr. Halse's description of the progress which the Free State had made within his recollection was quite astonishing, and reminded me of the strides in improvement and development that I had witnessed in America. He described to me a farm of 32,000 acres which he had bought for 65*l.*, when it was so overrun with game as to be perfectly useless. He afterwards sold it for 6000*l.*, and its value is now fully three times that amount.

In the neighbourhood of Dordrecht coal has been found and reported as easily workable; this cannot fail to prove of inestimable value to the inhabitants, for wood is scarce. Coal has been selling at 15*l.* the ton, and iron at 6*d.* the pound, solely on account of the great price to which carriage by bullock-waggon has risen.

In common with other towns in the east of the colony Dordrecht is improving. An officer of the police told me that he had purchased an erf of land there in 1873 for an old rifle, and in 1874 had sold it for 60*l.* Now probably it is worth 200*l.* or more. In the hills above are settlements of Fingoes whose small huts are now covered with tin roofs made from the linings of the boxes in which cloth and other goods are brought from England. These people are rapidly progressing in civilisation, a fact demonstrated by their purchase of European articles. No marriage now takes place among these natives without a present from the future husband of a gold wedding-ring. Bridal cakes made in England and sent to the colony frequently find a place at the marriage feast, and, indeed, these weddings are sometimes chronicled in the newspapers.

Marriage in high life, from the 'Observer': H.R.H. Mietge, one of the many daughters of H.H. Paulus Mopeli, was united in the holy bonds of matrimony at the Mission Chapel to —— ——, Esq. The young lady was gracefully attired in white, relieved by blue ribbons and sash, which gave a pretty contrast to her jet black complexion. The happy pair, after partaking of a collation, immediately left town to enjoy the honeymoon at Waaihoek.

Native women now are quite conventional in their dress. I saw one black beauty sitting on the bridge, trying on a new pair of stockings that she had just purchased at the store; whilst by her side was a dusky swain, whose entire costume —simplicity itself—consisted of a pair of Wellington boots, with a blanket gracefully thrown over his shoulders.

Near Blinkwater lies the famous Waterkloof, in which Macomo, the chief, so long defied her Majesty's troops in the Kafir campaign of '46, and in which so many of our men perished. After the war the Colonial Government appears to have permitted the nephew of this chief, Tini Macomo, to purchase the property, so that he has become a standing menace to the district, and he had broken into rebellion before I left the country, and a considerable force had to be despatched for the purpose of overpowering him. I was informed upon the best authority that in this location native meetings, dances, and orgies were periodically held by members of both sexes, and it is supposed that seditious plans were there discussed, which afterwards bore fruit in rebellion.

In the neighbourhood of Blinkwater are found a large

number of jerboas, or kangaroo hares, which are hunted at night with lanterns, and afford good sport.

The only other time that I ever saw them was when the Guards were marching up to the Russian batteries at the Alma, where they were running in scores along the line.

Here we saw the only milestone which I remember in the colony. At last we reached Port Elizabeth, having been nearly two months absent, during which time we had travelled 1600 miles. We all returned to Cape Town by the mail steamer.

CHAPTER XI.

FEDERATION AND COLONIAL DEFENCE.

DURING this journey my attention had naturally been particularly directed to two of the many great questions which await solution in South Africa. Upon the first of these I had a right, as an Englishman, to form an independent opinion. Upon the second it was my duty as a soldier to advise my superiors. These questions were, Federation and the military Defence of the colony.

It must be remembered that there is a specimen of almost every form of Colonial Government in South Africa. A responsible government in the Cape Colony, the two Crown colonies of Natal and Griqualand West, the semi-independent native locations of Basuto land, Namaqua land and Kaffraria proper, and the independent country of Kuti and the Pandos. In addition to these there were till lately two republics, the Orange Free State and the Transvaal.

As regards the Cape Colony and Natal it is to be observed that there is a high *ad valorem* duty of 12 per cent. on all goods which pass through their ports up country. The money thus raised goes to defray the Government expenses of these colonies, and it is not to be expected they will willingly forego the advantage it gives them.

Again, Natal would prove, if federated, a source of danger to the Cape Colony. Not only does it possess a black population of 300,000 as against 20,000 whites, but it has dangerous neighbours against whom the Cape Colony would be bound to assist it, in case of war or rebellion.

The people of the Transvaal dreaded two results of Federation, viz. loss of individual independence and increased taxation, and it was only the late war with the Zulus that convinced them of the compensating advantages they would gain.

The Orange Free State Republic feared that Federation would not only deprive them of the market they found for their products at the Diamond Fields, but would cause the same unrestricted sale of arms to take place in their country as has existed in the Cape Colony.

Griqualand West, on the contrary, was eager for annexation, by which not only would it gain protection, but it would have its present heavy taxes relieved by sharing in a portion of the customs dues.

One of the most talented members of the Natal House of Assembly, speaking of the Cape Colony, says:

> It looks to the north and sees in the three states that lie there much no doubt that is attractive, but much that gives cause for doubt. It fears Natal with her natives, and shrinks from the Transvaal with her debt. It dreads lest, by uniting its fortune with ours, it should imperil or sacrifice the position it holds. This is, perhaps, an unreasonable distrust, but I venture to think it is a feeling which is passing away.

If this be a true picture of the state of opinion of those who oppose Federation, it is clear that they are each looking rather to the good of his own part of the country than to the welfare of the whole. On the other hand, not only would the colonies be greatly invigorated by Federation, but the native question might really be settled for ever by the adoption of a well-considered vigorous policy and unanimity of action with regard to the Kafirs. Moreover it is obviously cheaper to have one military system of defence, than five isolated and fragmentary armies.

These were the views which Mr. Froude advocated on his mission to South Africa. Had it not been that the Government of the Cape Colony obstinately and, as I think, needlessly, did all they could to oppose him, he might have succeeded in carrying his point there and then. The seed he sowed, however, has not been lost, and his eloquent speeches are yet destined, I believe, to bear fruit.

The question is at present dormant. The recent expensive war with the Kafirs, the impending difficulties with the Zulus, the unsettled state of the eastern frontier and the Transvaal, have no doubt diverted public opinion away from it. As soon, however, as peace is firmly restored, a fresh impetus given to commerce, and security re-established, there is, I think, no doubt that the question will be brought prominently forward, and I hope that it will be settled by a Federation of the whole country south of the Limpopo. A union of all the colonies would not, I think, be so advantageous as a federation, as they differ widely from each other in their position and resources. A parliament at Cape Town would be ill-adapted for settling matters of local importance at Leydenburg; but a Federation which, while leaving minor points to be dealt with by local parliaments, would ensure unanimity in questions of universal importance, would, I believe, arouse patriotism, stimulate industry, increase the value of property, and secure peace.

The present political position of the colony requires some explanation. There has always been a conflict between the interests of East and West, and the eastern half itself is divided as to political views into three sections: Port Elizabeth, with its port at Algoa Bay; Grahamstown, with Port Alfred at the mouth of the Kowie; and Queenstown and King William's Town, with their port at East London. There is quite as much local antagonism between these sections as there is between the east and west of the colony. By adopting the maxim, " Divide et impera," and playing off the several interests against each other, the Cape Ministry can always find supporters in any measure they desire to introduce.

The East London, Queenstown, and King William's Town people give general support to the Ministry because they desire advantages to be conceded to them in preference to Port Elizabeth and the Kowie.

Grahamstown and Port Elizabeth fear to offend the Ministry lest advantages should be accorded to East London; thus, although I do not think that the east generally is by any means happy and contented under the dominion of the west, it lends a support to the Ministry which enables them to sustain their western influence.

In consequence of the immense sums of money which the present 1877 Cape Ministry have to spend in railroads, harbour works, and other great undertakings, their patronage has been much augmented.

They have therefore the power to reward and secure the support of very numerous adherents in the east. Had a dissolution of the House of Assembly taken place in 1875 and a fresh parliament assembled, after the programme of Federation had been brought on the platform, and before all these great works had been undertaken, the support to the Ministry would have been very different from what it is now, and the cry for Federation would have been irresistible.

In the west the Ministry are sure of support, because the cardinal interests of the west have no opponents within their area. These interests point principally in three directions, viz. to secure the customs' duties to the colony, to retain the parliament in Cape Town, and to see that the interests of that harbour should not be injured in favour of the ports of Port Elizabeth and East London.

As the west is perfectly secure from any native incursions, it is its direct interest to try to retain its natural advantages, and to discourage any system of frontier defence or other cause of expenditure.

In fact, though the west can not fairly be accused of wishing for a native war, yet so far from being injured, the people there are probably the better for it. They gain in trade a great part of what is lost by the east, and the military contracts, to a great extent, fall into their hands.

The best arrangement which could be made would, I think, be as follows:—

The Cape Colony should be divided into two parts, the east and west, by a line drawn from Cape Francis to Hopetown, the eastern boundary of the eastern province being a line drawn from the St. John's River in Kaffraria to Herschel on the Orange River. Natal ought to extend from the St. John's River to Zululand, embracing as much of that country as must eventually be annexed by the British Government. This would involve the addition of a considerable quantity of native independent country, but a great deal, I am convinced, must ultimately be annexed in any event. The fourth division would consist of the Transvaal, and the fifth of Griqualand West, to which, it is hoped, the Orange Free State would soon request to be joined. By this division none of the provinces would possess too preponderating an influence over the others, whereas, should the Federation consist of one rich and powerful colony and several small ones, the latter might possibly become mere dependents on the former.

I am not unaware of the difficulty of carrying out such a sweeping change, but I believe that some plan of the kind is essential to the interests both of England and of the colonies of South Africa.

But it is from a military point of view that I am best qualified to speak of the benefits of Federation.

The defensive state of the colony was, in my opinion, most defective. I have elsewhere mentioned the sale of arms to the natives, which the late Government, in order to gain a transitory popularity, so foolishly allowed, and which resulted in the possession by the Kafirs of upwards of 400,000 muskets.

During my command I repeatedly reported that the police, though of excellent material, were badly organised and ill disciplined, the Commissariat defective, the reserves of ammunition and war stores insufficient. Thus while the late Government were allowing the natives to obtain the means of creating a rebellion, they were taking no measures to provide for its suppression. As they often said: "The assegai is more formidable in the hands of a native than the musket; moreover, there will never be another Kafir war." The experience of the Boers against Secocoeni has proved the reverse, and common sense seems to indicate that a native armed with both a musket and assegais, must be more dangerous than one provided with assegais alone.

But enough of this Government and its follies! It has been dismissed for its incompetence, arrogance, and obstinacy, and, for the sake of the colony, I hope it may not again be heard of.

Federation alone, I believe, would enable the country to take such military measures as, while they involved the least possible cost, would prove efficient to secure life and property. It must be remembered that a colony like that of South Africa cannot afford to pay large sums for troops; taxes which would be easily paid at home, press hardly upon its rising trades. It is therefore above all things necessary that the military system should be cheap. But it should be effective. A bad thing is dear at any price, and I believe that the indirect losses caused by the late war, the paralysis of trade and the stagnation of enterprise, have had a most detrimental effect on the east of the colony. I do not say that absolute security to the colony could be obtained for nothing, but I do say that a good Federation system would enable the colony to maintain a military force, which would be far more effective in proportion to its cost than isolated bands of police or militia can possibly be. Well armed and equipped, it would be ready for immediate action whenever required, so as by vigour at the outset to stamp out incipient rebellion.

It is very satisfactory to read in the recent papers from the Cape of Good Hope, that the present Prime Minister is reported to have called the attention of the country, in his speeches in the provinces, to the advisability of a system of Federation. The following remarks in reference to the Transvaal are much to the purpose:—

Why then delay striving for that confederation under the British flag, which will confer upon us the blessing of real and true independence, the inestimable boon of good constitutional liberty, the glorious gift of security in the possession of our property and the peaceful enjoyment of our lives? The Transvaal will never know true liberty, never know genuine independence, never be safe from panic and trouble, until it forms part of a grand South African Dominion, powerful to suppress insolence and punish incipient rebellion wherever manifested among its subjects, able to maintain peace and remove all stumbling-blocks in the way of prosperity within its borders.

I approve unreservedly of the sentiments uttered in the Imperial Parliament by Sir H. Holland:

If confederation would strengthen the colonies, in no less degree would it strengthen the empire as a whole. And there are two other advantages of confederation. By confederation are secured uniformity of legislation upon all important questions affecting these great outlying dependencies of the empire. And by confederation we raised up a school of legislators in the colonies, who from the necessity of their position were forced to take a broader and more liberal view of the questions which came before them, and to take an imperial as distinguished from a provincial point of view. Their political area was enlarged, and they had a sense of the greater responsibility resting upon them. And lastly, he thought, that some day there would be a closer link between the mother country and the colonies by a more direct representation of the colonies in the Central Legislature of the empire; the West India Islands grouped under one legislature (as the North American provinces were), the great Australian colonies under another, South Africa under another. Nothing could be more moderate than the manner in which Lord Carnarvon had put the matter before the colonists. A universal assent had been given to the noble lord's proposal of a conference. The Legislative Council of the Cape, Natal, the Orange Free River State, the Transvaal, and Griqualand, had all agreed to the conference. Lord Carnarvon had been bound to submit the scheme for a confederation to the States, and they showed their entire appreciation of Lord Carnarvon's act.

BOOK II.—KAFFERARIA AND NATAL.

CHAPTER XII.

THE KOMGHA.

MY next tour of military inspection was to Pondo land and Natal. I reached Port Elizabeth by sea, and, having taken the rail as far as it was completed, proceeded to Grahamstown.

Crowded six in a small coach, we bumped along until near Nazar, where we overtook the preceding day's post-cart, standing by the side of the road, one of its wheels having entirely gone to pieces.

Our doubts whether we should ever reach Grahamstown were increased when, outspanning at a lonely hut in the wide "veldt," the only cattle we found in the miserable stable were three glandered horses. The driver directed four of the mail-contract horses to be spanned in, to which the passengers made no objection, though the Postmaster-General might possibly have done so.

The disease of glanders is becoming very prevalent in the eastern division of the colony. It has been found necessary to destroy many horses belonging to the Frontier Field Force. I imagine that the laws with regard to this dangerous disease are either too weak or, what is worse, are not effectually administered.

We reached Grahamstown on the evening of the 19th, in a

drizzling rain and cold wind, and were glad of the hospitality of the Judge.

On the following morning, when the grouse would be falling in the mountains of Connemara and Galway, we were again on our road.

We bowled over the firm ground in a new American carriage, which the Judge had lately bought in Port Elizabeth, behind four handsome bays, driven by the most expert whip in the country, and drove by two o'clock into Fort Brown. These American carriages (called spiders) are superseding the English covered spring carts so universally used here.

The roads which are common in the colony, and connect the largest towns, differ as widely from the road from London to Hounslow as the latter does from a Welsh country lane. But it is impossible to fix this in the understanding of an English coachmaker. He is not wise enough simply to imitate a model which would secure him a fine profit, but insists that he knows what the colonists require better than they do themselves.

After a hasty breakfast at Fort Brown, we entered the thick bush by a road which astonished even our Judge, and made his spider tremble, as it bounded over rocks and chasms for ten miles down a precipitous " kloof," a young moon serving to light our way.

At nightfall we drew up at Mr. Miller's farm, close to an old fort, which bore signs of having passed through many vicissitudes.

Mr. Miller had been engaged in every Kafir war since the year 1835, and his interesting stories secured our eager attention during the rest of the evening.

At early dawn the view was really beautiful; the Fish river winding among the precipitous deeply-wooded hills, studded with aloes, bearing at this time of the year their bright scarlet flowers, which were frequently mistaken by our soldiers in the war for Kafir warriors, and fired upon accordingly.

The kloofs I looked upon were the last resting-places of many a poor soldier in one Kafir war. Two soldiers, having strayed into the bush, and mistaking the fires of the enemy for those of their companions, fell into the hands of these devils, and were tortured, their dying screams being heard in the stillness of the night, without it being possible for their comrades to render them any assistance.

Attended by about thirty Kafirs, we ascended the hills, being posted in the best position to get a chance of a koodoo. This magnificent deer is almost extinct in the colony, but in Zulu land and on the Limpopo he is still common.

He manages his long horns most skilfully while dashing through the bush, carrying them almost level with his back, and on meeting with an obstacle quickly turning them into a sidelong position.

Soon a shout was given. A koodoo had broken cover, and rushed wildly towards the very bush behind which I was stationed. I fired through the brake, and grazed the back of the deer. It was a female, of no size; the male cunningly escaped scot-free.

Some smaller deer were driven out, such as bush-buck, raibok, and the tiny bluebok.

Attached to us on this occasion was a clever sportsman, a sergeant of police. His keenness as a shot, in my opinion, enhanced his qualifications as a soldier.

On Wednesday the 26th of August we left King William's Town, accompanied by an agreeable companion, the Commandant of the Frontier Force.

The country is open and undulating. We passed a mission station at Peel Town. Here, in the last war of 1846, it is related that the attitude of the Kafirs frightened the missionary, who retired to Alice. Having a well-replenished cellar, he directed a faithful Kafir to assist him in burying his wine previous to his departure. Some months after, to his horror, he read in a newspaper an account of a cheerful evening spent at Peel Town by some native levies and a Burgher force, and the handsome entertainment which they received from a Kafir left on the station; dozens of wines, brandies, &c., &c., having been placed at their disposition, the faithful Kafir-pupil of the missionary no doubt having his own share.

We lunched at Heath's Hotel, Hangman's Bush, the host of which was surrounded by all those comforts which make life valuable. He was an old soldier, who had served in my company in the 60th Rifles, when we were stationed at Corfu thirty years ago. It was pleasant to meet an old comrade in arms.

The name Hangman's Bush dates from an episode in the last war, when a traitor Kafir was hanged by order of General Eyre, a strict disciplinarian, whom I well remember in the Crimea, and whose determination was on many occasions of the utmost value to the colony.

We next outspanned at Mr. Kelly's, Draaibosch. Surrounding the house was a large number of natives, sunning themselves, and occupied in discussing the merits of sundry bottles of a white spirit known as Boer brandy. These wretched creatures spend all their money and much of their time in this way, and are fast degenerating from the noble savage into miserable beasts. It is stated that they have no difficulty in swallowing a quart of this vile liquid at a time. A short distance off were groups of women, who approached the canteen in long files, each bearing on her head a bottle. The spirit which they procured was used, I am told, for adding to their Kafir beer.

Near this is a lofty rock, from which in former days wretched people accused of witchcraft were hurled. This is reported to have been a daily occurrence.

On arriving at the Komgha, guards of honour were prepared to receive me—one from the Frontier army, and one formed of Mounted Volunteers under Captain Cowie.

The volunteer cavalry in this colony are a particularly fine body of men, formed of young and able farmers, thoroughly accustomed to exposure. They are accustomed to regard as an everyday occurrence what others might deem extreme hardship. It is this which makes the force so especially valuable, and the only points in which it can be considered inefficient are its weakness in numbers, the power of its members to relinquish their services at short notice, and their want of military habits.

We spent a very pleasant evening at the Komgha, and were hospitably received by the officers of the frontier army. The Komgha is the artillery station of this force. It is here that all the troopers are instructed in gunnery. For this purpose an officer of her Majesty's artillery has been attached. I was much gratified with the progress which had been made, which cannot fail to be of essential service. The guns, new breech-loading 12-pounders, were furnished with iron carriages, and, in my opinion, were of too weighty a pattern for effective service either in a mountainous country, or one devoid of roads. I am therefore in hopes that guns of a smaller calibre and pattern in future may be selected, as I am convinced they would be more appropriate for the uses to which they are likely to be put.

At the Komgha we received news which might have caused some anxiety regarding the Transkei. Her Majesty's Resident had sent a request that the Frontier Field Force might be held in readiness, their horses carefully foraged, and kept in a fit state for instant movement. The cause of these proceedings was that a number of Pondos, in the country to the west of St. John's River, under the chief Damas, had taken possession of a tract of land under "Umditchwa," the Pondomisi chief, and refused to move.

Umditchwa had lately, after continued application on his part, received a promise of our protection, so that war upon him was war upon us. The country which had been invaded was the very corner of Kaffraria which we should pass through, so that the interest, indeed I may say the excitement, was considerably heightened.

It was even doubtful whether my advance might not bring the question to an issue; but I calculated that in all probability it would be construed into a determination to settle this particular question, and that the thirty or forty cavalry soldiers who were to attend me would be magnified into an army, so that Damas would become alarmed, and direct his people to retire. My calculation proved correct.

These troops accompanied me, and as I was attended, if not by the artillery itself, by the commanding officer of that force, by a species of exaggeration common to these people, the advance of two separate armies was announced, and it was even reported that two camps had been formed, and that thousands of tents whitened the valleys.

Prudence then came to the councils of Damas, and orders were issued by him to forbid any further advance of the Pondos.

The next cause of anxiety to me was the position of the forces, it being said that a waggon had been detained at the Umtata river, one of the tributaries of St. John's, for four months during the last wet season, without the possibility of moving through the "drift." Moreover it would be impossible to turn back in case of rain, as the rivers behind would in that case become as impassable as those in front. The weather, however, gave every sign of continuing fine and steady, and we hoped our journey would be over before the wet season set in. We left the Komgha at 10 A.M. of the 27th of August. From this town I was accompanied by an intelligent and well-informed officer of the Royal

I

Engineers, and by an officer of the Frontier Field Force, who commanded my cavalry escort. We had two or three ponies each, our baggage being in a strong Cape cart drawn by six mules with three " mittous," and the excellent driver who had already been with us in the Free State. I much preferred ponies; but as it would be needful to have at least one charger to mount on special occasions, I purchased a strong and handsome dark bay for this purpose.

By midday we reached the Kei river, passing rapidly down a steep declivity to the bank, the frowning summit of "Murderers' Kop" looking over the drift. The mountain is named after a sad tragedy which happened when Sir P. Maitland was camped here. A party of young officers determined to explore the country. Mounting their horses after "tiffin," they rode to the top of the hill, obtaining an excellent view of the Transkei and the enemy's country beyond. Unseen by them, the Kafirs had noticed their presence on the Kop, and stealing up by a rugged by-path, they suddenly attacked the party, not one of whom escaped to carry the news of the disaster to the camp.

The Kei river is the boundary line between the responsible government of the Cape Colony and the people of the Kafir States, whose only law is might, and who practise the mystic rites of witchcraft (or smelling out).

It is requisite to watch these countries with unceasing care, lest their feuds should imperil the safety of natives residing within our borders and under our protection.

The jealousies of the tribes among themselves, if we fomented and encouraged them, would lead to their mutual destruction, and apparently to our benefit. After they had eaten one another up like the Kilkenny cats, we could easily step in and divide the land. I need hardly say, however, that besides being dishonest and unchristian-like, such a course would be very impolitic.

Our most prudent policy is to use our best endeavours to

soothe their animosities, and forbid party disputes. To be effective, however, our influence must be enforced by power.

The best course to pursue is, therefore, the one we are now taking, by placing in each country a Resident of capability, discretion, and courage, ready to hear the complaints of all parties, so that when the chief of a petty state, supported by the voice of his people, asks to be taken under our rule and protection, he may carefully consider and ultimately grant the request. In the discharge of such responsible duties there must, no doubt, be great discretion shown.

How such a boon is regarded by the native chiefs themselves will be seen in subsequent pages.

The natives of the Transkei may be roughly divided into four distinct classes: Pondos, Tembus, Galekas, and Fingoes.

The first are powerful, the second weakly, the third warlike, and the fourth industrious. The Fingoes, who were formerly slaves and much despised, have now more wealth and energy than any of the others. Besides these four, many small offsets and tribes have entered the country. Even amongst the four I have named, there are many authorities of different power, and, indeed, the people of the Transkei cannot be looked upon as a happy family.

The Kei is a fine river running between high mountains, constantly varying in the volume of its waters. In the dry season it is easily fordable at certain definite points; but during the rains of summer even its best drifts are dangerous.

On the other side of the Kei, the country which we next entered was Fingoland, which is under a resident magistrate. The Fingoes were formerly a race subject to other more powerful tribes. It was good policy to gather them together, and place them in a position to act as a buffer or check between our colony and the wilder inhabitants of the Transkei.

I was met by "Veldtman," a Fingo chief or headman, with about four hundred mounted men. As an attention, he had ordered a table to be placed under a wide-spreading tree, on which was laid out a simple repast, and his kindness was much appreciated.

Veldtman appeared to be a man with much strength of character; he is placed in a responsible position and seems to show much judgment.

At every 100 yards fresh horsemen joined the procession, saluting us by firing off guns or raising the right hand above the head, and calling out in a guttural tone " Buget," which, literally translated, is " Bring presents." Falling into the rear they swelled the train till it numbered at least 500. Although all of them could not boast of saddles, they formed a very respectable escort, when the general wildness of the scenery and the rudeness of the people were taken into consideration.

Temporarily allotted to me by the party was a " Bongo," or, as we call him, a trumpeter. The duties of this individual were loudly to extol the deeds of the great persons to whom they are attached. Some of his laudations were translated to me, and there was no feat of arms, from those of Don Quixote to those of the great Duke of Wellington, which my trumpeter did not declare that I accomplished daily. Fortunately the natives placed confidence in him, and did not call upon me to verify his assertions. The Bongo was a very old man, but he ran for miles beside my horse without apparent fatigue. I was told that he interlarded his flatteries with frequent appeals to the great men to give him a pony, saying that he was lame, and that they ought to be ashamed to allow a man of his talents to walk while so many ignorant men rode.

By midday we reached Captain Blythe's residence, a comfortable house situated on à hill-slope, well supplied with water. I much regretted the absence of the Resident himself, though every attention was shown me by Mr. Levy, who officiated for him. In the afternoon a great gathering of the people took place round the Court-house, where, through an interpreter, I complimented them on their improvement, and on their loyalty to her Majesty and the Government.

I had much pleasure in visiting the Fingoes. Evidently the pleasure was mutual.

Now that they are practically free, and by their energy rich, they are beginning to be proud of their position, and are equally capable of appreciating a compliment and of resenting a slight.

Personally I should have preferred visiting the renowned Kreli, chief of the Galekas. He was represented as a warrior of no common capacity and courage; but it was considered inadvisable. So great is the terror in which Kreli is held, that the Fingoes are most anxious to be permitted to enrol themselves for the purpose of carrying arms, as their country borders his state. The request seems not unreasonable, if dependence is to be placed on the report of the number of muskets daily procured by the Galekas. Even with Kreli a fear of the consequences appears to have some weight, for although he had at that time been threatening an attack upon his neighbours the Tembus, he had wisely refrained from carrying this into execution. I heard that Kreli was nervously anxious with regard to my visit, especially desiring to know the number of my escort, and my object in visiting the wilds of the Transkei.

At the Fingo Station I met Major Malan; the last time I had seen him was in the Crimea. Although a man of fortune and distinguished as a military officer, he had quitted the service from a feeling of devotion to religion, and became a missionary in these out-of-the-way wilds. He told me that the Fingoes were becoming too civilised to need his exertions, so that in a few days he intended to seek the wilder tribes now under Damas on the coast, between Kreli and the Pondos, who he hoped might profit by his instruction.

We parted each of us on his own road. I thought he

appeared to feel it, when we reverted to my present and his former profession. He took his solitary way with the dark natives in the wilderness, and I resumed my active duties with their responsibilities and pleasures. Each of us had his own cares. Although we were treading different roads, both, I trust, were leading us to the same goal.

CHAPTER XIII.

GANGALESWE.

EARLY on the morning of the 29th I awoke from a refreshing sleep—the flowers of Captain Blyth's pretty garden, especially the violets, perfuming the whole cottage—and after a delicious bath, for which his residence is famous, we were again on the road.

The inhabitants of the neighbouring kraals seemed to be in a thriving condition. Indeed, a beggar of any colour is never met with in South Africa, although plenty of idle, well-to-do natives may be seen. We outspanned for breakfast near the small stream Ixilingxa, where we met Mr. Wright, the magistrate attached to the Tambookie country, who accompanied us as far as Clarkebury. I must add that it is requisite to use some caution in drinking water at these streams, as they are infested with tadpoles which enter into the system, are difficult to extirpate, and are said to increase in size until they affect the body with fearful involuntary twitchings, like their own impulsive movements.

At the Idutchwa Reserve we were met by Gangeleswe ("as big as the world"), chief of the Tembus, accompanied by about forty followers, each with his gun or rifle.

Gangeleswe is a coarse-looking savage, about thirty years of age, and about 6 feet 2 inches high, dressed in a suit of well-worn tweed, with a cowrie shell stuck in the skin of one ear. He was meanly mounted. I own that what I had heard of him had not prepossessed me in his favour, and it corresponded with his appearance. Gangeleswe, the Tambookie, married a daughter of Kreli, the Galeka. Returning one day to his kraal, his young and pretty wife displeased him, it is said, by having made use of a word in which occurred one or two of the syllables used in spelling his name (a fatal offence among these people). Savage in word and deed, he raised his ever-ready knobkerrie, and, letting it fall with full strength, broke her leg. The poor thing crawled out of his hut, and, after hiding in the bush for two or three days, managed to meet with some friendly assistance, and ultimately reached her father Kreli's home. Gangeleswe now became much alarmed lest the wrath of the great chief should overtake him. He therefore sent messengers, and as an account of this is given in the native style it may be interesting :—

The messengers of Gangeleswe, having arrived at the kraal of Kreli, delivered their message. The first question was, "By whom had they been sent?" The answer was, "By the people and in pity to the motherless children." Question: "Where are the great men of the tribe, and where are so and so (four or five of Gangeleswe's wives being enumerated, who were said to have been killed)?" The reluctant reply was, "Dispersed and driven away by the chief." After much talk, Tonise was told to return and say, " A child had been sent by the Galekas to the Halas (Gangeleswe's branch of the Tambookies). After a while rumours of ill-usage reached the Galekas. The rumours were denied by different people. Feltman among the number. Eventually the rumours proved true, and the bones of the child of the Galekas returned. The matter was reported to Government, who said we might bury the bones, or otherwise do as we pleased regarding them; and is it reasonable that we shall now send back this skeleton to the man, who, according to your own admission, has driven away the great man of the tribe and maimed his wives, and who is now said to be cruelly using the orphans whom you profess to pity? Return, and say we sent our daughter to the Hala chief; her return to the Galekas has not been reported to us by the Halas. She is not here." Tonise, as in duty bound, expressed gratitude for the reply, stating that he would return again. To this there was no objection, and thus the matter stands at present.

The assertion that the woman is not with the Galekas may mean either that she is not publicly or officially there as becomes her birth and position, having crawled away secretly from her husband; or it may mean that, being maimed and disfigured, she is now but a shadow of her former self—in fact, "a skeleton," no longer fit to be the wife of a chief. She has returned to her father's tribe to be buried by them, and not by the tribe to whom she was sent.

When Gangeleswe made his first demand for the return of Kreli's daughter, the matter was reported to Government, and Kreli was informed that he might use his own discretion in reference to sending her back; and thus he says, "Government said he might bury her if he thought fit."

In the spring of 1873 Gangeleswe was accused of causing a waiting-maid of his wife's (Kreli's daughter) to be put to death, which on inquiry was found to be true.

The injury to Kreli's daughter was considered a cause of quarrel. Kreli attacked the Tambookies in the mountains near Clarkebury, and lacking courage to defend his country or his race, deserted by his warriors, Gangeleswe was found alone in a pitiable condition by the missionary. Kreli, obedient to the voice of good counsel, retired to his own land without following up his victory. Gangeleswe in his extremity implored our Government to take his country under their protection; but before his petition could be considered, seeing that the present danger was past, he begged to reconsider his request, and thus ruled some time longer, receiving an allowance from our Government.

An amusing story is told of a Tambookie warrior that reminds me of the Green Island, for many years my happy residence.

Two Tambookies running from the field of battle hid themselves in a hole, but the leg of one unfortunately protruding caught the eye of some wary Icalaka. They pulled him out, and were preparing to slay him, when he cried, "Spare me, and I will tell you something." They paused, and he said, "There is yet another man in that hole." The second hidden warrior hearing this, called out from his place of concealment, "Don't believe him, kill him at once, he tells lies, there is no one in here." But it availed him nothing, and, after the custom of Kafirs, the two prisoners were forthwith assegaied.

In the following year the Cape Colonial Government sent Commandant Bowker with a considerable force to settle their disputes, which, by his judgment and discretion, he seems to have done in the most satisfactory manner. The following is a short account of the facts:—

On the day following, the meeting took place, and was short and satisfactory, with very little excitement, as the effect of fire-water had passed. The Pondos then unconditionally accepted the announcement, and would let byegones be byegones. They broke up, and proceeded by invitation to see and hear Bowker's missionaries who preach peace. One of these, a small cannon, was taken to a spot, and under the able management of Captain Robinson threw some shells for the edification of the many Pongos who had assembled to witness the proceedings. At the word "fire," the gun responded by a loud report, and the shell hastened to its destination, which had previously been indicated, and then burst, to the no small astonishment of the natives.

N'gwilso ventured to look into the cannon's mouth. The discharge of a rocket was also the cause of much astonishment, and one of the spectators made a bolt. The chief N'gwilso remarked very naively, "No wonder that you English overcome us!" and proceeded to ask, "Who taught you these things?" We may state in conclusion that Bowker's mission has been successful in initiating a new and peaceful state between the Pondos and Halas, and the value of the mission may be guessed at by a remark which we heard N'gwilso make, and that was, "Come, Bokolo, fire away; you need not mind about wasting your ammunition; you have none to fight with; you have come in peace, and not to fight."

Gangeleswe was evidently most uneasy in his European dress. The only object which excited his attention was the instrument belonging to the trumpeter, which he was most anxious to obtain, saying that he would direct one of his councillors to play it for his amusement.

It is customary in South Africa on the occasion of a visit from a person of superior rank to present him and his followers with an ox. Should his party not be of sufficient number to consume the whole, the remainder is shared by the followers of the donor. Gangeleswe, though so powerful in his kraal, was unable or unwilling to provide the ox; he made great excuses to the interpreter, saying that it was coming; but finally two wretched sheep were substituted, and the chief himself, probably ashamed of his want of hospitality, vanished in the night without even taking leave of his guest.

After a lonely and somewhat fatiguing ride of thirty-five miles we reached the Ungwali river, immediately over which is situated the Mission Station of Clarkebury.

We encamped immediately on the other side of the river, as it is always wise to place a river behind one, lest before the morning it should be rendered unfordable by sudden rains. At Clarkebury I bid adieu to Lieutenant Robinson, who had accompanied me thus far. Parting thus with one of my *armies*, I continued my journey with the smaller escort.

The skins of nearly all the Kafirs whom we now met were of a polished Honduras-mahogany red. Both men and women used largely the red-ochre clay; it is said that they are thus protected from the bites of noxious insects and vermin. Fingoes use it as well as Kafirs.

The Commissioner in Basuto land has directed that this red clay should not be introduced into that country, at which the traders complain, as a considerable profit is made from its supply; but in Basuto land the blue coat, round hat, and corduroy trousers, have been adopted to a very great extent, more especially since the opening of the Diamond Fields.

CHAPTER XIV.

WITCHCRAFT.

THE natives whom we now met, both men and women, generally wore no clothing but a few slight ornaments.

An hour after leaving Clarkebury we reached the Bashee river, crossing it at a difficult and dangerous ford full of slippery rocks and boulders. Our only mishap was one to the cart, the wheels of which getting caught between two rocks received such a severe strain as caused the axles to spread at least six inches out of the level, in which condition they remained until we reached Natal.

We also crossed the Umtata river, noted for the slipperiness of its rocky drift. The water was low, but at other times it is deep and dangerous. Immediately on the other side we met an old man of the name of Kaye, who had served in the Kafir wars with the 2nd Queen's. I shall never forget his delight when he found my aide-de-camp to be the son of his old captain. "My boy," he said, "I look upon you as a son." He was doing well, being sober, industrious and steady, and he possessed good horses, sheep, and a large number of cattle.

Mr. Orpen, the Resident of the St. John's Territory, met us here. Although not previously acquainted with him, having read so many of his letters published in parliamentary documents on this country, I felt as if I knew him. I had many an interesting conversation with him, receiving an immense amount of information as regards the Transkei, Basuto land, the Free State, and the colony.

Contrary to the expectation of many, we had not seen one single head of game in this wide-spread country, neither did we see any, with the exception of half-a-dozen rei-buck, during our entire journey to Natal. The fact is, that where Kafirs live no game can long exist. They persecute them morning, evening and night, in and out of season. No sooner is a deer seen than a whole kraal turns out, and, surrounding the bush into which it is tracked, each armed with a bundle of assegais, they assail the unfortunate animal and destroy it.

We had now entered that portion of the country of the Pondos which is ruled over by Damas, the younger brother of Umquikela, the paramount chief. These two chiefs are both the sons of the great King Faku, who considered that Pondo land should be under the rule of the elder. But the younger, Damas, does not share this opinion, and bids his elder brother take it if he can. A few days ago they declared war, and some few Pondos were watching on the hills the advance of my "*army*." Otherwise the country was very quiet, so that the intention they had expressed of attacking the Pondomise had evidently been postponed.

We met a friendly old settler, Mr. Owen, at the Umtata. He had been a surgeon in the Old East India's Company Navy, but liking land better than water, and freedom in the wilds more than being cooped up on shipboard, he had exchanged the cockpit for a snug cottage in Pondo land, where he had now resided many years. He had the grazing over an unlimited range of country, and possessed many thousands of sheep and several hundred head of cattle, in addition to a store where everything that a Kafir could require was to be procured. No rents were demanded by the chief for grazing or occupation, but continued presents were expected, and indeed required. Lately a better system had crept in, and a rent of 5*l*. per annum had been arranged to be paid by each settler.

This rent cannot be considered excessive for such a range of pasturage. Mr. Owen gave us some home-made bread, a great luxury in this country; he could not procure milk for us. He had allowed his Kafirs to milk his cows after dark; the consequence was, he said, that no milk was forthcoming. A curious custom exists of always milking cows in presence of the calf, indeed a stuffed calf is sometimes kept in sight of the mother, otherwise no milk can be obtained from the cow. The settlers on the Umtata complained that they are constantly robbed of their cattle, but as they live on the borders of the Tambookies and not far distant from the Pondomise, it was impossible to say who were the cattle-lifters. How much this state of things reminded us of what we read regarding the Scottish Border in old times!

In Kafirs two great characteristics are noticeable, superstition and theft. The second, though almost a law of Kafir nature, is held under control by the first, which is often made use of for protective purposes. A settler on the Umtata having been robbed of some wood, a very valuable commodity in this country, and suspecting the Kafirs, bored some of his logs, and, having inserted gunpowder carefully, plugged up the holes. More thefts occurred, but a few days afterwards a report spread that the devil had got into all the wood used at this station. The owner of the wood naturally concluded that his gunpowder had something to do with this extraordinary circumstance, as from that moment no wood was missing.

In the Transkei, accusations and trials for witchcraft still prevail, and are a most profitable source of revenue to the chiefs.

In the protected states, where our Residents are the ruling authorities, it is gradually disappearing, but in Pondo land, both in Damas and Umquikela's division, we hear of it constantly. I was told that at least five men per week were "smelt out," their property confiscated to the chief and themselves put to death. The system is carried on in the following manner.

One person accuses another, unknown, of having butchered his child, &c. The medicine-man or doctor is then called in for the object of "smelling out" the accused; the accusation generally lighting upon some well-to-do person who possesses cattle. He is seized, and put to various tortures to make him plead guilty; and indeed it is of little use for him to deny it, as the power of the medicine-doctor is used with great vigour. Forthwith, by his prescience, the doctor discovers some sign which he declares proves the guilt. No sooner is the verdict given than the wretched man is seized and murdered, or possibly burned, his property in wives or cattle confiscated, a great portion going to the chief, some to the doctor, and some to the accuser. The best chance for the poor creature is at once to fly for protection to the missionaries, where he is usually safe. He is lucky if he escapes, even though he loses every earthly thing he possesses. The protection enjoyed under the missionaries is very great, for although they are not under the protection of the Government, yet, by custom, they hold a power which in these wild regions places them beyond the control of the chief, so that, without a gun in their possession, they rest as securely as if surrounded by a legion of warriors. It is dreadful that such horrors should exist close to our borders, but there is no way of putting a stop to them except by annexing the country.

" WITCHCRAFT AGAIN."—We are informed that a few days ago a most cruel murder was perpetrated in Kreli's country through witchcraft. It appears from what we hear, that one of the influential men of the tribe discovered or pretended that lung-sickness was among his cattle, and accordingly sought the aid of the witch "Doctor" to find out "the enemy" who had done this. A young man (possibly somewhat wealthy in cattle) was indicated by the witch "Doctor," and measures were of course taken to secure him; but, getting scent of the design, upon him, he absented himself from home during the day, and returning at night; alas! only to meet a most cruel fate. Myrmidons of the "Doctor," and his prompter were in waiting, seized the unfortunate young man, and after the usual tortures, he was stabbed to death in the most merciless manner. Such is the brief account of this sad affair as narrated to us, and respecting which we trust the British authorities will institute inquiry. It is a disgrace to civilisation that such abominable doings should be allowed to be practised on our very borders, a practice which those best informed on these matters believe is of very frequent occurrence amongst the tribes beyond the Kei. The murderer is said to have been taken up, but was simply fined a few head of cattle, which, for aught we know, may have been paid out of the spoil taken from his murdered victim.

A tragical scene has lately occurred amongst the Pondomise, the foundation of which is the powerful native belief in witchcraft. The circumstances are as follows:—A young girl manifests unusual wildness of manner, and frantically struggles, saying she is going to ——, and mentions the name of her lover. Her conduct is so boisterous that her friends are forced to detain her: she breaks away from them and runs to where her love is, in a partially naked state. Arriving there, she casts herself into his arms—he is very much astonished—her friends very much grieved. The oracle must be consulted, who is generally known by name of "Doctor." He states that the cause of this is that the girl has been acted upon by the lover with certain potent charms. The man—who has a wife and child—denies this; but public opinion is strong in the erroneous belief.

The man is so grieved by this persistency in spite of his declaration of innocence, that he determines to destroy himself, and in order thereto, loads his gun and then goes into his hut where his wife and child are sitting. He lays the gun down by his side and stretches for his infant, and kissing it, hands it back to the mother, who is shortly afterwards startled by the report of a gun, and by seeing her husband rolling about. Friends soon come in and find that he is not dead, the ball has passed through near his right breast. He can still speak, and says he shot himself because they would not believe his statement of innocency, and the accusation was painful to him. In a few hours he died, adding one man to the many past and yet to be the victims to this system of superstition.—'Frontier Guardian,' February 9th, 1875.

Quiet persons at home cannot believe the extent to which these horrid practices are carried.

It is indeed frightful to hear the stories which are related on the most undoubted authority.

WITCHCRAFT AMONGST THE KAFIRS.

It is astonishing to thinkers to find that statesmen in South Africa and at home have not looked into this evil amongst the Kafirs, and agitated for its suppression. Wonderful, truly wonderful! How many victims there are every year of this system of lies and cruelty in native territories adjacent to and connected with the colony, and yet little more than a passing thought is given to it! How loudly Englishmen talk of the evils of slavery, and what active and vigorous measures are employed to destroy it! Yet here is a greater evil than slavery, for it is manslaughter and murder, the result of a false and lying Priestcraft, practised in countries where the chiefs are paid out of the Government revenue. Take for example such chiefs as Kili, Ngangelizwe, Ndamase, and Umgikela, heads of tribes living in the country, from the Kei to the Umzimkula, and what do we find? They uphold and sanction this system of manslaughter based on some fanciful accusation, or, as they call it, divination. Take the following case as an example: A reim is lost from a span and cannot be found; recourse to a diviner is the next thing. He says, So-and-so's baboon (familiar spirit) took it, and So-and-so and another man have the reim between them. It is concealed; the accused are caught and tortured, and finally both are horribly and cruelly strangled for this imaginary fault, their families scattered, and their property plundered. Another man is accused of having a baboon which takes away his neighbour's calabashes. He is caught and horribly tortured and thrashed, laid on the ground and tied up to four pins in the ground, and fire applied to his most tender parts. Another is a woman; she is accused by the diviner of having intercourse with the god of thunder, "Impundula." In order to extort confession she is tortured, stripped and thrashed until her torturers are tired. She is next taken into her hut; a roaring fire is made and she is held by strong men to the fire, until she is scorched into an immense blister. Some of them die under the torture, and others faint with exhaustion. These things are of daily occurrence amongst the native tribes, yet our Government does not interfere. The subject only requires some able advocate, who should take the matter up and learn the particulars, after which an enlightened Government could not fail to take notice of such a cruel and fiendish system.

The way in which persons accused of witchcraft are killed is sometimes by placing an ants' nest on their bodies till they are devoured; sometimes, again, a thong is tied round their necks, stretched tight, and struck with sticks till the vibration dislocates their necks.

While speaking of these frightful customs, I must say a word about the marriage ceremonies of these people, of which I insert an account from a local journal.

    I went to see the marriage of the chief Faku, with the daughter
    of another chief from the Klip river district. Faku is a
    chief who did right good service during the rebellion, and he

is liked well. I was glad of an opportunity of paying him some mark of respect, went as an uninvited guest, and was right hospitably received. Well, sir, before this I was always under the impression that a Kafir marriage was a sort of bargain and sale, hop the broomstick affair, so many cows paid, and the woman handed over to the husband in the presence of the official witness; but I was much surprised to find it was quite a different affair, and one of much ceremony. In civilised society the gentleman usually settles himself and a dower on the lady, but here the dower is given to the father, and he brings the lady in much Kafir state to the husband. Proceedings open by a wild sort of dance, which announces the approach of the bride; in the meantime she and her bridesmaids were said to be washing and decorating themselves at a stream near by. After a short time the bride's party advanced, and was received by the husband and his people sitting down, a space being left of about twenty paces between them. All guests were on the husband's right hand, he and they being surrounded by the husband's tribe—men, women, and children—in a sort of half circle. The dances and songs open with the men on the bride's side, and after the dance the men deposit their dance shields one on the other in the centre of the space, the bride's father's shield, as chief, being placed on the top. The bridesmaids' dance and song then begins, the bride herself being still kept in the background. When this is over the bride suddenly appears in the centre of the bridesmaids, with her face veiled, a knife in her right hand, and a small shield in her left. The dance and song of bridesmaids begin again, all grandly advancing to the shields, and then stop. The husband calls to the bride to come to him, and she turns her back to him and dances with the rest back again; then again the men dance and sing. Several of the elders and wives of the bride's party run up in front of the husband and chaff him, tell him he is "no go," and not good enough for their girl. The men's dance then ceases, and the bridesmaids begin again. This time the bride's veil is lowered to the nose, and her eyes seen, and she advances beyond the shields. Induana, on the bride's side, sits down in a peculiar manner, indicating that the husband must give her plenty of milk, and so the dances go on till she comes up to the husband. He speaks to her; she turns her back to him; he asks her lovingly to give him her hand; she does so; and as she does so she looks over her shoulder at him.

"She gave him one look, but that look was a piercer."

More dances ensue, until at last she comes up unveiled. He asks her if she will be his wife; she says "Yes." She is then asked by the official witness if she is willing to be his wife, and to come and live with him, and she says "Yes." Other dances and ceremonies follow; but, as it was close to sundown, I had to up saddle and leave. As far as I could see, there was no constraint in the matter; on the contrary, from the look, rather a liking of the bride for the bridegroom. Everything was most orderly; beer (ubatywala) there was for the guests, but no drunkenness. The bride was one of the finest women I have ever seen in South Africa, six feet high, well formed, and very pretty.

I add an account of a case which came before one of our magistrates:

KAFIR WIFE SELLING.—In the magistrates' court at Alice, a couple of weeks ago, Quirana, a Fingo, was charged by Dingana, another Fingo, with the abduction of his daughter Noseki, aged about eighteen years, and keeping her a prisoner in his hut for three days against her will. Dingana said that Noseki was his daughter, that he had five months ago disposed of her to the accused for twenty-seven sheep and three oxen, but had not formally handed her to him, notwithstanding which defendant met the girl at a dance and took her to his house, where he kept her under guard till her mother found her.

Dingana admitted that he had sold the girl twice, first to defendant and afterwards to another man, for seven head of cattle; and that, having cancelled the first transaction, his object was to make the defendant pay for keeping the girl at his house for three days. Noseki stated that she was first handed over to defendant, who, after paying twenty-seven sheep on account to her father, met her at a dance and took her to his home, where, in his absence, she was guarded by the women of the kraal, until her mother found her and took her away. She was then disposed of a second time to a man named Inyaka, for seven head of cattle.

She preferred husband No. 2. Her father returned the sheep to No. 1. The accused stated that the present proceedings had been instituted by the complainant with a view of extorting cattle. In the first place he had given sheep and oxen for the girl, who came to his house as his wife willingly; afterwards her father got a better offer for her and sold her to another man; the girl had not been taken away by force, neither had she been kept a prisoner as alleged. The magistrate remarked that this was another example of the immorality attending the Ukulobola system. Here a father was bartering his daughter for sheep and oxen to the highest bidder, and after selling her to one man, hearing of another willing to give more, he cancelled the first transaction and handed the girl over to a second man. After failing to make the first purchaser pay for the girl's three days' society, he brought him into court on a criminal charge, which could not be sustained for a moment. Case dismissed.

At Kafir marriages a very curious doll is used. It is

made of a wooden cylinder about a foot long and four inches in diameter, covered over with beads. Representations in coloured beads are made of the eyes, nose, mouth, and hair, and little arms and legs are attached. Some of these dolls are reputed to bring good luck to the marriages where they are used, and some bad. If a doll is fortunate it is worth many head of cattle; and Commandant Bowker, the Chief of the Police Force, told me that they are prized so highly, that with all his influence he could not obtain one, but had to content himself with a copy made especially for him.

On the 31st of August we encamped at Gangelulu. Just before reaching the plain we killed an enormous cobra at least six feet long. I was cautioned not to go too near it in its death agonies, as it frequently spits venom into the eyes of any one near, which causes a temporary, if not permanent, blindness. One of the officers of the 13th Regiment was struck thus even at the distance of fifteen yards, and did not regain his sight for a week.

The stories which are told regarding snakes in South Africa are endless, many of them being as remarkable as those from America. Some snakes, it is asserted, have the power of coiling themselves into the shape of a spring, and, jumping from the ground, can light even on a passing horseman; while others, they say, putting their tails in their mouths, roll themselves along like a hoop, with the speed of a velocipede. Much to my regret, none of these singularly gifted reptiles ever presented themselves to me. Cats are said to be proof against snake-bites, as the following will show:—

> A green mamba was engaged in a fierce tussle with a big cat, in which the cat had bitten out one of its eyes, and in return got a wound in its face that swelled up to an enormous size, but beyond that he seemed none the worse for the encounter, and in a few days was well again.

There can be no doubt that the mamba is a snake of a savage and violent nature. One of my staff officers, engaged in purchasing horses, frequently passed the same spot, where a large snake, dashing out of its hole, cast itself many times against the carriage-wheel; but on one occasion, being prepared, he shot it.

Kafirs are by no means delicate eaters. When they have killed a snake they are sure to rip it up and extract a long, green bag, which they swallow with great relish.

The subject of snake-bites is one of no small interest in this country.

Liquid ammonia is, *par excellence*, the best antidote. It must be administered immediately after the bite, both internally, diluted with water, and externally, in its concentrated form. The "Eau de Luce" and other nostrums sold for this purpose have ammonia for their main ingredient. But it generally happens in the case of a snake-bite that the remedy is not at hand, and hours may elapse before it can be obtained. In this case the following treatment will work well:—Tie a ligature tightly *above* the bite, scarify the wound deeply with a knife, and allow it to bleed freely. After having drawn an ounce or so of blood, remove the ligature and ignite three times successively about two drams of gunpowder right on the wound. If gunpowder be not at hand, an ordinary fusee will answer the purpose; or, in default of this, the glowing end of a piece of wood from the fire. Having done this, proceed to administer as much brandy to the patient as he will take. Intoxicate him as rapidly as possible, and, once intoxicated, he is safe. If, however, through delay in treatment the poison has once got into the circulation, no amount of brandy will either intoxicate him or save his life.

'The Natal Mercury' relates an instance of a lady who lately awoke about midnight to find herself in the company of a large specimen of one of the most deadly of African snakes, the "ringhals," a kind of cobra. The lady was disturbed by feeling something moving in the bed, and on putting her hand down discovered to her horror the nature of her midnight visitor. Under such circumstances a terrified scream was excusable: her husband was awakened, a light procured, and search made for the reptile, which fortunately remained between the mattress and the sheet, where it was speedily despatched with a few blows from a stout stick. The "ringhals" is a bold fighter, and will stand erect and make rapid darts at an enemy, besides which, it is credited, in common with one or two species of African snakes, with the power of spitting a venomous saliva with considerable accuracy of aim.

The country of the Pondomisi, under the chief Umdichwa, is one of the protected States, and is gradually improving. We were now in a land inhabited by races as wild as any that are to be found on the continent of South Africa, and altogether unconscious of the instruction which so clearly marks the division between the savage and the civilised man, for the Kafir has no literature, no alphabet, and no knowledge of the art of writing.

Umdichwa was too ill to leave his kraal, but he sent us respectful messages. Previous to his receiving our protection he led a sad life. He truly described it as that of a dog. Since youth, he said, he had never known a quiet day or night. He was aroused at the barking of a dog, and thought his kraal was attacked by the Pondos—which, indeed, not unfrequently happened—his wives, cattle, and children being carried off and his young men killed. Now, however, he slept tranquilly, and was contented.

We were shown a mountain in which an old queen resided not long ago, who was the terror of her enemies. When attacked, she would place herself stark naked at the head of her warriors, and rushing wildly into the midst of the battle, scatter the Pondos to the winds, as much by her appearance and imprecations as by her blows, her husband the chief looking on with admiration.

We breakfasted at the Incolaha river, a very pretty spot, immediately opposite to a waterfall of no great size, but pleasing in appearance. Here we found a large quantity of wild asparagus, which was excellent.

While at breakfast we saw some families fording the stream, the mothers carrying their children, as usual, on their backs, which they seem to have no difficulty in doing for hours together, even while working all the time. They carry them in the same position that we have lately adopted for the knapsack of our infantry—very low down on the back.

The women pay but little attention to the dressing of their hair, or, indeed, to their appearance generally; but it is different with the men, who are very dandified, and have a great idea of enhancing their personal attractions.

Their heads are profusely rubbed with grease, wax, and sand, and the hair is then worked up into a sort of circular coil on the top of the head, something in the fashion of the pad used by a basket-carrier. In fact, it is difficult to believe that it is not a coil of gutta-percha. This is neither opened out, washed, nor dressed, except with more grease, for years, and must necessarily be very filthy. In this coil they store small articles, such as snuff or small coins. The lobes of the ears are cut into long slits, which are rendered exceedingly useful as save-alls, as some article of constant need, such as hair-skewer or a snuff-spoon is stuck through this slit on either side.

CHAPTER XV.

UMTHONTHLO.

THE mission station at Shawbury is beautifully situated a short distance from the banks of the river Kitsa. It contains a large area of ground well laid out, and is apparently very prosperous. On the following morning we ascended to the top of a neighbouring mountain, called Mount Cunynghame, and from this eminence we had a fine view of the celebrated falls on the river. Though hardly so grand as in the rainy season, they were most beautiful. The water, precipitating itself over a ledge of rock by a directly perpendicular fall 375 feet high and a quarter of a mile wide, whirling down into the abyss beneath, is carried off in a serpentine form through a deep channel between great red, scarped rocks. It is a noble sight, and one of the largest and highest falls in the world. At Shawbury the chief Umdichwa presented me with an ox which we had some difficulty in killing, for it ran away, after receiving one bullet, and required a long chase before it could be re-captured.

The hill that we ascended had not long since formed the camping-ground of the Pondos on the occasion of an attack. They had lighted a fire on a large rock. The heat made the rock split with a report like a cannon, which so alarmed them that they ran away in a body. On the opposite bank we met the chief of the second branch of the Pondomisi tribe, Um-thonthlo. He is considered the most daring warrior of the Transkei, and although he commands a comparatively small tribe, he has always been a terror to his neighbours. Whether in attack or defence, he is said to have no equal. He is surnamed the "Euphorbia," in consequence of a circumstance which happened to him when he was younger. Two of his wives whom he was desirous of putting to death were brought to his kraal. His father "Comtrees" would not allow him to do so; and to prevent it they tied him to the tree, the name of which, Euphorbia, he ever after bore. Others state that he was so named from his straight and manly bearing, which I should think the more likely story. The chief is a tall, strong man, with determination and cunning marked on his countenance. During his last war he had fought a battle with the Pondos upon the very spot upon which we met him. This is the story of it.

The Pondos, 4000 strong, came into his country, plundering as they went. Umthonthlo, cunningly retiring, and thus leading them on until they had got within a narrow strip of land with bush on either side, concealed himself in the retreat. No sooner had the victorious army passed than, rushing from the thicket in their rear, he attacked them with assegai and musket, routed their army, and put large numbers to death.

Umthonthlo is always accompanied by six followers, excellent shots, and armed with Winchester rifles, each loaded with their charges.

He not unfrequently uses these weapons against his own subjects when they displease him. A few months ago he was informed that a young man of his tribe had been presenting snuff to one of his wives. He summoned the lady, accused her of accepting this pinch of snuff, and added that unless she instantly gave up the name of the man he would put her to death. His body-guard stood with loaded rifles, ready to put the sentence in execution. Thus frightened, she gave up the name of the man who had paid her this trifling attention.

Umthonthlo summoned him to his presence, and demanded his reason for presenting snuff to his wife. The excuse not being satisfactory, he called for a Winchester, and, aiming at the chest of the young man, shot him. His sister upbraiding him for his rashness, he gave this remarkable answer, "Do not blame me, but rather the man that told me of it; he is the person in fault." This circumstance happened about the time he accepted our protectorate. He was therefore informed that he was now the Queen's subject, and that on the repetition of such an act he would not only lose his chieftainship but be tried for his life, which not a little astonished him.

These chiefs have an extraordinary idea of their power and dignity. Umthonthlo once requested Mr. Davis to make him a present of 20 pair of oxen and 100 blankets, as he said that his sister, the wife of Umgikela, was returning home from a visit she had paid him, and he was desirous that she should depart with fitting honour. He did not think he should be in a position to return these things, but he was willing to confer upon the missionary the honour of receiving them.

Umthonthlo is a sharp fellow. A trader thought to deceive him in some guns, and, showing him two, asked him his opinion on them. "Oh," said he, "this one is a Friday gun, that one is a Monday one." When asked to explain, he said, "Do I not know that all your artisans work well from Tuesday to Friday, and then all get drunk, and their Monday's work is worth nothing at all? Never show me a Monday gun again."

Nothing is more tiresome than talking to these native chiefs. They are utterly ignorant of any subject except cattle and extension of territory, which monopolises their whole conversation. Moreover, they think it dignified to remain silent for hours, which occasions some difficulty at a meeting. Some well-mounted and well-armed men attended Umthonthlo. They were dressed in soldiers' coats of different colours. Each carried on his head a monkey-skin cap, which increased the ferocity of their appearance. He was at this time in disgrace, on account of his having recently executed, without trial, a young woman who had been accused of witchcraft. She stated that another female had bewitched her, and that a spirit had appeared to her in the shape of an eagle, entering into her body, and transforming itself into a child.

A medicine doctor was sent for, who soon "smelt out" the whole affair, and recommended that the woman should be put to death, which was instantly carried into effect. These extraordinary delusions are fully equalled in India. At Cashmere, in the Himalaya Mountains, the soul of the Maharaja Runjeet Singh was firmly believed by his son to have entered into a fish, and, while I was there, it was death to any native of Cashmere to catch a single fish.

On one occasion Lord Canning told me that a bitter complaint had been made in consequence of some officers who had been fishing, whereby the soul of the Maharaja's father ran a good chance of being caught and eaten by an unbeliever.

We rode forward with Umthonthlo and some of his principal chiefs. One, an intelligent-looking man, carried the emblem of authority, the tiger's tail; this man was named "Many things." He carried this badge of distinction until we reached the confines of the country.

We now reached the country of the Amabacas. As there was a dispute regarding this portion of the country, it was deemed more prudent that Umthonthlo should return, especially as we knew that Makaula, the chief of the Bacas, was waiting on the other side of the hill to receive me. Although a fight between these two might have been interesting and instructive, I had no desire to be the cause of it.

We met Makaula on the mountains on the 3rd of September. He is a stout silent man, well dressed in dark blue. His escort was well armed and on good horses, and his cavalcade was the best turned out that we had yet seen in Kafir land.

Salutes in my honour were continually fired by the men we met. An immense train of mounted men joined the procession into Tshungwana.

Here a stately ox was presented in due form, and we were kindly received in the mission house. Immediately outside were some hundreds of natives in their war dress. I remained a short time to see them perform their dance by torchlight. Alternately advancing and retiring, brandishing their assegais and fighting in attack and defence with a supposed enemy, they produced a very imposing effect, especially as it was dark, and the torches flashed across their dark faces. The groans, stamps and howls of the warriors were quite enough to terrify any one. These men were dressed in feathers, with the tails of wild animals round their bodies, both behind and before; with amulets made of massive rings from the tusks of the elephant, and many a charm (or fetish) strung round them, together with garters and anklets of innumerable brass rings. Each had an oval shield and bundle of assegais. The assegai in the hands of the Kafir is what the hunting knife is to the Shekaai; there is no use to which it is not adapted, both as an offensive and defensive weapon, and in everyday use.

No Kaffir stirs abroad without a small bundle of these lances. With the assegai he eats, he fights, and does many useful things, and it is used as a surgical instrument. Carefully sharpening it, he uses it to bleed the human patient, and with it he inoculates his cow's tail. In the chase it is his spear, a deadly weapon in his hand, and a ready instrument for skinning his game.

We passed some good kraals of the Bacas, on our way to the Umsimbues river. The wicker-work roof is made of wattles, which are light and straight, and are bent over at regular distances. The kraals are well plastered and neatly thatched. The door is made rather small, the flooring hard and smooth, and at the upper end there is a raised ledge running right across, which serves as a cupboard where all utensils are placed. The firewood is neatly packed inside, between two grass copes which are fastened against the wall. The furniture is scant, but of native manufacture. Large clay pots, holding fifteen or twenty gallons of beer, stand inside.

It is singular enough that there are no regular cemeteries attached to any of the villages in this country. In no other nation that I have met with have I observed this want. The chiefs are buried within their own cattle kraal, as being the place of highest honour. Other persons are simply carried to the Veldt, and interred in the most convenient spot. Frequently the people do not take the trouble to wait until the man is dead, but when they see any one sick or old he is requested to walk into the bush. Here a hole is prepared sufficiently deep to receive a man in a sitting posture, and he is made to walk into it with his favourite walking-stick, but never with his money or anything that is valuable, after which the hole is filled up over him. He is thus spared future suffering, and his friends no longer have to attend to his wants.

Some of the stores which were offered to the Kafirs in this country were very poor. For blankets which could be purchased for 2s. in England—made of the flimsiest shoddy—10s. and 12s. were demanded. The paper blankets which have been lately invented will no doubt find a market here.

CHAPTER XVI.

JOJO—GRIQUALAND EAST.

We now reached the country of the Amatibi.

On nearing the Ingolo river, the chief Jojo met us, riding with many warriors, driving before them a very fine ox in capital condition, which he begged leave to present with the usual formalities. The natives who drove this beast into our presence were tall and well-formed, and the symmetry of their swarthy limbs was openly displayed. Their heads were singularly dressed, the natural woolly hair being so arranged as to have the appearance of a stout woollen cap, which looked like a Turkish cap and tassel, as some of them had tied the centre lock with a scarlet tuft. I was much pleased at Jojo's presenting the ox, as he is by no means a wealthy chief. It was a great contrast to Gangaleswe's niggardliness. Cattle are the greatest treasure of the native, being regarded as even more precious than women.

I may give an anecdote to illustrate the consideration in which they hold cattle.

A German presented Panda, the father of Cetewayo, with a watch. "What is the use of it?" said he; "To tell where the sun is? We can see it; when cloudy we remain in our huts, at night we sleep. Does it give milk?" "No." "Does it give calves?" "No." "Then take your watch away."

Poor Jojo is in difficulties, his country has been constantly the scene of attacks from the chief Umquikela, who considers

Jojo a rebel. The courage of this lesser chief has enabled him so far to be able to ward off the blows, and he declares that nothing shall now make him submit. He claims rights of independence, but by *some* interpretations of our treaty these seem to be doubtful.

Jojo's account of his own life was very interesting. Driven when a child from his home by the inroads of the famous Chaka (the Attila of the Zulus), he was carried to the mountains by the Amabacas and brought up by them. After the death of Chaka, he returned to his country, which was claimed by Umquikela, and war for years has been the result. Jojo now supplicates to be placed under our protection; an honourable petition, and creditable to her Majesty's Government, as demonstrating how much our rule is appreciated.

I encamped that evening by the river. The whole nightlong the followers of Jojo were stuffing themselves with portions of the fat ox. Looking out of my tent, by the light of the moon I saw in all directions groups tearing and cutting off junks of meat, which they swallowed with a grunt and a choke most alarming to hear. In the morning little or nothing of the ox remained. All that I saw left was in the arms of an old man who was fondly caressing the four legs, one protruding from under each arm giving him the appearance of a quadruped rather than a biped. He had evidently employed the night in mumbling the shank bone and intended to feast upon the feet at his leisure.

The quantity of meat which a Kafir can devour is miraculous. Pound after pound vanishes before him, nor does he appear torpid or less active in consequence. It is by no means uncommon for a couple of men to finish a small sheep in twenty-four hours. They are not at all particular what part of the animal they eat. Pieces which we should consider revolting meet from them the most ready appreciation, and apparently every portion is as digestible as it is palatable. I was told that a bullock that had been left by a transport rider was bitten in the tongue by an adder, while grazing. The ox, feeling the stinging pain, ejected the snake from its mouth, and an hour afterwards it was dead. It was skinned by natives and the meat eaten by them. Strange to say, none of the Kafirs suffered any ill effects. They are possessed of stomachs of extraordinary capacity, and apparently invulnerable.

The Kafirs, although ready to eat enormous quantities of meat when they can procure it, are frequently compelled to suffer from famine. In this extremity they tie leather rims round their stomachs. They call this the girdle of famine, and they fill up the vacuum by drinking water.

On the 6th of September we ascended the Ingali heights, obtaining two span of oxen to help up our mules on to the plateau. On our way up we saw a few roebuck, the only game which we had met with in the Transkei. One of our party breasted the tremendous mountain in the hopes of catching some. We watched his approach upon the deer, but when within a hundred yards of them, and while he was still hidden from their sight, something alarmed them, and they made off, having evidently "smelt the smell of an Englishman."

When we arrived at East Griqualand many Griqua farmers joined us and proffered their assistance. These men are half-castes between the Dutch and Kafirs. They were well mounted, and most of the horses were caparisoned with the shubragul, which, from a change of equipment, had been discarded by our cavalry. These were nearly new, and gave them a very dressy appearance.

Almost every cavalry regiment in our army was represented, Lancers, Carabineers, &c. Very few of the men spoke English, but one who did described many of their primitive customs, one of which is that their wives never sit down to table with their husbands, the former first serving the master, and then dining by themselves.

L 2

Passing over the ground which divides the lower country from the higher range, a fine view broke upon us in the foreground. Mount Currie stood well out of the plain with the lower ranges of the Drakensberg in the extreme background, while endless grassy slopes filled up the foreground of the picture.

The town of Kokstadt lay immediately below us, in a well-selected position; and although it did not show great signs of activity, its progress was sufficient to demonstrate that it would one day be a city. As we reached this, which is the capital of Griqualand East, Adam Kok, the Kaptain, met us, attended by a numerous escort. He received me most politely, regretting that through some error in the information he had received, we had arrived at least one day before he had expected us, otherwise a much more numerous body of his subjects would have been there to meet me. Finally, forming a procession, we crossed the Umzinthara river and entered his town.

In Kokstadt we were met by the head of the Scotch Mission Society, who invited us to his house, requesting us to be his guests during our stay. The Rev. Mr. Dower was a true type of a missionary; he can not only preach by precept, but by example; he gives both balance to the mind, and physic to the body. He inculcates industry, and at the same time practises it; and the comfortable dwelling in which he resides is an example of the result. He built, painted, glazed, and papered almost the whole house with his own hands. In my opinion a missionary who is able and willing to set such an example is worth a dozen of those who inculcate these practical things without energy or knowledge to put them into execution. A cheery room with a spotlessly clean bed was given me, looking into a garden, where crowds of avadavats chirped merrily among the flowers.

The cannon began to boom its salute while we were enjoying a hasty meal.

Griqualand East, formerly called No-man's-land, was some years since a sort of neutral territory between the Zulus who inhabited Natal, the Pondos, the Pondomise, and the other tribes who lived in Kaffraria proper.

After Chaka, the great warrior who overcame Kaffraria, had been driven back, the country remained uninhabited; and indeed it was still in the state long after the Dutch had settled in Natal, and after we had assumed its government, taking it from the hands of the emigrant farmers.

At the time the Dutch Boers left the Cape Colony, when they emigrated into the Free State, these "Grikas," or "Bastards," held a large tract of country to the south-west of Bloemfontein, called Griqualand West. They were an industrious people, and far more advanced in civilisation than any other native tribe. They had large flocks of cattle and sheep and were wealthy, with good furniture and houses.

This excited the desire of the Boers to possess these good things and the result was constant vexation to the poor Griquas. Under these circumstances they determined to "trek" and relinquish their country, provided they could place themselves in a secure position in a new land. They mentioned their wishes to the Governor of the Cape Colony, and met from him a ready response in the offer of No-man's-land.

Adam Kok, who had been elected their chief, was invited to look at the country. He did so, and thinking that it would suit the purposes of his tribe, he determined to move them into it at once.

The exodus commenced. Many hundreds of families and waggons, cattle, sheep, and household goods, formed the procession, and they commenced their journey towards the Promised Land. Marching east, they first crossed the Caledon river; next the Orange river, at a drift now known as Kok's drift; thence passing through the country now called Wodehouse, they arrived at the lower range of the Drakensberg.

Here they crossed the mountains at what was subsequently named Kok's Pass, and, moving onwards, took up their "lager" at the southern foot of a fine mountain, called Mount Currie, in honour of Sir W. Currie, a very distinguished veteran, who commanded the Frontier Police.

Great dangers and difficulties were encountered in their progress; an immense lot of cattle died, but the exodus was finally accomplished. Two 12-pounder brass guns accompanied them, the very name of which proved a terror to the natives. But for them the Griquas might have encountered much greater difficulties and interruptions.

For years the Griquas seem to have had much trouble in holding their own in their new country. The Pondos attacked them from the south, the Amabacas from the south-west, the Basutos from the north; and the Government of Natal, being anxious to absorb a slice of their country south-east, were not over friendly to them. Nothing caused them more uneasiness than when a Lieutenant-Governor of Natal crossed Griqualand. without even presenting his compliments to its ruler. Had they not met with protection from the Governor of the Cape Colony they could scarcely have continued in existence. Still they hold their own, and within the last two years they have shared in the general prosperity of the colony caused by the Diamond Fields. Leaving their "lager" at the foot of Mount Currie, they are now taking up their abode at the new capital, Kokstadt.

Poor Adam Kok left his affairs in Griqualand West in the hands of an intelligent Englishman, whose intelligence was so energetic as completely to have exhausted all Adam's resources in that country, property to an immense amount having, it is said, been absorbed, and no explanation given.

No-man's-land, now called Griqualand East, possesses a fine climate, the land being well watered, both for sheep and cattle. It is singular, therefore, that the cows are so badly managed that no butter is to be obtained except that which is brought either from Natal or from home, and no milk except preserved milk in tins.

The upper portion of the country is excellent for wheat. It contains on its eastern borders fine forests of yellow wood, stink wood (the African mahogany), and other trees. On its south-eastern borders there is good land for "mealies" (Indian corn). The water-power in the rivers might be turned to account, as many are never dry, and from the peculiar position of the hills and gorges, they could readily be dammed up to serve as reservoirs. Nothing of this has yet been attended to. A large number of horses are bred, small, but strong, hardy animals. The configuration of the country is such that it is easily defensible on all sides.

In the afternoon we attended the native service, carried on in the Dutch language. It was impossible for me to follow it; in fact, the discovery that the sermon related to the Prodigal Son formed the limit of my knowledge of what was going on. The congregation appeared attentive, and the clergyman in earnest.

The following morning we called upon the Kaptain (as Adam Kok is called). He showed us his brass field-pieces, of which he was justly very proud. They had been made in England, and were ornamented with a cock rampant (in allusion to his name), and mounted on high carriages. These two guns were delivered to him, with a certain amount of ammunition, for 3000l. The Kaptain was entitled to set some value upon what had been so costly a bargain to him.

Many new public buildings, churches, schools, and houses, are in course of erection.

Sanitary arrangements are little understood or appreciated, and nothing can induce the people to adopt a drainage system in their houses. Their fathers had none, and why should they? Many new stores have been put up. They are of large dimensions, and are built of wood, covered with corrugated iron roofs. The profit from these speculations is considerable.

No doubt the charges for English goods are high. To obtain a pair of boots they say that it is requisite to sacrifice a sheep for each foot.

A large number of guns and Enfield rifles are in the market, which sell among the Pondos at the rate of a bullock per barrel.

It is customary for all farmers who can afford it to erect a shed in the town to contain their waggons and families when they come in for the purpose of attending divine service and making their purchases, as they remain on each occasion for several days.

The financial budget of this little State is said not to exceed that of a moderate fortune. The entire revenue from taxation is estimated at 500*l*. per annum, with an annual expenditure amounting to about the same sum.

There is, however, no public audit of accounts, all this being arranged between the "Kap" and his Secretary. This state of matters appears to have created great uneasiness, which, if continued, may cause serious difficulties in the Liliputian kingdom.

We were presented with some postage stamps, which would be rare in any collection.

No one could be kinder in his small way than the old Kaptain. Though the ruler of his own people, with powers of taxation and of life and death, which he has enjoyed for many years, he is certainly a humble and modest potentate.

The cares of state weigh heavily upon Adam Kok, although he insists on the performance of them, and the junior members of his family are said to cause him annoyance from their irregularities. If allowed to exercise his own judgment, I have no doubt he would prefer to retire upon a salary paid with British regularity rather than live this uncertain and precarious life, surrounded by the troubles which have pursued him in his chequered career from boyhood.

Not very long after my visit, it was decided that this was the time to re-annex the country and a Commission was appointed to take it over. Adam Kok could not relinquish it without some show of dissatisfaction. Nevertheless, on the day appointed he paraded 500 mounted men and 200 armed footgangers; after which there was a meeting of the people on the Market Square in Kokstad, where opinions were expressed on the acts of the Government, and the people's forebodings of the future expressed. Kaptain Adam Kok, who was the first speaker, after thanking the Commission for their attendance, and recapitulating briefly the circumstances of the Griqua trek, and also of his meeting with Mr. Orpen in June 1874, and in October with Sir Henry Barkly, complained of the hasty and arbitrary manner in which Government were assuming authority in his country. He denied that he had ever called them in to take authority, saying that from June, when he asked Mr. Orpen to define his position, until Sir Henry Barkly came and annexed the land, no word from Government had ever reached him. Government could not take exception to his people having formed an idea they were independent by the way in which they had been left to their own resources. They, the Griquas, on leaving Philippopolis, knew that they were going to a British country, and expected, as stated in Sir George Grey's condition, that they would have a Resident, who, if he had been with them, would have been of great assistance in checking plundering by Basutos, and in settling boundary questions with their neighbours. They had, on the contrary, not had the slightest assistance in advice or money from the British Government. They had their own cannon, fire-arms, and ammunition, bought with their own money; and after being left for thirteen years entirely to their own resources, without any preliminary notice the Government stepped coolly in and took possession of them and their property. This property Adam Kok considered ought to be paid for.

When the Government laid out the Kat River Settlement of Hottentots, they gave the settlers seed-corn, ploughs, and various other things to help them. But what had they done for his people? They came to this land naked. His people, and he, and his father, and his grandfather, had always been faithful allies to the British, and he considered he ought to be looked upon now as an ally rather than a subject, and not taken over without ceremony, as he had been. He had been left to govern his people with their own assistance only, the whole of his life; perhaps, in other people's opinion, in a stupid manner; but it had always been his aim to do justice to all, white, brown, or black; and in this he had worked to the utmost of his judgment. His acts, therefore, during the period until October 16th, 1874, must be looked upon as legal and confirmed by the British Government. If they persisted in annexing him and his people, he insisted upon the fulfilment of the condition to the letter as given by Mr. Brownlee to his messengers, and he would then be satisfied, otherwise not. At the same time, he would suggest that his people, not being so far advanced in civilisation as the colony, should now be governed in accordance with their own customs and habits until further advanced. He hoped he had said nothing to affront the Commission, whom he personally respected; but the Government must understand that his mind was fully made up on the question of subverting his past acts of government.

Adam Kok was pensioned off with 1000*l.* a year. He has since been killed in a carriage accident.

I much regretted that before leaving Adam Kok's country I could not visit the range of the Drakensberg, particularly the pass by which he had entered, so as to have made myself acquainted with the Basuto chiefs now settled there, especially with Nehemiah.

At the revolt of Langalebalele he was taunted with not assisting him, but he answered, "if you had lived for years the life of a dog, pursued at every turn by English bloodhounds, and finally run into, you would not recommend me to place myself in such an unhappy position for the sport of such a wretch as Langalebalele." A superior Basuto chief reproached Nehemiah with being thin, upon which he replied, "I have worried Major Bele, the magistrate; now do you go and do the same, and see if he does not make you grow thin also."

At Stafford I was met by the hospitable owner of the location, who invited me to an excellent dinner, and put us up very comfortably. Round this store were numerous Kafirs, occasionally entering to make purchases. I was particularly struck with one fellow who had just received his month's wages, amounting to 8s. or 10s., and who was scraping out the remains of a 4s. 6d. pot of jam which he had purchased that morning, with his dirty fingers, and sucking them. This was the happy result of more than fourteen days' labour.

We were here shown some excellent sugar and coffee, grown by natives; so that with a good government these men are capable of improvement, but under such rulers as the chiefs, and with such a system as witchcraft, it is impossible for them to thrive.

We were very kindly received at Mr. Button's Church of England Mission Station. The property had lately been purchased by the society. It consists of 4000 acres of land, a large amount of which is well watered and productive. There is a tolerable dwelling-house upon it, with a well-stocked garden, full of peach and other trees. For the whole of this property they had paid 250*l.*, which I think no one can consider excessive. Mr. Button was taking energetic steps to improve the property, well knowing that in doing so, he was doing much for the poor barbarous people surrounding it. He appeared a sensible man, appealing to the people by precept and example, and endeavouring to civilise them rather by useful acts than by thrusting "learning" down their throats. Here I was introduced to Mr. Hully, an old gentleman not far from 78 years of age, who had been present immediately after the great massacre which Dingaan (the Zulu King, Cetewayo's uncle) perpetrated on the Natal settlers. He was friendly with Dingaan, who said, "Well, Hully, I have destroyed the Dutch, what do you think of it?" Hully answered, "You have finished the beginning, but what of the end?" Dingaan lost Natal, and was murdered by his brother (Panda, Cetewayo's father).

Most of the natives in this part of the country are originally from Zulu land, they are said to be more industrious than the Pondos or Pondomisi. They are obtaining a considerable quantity of arms, some of which they retain, bartering others. They now begin to understand the relative value of a good and bad article; formerly they accepted any gun offered to them, but lately they are more difficult to please.

CHAPTER XVII.

PIETERMARITZBERG.

I now entered the colony of Natal, having passed through these native states with less difficulty and fewer adventures than in many countries in which I have travelled in Europe. The predictions of those in Cape Town who looked upon my expedition as foolhardy were happily not verified. I fully believe that this country is less advanced than any south of the Zambesi river, and even the natives opposite the coast of Zanzibar, I am given to understand, are more civilised than those in the Transkei, with the exception of the Fingoes.

In the afternoon of the 10th of September we were descending the slopes of the Umcomas river. The vegetation on its rugged banks resembled that of the Fish river bush, and would present very serious difficulties to an invading army. The banks of the Umcomas are said to be more infested with deadly snakes than any other part of Natal. It is here that the poisonous mamba assumes great proportions and most vicious propensities. There are probably few countries in the world which possess a more dangerous reptile. Near the Incopo river we passed over Puff-adder hill, and near Umcomas Satan's mountains, both noted haunts of these dangerous creatures.

On the following morning we reached the pretty town of Richmond, the first spot surrounded with European civilisation we had met with since leaving King William's Town.

It possesses a handsome Ladies' College in a tolerable state of prosperity, though much anxiety was felt during last year's rebellion in the mountain, as it was reported (though probably without truth) that the Kafirs in the neighbouring kraals had made their selection of future wives amongst its young and handsome inmates, after the bright days of their successful rebellion should shine propitiously on them.

The pretty hedgerows and well-divided fields had a most pleasing appearance, and Mr. Lloyd's beautiful gardens and orange-trees profuse in bearing were very refreshing to the eye after the arid plains we had left.

Pietermaritzberg is the capital of Natal. It is a nice-looking town, well situated on the river. Its name is a conjunction of those of its two founders, Peter and Maritz. The streets are wide, a fair amount of trade goes on, and there are large sales of forage in the market-square, where the House of Assembly and other public buildings are situated. The morning after our arrival I took the opportunity of attending the Cathedral Church of Bishop Colenso. I much regretted not being able to meet the Bishop. He was absent, in England, endeavouring to persuade the British people that Langalebalele and his tribe are not perfidious natives, but mild, inoffensive, hard-working, laborious, and much-injured individuals. The sermon I heard was very interesting, but mainly directed to induce persons not to believe implicitly all that was handed down in the Old Testament, but to take a liberal view, and consider these histories in a typical sense.

No one in South Africa has worked more energetically than Bishop Colenso for the benefit of the black race, but it seems doubtful how far he has met with success. He has often suffered disappointment. In one instance, a young man whom the Bishop induced to put away his wives, and adopt European habits of industry, became converted, and displayed considerable ability in printing and other arts. Some time elapsed, and one day the young man came and said farewell. The Bishop was much vexed that he should leave him; but on inquiring his reasons he received this reply, "You have separated me from my wives; the one wife you left to me has dishonoured me, and I leave you for the bush and the blanket."

It struck me as singular that there was not one old or even oldish man in the church, not one with a grey hair in his head except myself.

I attended some of the debates in the House of Representatives, which were exceedingly well conducted, the members possessing considerable power of speaking.

A review was held in which the volunteers, both cavalry and infantry, joined; one cavalry corps was composed of young cadets, about eighteen years of age; they rode extremely well, doing the greatest credit to the colonists of Natal, who are noted for their skill in horsemanship. Towards the termination of the review the heavens showed that a severe thunderstorm was brewing. On the same spot some years ago three soldiers of the 20th Regiment were struck dead on parade, their bayonets having been imprudently kept fixed during a storm, by order of the commanding officer.

Fearful accidents continually happen from lightning in South Africa. In the Orange Free State, at certain seasons, every post will bring tidings of fresh disaster. On one occasion, when I was at Bloemfontein, it was reported that on the Modder river, but a few miles distant, four Kafir lads had been struck dead with their dog. At Harry Smith, about the same time, three gentlemen were playing billiards, when two were struck, one killed dead on the spot, and the room destroyed. Lightning conductors are now extensively used. There is nothing of which natives are more afraid than lightning. To avert it they place a pink feather of the flamingo above their huts, which they rely upon as a sure specific against the danger. A chief would be willing to give ten oxen for a flamingo rather than be without it. I was amused at the story of a blacksmith who, being desirous of saving his property during the war, had put up a hammer in front of his house, taking care that all the Kafirs in the neighbourhood should be informed that this was his lightning conductor, and that any one who touched it would certainly be struck dead. The manœuvre was declared to have been quite successful.

Durban is a large and flourishing town, and commands a considerable commerce. It is the only port of the colony of Natal, and through it much of the inland trade is carried to Pondo land, Griqualand, Basuto land, the Free States, Griqualand West, the Transvaal, and even to the Zambesi, while the wild tribes of Zulu land are almost wholly dependent on it for their European supplies.

The town of Durban is built upon a belt of sand which to all appearance has risen on the banks of the estuary itself. The port of Durban, although so much depends upon it, is by no means satisfactory, as large sand-banks are forming not merely in the basin, but in the throat of the harbour, while the bar at its mouth is shifting.

To mitigate, with some hope of eradicating, these difficulties, various schemes have been adopted, but none steadily pursued. A comparatively inexpensive plan was first tried, but when success was attending its execution, it was superseded by one which was quite gigantic, but which broke down in its turn from a collapse in the funds of the contractor. Should the views of Sir J. Coode be carried out, a perfect success may be looked for. In consequence of the position of Durban, which lies in a low swampy spot, it might be inferred that it would be unhealthy, but the contrary must be the case, for the troops enjoy excellent health. Wounds heal rapidly, and it is reported that when the 20th Regiment were besieged by the Boers on the first occupation of Natal, that the wounded, although deprived of almost every comfort, and having undergone the most frightful privations, recovered in a marvellous way. Bronchitis is almost unknown, and this renders Natal a very favourite resort for many of our countrymen at home who are afflicted with this painful complaint. There is, however, one serious evil, the impurity of the water. The Umgani river is said to contain a small and dangerous animal, not well known as yet to medical science, which secretes itself in the neck of the bladder, causing a very serious disease.

The accounts of the siege, above referred to, are very interesting. Captain Smythe of the 20th appears to have been a very brave man, but somewhat imprudent. Not contented with beating off the enemy from his entrenched position, he made a night attack upon them, when, either through a mistake in his approach or by the treachery of his guides, he was forced back by superior numbers, his men got entangled in the mangrove swamps, and almost the whole of the attacking party fell. A Mr. King then volunteered to ride with the news of the disaster to King William's Town, a distance of 458 miles, a wonderful feat, which he accomplished through this wild country in nine days.

Whilst at Durban an amusing story was told me regarding the native police. A Kafir bought 3*d.* worth of bananas, for selling which on a Sunday a coolie was fined 5*l.* The nine o'clock bell referred to is a sort of curfew, after which natives are not allowed to be about without permission.

Before the magistrate the Kafir made the following deposition:—

I am the Kafir who bought the bananas for a "*pen*" (a penny) My name is Ji-Ji. My mistress at the Umhlali taught me to write, but she could not teach me to be a Christian, because I too much stupid. One day I came to town to work for money to pay the hut tax. I wanted money very

M

much because Mr. —— not give me any more skredit. When I got into town the sun was quite dead on Saturday, and I was very hungry.

I went to see my brother; my brother's name is Kitchen, he works for the white man that kills the ships, and builds houses with them. My brother say, "White man not like you sleep here; not like you eat scoff."

By-and-by white man came on and kick me three times, hard, and I ran out into street and heard the 9 o'clock bell cry. Then I ran very quick and got into a railway carriage to go to sleep. By-and-by four white men come and say they sleep in that carriage, and kick me out. Me very sore and my heart tell me to die. So I lay on the ground. Then coolie came out of another carriage with a light, and said: "You give me 6d. and you sleep in my carriage; you no give me 6d., you go to jail." I gave two pens, I go in, I go to sleep. I wake, I look, it is light; coolie gone, money gone, I there alone, I berry much afraid, I go out. By-and-by bells cry much and people go to church. I sit near white church and see the people go in. They sing loud and I go into town. I go to house of Fundisi with long coat. Boy in kitchen tell me Fundisi soon come on and give me scoff. Fundisi come on with long coat and black book, Fundisi say mealie meal twenty shillings a muid, then he kick me twenty times and shaia me with black book on head; then I ran away very sore. Good boy lend me one pen. I walk in street three streets. I see shop with bread, I go in and say, "Bread for pen"; white man say, "This is Sabbath," and kick me out. I go on. I see Coolie Store; I buy bananas for pen. White policeman come on. Kafir policeman come on. He hit me on head with knobkerrie and take bananas. He eat five, white policeman eat ten. I run away. I see Tom who works for Frenchman. We go to his kitchen; I eat scoff. Frenchman come on and say, "You black thief, I catch you now." He give me to policeman. I sleep in tronk. Next day magistrate tell me, "You break bye-law; you go jail one month." I go jail; I come out. Durban no good, no good at all.

(Signed)   Jɪ-Jɪ.

CHAPTER XVIII.

THE TUGELA.

As there was no steamer starting for some days, I made arrangements with Captain Elton to visit the eastern portion of the seaboard towards the Tugela river, to see the sugar and coffee plantations in that district.

Captain Elton very kindly provided for our use a carriage with four smart horses. We first crossed the Umgani river, now nearly dry; but from the debris of a fine iron bridge which had been broken to pieces and still encumbered the banks of the stream, it could be seen that the river sometimes became a raging torrent, overflowing its banks and carrying all before it. Here we saw a steam-power ice-making machine, which the owner said would pay very well, provided he could obtain intelligent labour at moderate prices. Native labour, however, was not intelligent, and European was costly and the men drunken in their habits, so that he thought he must close the business.

On crossing the Umgani, we were shown a spot on the river-bank from which a sea-cow nightly emerged to eat the sugar-cane. This animal is, however, so cunning, and has such wonderful scent, that they could not kill it. There are also crocodiles in the Umgani, though they do not seem to attain any great size.

We started for Verulam beyond the river. The road winds through an undergrowth of luxuriant shrubs, occasionally giving beautiful peeps of the sea beyond.

We met parties of Kafirs working, either going to or coming

from the plantations. Almost all of them, of both sexes, were without any clothing; some of the women's only adornment being armlets and waistbelt. I mentioned this to a gentleman of high position, well acquainted with the natives, and he told me an anecdote which was interesting. On one occasion he was talking to a Kafir chief, and asked him why his young daughter was not clothed: "Master," he replied, "she is clothed in the garb of innocence, she does not know that she is naked. Would that all in the world were like her!"

We continually passed large sugar and coffee plantations, and in one instance a small tea plantation. The plants were thriving, and promised to be a great success. As a rule the coffee plantations in Natal have not proved very successful. The introduction of the Liberian coffee-plant has been recommended, as the species appears to live well at a low level. The Arabian coffee-plant is said to thrive best at a level of from 4000 to 6000 feet above the sea. The tobacco-plant also grows in Natal with great luxuriance.

Verulam appeared a flourishing settlement, the houses and stores being built principally of wood brought from Sweden and Norway; everything, in fact, but meat, coffee and sugar being a foreign production.

Upon this subject a great political discussion had lately been going on in the Cape Colony, in consequence of Mr. Froude's speech at Bloemfontein and the Diamond Fields, as to their not being self-supporting. Why did they bring planks from the Baltic when they had a forest like the Nysna; butter from Holland, when pasture land abounded at the Cape; fish from Newfoundland and Scotland, when plenty was to be had on their coasts? The answer is, that labour is so high here, that those articles are dearer when made on the spot than if brought from thousands of miles distant. Coals from Newcastle in England are infinitely cheaper at Pietermaritzberg than if brought from the Newcastle in Natal.

The labourer is employed in producing raw articles of commerce, such as wool, skins, iron ore, diamonds, gold, &c., which pay very much better.

The sugar-cane bears well, and is reckoned to produce a good yearly profit, even where money is borrowed at 8 or 10 per cent. Frequently, however, 12 or 15 per cent. have to be paid, when it is scarcely possible that a sugar estate can be profitable.

Apparently there were were about as many Kafirs working on these properties as there were coolies from the East Indies. The labour of the latter is more certain, because they never leave the estates, whereas Kafirs go and come at their own pleasure. The great risk in sugar planting is the uncertainty of labour.

The best method of ensuring a supply of Kafir labour is to obtain possession of an estate in the interior, and to bring labourers down to it in relays. This plan has been found to answer well, the privilege of squatting on the grazing farm being accorded on the condition of work with payment on the sugar estate.

On the sugar plantations on the coast the best of cotton could no doubt be grown. A table-cloth made of Cape cotton which was shown in the Philadelphia Exhibition was so fine that the judges would not believe it was all cotton, and had a piece cut off to have it tested. But the price of labour is a very material consideration in cotton growing.

In the afternoon of the following day I inspected the mounted volunteers by invitation of the Government. The troop was not numerous, but the young men were strong, rough, and ready; they were well mounted, and rode with a firm seat.

On our return from this inspection we prolonged our ride brough some of the plantations. On descending a hill we were met by a witch doctress, who came dancing along the road. With the exception of bracelets, armlets, and anklets of brass, she was otherwise almost naked; she had long scarlet streamers in her hair, and a bunch of feathers suspended from her girdle.

Such women have great influence, and it is most dangerous for natives to thwart their wishes.

In Durban the planters from the estates who visited the club, of which I was kindly allowed to become a temporary member, were very attentive to me; but amongst themselves they are somewhat boisterous and noisy in their jokes. One night I heard a terrible uproar, which was explained to me in the morning, a gentleman having found a snake twelve feet long in his bed.

During my detention at Durban I was appealed to by a raw Kafir. It appeared that he had been sent by his master with a message; but the first shopman of whom he made inquiry as to the residence of the person for whom the letter was intended, being desirous of sending round some notices, thrust them into the man's hands. The Kafir started on his way, eagerly showing the notes and asking of every passer-by the whereabouts of their destination. While delivering them, more letters and advertisements were continually added, so that he was kept running all day, wondering, of course, at the extraordinary result of his first message, while his master was raging at the long absence of his servant.

The large numbers of skins of wild animals which lay in the storehouses at Durban ready for exportation, were surprising— those of the giraffe, zebra, buffalo, and buck being innumerable. A large portion of the two former had been sent from Zulu land by Mr. John Dunn, who has sent regular parties of hunters out for years for the purpose of killing wild game. This gentleman has lived many years in Zulu land.

Cetewayo appears to have great confidence in him. He is well known to many of the colonists in Natal, and also to European sportsmen, officers of her Majesty's Guards having accompanied him in former years in sporting expeditions in the interior. He now receives 300*l.* a year from the Natal Government, for acting as a kind of political agent to the Zulu King. It is said that through his instrumentality large numbers of guns have been introduced into Zulu land; but if the King insists upon arming his troops and has cattle to exchange, he needs no John Dunn to carry out his wishes.

Whole regiments of Zulus have been marched into the proximity of Lorenzo Marques—each man returning with two muskets, and it is said that Basutos are employed at the chief's kraal in making gunpowder.

We spent two very pleasant days at Port Elizabeth, and then embarked in the *Kafir*—a coasting steamer which was returning from Delagoa Bay.

The terrible rolling qualities of this vessel were proverbial, but the pleasant manners of the commander did all that was possible to make amends for them.

A curious circumstance had happened with regard to this ship on her way up the coast. She was carrying a number of Zulu Kafirs who had been employed on the Western Railway works. Some of the sailors becoming mutinous, a passenger who spoke the Kafir language told the Zulus to give their assistance to the captain, as the sailors were going to throw him overboard, and if this happened everybody must perish, as he was the only person who knew the paths on the sea.

The Zulus were greatly alarmed at this information. They sprung below, seizing their assegais and surrounding the crew, who in their turn were terrified beyond measure, and immediately hastened to obey all their captain's commands.

This was my second long tour in South Africa. Since then many chiefs I have described have undergone numerous vicissitudes of fortune.

In November 1875 Gangaleswe was placed under a British resident magistrate. Makaula, the chief of the Amabacas, persuaded our Government to take his country under our rule.

Umthonthlo was warned against too liberal a use of his Winchester rifles; and Umquikala, Damas, Moni, and Kreli were severally told that we would not permit the pastime of war to be carried on in or near the countries which we protected. Kreli is now a fugitive with a price on his head. He is believed to have gone into Zulu land.

Poor Jojo was for some time longer left to his fate as dependent upon Umquikala the Pondo.

This tour had opened my eyes to many facts, not the least serious being the dangerous extent to which the natives are becoming armed, not only with old smooth-bore guns, but with excellent modern rifles.

For what purpose, then, is this insatiable craving for arms? It is to possess the all-powerful weapon with which the white men conquered and brought them into subjection, but which they hope to employ in their turn against their conquerors. Then, of course, the British soldier will be implored to come to the assistance of the colony, generous Old England will be asked once more to pay the bill, and the colonists will be ready to send waggons, and teams of oxen, with supplies at fabulous prices, and to undertake all the necessary contracts for the supply of the troops.

The following article from the 'Free States Newspaper' will demonstrate the state of public opinion there at the extent to which this traffic in arms is carried on:—

> Our British neighbours have established at the Diamond Fields free-trade in guns and ammunition, in spite of all treaties with the Republics, and even in spite of their own professed policy in the Cape Colony.
>
> Griqualand West permits the supply of guns and ammunition to the natives, Zulus and Basutos, without hindrance; and

whilst Earl Carnarvon requests all South Africa to meet in a friendly conference, because of the native question and Zulu difficulty, British traders supply her Majesty's enemies, and our enemies too, with guns and ammunition to any extent, in order that these enemies may be better prepared to fight us when the next struggle may commence. And, worst of all, British commerce, represented by colonial shopkeepers and merchants, who to fill their own pockets would not for a moment hesitate to bring ruin upon the colonial farmers and republican Boers, cry out that it is preposterous to stop the trade in guns, and, unmindful of the peculiar circumstances of the country, they talk grandiloquently of " free-trade principles," and so forth. Now, either all their anxiety about unity in order to withstand the natives is hypocrisy, or else the unlimited supply of arms and ammunition to our common enemy is a crime of the blackest dye.

On the 6th of October we arrived at Table Bay. I could now fully understand that there is no part of Africa so beautiful as the back of Table Mountain.

This is mostly owing to the oaks and other trees in stately avenues planted by the Dutch near their residences, which, backed by the grand old mountain, make up a picture that would compare with almost any in the world.

BOOK III.—THE DIAMOND FIELDS.

CHAPTER XIX.

GRIQUALAND WEST—THE DIAMOND FIELDS.

I HAVE told the tale of the emigration of the Griquas from Griqualand West into Griqualand East, whither they fled to enjoy greater tranquillity than they had found in the former country. Not long after they departed, diamonds were discovered. The story of the finding of diamonds, and of the difficulties which attended the owners of the Great Kimberley Mine, has been so often told that I shall not repeat it.

When gold or diamonds are found either in South Africa or any other wild country, there is a tendency for private rights of ownership to be invaded. There is a "rush" of lawless diggers to the spot, who begin with frantic eagerness to tear up the soil. A Committee is appointed to mark the place roughly into "claims," and any protest the owner may make is only respected so far as to give him some fixed share of the plunder. As for considering all the diamonds his own he would be a rash man who should dare to broach such a theory of property. It is a case in which a sort of "jus naturale," supported by revolvers and bowie knives, overrides all ordinary rights of ownership. So it was in this instance. The country had only very recently been placed under English rule, and in fact it was a sort of No-man's-land, with no settled Government.

Most of the occupiers of land, especially in those parts

where diamonds had been discovered, were Dutch farmers whose fathers had left the colony in disgust at the liberation of the slaves in the colony. Although a liberal sum for the enfranchisement was awarded them, yet in consequence of some mismanagement in regard to its payment, in which delays occurred, they thought they should never receive it, sold their claim for a comparative pittance, and trecked into the African Wilds, seeking and obtaining from the native chiefs and rulers beyond the Orange river, the freedom which they could not enjoy near Cape Town.

On the discovery of diamond deposits on their lands, these Dutch farmers, seeing an invasion of Englishmen, grew greatly alarmed, and were ready to sell at prices which seemed enormous, but proved in the sequel not to be a tenth of the value. The individuals and companies who bought, unable to treat the diamonds as their private property, contented themselves with a rent on each claim.

Unfortunately, the Government, instead of at once stepping in and purchasing the mines, allowed them to be sold to sharp men who foresaw their eventual worth. The Colesberg Koppie or New Rush was purchased for 6000*l*. from a Dutch farmer who had probably bought it for less than 100*l*.

In 1875 the Government became the purchasers at 100,000*l*. It had yielded a rent of about 30,000*l*. a year. As soon as the diamonds were discovered tents were suddenly erected, and digging commenced first on the river Vaal, at P. Neil, now called Barkly, at De Toits Pan, 25 miles to the east, and subsequently at the Colesberg Koppie or the New Rush, which last has proved the most successful.

For a time anarchy prevailed. But as there must be some law in every community, a Diggers' Committee was organised. The most heinous crime of all was theft, and thefts by natives were those of the blackest nature. Then followed a period of working, fighting, drinking, gambling, losing of fortunes and making them—in fact, all the phenomena of a rush for gold. Side by side the Cambridge honour prizeman and the smart cavalry officer, once the darling of drawing-rooms, worked with the Australian bushranger or the escaped felon. The motley crew that was assembled there to struggle for wealth could only be seen on such an occasion.

In the year 1875 the diggers had been at work at the Diamond Fields for nearly four years, during which time about three and a half millions' worth of diamonds had been extracted.

This sudden accession of wealth had been most opportune. Farmers were enabled to pay off their mortgages, merchants to prop up their failing houses, and lands to be enclosed and cultivated. I trust that the great impetus given to the colony may be more than transitory, but I cannot help fearing that a reaction similar to those seen in England may take place, and that bad times may succeed the good.

Disputes took place between the diggers and the Government. Commissioners were sent down to settle all these quarrels. In this they partially succeeded, and partially failed.

When the English law suited the diggers, they swore by England; but when the Dutch law suited them best, they declared that they would join the Free States.

The diggers were generally Englishmen of education or Dutch farmers, for a digger is not a man who digs out the stones, but one who superintends natives, and employs Hottentots, Kafirs, Zulus—any one he can find to dig for him.

Moreover, repeated disputes arose as to what the rights of the proprietors were, and cases constantly came before the Recorder, who was sent by the Government to act as Judge.

His difficulties must have been very great. According to the strictest law, the owners of the soil possessed absolute power to do what they pleased with it and to eject the diggers.

To have a pronounced decision in conformity with this would have produced a revolution. Moreover, blacks and whites were on an equality in the eyes of the law, but the whites firmly set their faces against purchase of claims by natives, and to have attempted to carry out this principle against the will of 5000 determined diggers, well armed and accustomed to deeds of violence, would have required a small army.

In the Free States, six miles distant, there was no such difficulty. There no native could hold land or other property. All blacks can be sent to the field cornet and receive a round dozen or so on vague charges and unsupported assertion, a justice which the diggers complained could not be meted out on British soil. Many wished that the British flag should be hauled down, for one with "Why should not every man whop his nigger?"

Moreover, niggers who were allowed to work for themselves at the poor or worthless mines used to work for masters at the richer ones, secreting diamonds there, carrying them off to the poorer mines and pretend to find them.

In the spring of 1875 the discontent of the diggers grew dangerous. They proposed either to join the Free State Republic, where every man could thrash his nigger as he liked, or to haul down the British flag and form a Republic on their own principles. They formed a Diggers' Association and held secret meetings.

It is said that in April these would-be rebels numbered from 600 to 700 men, all armed, and formed into companies, battalions, and squadrons of cavalry. They drilled openly under German and Irish Fenian officers.

They resisted the arrest of a man, who was sent to gaol for purchasing arms without a licence, and a scene occurred in front of the public offices, which, by mere accident, did not end in bloodshed.

The Lieutenant-Governor then thought it was high time to interfere. The uncertainty at Cape Town regarding the real state of affairs caused some delay in sending up the troops, but the Governor finally requested me to dispatch a force.

I directed that it should consist of 250 infantry, 40 mounted infantry and two Armstrong guns, with 25 Royal Artillerymen.

Having no cavalry at my command, and no horses, my first care was to supply the deficiency, by mounting 40 men of the 24th Regiment, and to purchase horses for them and for the two guns.

These measures caused some amusement at the time, as it was supposed by those who were ignorant of military affairs, that infantry soldiers could never be turned into cavalry.

My experience has always shown me that *picked* officers and men from foot regiments can in a very short time be turned into mounted riflemen of the very best desciption.

In the meantime very reliable information was received that the associates had procured two Armstrong guns, and that they had stated their intention of meeting the Imperial troops on the river Modder, and disputing the passage.

This was the exact state of things when I left Cape Town on May 25th. The Governor, placing the most serious responsibilities upon me, at the same time gave me the fullest latitude of action in confidential instructions. The distance we had to march was about 700 miles.

The most direct route from Cape Town is through the Karoo, a tract of country covered with very little else than stones, with scarcely any water, and no wood except the Karoo bushes. The accounts which I received from those who were considered the most intelligent men in Cape Town were appalling. It was said that I could not move troops through this district, that they would die by the road of starvation and want of water, and that the expedition would collapse.

I always found that there were two parties at the Cape, one who declared that there was no danger or difficulty in any undertaking whatever, and the other who magnified every molehill into a mountain.

It is true that a march of 700 miles through a wild country requires prudence, especially when economy has to be studied. Of course, anything can be done with money, the difficulty being to do it when your means are limited.

The usual and much the least costly mode of conveyance of the supplies of a force in South Africa is by bullock waggons. They proceed easily at the same rate as the men can march, but in the present case, two obstacles presented themselves to this mode of conveyance. No bullock could live in the Karoo for want of grass to eat and water to drink. It was requisite that the troops should move quickly, their presence being required immediately at the Diamond Fields, and twenty or thirty miles had frequently to be got over in the day, otherwise the troops would have had no water.

The difficulty was to obtain transport. As soon as it was known that we desired mule waggons, the prices rose to a most exorbitant height. Finally, however, we made arrangements for 10 mule waggons with 10 mules in each for the first party of 100 men, and 23 waggons with an equal proportion of mules for the second party of 230 men. Each waggon was hired at about 7*l*. 10*s*. per day, the mules to be fed by the owners. When the high rate of freight is considered, the bargain was by no means a bad one. Each waggon was calculated to carry 6000 lbs. weight besides forage.

For the conveyance of myself, staff, servants, and baggage, I hired a spring waggon with eight horses and a cart with four horses.

CHAPTER XX.

START FOR THE DIAMOND FIELDS.

On the morning of the 25th of May we arrived at Wellington, seventy miles distant, going ourselves that distance by rail.

The line of railway was progressing very satisfactorily, the colony being rich and the money readily forthcoming. The sale of spirits to the black man as well as to the white was sad to witness. Fights, in which the English navvies took an active part, continually occurred. The Dutch Boers could not understand who these strong men were, or from whence they came. They said they had heard of many countries, but to what country did the navvies belong? What a terrible nation they must be!

For conducting each of our waggons two men were required; one to hold the reins and work the break, the other to use the whip, by means of which alone the horses are guided. It exactly resembles a seventeen-foot salmon rod, and is used with all the practised dexterity of a first-rate fly-fisher; its pointed thong of hide being, by the skill of the driver, placed exactly on the selected tender spot of any of the eight horses of the team. To the waggon was attached a little boy, whom we called Flibberty Gibbet, who was curiously dressed. Beneath an old English tall pot he wore a coarse red night-cap, with a yellow border. His face was black, his coat dark red, he had short blue breeches and shining black legs, hardly distinguishable from black silk stockings.

At Wellington we found the waggon packed and waiting for

us, and placing our light baggage in it, we were soon upon our road to the interior.

The first part of the road immediately on leaving Wellington is up a very high mountain, by a gorge called Baine's Kloof. There a large body of convicts were employed for some years in cutting a passage through the rocks, and have accomplished a very satisfactory result. The railroad now in progress circles round the mountain through which this road is made, joining it in the valley beyond. When finished, this piece of work will probably be allowed to go to ruins.

This was the fate which was predicted by the landlord of the small inn at Darling, immediately below. He was considering what repairs he should execute on his house, so that it might last the exact time required, before the railway was finished so far, when, as he stated, he should "skedaddle."

Arrived at Darling, we outspanned horses for a short rest, and subsequently trotting merrily along, we reached Worcester, forty miles from Wellington, by 7 p.m.

During our journey shelter was not unfrequently refused. When it was granted, 1*l.* was generally demanded for the use of the mud floor of a cabin for the night, with a small amount of firewood.

At Constable we came to a sort of oasis in the desert Karoo. The landlord had let four waggons to the service, receiving 32*l.* per day for them with their thirty-two mules, but including their feed and the payment of the drivers.

The feelings with which some of the Dutch Boers regarded the expedition were singular enough. They pitied the soldiers, who they said were destined never to return, as they would all be killed by the Dutchmen of the Free State and the Transvaal. We endeavoured to explain to them that it was not our intention to go into the Free State, or near the Transvaal, but nothing could make them believe us. As far as truth is concerned, morality in South Africa is at the lowest ebb, and they naturally look upon any information they receive with the same suspicion as that which they give generally deserves.

With the passing troops was a staff-officer, with one of the new regulation spiked helmets; on observing which an old shepherd said he knew which of the soldiers would be most successful with the rebels—pointing out the officer with the helmet—"A pretty ramming he'll give 'em."

Wretched hovels now succeeded each other at every nightly halting-place; but we preferred to use them rather than have the trouble of pitching our tents, which always involved a delay in the morning.

At Blood River the house was kept by an Englishman, who entertained us well. As it was plentifully watered, his garden was well stocked with vegetables, and with oranges and other fruit.

This night we slept in the middle of the soft dusty road, the owner of the small farm at which we outspanned refusing shelter either to ourselves or our horses. We chose the middle of the road, because the stones had been well pounded into dust, and were much softer than at the sides, which were rocky, the only danger being that a waggon might run over us in the dark night. As it is very difficult to stop the bullocks on such occasions, this was not altogether an imaginary danger.

Beaufort is a nice clean town. It owes its advance principally to some neighbouring hills of excellent pasturage, and to a fine dam of water, about two miles across. The dam, however, had not long since broken down, owing, no doubt, to its faulty construction. A large number of convicts are now employed in its restoration.

The prosperity of Beaufort is evidently on the increase; and no doubt it does not suffer from the fact that its parliamentary representative is the Prime Minister of the colony, owning a magnificent farm, said to contain 60,000 or 70,000 acres, in its immediate neighbourhood, with more than 30,000 sheep on it.

There were some nice farmhouses occasionally by the roadside, the owners of which showed no friendly feelings, being persuaded, as usual, that the ultimate designs of our advance was an attack upon the Free State—or the Transvaal—inhabited principally by their fellow-Dutchmen.

They allowed us the use of their rooms and kitchen, and supplied us with a little bread and milk, and sometimes coffee, demanding from one to two sovereigns for this meagre entertainment. It must however be remembered that the rush of diamond-diggers through this country has naturally stopped indiscriminate hospitality to all comers.

At Kruidfontein we overtook a convoy of four Cape carts, going northwards on a venture. For these were demanded 70*l*. or 80*l*. each; they certainly could be purchased at home for 25*l*. They are two-wheeled, and carry four persons, and have a fixed hood.

By the roadside were numerous wild melons, like twenty-four pound shot. They were attached to the ground by a thread-like stem, scarcely discernible, especially where it had become withered by the drought. These melons, I believe, are unfit for food, even for animals, although their appearance is very tempting.

On the 3rd of June we reached Murraysburgh. It was here that the President of the Transvaal was born, and held a cure as minister of the Dutch church. This is a very pretty rising town, and apparently well supplied with water.

From this district all the wool and other produce goes to Port Elizabeth by way of Graaf-Reinet.

We passed Richmond, a wealthy district, with some of the finest farms and richest proprietors in this region; indeed, the Government taxation amounts to about 16,000*l*. per annum, while the local expenditure is not more than 1000*l*.

A DUTCH FARMER'S TOWN HOUSE.

We were now in the eleventh day of our journey, having travelled each day from dawn to dark. The distance covered was about four hundred miles, or that from London to Edinburgh. On a rough calculation this journey had taken just eleven times the time required, as well as eleven times the expense which it would have done by railroad.

Hanover has a grand appearance: the Dutch minister's house, standing in the centre, being quite a palace. It was built by the subscription of his parishioners. The honours which the Dutch lavish on the ministry are worthy of remark. In all the distant central towns in this colony it is the habit of the Dutch farmers to purchase a plot of ground, upon which they erect a small two-roomed house. Here they meet at festivals, and baptise and marry. In addition, they do a certain business in wool; while the good wives purchase stores for the following months' supply. When they leave the town they lock the doors, and the house remains empty until the next time it is required.

On the great high-roads to the Diamond Fields open house to all passers-by is not now the rule, nor could it be expected; but in other parts of the colony, particularly those more distant from the large towns and off the post-roads, open house is still kept for all. A hearty welcome is given at each meal, where the whole family sit down at one large table, the choicer wines and dishes being placed before the master of the house, above the salt.

Coffee is served in the morning, with little else until one o'clock, when there is a substantial dinner, and, late in the evening, supper. Coffee is served universally with each of these meals, and occasionally, in the better houses, some Cape sherry. The universal use of coffee throughout the colony is no doubt owing to the constant communication which was formerly held between it and Batavia, as no coffee is grown in the colony itself, and that which has been produced in Natal has not hitherto proved a success.

Before the family retire to rest the large Bible is opened, and the chapter appropriate to the day is read.

This Bible is frequently a very curious and ancient volume, containing the history of the family for some generations, with records of the marriages, births, and burials of all the members of the family from the period of their emigration from Holland.

The cocks at Hanover crowed so pertinaciously all night, that even my twelve days' travel did not make me proof against them. In the morning I found that the yew trees surrounding the house were converted into a roost. The cultivation of poultry appeared much in vogue here; each household adopting its own colour, which was painted on the back of the animal's head. At first I took these birds, particularly the ducks, to be some new description of fowl, until the matter was explained to me. I was much disappointed, for I thought I had recognised some new and extraordinary species, which, if imported, would have been considered a great rarity.

Philipstown is a very unattractive place. Ostrich-farming in the neighbourhood is reported to be most productive—one farm having this year sold nine young ostriches at 20*l.* each. The expense of rearing them could not have exceeded 100*l.* Artisans of all trades are doing well. The price of the necessaries of life, bread and meat, does not exceed that at home, groceries being somewhat dearer, lodgings at least twice as high, and clothes costing half as much again; but he must be a poor mason or carpenter who cannot earn his 12*s.* per day, if he will only keep from Cape brandy.

On the 6th of June we breakfasted at Gaspan, a very nice house and a fine farm. Mr. De Villiers now breeds sheep, finding it more profitable than horses.

It is singular enough that the name of De Villiers, which is associated, in England, with so many historical recollections, should be pronounced in the colony "Filgee." I never could obtain a satisfactory explanation. Another curious fact is that the Jewish Rabbi, whose name is Radowick is called by the Dutchmen Straubenzie.

Late in the evening we reached the tent at Aasvogle (the Vulture's Hill). This was the residence of a rich Dutch farmer, who refused us admission to his house and would not even sell us an egg. Having been made aware of his usual incivility, we had provided ourselves with all we wanted, and in a brief time our tent was pitched, and a comfortable fire and dinner prepared. We were thus independent of the lanky Dutchman, whose tenement I do not think even the powers of a George Robbins could convert into anything more magnificent than a tumble-down wreck, such as is scarcely seen even in the bogs of Galway.

Dressed in an old corduroy jacket, he watched us eagerly, lest we should run off with a mite of his property. Yet this man had 12,000 acres of land and at least 500 sheep!

Late in the evening the sounds of the evening hymn floated over the plain, the nasal twang of the patriarch being distinctly heard leading the choir, while female voices with their plaintive notes chimed in.

It is pleasant to hear in these lone lands such evidences of a religious sentiment pervading the community, and it is an assurance that the people are contented and happy.

June 7th.—As usual at this season the morning was beautiful. We outspanned at Karoo-bosh, a large pan almost destitute of water. The owner of the house had a number of beautiful skins of kooboo, hartebeeste, eland, &c., which he had shot some years ago in the neighbourhood.

In the afternoon Hopetown church was visible in the distance, and after a hard tug in the sand we reached the town at 4 P.M., and were tolerably well lodged at Smith's Hotel.

The advent of our little army caused no small stir in the place. Certain stores were still wanting to complete the equipments; the medical officers recommending an increase of warm clothing. Thus an additional impetus was given to trade, beyond the contracts of the commissariat. Everything but meat was at an enormously high price. I inquired the price of a plank of Swedish pine timber that lay outside a store, 20 feet long, by 12 inches wide and 3 inches thick. Its price was 6*l*. 10*s*. At this rate building must indeed be expensive. But it had come from Sweden, and been brought up by waggons, probably at 4*d*. or 5*d*. the pound weight.

For four-pound bundles of straw 2*s*. 6*d*. was demanded, other prices being in like proportion.

Hopetown cannot be said to be improving as fast as formerly. Standing as it did on the verge of the colony, it was the starting-point for all native traders to the interior, and the point to which they brought all the successes of their ventures inland, their ivory, ostrich feathers, gold dust, and a few stray diamonds, and more than one wealthy firm made immense profits thereby. Indeed, it is said it was no uncommon circumstance for traders to come loaded with 40,000*l*. worth of ostrich feathers and ivory, to dispose of their wares to the merchants of Hopetown.

We had now reached the Golconda of South Africa. Close to Cape Town we saw on the river bank a fine vein of crystals. Not a few miles from this the famous " Star of South Africa " had been found. This diamond was at first sold for 150*l*., and immediately afterwards for 1100*l*., but I am told that it has since not been considered so valuable.

Mr. Watermeyer of Cape Town told me that many years ago he had received some pebbles from the Vaal river, which were supposed to be crystals, and that he gave them away to a person going to England. Some time afterwards he received, anonymously, a very handsome diamond ring. He never knew from whence it came, but supposes it must have been in return for the stones, which probably turned out, many of them, to be diamonds.

MOUNTING THE INFANTRY.

As I have said, the bright days of Hopetown are now comparatively eclipsed, in consequence of the formation of Kimberley, which, although even now, no more than a canvas city, has naturally become the greatest centre of trade in the northern part of South Africa, as the traders, who formerly considered Hopetown as their base of operations, now rely upon Kimberley.

By the 14th of June the small force under the command of Colonel Glynn had assembled on the south side of the Orange river, at the Langford Ferry.

The occupation to which we now devoted ourselves was the purchase of horses for our two guns, and for the body of mounted infantry, which I had determined to organise.

With great exertion this was accomplished in eight days, and the column consisted of 2 Armstrong guns, 25 Royal Artillery, 15 horses, 40 mounted men, 24th Regiment, and 250 infantry, 24th Regiment.

Nothing could exceed the energy with which the officers seconded my endeavours to procure horses for the men that were to be mounted.

Lieutenant Carrington travelled 300 miles in little more than six days, and spent each night under his cart in the open Veldt. He was rewarded by getting some very good animals.

We then crossed the Orange river at Rustall's Ferry: a very good punt being kept by a successful man, said to be a Malay, who, not many years ago, came up as a servant. He now possesses a valuable store and thousands of sheep.

The care of the store was thrust upon him last year. Previous to that period he had let it to two Germans, who had a native boy in their employment. This youth roused their anger by his carelessness, or peculations, or some other cause. Charging him with some offence, the savage barbarians tied him and flogged him, on and off, for four hours, and not content with this, got a boat and dragged him through the river. The poor wretch, at his last gasp, lay on the colonial side of the drift, and calling upon the Deity, which he had hoped would have protected the black man, gave up the ghost.

The storekeepers fled, the tardy operations of justice, consequent on the absence of Federation between the provinces on either side of the river, enabled them to escape, and for want of an owner the store fell into Rustall's hands.

The post office and Customs arrangements were under the care of a fine old officer, late of the Cape Mounted Rifles. He had that morning passed through some waggons laden with the produce of the interior, elephants' tusks, karosses, worked skins, and ostrich feathers, the value of one load being estimated at 30,000*l.* The feathers of the wild bird are far finer than those of the tame.

In consequence of the Customs' duty arrangements an occasional examination of baggage is necessary on the frontier, for it sometimes happens that guns and gunpowder are introduced on fictitious invoices, and in packages of other goods. It was especially desirable now to put a restriction upon this contraband trade, in which I am afraid the merchants of the colony occasionally indulge. It was stated that at the auction at Cape Town of the wreck of the *Celt* fortunate purchasers of some cases marked "boots," discovered watches, jewelry, and pistols, concealed in the lots which they had bought.

I halted one whole day at Belmont, where I held an inspection of the troops, a sight which had never before been seen there.

Nothing could be kinder than the reception given to myself and my staff. In the evening Mr. Wheland attended me on the plains, when we saw many bucks. I had the good fortune to kill one springbuck, placing a ball right through his heart at 300 yards' distance.

We saw many diminutive Griquas acting as farm-servants,

and some Bosjesmans, or Bushmen, from the deserts of the Korana. These little people are now becoming tame on this side of South Africa. Formerly they were the terror of the Dutch settlers.

The Bushman is wonderfully clever at the destruction of all game. His favourite method of approaching ostriches is to clothe himself in the skin of one of these birds, in which, taking care of the wind, he stalks about the plain, cunningly imitating the gait and motions of the ostrich until within range, when, with a well-directed poisoned arrow from his tiny bow, he can generally secure it. These insignificant-looking arrows are about two feet six inches in length; they consist of a slender reed with a sharp bone-head, thoroughly poisoned with a composition of which the principal ingredients are obtained sometimes from a succulent herb, having thick leaves yielding a poisonous, milky juice, and sometimes from the jaws of snakes. The bow rarely exceeds three feet in length; its string is of twisted sinews. When a Bushman finds an ostrich's nest he ensconces himself in it, and there awaits the return of the old birds, by which means he generally secures the pair.

Some years since, when everything from South Africa was looked upon as strange, a knowing Yankee conceived the idea of bringing home a party of Kafirs to astonish the citizens of London. Very wisely, instead of going into the wilds to find them, he contented himself with procuring some Kafirs from within fifty miles of Cape Town, and having instructed them in native dances, and clothed them in the skins and the war paint of the Fingoes, he brought them to London. At that time a Kafir war was going on, and the tax-payers were reminded of South Africa by seeing a pretty considerable item introduced yearly into the estimates. These wild Kafirs, therefore, for a time became the rage. A Dutch farmer named De Beer was in England on the grand tour. Seeing a placard advertising these Kafirs, his curiosity was not unnaturally excited, and paying his shilling, he went into the hall in Leicester Square. For some time he remained a quiet spectator of the scene, until an evident excitement took place amongst the actors, and suddenly, much to his annoyance, two of the wild Kafirs rushed from the stage, and, clasping him round the neck, shouted out in Dutch, "Why here is old Papa De Beer." With difficulty releasing himself from their greasy embraces, he discovered that these warlike savages were no other than half-a-dozen of his own labourers, who had left his service some six months previously, for some purpose that he had vainly endeavoured to discover. Great, however, was the consternation amongst the audience, who imagined that the savages, out of some mad perversity, had determined to throttle one of the audience. Each spectator fearing that he might be the next victim of their deadly intentions, a great disturbance was the result.

We had now some bad weather, always an unwelcome accompaniment to a march, but we soon reached the junction on the Modder river.

Here, as has been said, the Associates had declared that they intended to dispute our passage, with 400 or 500 men, 40 or 50 cavalry, and two Armstrong guns. We found the river and the ford entirely unoccupied, and wading through the stream on a rocky bed, the whole force about knee deep, we soon passed over, and formed camp on the northern bank.

At a canvas-built canteen, on the southern bank, resided a tall Dutchman who had recently undergone imprisonment for robbing the mail-bags of a considerable number of diamonds of great value. It would appear that the bag got detached from the cart, and, falling into his hands, the temptation was beyond his power to resist. He opened it, and appropriated its contents, but was detected without much difficulty.

It is worthy of remark how seldom anything of this kind has occurred. A large number of diamonds leave by almost every mail. Yet during the first three years after the Kimberley mine was first opened, I believe I am not wrong in saying that only three instances of mail robbery occurred, and not one of them was accompanied by violence.

This is the more surprising when it is borne in mind how many needy, disappointed men frequented the diggings to improve their fortunes.

Three times a month a diamond bag is formed at Kimberley, and the weight of the package is about 28 lbs. Taking 5 lbs. as the weight of the wrappers, there is left 23 lbs. weight of actual diamonds sent by each of these mails; which, on a rough calculation (and it is utterly impossible to make other than a very rough one, as the diamonds vary so much in size and colour, and consequently in value), may be estimated as worth from 30,000*l*. to 40,000*l*.

This, together with the common letter bags, is placed on the mail cart with a driver, and no guard, and proceeds night and day, at about eight miles per hour, the entire distance (about seven hundred miles) to Cape Town.

It must be perfectly well known on the road what treasure this cart conveys, and yet it has never once been stopped and plundered. I very much doubt if a daily mail of such value were to travel seven miles, instead of 700, through the City of London, under similar circumstances, the treasure would be so successfully conveyed.

In 1876 the packets of diamonds sent in this manner amounted to a weight of 773 lbs., and in value to 1,414,590*l*., which may be calculated at about three-quarters of the value of the whole diamonds dug up in the mines during that year.

I said that the occasions on which a robbery had taken place were very few—indeed I believe only three. One was committed by a man who watched the postmaster leave his tent, and, looking through the window, saw a packet within reach of his arm. Breaking the glass, he appropriated it; so slight were the precautions taken for its security.

On the second occasion, the driver opened the packet, by which some of the stones were strewed along the road. These, being found, caused a diamond rush to the locality, which continued until the robbery became known.

In the third instance the mail dropped from the cart. The Kafirs, though they will often steal, have something of the dog's nature as regards their fidelity in guarding property given to them "on trust." As a proof of this, a gentleman at the mines told me that he had sent 10,000*l*. worth of diamonds by a Kafir to Hopetown on the Orange river, without fear of the result. Most robberies by natives, I believe, are instigated by three causes: the temptations placed in their way by lawless buyers, the desire of obtaining arms, and the obligation which is laid upon them by the chief, in whose power they have left their families, to bring something on their return. Considering that Secococni has had some 20,000 natives working at the mines, each of whom is bound to bring home a stone, he must have a great store of diamonds.

At the Junction some wild bustards were shot by some of the officers. These were magnificent birds, weighing thirty or forty pounds each, and excellent to eat. They were killed with a single ball from a Martini-Henry express rifle.

It was fortunate that I had taken the precaution of bringing a forge with the troops from Cape Town, for prices are startling in Griqualand. One pound was charged for shoeing a horse. It will be readily seen what straits young subalterns were put to on 5*s*. 3*d*. per diem.

We had a very cold Sunday at the Junction, but fine weather. Unfortunately one obstinate mule of our team led seven more back through the river. We hunted for two days on the north side, when news met us that the truants had taken a southern course, and it was not till two days afterwards that they were recovered at Honey Kloof. They rejoined us on the fifth day. The accident caused us some worry and inconvenience; but such things are too common in South Africa to cause any comment.

A section of country between the Modder river and Kimberley had become a subject of dispute with the Free State. They had detained some waggons, and a cause of complaint was thus established against the Republic, and 600*l.* damages claimed. Determining, therefore, not to raise a question as to my marching her Majesty's troops on Free State soil, I directed them to proceed on the following morning in the direction of Barkly, on the Vaal river. On the 20th I halted by a dam in Wolverdam, where the Lieutenant-Governor came out to meet us.

I had now some doubt which would be my best course to follow, whether to march upon Kimberley or to deviate towards Barkly on the Vaal river, there to encamp the men and wait the course of events.

By marching upon Kimberley, I feared lest the presence of the troops might irritate the disaffected, and induce them to commit some violent act upon the canvas city, such as burning it, and retiring into the Free State, only six miles distant. I was also somewhat afraid of desertions taking place among the troops.

On the other hand, if I avoided going into and through the city, my not doing so might be imputed to a fear of attack, an imputation which ought not to be allowed to rest upon her Majesty's troops.

Again, I thought that by taking the soldiers to see these extraordinary mines, they would be less tempted to desert than if rumours reached their ears of unbounded riches near at hand, which they were forbidden to see. With the English soldier confidence begets confidence, and I have never found it betrayed when it is given freely.

I therefore intimated to the Lieutenant-Governor my intention to march through Kimberley. This resolution gave him much satisfaction.

Some care was required not to allow the natives to loiter in camp, for while sitting down, apparently intent on idleness, they will purloin even the smallest article.

A gentleman near the Modder river told me that while he was once stopping to have something repaired in his cart, the blacksmith had thrown a bolt on the ground to cool. A Kafir, not thinking that it was nearly red hot, dexterously seized it between his toes in passing, intending to make off with it. It may be imagined how he screamed with pain when he discovered his mistake. The iron had become wedged so tight between his toes, that he could not release it with the aid of his fingers, and awful was the plight in which the thief rushed bellowing into a neighbouring pool of water.

On the 21st we started by call of bugle, marching off at 8.30 A.M. The weather was dreadfully cold, especially during the night; but the soldiers had become very hardy in their march through the Karoo.

A bivouac without tents each night had inured them to 30° or even 25° of cold. Those who were on picquet were sometimes sorely tried; but there were no complaints, and every man looked more healthy daily. A canteen was kept, where a regulated amount of wine and spirits was to be obtained—but no excess was permitted. To this regularity, with the cold weather and exercise, and a liberal ration of meat and bread, the extraordinary health the men enjoyed may be attributed.

On Tuesday, the 29th of June, the force camped in a small valley within two miles of Kimberley; but so sheltered was this spot by the rising ground, and so unexpected was the flank march, that the citizens were not aware of our whereabouts. Although buggies, carts, and omnibuses were at premium prices to meet or see the troops, some going south and some north, greatly to their disappointment the army was invisible.

On Wednesday morning, by 10 A.M., the force was paraded in the Park, and from thence, detaching the baggage to the Homestead, the cavalry, guns, and infantry moved into the heart of the city. Although there were many ugly faces, and some of the ringleaders were pointed out among the crowd, public opinion was now evidently on the side of order. Hospitality was freely bestowed on the soldiers and officers. The men marched in two successive parties to the edge of the Diamond Crater, where the extraordinary qualities of the wonderful abyss were explained to them by Mr. Hall. It was most satisfactory to witness the interest which was shown by the men at the sight.

As to ourselves, we were most sumptuously entertained by the Lieutenant-Governor, and in the evening a beautiful ball, given by the Masonic brotherhood, ended the day.

On the following morning, before 8 A.M., the ringleaders of the revolt were arrested.

They were permitted to go at large on heavy bail, and thus ended the Diamond Field revolt. There is no doubt that, if it had been allowed to proceed further, it would have assumed dangerous proportions. As it was, Sir Henry Barkly arrested the mischief at the right moment.

Substantial evidence was produced that it was the intention of the ringleaders to have deposed the Lieutenant-Governor of the Diamond Fields, to have seized the reins of government, and then to have offered the country to the Free States, and, in default of their acceptance, to have created a Republic—for themselves.

CHAPTER XXI.

THE KIMBERLEY DIAMOND MINE.

THE singular appearance of the great mine of Kimberley has been so often described that I will not dwell upon it. It is about the size of the New Square of Lincoln's Inn, and twice as deep as the houses there are high. The whole area from its sides to the bottom was interlaced with countless wire-ropes; buckets ascending and descending. At the edge were thousands of black natives, some attending to the buckets on their arrival, others employed at small windlasses in wheeling the blue clay to the surface. All seemed noise and confusion.

At the bottom of the mine was what appeared to be a ruined city of roofless houses. The claims had been measured into exact rectangular blocks, and the miners in digging had left their party-walls between their respective areas. The clay is stiff, and will stand many feet in height, so that this is the cause of the singular appearance.

Thousands of natives were working on the margin of the crater. These men at first sight appeared like a body of soldiers; in fact, they constituted a *part* of the British army. Every one of them was clothed, as far as his jacket went, with a cast-off tunic—the Royal Artillery, Hussars, Guardsmen, and Horse Artillery being all represented. What added to their curious appearance was their tight-fitting black pantaloons, which, however, on a nearer inspection were evidently those of nature. At the dinner hour, when they temporarily ceased work, the scene was very singular, for many of them, having just arrived from the far interior, had no ideas of civilisation. It was amusing to see how they employed their leisure. Their general occupation seemed to be to attend to their hair, on which they had been accustomed to expend a great deal of their superfluous time in the wilds. I was much amused by observing a native from Lo Benguela's country undergoing the operation of being shaved by his companion, the substitute for soap being his moistened finger, and the razor being a piece of a broken bottle. The march of civilisation amongst the natives has since made great strides, for now not only nigger dining-halls and canteens, but nigger billiard-tables, all of which are said to be in constant use, are frequent amongst the corrugated iron dwellings.

On my subsequent visits large horse windlasses and iron buckets of great size had replaced the smaller ones. The adaptation of this horse machinery, and in some cases of steam windlasses, reduces the number of the natives employed at the upper edge, so that, instead of the hill appearing like a huge ants' nest when disturbed, it subsequently bore a look of order and regularity.

The matrix in which the diamonds lie imbedded is a species of blue clay deposited in the large caverns of rock; once therefore this clay is removed, it is assumed that no more diamonds will be found there, as there would be nothing to hold them. It is impossible they should exist in the rock itself. Here therefore lies one of the speculative elements of this industry. As yet the bottom has nowhere been reached, except where the rock is shelving inwards. Symptoms have occasionally shown themselves which were supposed to indicate that a bottom would shortly be arrived at, but these have again disappeared, and still greater riches rewarded the diggers. Not only is a better diamond now extracted than at first, but less of the yellow or tawny-coloured stones are dug out.

The word "digger" does not imply that he is the working

labourer; in fact to dig is just what the "digger" does not do. It is he who superintends natives in this work, warily watching as far as he can that they do not conceal such stones as show themselves when breaking the clay at the bottom of the mine; for although by far the larger portion of the diamonds are found in the clay which is taken out of the mine and sorted at the top, yet it naturally will happen (more especially with the larger, and consequently more valuable stones) that some will reveal themselves to the spade and pick at the bottom. This is a fertile cause of many of the thefts which occur. The natives frequently conceal such stones, and there are many persons who make a trade of purchasing diamonds surreptitiously from those who have done so. The prices they pay are not, perhaps, a fraction of the real value; but even at this reduced rate the native who a few months before in the loftiest flight of his imagination could not have conceived the possibility of possessing enough to purchase even one Birmingham musket, might suddenly find himself able to purchase a whole stand of arms. It thus becomes requisite to make the severest enactments, not so much against stealing the diamonds as against inciting others to do so; and cases have occurred in which when the crime has been committed, though the guilty parties have succeeded in reaching Australia, they have been followed and brought back to justice.

Some few instances have occurred in which harshness and even great cruelty have been exercised towards the natives to cause them to confess their concealment of stones. There was a case of this kind shortly before my first arrival.

Some persons were accused of beating a Kafir by slow degrees to death; and so clear did the evidence appear that an offer is stated to have been made by one of the accused of 10,000*l*. for bail, which was indignantly refused.

The temptation to these poor black fellows is very great, but the profits by the illicit buyers are so large as to be quite irresistible. For instance, a case is well authenticated of a diamond having been sold by a native for 15*l.*, which was again sold for 350*l.*, and eventually realised the sum of 1160*l.*

These frauds reminded me of an amusing anecdote which I read in an American paper, showing that diamond smuggling is not confined to South Africa.

A New York Jew, who was reputed to be in the business of smuggling diamonds, used to cross the water on the Cunard line from three to four times a season. Two years ago, in the early part of the season, he was seized upon his arrival and taken to the searcher's room. Nearly a thousand dollars' worth of precious stones were found secreted in the lining of his boots. He returned to Liverpool by the same steamer, and four weeks afterwards again landed upon the Company's wharf on North River. He was again seized and subjected to the same rigorous search, but with no success. The Jew took it smilingly and philosophically. When he took his leave, he said, "Better luck next time, gentlemen; I shall go back by the same steamer on business, and when I return you can try it again." The officers mentally determined if he did they would try it again. Upon inquiry it was found that he really had engaged a return passage, having kept his state-room for that purpose. Two hours before the sailing of the steamer he was driven down to the pier in his carriage, his wife and daughter with him to see him off. When they returned they carried with them over ten thousand dollars' worth of diamonds which had lain secreted in his state-room during the whole time the steamer had remained in port. Before his return to New York the collector was notified by one of the revenue agents abroad that "Max Fuscher would return with several thousand dollars' worth of diamonds by the steamer which would leave Liverpool October 25th." In due time the Jew arrived, and for the third time he was escorted before the searcher. He was evidently not prepared for such persistent attention; he seemed nervous and agitated, and finally attempted to compromise. He was politely informed that that was out of the question. He was again put through the searching process. His pocket-book, which was first investigated, revealed a memorandum showing the purchase of eighteen diamonds of various sizes and prices, amounting in all to about twelve thousand dollars. When this came to light the Jew begged with tears to be allowed to compromise. A deaf ear was turned to his entreaties. His coat was removed, and the lining examined. Nothing there. Then the waistcoat. As the searcher passed his practised fingers along the lining his heart gave a tremendous thump as he recognised the "feel of something pebbly, like little rows of buttons." The garments were hastily ripped, a strip of chamois skin withdrawn and unrolled, and there lay one, two, three—eighteen! All there. "You can put on your coat and waistcoat again, Mr. Fuscher," said the searcher, blandly. "Good day." Without a word the Jew departed, took a horse-car home, kissed his family, ate a rousing dinner, repaired to the bathroom, and after soaking a rather capacious plaster across the small of his back for a few minutes in warm water, peeled it off, and with it "eighteen diamonds of various costs and prices." What the searcher and collector may have said or thought when they found their seizure to be nothing but clever glass imitations, worth from ten to thirteen cents each, nobody knows. Although the seizure was loudly heralded, the finale was never made public.

Perhaps there is no property so fluctuating as diamonds. Many instances have been stated of their having increased or diminished in value as much as 50 per cent. in one week; and those who one day perhaps refused three or four hundred pounds for a stone have been glad on the following week to accept the half of it.

I insert an extract which was taken from evidence on this subject at Kimberley, where it was stated that 65 per cent. profit on a purchase had been made.

If the parcel had cost 25,000*l.* in February or March 1876, witness would consider 13,000*l.* a fair price in August, when there was no market for them. Told Lejeune that if he had held the diamonds so long as plaintiff did he would not have sold them. Would not have taken over the purchase from defendant because the market was so bad then. 6000*l.* was not an extraordinary profit on these diamonds at that time. Had frequently made as large profits on diamonds bought in the open market through brokers and diggers. Profits in that August reached 65 per cent.

Again claims which have been purchased for hundreds of pounds may, from the despair of the digger at finding no return for a long period, be sold for a few pounds, and may scarcely have passed out of hand before successful finds of rich stones may again be made.

It is indeed extraordinary to be shown a small space, perhaps 5 feet square, said to be producing to the owner not less than 100*l.* a week of clear profit.

One gentleman's claim was pointed out to me from which it was stated that in two years he had cleared 45,000*l.* He then sold it, reserving the returns of one-third, from which he was said now to be receiving as his share, 500*l.* per week.

It was impossible for me to verify all these accounts, but if the half of what I heard be true it is quite wonderful enough.

There can be no doubt but that frauds to a considerable extent as regards imitation diamonds have been practised. The French appear to be particularly skilful in the art of imitating them.

A most cunning device would seem to be practised, which is called the "doublet fraud:" it is the combination of a well-cut crystal with the facing of a genuine diamond, the latter so thin in itself as to be comparatively worthless; but when cemented with a colourless cement on to the face of the crystal, it is likely to deceive the best judges and enhances the value 1000 per cent. The file ceases to be a test unless the stone is taken from its setting. Then an application of the steel instrument to the edges resolves any doubt.

The following is rather an interesting account of the adventures of a diamond digger, and it may be looked upon as a case of by no means rare occurrence. It is taken from Boyle's 'Savage Life:'

He then went to try his luck at the dry diggings of Du Toit's Pan and Bultfontein. He sent his furniture, packed in the canvas of his tent, under the care of a Boer returning to the former place, and, accompanied by his Kafir Charles, he traversed the distance of twenty miles on foot. They walked all night, with the exception of two or three hours' rest at the halfway-house canteen, and, passing through New Rush Camp, reached Du Toit's Pan at 5 o'clock in the morning. Aided by a friend, though with some misgivings as to the honesty of the process, he obtained a "jumpable" claim at Bultfontein, where he worked so successfully that on the 1st of April, about three months after he left Pneil, he had 726*l*. in hand. He then sold the claim for 274*l*., in order to make up 1000*l*., with which to start on a fresh speculation at New Rush. There with two partners he purchased the right to a three-quarter claim excavated beneath a road, which he was to clear and build a bridge across in ten days. The road, however, caved in on the second night after the work began, and when the author arrived at the scene of the disaster, some of the diggers began to scramble down to search among the precious débris. Loudly asserting his right to whatever was found in the heap of stuff, he attempted to stop one of the men from descending, and, losing his hold, fell down the precipice. He received fearful injuries, every bone being apparently broken; and he remained prostrate for months from the illness that ensued. At great risk he was removed at the end of July to the hotel at Du Toit's Pan, and attributes his discovery mainly to the news conveyed to him by one of his partners that, although their right to the claim of the wreck had been disallowed, yet that forty-seven diamonds, valued at 2800*l.*, had been obtained from the stuff already cleared, and what was left *in situ*. Finally he gives as the sum total of his story: at Pneil he cleared his expenses; at Bultfontein he made just 100*l*. with diamonds and claim; at New Rush 1115*l*. net. His year upon the Diamond Fields, all expenses of travel and illness cleared, returned him 2000*l*.; but, he significantly added, the price he paid was heavy.

The advantages which have accrued to the Boers who had settled within an area of fifty miles from Kimberley can hardly be over-estimated.

Their garden produce, their wood, their game, all find a ready market at excessive prices; and they have become less simple in their transactions, as the following anecdote will show:

Mr. Louis Keefer, a dealer in the Du Toit's Pan Road, has made the Boers who come to Kimberley understand that he gives the highest price for fresh eggs, and that the test of freshness is that when the egg is shaken the inside is solid, and does not shake loosely in the shell. A few mornings since a Boer brought Mr. Keefer seventy-two dozen of " beautiful fresh eggs," and they did look as if fresh laid; the shells were clean and white, every egg was solid, and there was not a shake in it. Mr. Keefer sent round to let his customers know that he had such a prize in fresh eggs. The seventy-two dozen went off like lightning at 6*d*. a-piece. Custards were a momentary weakness in the neighbourhood. Housekeepers cracked their eggs at the side of their custard moulds, but no white or yolk appeared. The farmer, to prevent the eggs shaking, had boiled them, and, to make them look white and clean, had washed all the shells. Mr. Keefer had purchased seventy-two dozen of hard-boiled eggs, and the Boer had ridden off.

But it is very requisite for the Boer to be wide-awake in his dealing with some of the Hamburg fraternity. It was told me as a good joke, that, in summing up accounts with a wool-dealer, a Jew, had misreckoned in his calculation; the Boer pointed this out, verifying what he was saying by producing a ready reckoner. Not in the least taken aback, the Israelite at once said, "Oh, but yours is a ready reckoner of last year's date; it is all wrong for this year," and threw it on one side, upon which the Dutch wool-seller, abashed, went his way in apparent content.

The prices for European luxuries appeared large, but nothing is too high for the successful digger; 1*l*. per bottle was the charge for champagne, and 5*s*. for Bass's beer; but it must be borne in mind that the carriage from Capetown was about 8*d*. per pound weight, and that these goods were at least two months on the road. It is a curious fact that fashion in such matters as champagne reigns supreme at Kimberley. I was informed, for example, that no one would drink any but a particular brand. So that if Perrier-Jouet was the rage, you would have to change all the labels on your stock of "Moet et Chandon."

There were two other diggings in the neighbourhood of Kimberley—Old Dr. Beer's and Du Toit's Pan; the last named has latterly become very much more profitable.

The river diggings are totally unlike those I have described, for here diamonds are discovered generally in a sort of blue clay, on the banks of the river.

It is concluded that they were originally formed in volcanic craters, which, in consequence of some deluge of water, burst their bounds, so that the diamonds have been swept down the river and deposited here and there in the vicinity of the river banks.

A few days later the whole of my force was encamped in an excellent position at Barkly, on the north side of the river Vaal. This town had formerly been known as Klipdrift, and was the location of the early diamond diggers on the river before the great diamond mine at New Rush had been discovered. Barkly is perhaps the prettiest spot in Griqualand. The town is placed on the banks of the river, which is here winding and picturesque, and well wooded; and care is now being taken that the timber shall not be shorn off the face of the earth, as it has been throughout the entire country of South Africa, wherever it was possible to do it.

I accompanied Mr. Palgrave on a visit to the river diggings at Winter Rush, about fifteen miles below the town. It is impossible to say what success attends the exertions of the miners, for with much prudence they refuse to disclose their finds, lest hundreds should rush to the spot to share their good luck. They put on lugubrious faces, but when a question of purchasing a diamond arises, especially by one evidently ill-acquainted with the matter, little bags are instantly produced from the pockets of the diggers, each of which contains one or two stones.

There appears to be some virtue set upon these bags, for they are beautifully made; some of skin, others of cloth, worked and braided in fancy colours.

Stones of four, six, or ten carats are shown; some pure white, some coloured, and all more or less perfect in shape. They are seldom larger, for as soon as a fine stone has been found, it is beyond the power of the finder not to brag. Thereupon diamond buyers from Kimberley—Jews and Germans—instantly take cart and pursue the possessor, gradually raising their offers, as he is reticent and can afford to refuse them.

Although the price of off-coloured stones and small white ones has very much fallen in the English market, principally in consequence of the large number which have been found, the produce of the New Rush Mine alone being of the average daily value of 3000*l.*, yet fine white ones of anything above twenty carats are very rare.

Peace and tranquillity now appeared to have been restored to the Diamond Fields. The dangerous spirits who had created disturbances had deemed it advisable to leave. They had gone to the Gold Fields in the Transvaal, to Leydenburg, and to Pilgrims' Rest. Things were settling down. The diggers felt a greater confidence, more especially when they understood that the Governor had strongly recommended to Lord Carnarvon the purchase of the New Rush Mine.

Passing out of Kimberley by the Western Road, I saw numbers of hulking brawny black fellows idling by the side of the road, their only dress being a linen waist-cloth.

Some of the officers and men worked hard at digging for diamonds, but although the spots they worked were in close proximity with the holes from which it was known a large number of fine stones had been extracted, their labours were but ill-requited; only one diamond, indeed, being extracted, which was of small size and slightly flawed.

The health of the troops was excellent. Every attention had been paid to their wants. The best of meat rations, and as good bread as it was possible to provide, had been obtained for them. Not only had they beef and mutton, but occasionally venison, which the Commissariat purchased at 3*d.* per lb., in consequence of its plenty, and served as rations. The proximity of the camp to Pebbly Bottom and Five-river Vaal had enabled them to indulge in bathing and swimming, which are agreeable and healthful in this country.

At Barkly we obtained some beautiful karosses; one was

presented to me by Mr. Palgrave. The skin was supposed to be a sure protection against rheumatism. It accompanied me through all my future wanderings in South Africa, and, exposed as I was to all the vicissitudes of the climate night and day, I never suffered from a rheumatic attack, though I cannot say that I think the particular nature of the skin had much to do with the matter.

I now placed the force under the command of Colonel Glyn, and started on a journey of seven hundred miles to visit the troops at the eastern portion of the Cape Colony, on the boundaries of the Kei river. The entire expenses and detention of the troops during the six months amounted to the sum of 19,600*l.*

On the 14th of July we left on an expedition to the hunting grounds, in a country between the Vaal and the Sand river, where we were assured that we should meet with large herds—blessbuck, wildebeest, springbuck, and perhaps with a quagga.

We encamped at ———, a farmhouse belonging to a settler, formerly a sergeant of the 85th Regiment. By his industry he had gathered together a considerable amount of property—houses in Queenstown, and a fine farm of six thousand acres in the Free State, with cattle, horses, and sheep. His property cannot be computed at less than 6000*l.*, and perhaps it is worth a great deal more. His graphic explanation of how he obtained it is summed up in a single sentence. He said, "Any man can get along here who does not drink."

On our drive this day we met with the original owner of the New Rush Mine, who had sold it about the year 1872 for 3000*l.* In 1875 the Government gave 100,000*l.* for it. He was driving an ox-waggon. His manners were by no means courteous, and they did not improve upon further acquaintance.

The night was very cold, and after our long ride and drive we were anxious to get our late dinner, but a singular accident delayed it. When it was about half cooked, my Mussulman cook discovered that he had lit his fire upon a grave. Nothing that our English servants could say would prevent him from putting it out and recommencing his culinary arrangement in another place. He affirmed that the spirit of the departed would assuredly rise up in the night, to avenge the sacrilege, and to give us an indigestion. Nearly an hour was wasted in deference to his principles.

In the morning we moved on to Quagga Fontein. This is a fine farm, of about eighteen thousand acres. Twenty years since it is stated to have been sold for a span (or pair) of oxen. Now it is worth at least 7000*l*. In the garden near the house, and where the land is plentifully irrigated, a large amount of green forage is grown. It was estimated that a profit was derived from about twenty to thirty acres of this land of more than 500*l*. per annum. The forage is chiefly used for horses, and is the more valuable as a good market for it is readily found in Bloemfontein, to which the farm is so near.

Mr. Chatfield, the owner, had answered to the call when volunteers were demanded by the State in the Basuto campaign. He had been attached to a command. He had a narrow escape of his life in action. One night near the Caledon river, when asleep in his small patrol tent, a short distance from his companions, the camp was surprised. He was suddenly awakened by the most diabolical shouts, his tent being rolled over him, and half-a-dozen assegais stabbed into his body. Though weak from the loss of blood, he managed to crawl out of his tent, armed with his revolver, and fired into a black mass of men. Thus attacked they gave way, and he staggered into camp. The shot alarmed the whole command, who were now fully sensible of their danger. They rallied, and, firing in their turn, killed twenty-five Kafirs, thus escaping the penalty of their neglect.

After the war a Kafir told Mr. Chatfield that they were so

numerous that they could have destroyed every white man, but that seeing him walk away after being stabbed in at least a dozen places, they thought that his party were spirits and not men, so that they were glad to leave them alone.

At Quagga Fontein we saw a little imp not four feet high, one of the diminutive race of Bosjesmans. He was said to be perfectly wonderful on horseback, clinging to a horse like a monkey. The universal forage that is given in South Africa is oats, or barley straw with the ear on. Our evening meal for the team of four horses was charged 22s.

Although hundreds of thousands of acres of fine grass land are to be seen on all sides, no attempt whatever is made to convert it into hay, but it is always allowed to go to waste. It would now be too expensive to save it, as the labour of the mowers could not be had for less than 10s. per day to each man. In a few years, when emigration has filled up this country, the mowing-machine will soon bring this valuable crop to some use.

At 4 P.M. we reached Moi-mais-Fontein, or the Spring of the Pretty Maiden. It was here that a fight had taken place about a year before between the Free State police and some Basutos. These Kafirs had been paid for their labour at the Diamond Fields, not in money but in firearms. With these they had started to march across the Free States, to their own country. It being contrary to the law for a native to enter the Free State with guns, the police determined to disarm them. The natives resisted; fighting ensued, and some were killed. The affair gave rise to some ill-feeling between the Government of the Free State and the Cape Colony. In my opinion no blame could be attached to the Free State. Their law prohibits the natives from carrying arms, and the wisdom of such a prohibition has been most clearly shown. The Free State had therefore a perfect right to insist on its enactment being respected.

On the plains we met some huge herds of game, and had splendid sport. On one occasion I wounded a buck, which soon lagged behind the rest, and if left for a short time would no doubt have laid down, so that, when stiff, it could easily have been approached and despatched. But to my amusement I saw Johnny, our Mussulman cook, following him with desperate speed, crying out, "Master no fire!" Poor Johnny was too good a Mussulman to eat any meat unless it had been killed by a Mussulman, and in the name of the Prophet; and although plenty had reigned in the camp for some days, and the Kafirs were actually gorged, he had religiously abstained from tasting a morsel until, as on this occasion, he could kill it himself.

We were always glad to see the Dutch farmers of the district, and entertain them with the same fare which we enjoyed. This day two of them joined us. Although the night was bitterly cold, they did not seem to be in the least incommoded, though they brought nothing with them but the clothes they rode in, not even a blanket to cover them when they lay on the ground under our cart.

I have often remarked the hardihood of these Boers, and whether for bearing cold, heat, or deprivation of food, or for power to continue in the saddle, I look upon them as quite equal to the Cossack of Russia, and very far superior to him in the use of the rifle.

It is not surprising that they should generally be very good shots. It was not in taking aim that they showed their superiority, but in judging distances. The art of judging distances is one of the cardinal points of good rifle-shooting. Under any circumstances it is most difficult to acquire; in wide extending plains it is tenfold more so.

I found it expedient to have the fore-sight of my rifle protected by a ring, after the manner of a wind-gauge ring, but fixed, through which I aimed. The back-sight I had constructed after the old Dutch model; a separate sight, very legibly marked, for each distance, which I could alter in one moment, as the game advanced or receded. The advantage of these expedients in rapid firing at game cannot be too highly estimated. The hunting-knives which we bring from home are far too large, and the blade too long, rendering them cumbersome and causing them frequently to be lost. Experience assures me that the most useful hunting-knife is that which has a blade four inches long, very stout at the back, and made of course of the very best steel. This should run into a sheath, the handle being protected from falling out by a loop.

Even with the greatest precaution, we continually lost our knives during the severe gallops of four or five miles we took over the rough country. Nothing is so annoying as to find oneself beside a wounded animal, and unable to put an end to its misery. One out of every three or four sportsmen should be provided with a small, strong, wide-bladed axe, fastened on the saddle. It is most useful for cutting up the game and enabling it to be more easily carried.

In the farmhouses we were always very kindly received. They are built almost invariably upon one model: a large parlour with a sleeping-room on either flank, and a kitchen in the rear. One room is set apart as a guest chamber, which was invariably given over to our use. We were welcome to a place at the board at each of the daily meals; but as we had our own stores and coals, we preferred to accept the use of the room, and to invite the owner to dine with us, which he generally accepted. On leaving, payment would have offended the master; but we usually paid a liberal price for all we purchased in forage, fowls, &c., and as we were a large party, the payment generally amounted to a considerable sum.

On the following morning we had some tremendous gallops after the wildebeest, and brought down several. Never shall I forget the death-struggles of this animal or the wicked

P

attempts which he makes to drive his horns into anyone that approaches him. He stands with his cloven feet thrust firmly to support his body, and tosses his shaggy head from right to left, his eyes gleaming with fire, while torrents of blood rush from his mouth.

No sooner is a deer wounded than the quick-sighted vultures hover over the poor animal. Should he lie down exhausted, they wheel in circles above him, collecting from distances quite beyond the sight of man, and with a rapidity quite incredible. By watching the spot round which they hover, the position of dead game may be discovered, but delay is fatal, as they collect in such numbers and are so greedy, that nothing but the remnants in the shape of bones and horns will remain upon the ground a very short time after they have commenced their operations.

In the afternoon a Kafir boy brought a letter from Boshof, fully thirty miles distant over the hill, and appeared very well satisfied with the half-crown which was given him. He immediately set off on his return home, taking, however, a different route for the purpose of visiting a canteen which lay twelve miles distant.

Before leaving Boshof an amusing story was told me of a circumstance that happened there shortly before our visit.

A Dutch wedding party was to take place on a large scale. Invitations had been sent far and wide, and the number of guests was great. Old, young, married and single, rich and poor, were welcome, so long as there were no English. For miles the farmers came in their carts. The wives were brought that there might be chaperones, and the nurses and babies could not be left behind. A room upstairs was appropriated to the babies, who were put to bed, while the mothers and nurses danced.

During the dance some mischievous young men, aided perhaps by some of the girls, went upstairs and changed all the babies, not only removing them from one cot into another, but taking off their clothes and putting the dresses of some on the bodies of others. When the parents and nurses had well danced, and eaten and drank, they sleepily took up their children and started in the night to go home. It was when the morning sun arose on the Veldt, and they became able to see more clearly, that they discovered the dreadful trick which had been perpetrated. It is said that the exchanging of babies from one district farm to another took eleven days' hard work, and that even still there are two young ——— who are suspected not to be the children of the parents who own them.

While speaking of the eccentricities of the young men of the Free States, I may mention another anecdote of their doings:—

There were a good many people made April fools of on the first
of last month, but the worst case heard of was that of a
cleaned and trussed monkey which was sent to a bachelor's
hall, and eaten by several new-comers under the assurance,
as per accompanying letter, that it was a bluebok. They
spoke highly of the flavour of South African game.

I then quitted the Free States and proceeded to Cradock. The surrounding country appeared to be some of the finest grazing land in the colony; but it is reported to be overstocked with sheep, and in consequence a great deal of disease exists amongst the flocks. Professor Bandford, in his report, says:—

The deteriorated veld is overstocked, and the impoverishment of
veld and stock goes on together. So we are going downhill
at an ever-accelerating pace, and using up our resources in a
most thriftless manner. Not content with using up, we take
pains to rob the soil of its proper nourishment, and so prevent,
as far as we can, the natural process of recovery. The dung
which would give life to the soil brings death to the animals,

yet instead of spreading it abroad on the land, by our system of heading the cattle we pile it up in sleeping grounds for the sheep. When rain falls, this sleeping ground becomes a fetid dung-bath, and the poor sheep may be seen standing up to their very bodies in slushy, fetid matter. Those that, weary with the long day's roaming, lie down, saturate their fleeces with the filth, and for days they carry about their bodies a load of their own dung.

The Professor vehemently asks, How in the name of goodness can health be expected in animals exposed to such "influences?" The dung heap which forms their bed is an excellent nursery for the parasitic creatures that seek the enfeebled and sickly body. So by violating the order of nature we accomplish three distinct and serious evils—we starve the veld, predispose the sheep to disease, and encourage parasites.

All these evils, no doubt, arise from the system of herding the sheep every night in kraals; but it is easier to condemn this system than to alter it.

Where the entire face of the country is open and undivided it would be almost impossible to fence, more especially where wood is in general so scarce. Not only is iron wire very expensive, but European labour, by which it must be put up, cannot be procured much under 10s. per day. How, then, can it be expected that the sheep should be fenced in? Again, in the same localities, many sheep are affected with fluke; these sheep appear fat, but soon fall off.

The natives frequently own good herds. Their power of counting the sheep is quite extraordinary: they can count a thousand sheep when starting out of kraal without a mistake, but many of them are great thieves, and their robberies are a serious loss to the farmer, from which it is loudly complained that the law as administered is by no means a sufficient protection. This is a farmer's complaint.

Allow me to introduce a neighbour of mine, Mr. Zete:—

For years Zete has set the law at defiance. A paternal government has located him in the very best place for the profitable exercise of his profession. I am afraid to state how many times Zete has been caught and discharged. I myself, with some other farmers, saw thirty-eight stolen sheep in Zete's kraal, all marked with paint most unmistakably. They were claimed by a farmer, and were stolen from him while on the track. Zete was tried and acquitted, the sheep not having been found about his person.

He is now in again for eleven sheep, but we all expect he will escape, as usual. I have frequently said to this man's neighbours, " Why do you not rid yourselves of such a fellow, who brings trouble on the whole of you?" "What's the use?" they reply; "we have caught him stealing over and over again, but you English let him go again." The Kafirs tell me that, whenever Zete has committed a theft, he prays to a tree. This tree he calls by his father's name. After this he chews some "bosjes," and is then law proof. But should he be taken his mother, who is a witch, stands in the gateway of his kraal, and calls upon his name. She then sends one of her sons, who carries a bush in his hand, along the King William's Town road. He also calls out, " Bawo yisa n'duja ku kumbula." Next morning Mr. Zete is in the bosom of his family again.

The Kafirs firmly believe all this: I don't believe it myself. I account for Zete's success in another way. He must have gained possession of one of " Finnygan's " cast-off wigs, and has thus become so saturated with Cape criminal law that he can bid defiance to his enemies.

Now, I would ask, of what use are laws, and, I may add, judges, when a conviction cannot be arrived at in such cases as I have cited? The law at the Cape, which is compounded of English and of Dutch-Norman law, is, it must be owned, very technical, and has hardly kept pace even with English tardy improvements.

Although the neighbourhood appears to be more pastural than agricultural, its soil has great capabilities. Potatoes flourish admirably and grow most rapidly, and pumpkins attain an enormous size. I saw one of more than 80 lbs. weight grown in this neighbourhood.

There is also a pith which is taken from the underground skin of the thorn. It is a quarter the weight of cork, and is one of the lightest solid substances known; a shoe sole had been made of it for a little boy, one of whose legs was shorter than the other, and helmets that have been made from it have worn well.

Cradock appears to be one of the most rising towns in the Cape Colony. There is a fine church there, which must have cost a considerable sum. The streets are broad, and the situation of the town is very good. The position of Cradock, as regards South Africa generally, is central, and it is by no means impossible that it should become the political capital of the future Confederated Colonies. Railroads, one of which is already approaching it, will place it in direct communication with Port Elizabeth, and ere many years it will be in communication by rail with both east and west.

CHAPTER XXII.

THE LOVEDALE INSTITUTE.

We next came to Alice, near which the Lovedale Institution is situated. I visited this with very great satisfaction.

Cart and waggon building, and carpentering were progressing satisfactorily, while the more experienced men were employed in type-setting and printing, and telegraphy.

It is very much to be desired that mission stations should be more generally established on these principles, and that reading and singing the Psalms should not be the beginning and end of education of black men.

The account of a visit to Lovedale, which I read in one of the daily papers, is so interesting that I trust I shall be pardoned for inserting it here:—

After kindly welcoming me to Lovedale, he invited me to have a look over the place, and here it was that all the arguments that I had prepared vanished, as chaff before the wind. For one of the first observations that the Doctor made was this: "Our object, Mr. ——, is to teach the native to work; work he must, a certain portion of the day, or go. We cannot afford to keep idlers here; lazy fellows soon must leave us. We endeavour to civilise, and teach them to fear God at the same time, and hope that some at least may turn out useful men and women." I could scarcely avoid applauding the Doctor's sentiments with a hearty "hear, hear," having all the ground knocked from under me. I proceeded to examine the workings of the institution with less prejudice. The Doctor leading the way, first we entered the printing compartment. Here was one white man and several black boys hard at work at the press, running off the 'Christian Express.' They appear to be well up to their work, the type being clear, and equal to any I have seen. The next was the telegraph office; this is worked by two black boys. The Doctor remarking, "Of course you understand the working of the telegraph, Mr. ——?" The "Oh yes" came out without thinking, and I felt foolish while the Doctor was explaining. He, however, was generous enough not to notice my blushes.

Then we examined the carpenters' shop, where the Doctor told me there were twenty-four natives learning the trade. Then came the waggon-makers', where eleven boys were at work. Blacksmiths and farriers came next, where an equal number of boys were being instructed. While thus employed, the strains of music reached our ears, and in answer to my inquiry as to its meaning, I was told that the brass band was practising, having been asked to head a procession the next day. The Good Templars were about to celebrate a something or another, and intended marching through the town, headed by the band. The band consists of native lads, with the exception of four white boys. As far as I could judge, they performed correctly. While they were blowing like fury a Good Templars' march, the Doctor caught me by the sleeve, and took me rather hurriedly outside, just in time to witness about a hundred native boys passing with their picks and hoes returning from work, the Doctor remarking, "It's not all band-playing, you see, sir." I was astonished as well as delighted, and could not help wondering at the mistaken ideas many have of the Lovedale Seminary. We next examined the dormitories. Here my entertainer remarked, "Every article of bedding is found by the boys, only the bedsteads do we provide." I expected to have to bolt out with my handkerchief to my nose, but what was my surprise to find everything as clean and sweet as one could desire! Now we entered into the dining-room, where supper was preparing. Long tables were laid for three hundred boys. Each boy was provided with a tin mug, ditto plate, and spoon. The supper consisted of maize, or mealies, and churn-milk, with bread. These boys are not stuffed with meat; having to work moderately hard, they are blessed with a good appetite, and Dr. Stewart considers mealies and milk good wholesome food, and less expensive than meat. The bread-cutter amused me. It is on the same principle as a lever tobacco-cutter, but on a larger scale, and works with a spring; a loaf is nipped up in slices of equal thickness in less than no time. The last peep was at the kitchen. Here were five to seven large soap pots, boiling as for dear life, and I was about to exclaim, " Why, Doctor, do you go in for soap-boiling ?" but I was stopped by that gentleman remarking, "Three and a half muids of maize are used daily, so large pots are necessary." It was now time to retire. Thanking the Doctor heartily for his kindness and trouble in showing me over the establishment and pointing out all the minute details of the working, I left convinced that the institution ought to have every support and encouragement, and I trust that some—ah! many—will, after perusing this short and imperfect, yet true description of the workings of the establishment, forward Dr. Stewart subscriptions in 5*l.* notes and upwards, to enable him to carry on this praiseworthy institution. I may mention here that all the boys pay a fee of from 5*l.* per annum and upwards, as their circumstances will allow. Still the establishment is not quite self-supporting, and a little help from outsiders would be thankfully received. The buildings also require enlarging, for which purpose funds are required.

CHAPTER XXIII.

THE ANNEXATION OF THE TRANSVAAL.

I HAVE shown how requisite it was that South Africa should become one united dominion.

In 1876 circumstances occurred in the Transvaal Republic which caused a deep agitation throughout the whole colony. Mr. Burgers, the President of that Republic, had visited England, and other European countries. He had gone there with a desire to make the Transvaal Republic better known, and to obtain funds to make a railway from its nearest port, Delagoa Bay.

He was full of confidence that he had gained the good wishes of Holland and of Portugal, and appeared quite independent of the help of England or of her good opinion; indeed, he seemed rather to pride himself upon this independence, and returned to the seat of his Presidency full of hope for the future.

There is one peculiarity in the institutions of the Transvaal which has deeply affected the progress of that country—the custom, which had become law, of granting to the son of every settler a farm on attaining the age of sixteen years, or thereabouts. Certainly the country was wild and extended, and the people few, but the lands which the Boers could at all lay claim to, or protect, were not large enough to allow the Republic to give every male in the State a plot of land nominally 6000 acres, but averaging from 6000 to 12,000. Consequently, the only resource open to the authorities was to grant allotments on the lands which the natives declared they had not alienated; when, therefore, those who had received Government grants attempted to settle upon them, they were repulsed, and quarrels and bloodshed were often the result.

The only way in which the President had been able to obtain money for carrying out his pet scheme, the Delagoa Railway, had been by granting concessions of land to those who would advance the capital.

When, therefore, the natives resisted the attempts of the Boers to settle on the lands which had been allotted to them, the President and his advisers were compelled either to relinquish altogether the right which they had assumed, or to insist upon it by force of arms.

For many years the Boers, though occasionally they had suffered in bloody reprisals, had been accustomed to carry all before them.

With their double-barrelled guns and the long roer they had terrified the savage armed only with the assegai, and when they had met with opposition, had quickly subdued it, after the manner of Cortes and Pizarro, putting the men to death, and carrying the women and young children to their farms to work as "apprentices."

Mr. Rosalt remarked that—

> It was a singular circumstance that, in the different colonial Kafir wars, as also in the Basuto wars, one did not hear of destitute children being "found" by the commanders, and asked how it was that every petty commander that took the field in this Republic invariably found numbers of destitute children? . . . .
> He gave it as his opinion that the present system of apprenticeship was an essential cause of our frequent hostilities with the natives.

Mr. Jan Talyard said—

Children were forcibly taken from their mothers, and were then called destitute and apprenticed.

Mr. Daniel Van Vooren was heard to say—

If they had to clear the country, and could not have the children they had found, he would shoot them.

They did not make slaves of these children, as it would have been contrary to the convention which had been signed on the Sand River with the British Commissioner, but they "apprenticed" them for terms, say forty years or so, to work on their farms.

Mr. Burgers and the Government of the Transvaal Republic continued allotting the lands belonging to the natives until at last they roused a determined opposition, and the Kafirs took to arms. Commandoes were now assembled, and marched to the disputed territory to which the Republic laid claim, which in this instance was Secocoeni's country.

Secocoeni's city, as his Induna loves to call it, is situated about seventy miles from Pilgrims' Rest, in the Drakensberg range, upon a triangular flat surrounded by rocky hills, not higher than those round Pilgrims' Rest, and in some places much lower, but rugged, steep, and very difficult of ascent. These hills are fortified by thick stone walls, one behind the other, and divided into sections or squares by narrow footpaths forming the ingress and egress for the women to the laagers erected on the summit of the hills. I cannot better explain the plan of these stone walls, than by comparing it to a pew in a church or amphitheatre. The entrance to the city consists of two passes or ports, one approached by a footpath, which is barricaded at a deep gully which it crosses, the other protected on a rocky hill, fortified on each side by stone walls and a thick prickly-pear hedge, the gaps of which have been strengthened by camel-thorn trees, and with a gate closed every night. The city itself is surrounded by a camel-thorn hedge about six feet high, with only one gate, also closed every night. Everything was well looked to at Secocoeni's. The women left the city for the laagers on the hills, where plenty of mealies and corn were stowed away. About four thousand head of cattle were sent into the ravines and kloofs round the city, also a great number of goats. The rest of the cattle were sent across Olifant's River. Watches were placed by night and day on the hills close to the Commando, which was not more than 1000 or 1200 strong.

Secocoeni said—

I think I will beat the Boers and burn Leydenburg, and all the homesteads down to the Comatic; but if unfortunately I should get beaten, I shall follow at once the example set by the late chief Moshesh, and apply to the great chief at the Cape to become a British subject. I would sooner give my country to the English than one inch of ground to the Boers.

Secocoeni had no dislike to the English, but quite the reverse, as the following message, which was sent by him to the Gold Fields, shows:—

Secocoeni has heard that the Englishmen at the Gold Fields are building laagers; and he has also heard from Johannes' men that Englishmen fired at his boys at Kruger's Post, that the Englishmen at the Gold Fields are afraid of an attack from his boys; but he can assure them that that is not his intention, and that he has given strict orders to his people not to molest the Englishmen, nor to take anything belonging to them. Secocoeni has asked ——— to tell the Englishmen to come and trade with him; he will send ten men to the boundary to bring them safely to his place, where they will get protection. Powder and lead they must not bring, as he has plenty; but they must bring plenty of blankets and picks for his boys. Mealies he cannot promise them, but he has money; for the mealies his boys must save, as the war won't allow them to plough this year. Now Secocoeni regrets to hear that his boys have captured two waggons belonging to Englishmen; it is against his orders, and if the owners will apply to him after the war he will repay them. Now that Secocoeni has said all he wants to say, he will also say this—that he loves the English at the Gold Fields, and he hopes they also love him.

These were not the feelings of Secocoeni only, but of every chief in the country.

Many of them said—

We regard the Queen as our mother; we are children of the Queen. Come then, and relieve us from our tyrants.

Now that they were so extensively armed, even better than the Boers, they felt that their day of revenge had arrived, a day which they by no means consider yet to have gone by. The result of this Commando was as follows:—

The Boers attacked Secocoeni's Mountain in two wings. The whole army numbered 2900 men. Of one wing only 40 men exposed themselves to fire, and all the commandants and officers of this wing were subsequently fined 5*l*. each for cowardice.

The attack on the mountain was repulsed, two Irishmen being killed, and some six or seven wounded. Not a Kafir was to be seen, all being hidden behind the rocks. After the repulse the Boers refused to fight any longer. They went in a body to the President and announced their determination to go home. The President is said to have asked his men to shoot him, and not let him survive their disgrace.

About the same time that Secocoeni's position was assailed the Boers had attacked Johannes' Kraal, a native town about twenty-five miles from Leydenburg. They had shown a great dislike to approach the fortified position, and were accused of screening themselves behind some rising ground, while the Amaswasi, a tribe that were friendly and were assisting them against Secocoeni, bore the assault. An account was given of this action, from which the subjoined is an extract:—

The following is the result of the action at Johannes. Killed, 47 men, 19 women, 13 children; and wounded, 16 men, 4 women. I've gathered the following from Johannes, who sent for me to see if I could do anything to his wounds. I arrived at his place about ten or twelve hours after the action from Steelport River. He says, " We were taken unawares. We saw the Boers approaching, but not the Zwasies. The women asked me if they should go into the cave, but I told them they were only the Boers coming, and they are sure to run away at the first shot. At about three thousand yards from my place they came to a standstill, and I gave orders to my men to go and meet them, which we did, when the Zwasies, who were behind us on the hill, charged the laager. We rushed back to the laager, but they came in such numbers over the walls, that after our first shots were fired we had not time to reload, but had to fight with the butts of our muskets. The Zwasies fought well, but the Boers were afraid to come on. They stopped where we left them." Johannes got a stab from an assegai in the right breast, and another through the groin of the left leg. He died two days after. Before he died he called his brother and said, " I am going to die, I am thankful I do not die by the hands of these cowardly Boers, but by the hands of a black and courageous nation like myself. You are now chief here; promise me that you will never give up this piece of ground, but that you will die defending it." His brother said these words: " I promise you the Boers shall get this ground after they have killed me." Johannes said, " That is good." He then took leave of his people, told his brother to read his Bible, and expired. The Boers and Azawasi were repulsed.

The truth is, that the Boers had become conceited from their constant successes. Hitherto they had only been opposed by natives armed with assegais. When they found themselves confronted by the old Enfield rifle, and other far shooting muskets, which had been sold to the black man in return for his labour at the diamond mines, they discovered, to their cost, that it was no joke to attack even the most moderately fortified place defended with these weapons.

Men from the Commandoes poured into Pretoria, pursued by the Kafirs of Johannes and Secocoeni; and the Amaswasi, who had borne the brunt of the fighting at Johannes' kraal, were so enraged at the cowardice of the Boers, that they threatened to burn Leydenburg, and were only appeased by presents from the various stores in that place.

At this crisis the Volksraad assembled, and, quite incapable of action, they disputed as to the causes of the failure of the Commandoes; and when asked to raise a fund to carry on the war, pointedly refused until the reason for every penny of the expenditure had been fully explained to them. Some said that no attack should have been made; others that Secocoeni was a rebel who ought to be punished, while others declared that he was an independent chief, and that his country did not belong to the Republic at all.

At this juncture a despatch arrived from Lord Carnarvon, who had received information of some of the proceedings in the Transvaal, and who was justly apprehensive that they would lead to very serious evils to the whole of South Africa.

In the meantime the most revolting accounts of the doings of those composing the Commandoes (the Filibusters) were being sent down to Cape Town. No doubt many of them were exaggerated, but they impressed the public with the justice of Lord Carnarvon's remarks, and with the necessity for interference.

Two specimens of these reports are here subjoined :—

Von Schlickmann has since fallen fighting bravely; but there is no longer the slightest doubt as to the murder of the two women and the child at Steelport by the direct order of Schlickmann; and in the attack on the kraal, near which these women were captured (or some attack about that period), he ordered his men to cut the throats of all the wounded. This is no mere report. The statements are based on the evidence not alone of Kafirs, but of whites who were present.

There is a field cornet who recently visited a kraal of friendly natives, when he off-saddled and partook of the hospitality of the people, the chief giving him a goat to slaughter. Thirteen natives were commandeered from this kraal, and accompanied an expedition commanded by Abel Erasmus. On the third day the men were told by Erasmus to go home, as he intended returning; and, after they were deprived of the ammunition in their possession, they went back to their kraal. Not suspecting any danger, they were sleeping in fancied security, when about dawn the next morning Erasmus attacked their kraal, killed three old men who were sitting round a fire, wounded a man and a woman, and took six women and eighteen children prisoners. He also captured a number of cattle, and threatened, if more were not given, to kill the chief and all his people. It is this same Erasmus who, according to the telegram we publish to-day, has attacked another friendly chief, and shed more innocent blood.

Many cases were freely mentioned in the newspapers of the day, which, if one hundredth part of them were true, would put upon England a positive obligation to annex the Transvaal. I quote a few of them:—

On the 25th of August a party went out from Steelport to scour the surrounding mountains. The party on their way to a kraal met some women who had been for mealies. The first was quite a young woman, who was first wounded, and then shot through the head as she lay upon the ground. Whether any more women were killed before the horsemen entered the kraal we cannot say. Several were killed in the kraal. The number of ten has been given by a camp Kafir. Two women were caught outside and sent to the rear in charge of two Kafirs. They were questioned as to whose the cattle were, and were promised that their lives would be spared on condition that they told. They gave the information required, but the filibusters did not overtake the cattle.

The two women were taken to the Steelport laager, and a council of war was held as to what should be done with them. It was decided that they should be set at liberty, as two other women had been previously. They were accordingly sent out under an escort. They were accompanied by two of the camp Kafirs. When they arrived at the river, one of the chief filibusters is said to have told the Kafirs, "Now you are to kill these women, and to know they are dead I must hear the shots." The women were accordingly followed. One of them put her hands together and besought the Kafirs, whose intention she appears to have divined, not to shoot her. She had a baby on her back.

Supplication, however, was of no avail. The man levelled his gun. The ball went through the baby's head and into the woman's shoulder.

The other woman was shot by the other man through the back, and after they had stabbed their victims they returned and showed the blood upon their assegais.

There was, we hear, great outcry amongst the more decent men of the laager, but we do not hear of their having taken any steps to prevent such atrocities in the future.

The leader of the filibusters is said to be more anxious to kill the women than the men, because, he says, they pick and sow, and thus are the chief instruments in prolonging the war.

The above details have been brought into Leydenburg by several parties from Steelport, and have been fully corroborated by one of the Steelport camp Kafirs.

This Kafir also says the women begged hard for their lives, and offered to show where there was a lot of grain hidden. The Kafir murderers themselves have also told the horrible tale.

Fort Bergers, Dec. 26th, 1876.

Slaves are sold here every day. There are plenty of witnesses to prove all I am going to say . . . bought a salted horse (that is, a horse which has had the sickness), from a farmer for two little Kafirs. I believe the father of the Kafirs was first shot, and then the Kafir that was sent to shoot him said, "Now that the father is dead let us kill the mother, or she may tell tales." D. S. bought another slave—in fact all the farmers trade in them.

The prisoners at Kruger's Post have been shot in the night, sooner than take them to Leydenburg. One was killed at 3 o'clock in the morning, and the other was taken away and killed at Spekboom at 11 o'clock at night. They wanted to put him up for a target, but it was said the English people at Kruger's Post would not allow it. Next a Kafir going into Leydenburg with a flag of truce was shot. The other Kafirs ran away, but three or four days after they gave themselves up. These three Kafirs were shot in a most brutal way; for if they got into Leydenburg they would have told the English about shooting at them when going in with the white flag. The prisoners were sent to Leydenburg in charge of the very worst hands in Kruger's Post. From Kruger's Post to near Spekboom three farmers kept with them until going into Spekboom, when —— rode about to see if no Englishmen were about. The other two farmers stopped behind about a quarter of a mile. The two Kafirs in charge had orders to shoot down two of the prisoners with the first two shots, which they did; the other one ran away with his hands tied behind his back; then one of the farmers rode up and shot him. One of the three farmers always took out with him about fifty or a hundred Kafirs to do the dirty work, such as killing women and children.

[In the original the names of these farmers are given.]

These atrocities were very naturally denied by the President, who intimated that witnesses were required to prove their truth; but as an indictment for high treason awaited those who were bold enough to denounce them openly, no one was ready to undertake the hazardous duty.

While I was at Pretoria, the officer commanding the mounted infantry was encamped about the town. A native attached to a waggon-party which was passing by, seeing the British flag rushed into the camp and implored protection. He said that he had been at the Diamond Fields, and as he was returning thence, about a year and a half ago, with the gun he had purchased by his labour, and which he had a permit to carry, he was seized and made a slave of by a Dutch farmer, on whose farm he had been obliged to remain since that time. British protection was of course extended to him.

Sir Theophilus Shepstone was directed to go to the Transvaal as Commissioner and try and restore order. Secret powers were given him to annex the country if he thought it needful. In January 1876 he arrived at Pretoria, accompanied by a small party of Natal police. He found the affairs of the State in a very bad condition. The failure of the Commandos raised against the chief Secocoeni had demoralised the people. They refused to fight for the defence of their republic, and when called upon to contribute to the payment of the expenses incurred by the war, declined to pay the war taxes. The

President was forced to accept an inglorious treaty of peace with the native chief whom he had sought to humble; but there was no guarantee that the peace would be long continued. Besides this, the treasury of the Republic was empty and the credit of the Government gone. Sir Theophilus Shepstone then placed before the President (Mr. Burgers) a proposal for a confederation of the Transvaal with the other British colonies. The Local Parliament or Volksraad was summoned to consider the Commissioner's proposals. During the animated discussions which ensued, the President endeavoured to bring the members and the people to a sense of the condition of the Republic by the most bitter exposure of its weakness. He derided them for cherishing a mock independence in the face of calamities which must inevitably crush and destroy them, and proposed as the only remedy a change in the Constitution, by which the President would virtually become a dictator for five years. But the Government under Mr. Burgers' auspices had not been so successful as to encourage the people to desire five years more of it. Finally the Volksraad broke up without having done more than agree to certain oppressive measures, the most grievous of which was the levy of a war tax far heavier than any preceding impost of the kind. Meanwhile Secocoeni, the chief who had been at war with the Transvaal, again assumed an offensive attitude, and repudiated "the terms of submission" which it had been understood he had accepted. The Zulus, moreover, showed signs of their intention to attack the Boers. During his stay in Pretoria Sir Theophilus had abundant opportunity for observing the helplessness of the country and the impotence of its Government. At length the period arrived at which he considered he ought to act upon his secret instructions.

On the 6th of April he apprised the President that he should wait no longer, but at once proclaim the Transvaal to be British territory. Three days later a Gazette Extraordinary was issued containing the Royal Commissions, the Special Commissioner's Proclamation of British rule, with the reasons therefor given at considerable length, Sir T. Shepstone's Proclamation assuming office as administrator, a long address to the Burghers of the Transvaal "appealing to them as a friend," and justifying the act of annexation out of the mouth of their late President, and a proclamation suspending the operation of the law by which the obnoxious war levy had been imposed.

Sir Theophilus thus expressed his views upon the situation. He said that—

The purposes contemplated by the mission were purposes of good will to South Africa generally; and, in regard to this country in particular, her Majesty's Government had no objects except such as would promote its real prosperity and advantage in every way. These objects, however, it was earnestly desired to accomplish by and with the concurrence and co-operation of the people and the Government of the country itself. But, besides and beyond these latter important objects, her Majesty's Government had felt bound to look at the position of affairs in South Africa generally, which for some time past had caused considerable anxiety, especially in regard to native affairs and complications and possible eventualities arising out of the condition and line of action adopted by the Transvaal Republic, which would very soon and very seriously affect the British colonies and the whole of this portion of the African continent. The tendency of what had been going on in this neighbourhood for some time past had been to damage very much the influence and authority of the white man, upon the maintenance of which the very safety, lives, and property of all the inhabitants of South Africa depended—surrounded on all sides as the white population are by overwhelming masses of natives, most of them in a state of barbarism. It was to be feared that they had of late come to think it quite possible to oppose the white man, and that successfully, and that unless preventive measures were adopted, they might combine to a very dangerous extent.

The position, both of the Cape Colony and of Natal, especially the latter, was in such circumstances as to demand that steps should be taken to obviate this possibility. In that view the great point was, that the various civilised communities of South Africa should be united among themselves; that, abandoning jealousies and a line of conduct which kept them apart, and rendered joint action impossible, we should present a united front to the masses of natives around us. For the accomplishment of these purposes the British Government had resolved upon this mission to the Transvaal, and, considering the very long term of service which Sir Theophilus had had, and his consequent experience and knowledge of native affairs, customs, and complications in South Africa generally, had determined to place him at its head, in the first instance somewhat against his own wishes. But he had not felt at liberty to decline the duty which the British Government desired to impose upon him. He earnestly hoped that the objects of the mission would be thoroughly and quickly accomplished. It seemed absolutely necessary that the different colonies and states should very soon be united under one general bond for the protection and promotion of every civil, social, and religious interest. To that object his earnest and determined efforts were being now directed. He hoped he should receive as he needed, the sympathy, support, and co-operation of the people generally in order to carry out what he had in view in the best, simplest, and most natural manner. He had determined if possible to succeed, and he hoped that he would have the assistance of the Government in carrying out what was in hand, upon terms fair, reasonable, and beneficial to this country in all its interests.

On the 12th of April the annexation was formally made, a day memorable in the annals of South Africa and indeed in those of Great Britain. The change of government was effected without any disturbance. It was known that British troops were on the borders of the adjoining colony of Natal, but none were in the Republic. A number of the inhabitants of Pretoria who supported the Special Commissioner's proceedings formed a protecting force and offered their services to maintain order, although fortunately there was no call for them.

The President entered a protest against the annexation—in fact, he could scarcely do less *pro formá*—but it was quite evident he saw that the Republic could not stand alone, and I believe that, seeing this, he felt that it was infinitely the best for its real interests that it should fall into the hands of England.

Under the circumstances I think it will be allowed that a reasonable pension should be given him, and I sincerely hope that this may be done.

A greater danger to the tranquillity of South Africa than any reprisals from Secocoeni or other northern tribes was the animosity of Cetewayo against the Boers generally and against the Transvaal Government in particular. The special cause of this feeling was a dispute which the Zulu king had for some years had with the Republic respecting certain lands on the Pongola river, east of Newcastle in Natal, and of Utrecht. The Boers claimed a large extent of country which they stated had been sold to them by Cetewayo, the sale of which he altogether denied.

The Transvaal Government had already alienated this land to certain of the citizens. It was undoubtedly purchased at absurdly low prices, for a gentleman told me during my tour in the Transvaal, that he had bought 70,000 acres of fine land for less than 1000*l*. The purchasers claimed the protection of the State in their occupation, which the Republic was quite unable to grant, and the occupiers were consequently driven from their farms.

This disputed country had been offered by Cetewayo to the British Government, but while there was a dispute concerning it with the Boers, it would naturally not have been proper for the British Government to have accepted it, however much (now that the annexation is completed) we may regret that we did not do so. Cetewayo then threatened to attack the Boers, and seeing how abortive their attempts against Secocoeni had been, and hearing of the contempt with which they were regarded by the Amaswasi, who accused them of cowardice at Johannes' kraal, he determined to execute his threats and carry fire and sword into the Republic.

Cetewayo and his army felt themselves strong, they were numerous, united, and well-armed. On the previous year I had met some of Cetewayo's Indunas at Pietermaritzburg. I had an interview with them, and they informed me that his army consisted of more than 20,000 men, all armed with muskets, and that 4000 of them had rifles, of which 2000 were breech-loaders. Subsequent accounts do not belie the accuracy of these statements.

The great danger of an attack on the Republic by the Zulu king was averted, just in time, by the annexation of the Transvaal. Had Cetewayo attacked the Boers, the intimate acquaintance which I subsequently made with the country, assures me that the Transvaal Republic would have become a scene of bloodshed, fire, and rapine from one end to the other.

Cetewayo, however, saw things in rather a different light. Greedy for land, as all natives are, he gave Sir T. Shepstone the credit of being animated by this passion alone. He considered that the Commissioner was treating him basely, first by preventing him from overrunning the country, and then by occupying it for the British. He felt especially grieved that this should be done by Somtsen (the native name for Sir Theophilus), whom he considered as his father, and who had crowned him at his coronation. Report said that immediately on the news reaching Newcastle that the Transvaal had been annexed, the chief native constable was sent off according to instructions received from Sir Theophilus Shepstone to Cetewayo to inform him of it, and to tell him, on no account, to attempt the invasion of the Transvaal. On the delivery of the message, Cetewayo flew into a rage, and ordered the messenger to be put to death at once. One of his principal Indunas, however, interfered, and told him that they (the Indunas) could not allow it to be done, as he had only delivered the message he was sent to deliver, and it was not his fault if that message was offensive.

Cetewayo then ordered the Induna to be killed; but the other Indunas objecting to this very strongly, he was obliged to relinquish his intention, and walked off to his hut in a passion. He said that the Natal Government had deceived and outwitted him in annexing the Transvaal, that they had prevented his going to war with the Boers; that they might take the Boers' country to themselves, and close him in, so that there would be no path for his armies to go out to fight with other Kafir tribes. Since this Cetewayo has submitted the question of peace or war to his army. A majority is said to have decided in favour of peace, but these wiser councils having been overruled, and the British Government having sent an ultimatum to Cetewayo, has commenced hostilities against him.

In a few words I have thus endeavoured to explain the necessity which compelled us to annex the Transvaal. Some of the inhabitants resented it, and sent Paul Kruger, formerly a General in the Republican service, with a petition to England against it, but the majority, especially those on the eastern side, knew their danger, and that the Republic was perfectly unable to defend itself, so that although a few spoke against the measure from national pride, they were deeply grateful in their hearts to the hand which had saved their homes from destruction.

It may interest my readers to quote a few words from Mr. Fynney's report of an interview which he held with Cetewayo about this period at the request of Sir Theophilus Shepstone. Mr. Fynney says that the King sent most of his chiefs and all his men away, saying, "he had a word for Mr. Fynney's ear alone":—

I wish you to ask Somtsen (meaning Sir Theophilus Shepstone) to allow me to make one little raid only, one small swoop; it will not be asking much. Why will he not listen to me? He knows where I want to go, and so do you too, only you won't admit it. It is the custom of our country when a new king is placed over the nation to wash their spears, and it has been done in the case of all former kings of Zulu land. I am no king, but sit in a heap. I cannot be a king till I have washed my assegais.

Cetewayo had never seen a revolver-pistol. Mr. Finney, having shown him one, fired it at a calabash. The chief was much surprised at the power of so small a weapon. "How destructive will it be," he said, "when it has grown up and become a mother?"—which must be understood as meaning a cannon.

In Zulu land it is considered a great privilege to be made a soldier. All the sons of Cetewayo are made soldiers at the age of six years or thereabouts, and all the children who are born in the same year are also made soldiers at the same time as the dignity is conferred upon the prince of whom they are contemporaries.

Wives are a very valuable property in Zulu land, partly, of course, for the reason that the greatest reward of a soldier is to receive a present of a wife.

The lot of a native wife is often a most unhappy one. Considered as property, and treated well or ill according to the caprice of her husband, she not unfrequently attempts to escape.

The Zulu laws to prevent these escapes are most barbarous. If any woman runs away, either to Natal or any neighbouring tribe, Cetewayo orders the execution of all the men in the kraal, confiscates the women, and bestows them as wives on his soldiers.

The following story was related to me concerning Cetewayo. Dr. Drummond had lately been invited, at the instigation of Mr. John Dunn, to visit Cetewayo at his great place in Zulu land, to give medical advice to the chief as to his health.

Upon a careful consideration of the circumstances of the case, Dr. Drummond could find no better recipe than a liberal allowance of oysters and porter. Cetewayo was so pleased with the advice that he ordered three hundred head of cattle to be at once presented to the doctor, and that Mr. Dunn should see to it. The value of the cattle may be estimated at about 5*l*. each—a royal reward, no doubt, and fairly earned. But Mr. Dunn had made a private arrangement with the doctor to give him 100*l*., whatever the remuneration might be. Dr. Drummond only got his 100*l*. The person perhaps most pleased with the recipe was Mr. John Dunn himself. Had the doctor ordered even the most nauseous compound, Dunn would have been obliged, according to custom, to swallow a considerable portion of it in front of the chief, to prove that it did not contain poison. In the present instance his duty was easy and agreeable.

There is no doubt that the Zulus are the most warlike tribe in South Africa. Their conquests have been extended further than those of any other; and but for the arms and organisation of the white man, it is by no means improbable that they would have come as conquerors even to the walls of Cape Town.

They are reported to be ready to offer sacrifices when they consider that their military enterprises will be benefited by them. In Zulu land there is said to be a locality where Chaka buried all the brass ornaments of his tribe, having ordered his Zulus to wear none in future but those made of iron.

CHAPTER XXIV.

TOUR TO THE TRANSVAAL.

Though the Cape Colony has no more to do with the Transvaal than England has with France, the annexation made the Governor at Cape Town Governor of the Transvaal also, and the English troops were charged with protecting the lives and property of the Transvaal colonists no less than the lives and property of the inhabitants of the Cape Colony. As soon, therefore, as the Transvaal had been annexed, it became my duty to propose arrangements for its defence. Early in the spring of 1877, Sir Bartle Frere arrived at Cape Town. I placed before him my views upon the subject, which he entirely approved. I then started for the Transvaal in order to make sure that the arrangements which I thought necessary should be properly carried out.

I will not narrate the incidents of my journey to Natal. Suffice it to say that, having passed through Pietermaritzburg, I reached Frasers on the 31st of May. The British troops under my command did not immediately accompany me, but followed by a somewhat different route. In case of an outbreak I established a military post at Newcastle, a commanding position, and the troops, having reached that point, proceeded to the Transvaal. On the north-east of Frasers is situated the tract of country called New Scotland, which had been purchased by a Scotch company. I was given to understand that it comprised 300 farms, in all about 1,800,000 acres. It is said to have been bought at the rate of 1s. per acre, and paid for in bank notes of the Republic, which could be purchased at the time for about 2s. 6d. to 3s. in the pound. If so it was bought, not at 1s. the acre, but at 1½d. Shortly after I left the Transvaal, Mr. Robert Bell, who was carrying on the agency of this large estate, was murdered.

A young Kafir had committed some act of disobedience to his chief, who resides on Mr. Bell's farm, being an Amaswazi refugee of some eight months' standing. This chief had seized cattle belonging to the young native. He appealed to Mr. Bell, who, after consulting Sir T. Shepstone, went unarmed to recover the cattle at the kraal of the chief. He was accompanied by some eight or ten native policemen. The restoration of the cattle was peremptorily refused. Mr. Bell then directed his men to seize the person of the chief, but before they could do so he signalled his followers to attack Mr. Bell and his people. They rushed upon the little party, and assegaied all but two, who managed to escape. When last seen by his policemen, Mr. Bell was down on one knee apparently remonstrating with the savages, and endeavouring to ward off the assegai stabs. The resident magistrate at once visited the kraal. He found only Mr. Bell's body stabbed through the heart. The Kafirs had all made off.

On the following day I proceeded to Standerton, a well-situated town commanding the ford across the Vaal river. My object was now to select some station on the high veldt, where the cavalry could be posted, but it was requisite that it should fulfil certain conditions. It must be so placed as to be of easy access to Utrecht to the east; or, in case of any demonstration from Cetewayo, to the north, to give ready help to Leydenburg, or any party operating against Sccocoeni; to the south-east, in connection with Newcastle; to the west, in case of disturbance in Potchefstrom; and to the north-west to be well in communication with Pretoria. Moreover, it should be upon the direct road from Natal to the capital of the Transvaal, and, if possible, about half way from the station which I had formed at Newcastle. It was difficult to secure all these conditions at once, but singularly enough I found them combined in Standerton, which I at once determined in my own mind to make a cavalry station. I say in my own mind, because had I promulgated the fact, the value of land would at once have risen so as to cause the Government probably a much increased outlay.

In consequence of the horse sickness which affects all horses during the hot season in the plains, it is a wise precaution to place them on the elevated plateau during the rainy and hot season; and as Standerton stands more than 4000 feet above the sea level, it possesses an advantage in this respect scarcely shared by any other town on this route.

At Standerton we were kindly received and most hospitably entertained by Madame Swikkard, a German lady, who, poor thing, had just lost her husband, an officer who was formerly in the Prussian service, and had left behind him a charming and clever family of small children. I say clever, for they all spoke German, English, Dutch, and Kafir with fluency, which gave them an immense advantage over the settler from home, who knows no language but his own. The Deputy Commissary General engaged one of the eldest to assist in his department, in which his services proved very valuable.

Standerton was first formed by vote of the Volksradt, at the investigation of a General of Pretorius's army, who had commanded a part of the force opposed to Sir Harry Smith, at Blomplatz. He was residing near the town, and I took the opportunity of calling upon him. He seemed very much gratified with the attention, having been under the impression that his reception by a General of our army would be the reverse of agreeable.

At Standerton the officer commanding the march of the troops was met by an anxious Dutch Boer, making inquiries regarding our intentions in the Transvaal. He came to camp from his location at some miles distant, well attended by servants and spare horses, and was evidently a large proprietor. He said he had been informed from Pretoria that our intentions were to take the lands; to conscript the young men and place them in the Grenadier Guards, and send them to fight the Russians; and to levy a war tax in the Transvaal, in order to pay the expenses of the war in Europe, while giving them no share in the Government of their own country. When assured that this was all false, and that it was the intention of the Commissioner of the Transvaal to remit the war tax, he went home quite contented, saying that from that moment he would support the English, and added, "Pray take a glass of Schiedam, Colonel, we are now all English."

There are no finer young men in the world than the young Dutch Boers, who are generally of immense height and size, and very hardy. Their life is spent in the open air by day, and frequently at night they sleep on the veldt, with no tent or covering; men more fit for the Grenadier Guards, as to personal appearance, could not be found. Some of them are plucky; a Boer had part of his hand blown off by the bursting of his gun. Having no doctor near, he directed his son to bring his hammer and chisel and shape off his fingers.

There was one fact in our favour, which was that we paid for everything, not in bank notes, which were looked upon with much suspicion, but in solid gold pieces, to which the people had long been strangers, and at the sight of which they showed equal astonishment and gratification.

There were a few in different parts of the State who still spoke of their wrongs, and were inclined to make mischief. Against this species of disaffection the Volksraad had passed most stringent penalties, declaring the act of "speaking against Government" to be high treason. As we had now inherited their laws a copy of these enactments was directed to be sent to them, which caused them much uneasiness.

Having made a detour for the purpose of inspecting the country, I found when I arrived at Pretoria that the troops had already arrived there and that a camp had been formed.

Pretoria is well situated and well supplied with water. The President Pretorius, after whom it was named, first settled the capital of the Republic at Potchefstrom, some 100 miles to the west; but having granted to himself a considerable farm at the site of Pretoria, he one evening packed up all the public documents, without giving any notice or warning to his councillors, started off and unpacked them at Pretoria, calling the future town after his own name, and establishing it as the capital of the Transvaal Republic.

The position of the camp had been well chosen in a spot above the town, and the troops were healthy, except for a few cases of illness, said to have been caused by drinking stagnant water on the march up.

The temporary Government House was the best in the town, and the best situated, possessing a garden sufficiently extensive to enable the Governor to place his police escort within it, as he did on his first arrival, when he was seriously threatened by an attack from a faction, who desired to retain the old wild sort of government as more favourable to their own interests.

A curious circumstance had occurred as regards the king of the Zulus. On the march of the troops from Newcastle he had sent native emissaries to follow them in order to give him information should the Queen's troops be attacked by the Boers.

This is the story told by these spies.

Upon arrival in Pretoria we exchanged our clothes for blue serge coats and trousers, obtained from a retired policeman.
Upon consultation we determined to wait until her Majesty's birthday. We had no difficulty in obtaining work in Pre-

toria, being old hands, and understanding a little English and Dutch, picked up on the Diamond Fields. We were surprised to find such a large dorp in the interior, but found every store belonged to Englishmen, and all the people talked against the late Government; therefore we considered there was no chance of fighting, and our mission at an end. Her Majesty's birthday passed off very orderly, much to our disappointment; we noticed very few Boers, but hoped they would show up with their generals and attack the red-coats scattered all over the hills. We came to the conclusion that British infantry look very well at play, but doubt their abilities in bush countries—we, for instance, could in five minutes massacre that little body in our country. We were much impressed by the rapidity of the artillery; they were well backed up by those ferocious-looking fellows the mounted police, who report says are regular "Iblabana," or "blood-suckers," and would prove to us very tough customers. We supposed Somtseu had his mabutos out to frighten the Boers, and they certainly did so; as on our return we met numbers of them trekking northwards with their stock, and passed numerous deserted homesteads. Somtseu and his Bantshla looked very fine, they had on all their talismans of war.

We did not see the late President; we heard he was afraid. Sir T. Shepstone intended sending him to the island where Langalebalele is, under an escort of the blood-suckers; but he, hearing of it through one of his Holland officials, who had accepted service under the British Government, and not trusting "Paul" and "Galankulu" to rescue him, fled to the Free State.

We tried hard to get a look at the machine which they say 'inva inhlamvu' (the Gatling gun) by the handful, but that building and corner street were always watched by some ugly fellows who we were told had just returned from murdering and impaling Sccococui's poor women and children.

There were numbers of Basutos in to witness the "Umhosi," and they never having seen British soldiers were very much astonished. We also noticed the head Induna from Swasiland and his followers. We tried hard on several occasions to pump the latter on their mission, but without much effect, but we are sure they are now English.

We left Pretoria about the end of May by the Middleburgh road, making a detour to obtain passes at half-price. In Middleburgh we met some German wood waggons returning to Pongolo, and fortunately obtained passages.

Our king seemed perfectly satisfied with our report, and presented us each with ten head of cattle.

The conduct of the troops had been all that could be desired, and the inhabitants appeared in every way satisfied with their presence.

Nothing but the firm attitude of Sir T. Shepstone could at this moment have saved Pretoria from a civil war and its consequences. The Zulus who were in the employ of civilians simultaneously left the city and congregated in a neighbouring valley, where they came to the determination to attack the Boers, in defence of their Father (the Administrator). They were employed in sharpening their assegais and other preparations to pay their old masters out, and but for Sir T. Shepstone's influence, bloody scenes would assuredly have been enacted in this city.

The value of property in Pretoria has risen about 400 per cent. during the last two months, clearly demonstrating the unceasing confidence in our occupation. Previous to the proclamation, whereby it was placed under our flag, no taxes had been paid, and consequently no salaries received by public officials. When the Administrator requested to know what more there was in the public chest, he was told that it had all been lent upon good interest by the treasurer, but would be paid back as soon as received. I understand that the whole sum which could be credited to the public use did not amount to more than a few pounds sterling while the debts and obligations were very considerable, and the credit *nil*. To set the State going, a loan of money was a positive necessity.

Having made all possible arrangements for the present at Pretoria I was desirous of visiting the Eastern frontier of the Transvaal, especially the Gold Fields, and on the 21st of June we left for Middleburgh.

Starting in the afternoon, we only reached Bothu, and the following evening we slept at Forster's—where one of our best mules succumbed. His body was drawn into the veldt by the remainder of the team as the dead horse is dragged out of the Corrido del Toro at Madrid. This was a great loss to us, as the price demanded for mules in this neighbourhood was too high to justify me in purchasing another. At the neighbouring farm at Lumbengs they asked 100*l*. for a pair, and beyond Middleburgh 150*l*. These mules possessed an advantage, especially for this country, which very much enhanced their value; they had undergone the process of *salting*, which signified that they had each had the horse sickness, from which they had successfully recovered. Thus, they were almost safe from a future attack of that disease, and their value was trebled by the fact.

On the 23rd we reached Middleburgh, and remained there during the following day. In the afternoon we drove over to one of the largest and most interesting mission stations in South Africa. Botse Bello is situated about eight miles north of Middleburgh, the river having to be crossed on leaving the town.

CHAPTER XXV.

BOTSE BELLO.

THE first object which met our view on leaving the station of Botse Bello was a beautiful church, surpassing anything to be seen not merely in the Transvaal, but in any part of the colonies, with the exception perhaps of Cradock. Around it were some excellent houses, with orchards and gardens of considerable extent and trees heavy with fruit; below was a walled native town, with three or four watch towers to command the approaches, the river winding underneath.

The residence of Mr. Marensky, the superintendent, is a charming house with fine rooms. I very much regretted his absence—we were informed by his lady that he was employed on a tour in the Zoutspanberg district.

We visited the military works which he had caused to be erected on the hill above the town. They were excellently planned and of considerable extent, and evinced a great knowledge of military science.

I was of opinion that Mr. Marensky had shown great foresight in these precautions, for, in the state into which the country had drifted through the miserable incompetence of the late Government, it was impossible to guess the day or even the hour when an attack might be expected from the Zulus or the Amaswasi.

But in making these works, a large amount of instruction had been conveyed to the natives, who appeared not to have been slow in availing themselves of it; for I was given to understand that Johannes, who successfully withstood the attack upon his kraal by the Boers in Secocoeni's country, had been for a considerable time at Marensky missionary station, and had there gained the knowledge he used to fortify his town.

Around the church there were shops for all trades. Blacksmiths, masons, carpenters, and numerous natives had profited by them. Large farming operations were being carried on; many hundreds of acres were carefully walled in; in fact, Botse Bello had advanced far beyond what I had previously seen or expected. We visited the native huts, which were well built and scrupulously clean, with nicely arranged courtyards to each. The number of children was quite extraordinary, and evinced the prosperity of the station.

I understood the work to be conducted upon a system of sharing the profit, a very considerable portion going to the superintendent for the expenses of the institution.

This, then, seemed to be the correct method of civilising the natives; first causing them to know their wants, and then teaching them how to supply them. I could not doubt that Mr. Marensky must be a man of great energy, or fail to wish him the success which he so well deserves. I think that if such a system were adopted in all missionary stations as those at Alice and Botse Bello, more speedy results as to Christianity and civilisation would be the consequence. They are founded upon principles which appear to me to appeal to common sense rather than to the ideal; the first being within the range of the mind of the savage, the second elevated beyond him.

Middleburgh, formerly called Nazareth, shows evident signs of becoming a large town in the future. The Boers are very fond of Scriptural names, and it seems a pity that the title of this town was altered, though its present name is appropriate, as there can be little doubt but that it will become the centre of a thriving district.

Property is increasing in value here with marvellous

rapidity. I was shown one farm but a short distance from the town, for which the owner, a resident in Middleburgh, had a few months ago refused 120*l*. He had purchased this farm three years before for three bottles of brandy and a bag of sugar and coffee!

At Middleburgh we made the acquaintance of Mr. Essell, who was in Government employment. His anecdotes regarding the northern portion of the Transvaal and the Zoutspanberg were very interesting. He said that when residing on the northern border, Paul Kruger being in command, the natives in large numbers surrounded a well-built village containing a considerable number of houses and many stores. A black spokesman advanced and told him that by Monday next every soul must leave the village, as they intended to burn it down. This being, as he said, on a Saturday, they had not much notice of the coming destruction of their property.

The Kafirs, however, evidently meant what they said. They were in war paint and armed, performing their war dances, brandishing and hurling their assegais. The inhabitants appealed to Paul Kruger, who said he was powerless to assist them; that he had not sufficient force at his command to ensure their protection, and that they had better pack up their effects as soon as they could, and be ready to start; and if they wished to accompany him they must be prepared to move on Monday morning. On Saturday and Sunday they packed all their things in waggons, the natives sitting round the town, drumming, but not interfering. On Monday morning the people assembled in the market-place,—the savages watching them from the neighbouring hills,—and started for the lower country, leaving their houses and gardens and such stores as they had not been able to pack up. No sooner had they left the village than the savages rushed upon it, each with a lighted brand, and before they were many yards away the town was but a heap of ashes. He said that this wanton assault was never avenged; the savages had been pressing on for some years, retaking from the Boers many and many a farm and thousands of cattle, the Boers being powerless to protect themselves.

Near the shortest road to Leydenburg, which was represented as so bad that no carriage could possibly travel along it, there exists a mine, the property of Sir Maurice Barlow and some others, who had bought it from its Dutch owner. Not knowing what the mineral was, they sent a specimen of the ore to England, when it was declared to be cobalt. There are said to be only three cobalt mines in the world,— in Russia, in Hungary, and in the Transvaal. The ore from this mine now realises 130*l*. per ton, and the company now makes about 4000*l*. per annum. Singularly enough, the Dutch Boer who was the owner of the land now acts as overseer on his former farm.

Before leaving Middleburgh I paid great attention to the position of the town, as I clearly saw that in the event of future difficulties in the eastern part of the Transvaal it would be a valuable and necessary position for troops. Within twelve months a force from Pretoria was despatched there.

We started from Middleburgh on the way to Pilgrims' Rest on the morning of the 25th, but with the intention of remaining a day or two at Hortogh's farm, about fifteen miles distant, at which we arrived about noon. It was unfortunate that we had not sent some of our shooting horses forward. We had understood that there was very little game in this neighbourhood, whereas it turned out that the whole country was covered with wildebeest and blesbok. Mr. Hortogh was good enough to lend me one of his horses, and before evening we made a reputable bag.

In doing this I had the opportunity of looking at some of his farms, each of about 6000 acres of land, but most of them lay in a state of nature. His runs for sheep and cattle appeared excellent, but at present they held nothing but game. We met with many fine pans of water, at which the gnu and the antelope alone slaked their thirst; and Mr. Hortogh assured me that he had discovered on his land coal, iron, lead, silver, brimstone and saltpetre; but what did not exist was people to improve the face of the country. He was most desirous of obtaining emigrants. He said that he would give up four farms in this district, of 6000 acres each, lend ploughs and oxen, and give seed, on the terms of his taking half the produce for ten years, at the end of which time the farm would become the fee-simple property of the settler without any payment. I carefully noted what Mr. Hortogh said, because the terms appeared so advantageous to any emigrant who might have the means of finding his way to Middleburgh at his command, and the more strong young children he could carry with him the better.

The soil round Mr. Hortogh's four houses was wonderfully rich and productive. Two rows of blue gum-trees gave the place a pleasant appearance, and although they had only been planted for three years they measured more than forty feet high, and the standard peach-trees of the same age were in full bloom, and of the size and height of apple-trees at home. Such peach-trees would take from ten to twelve years to attain the same size, even in Stellenbosch, near Cape Town.

The potatoes which he was then digging from his garden were magnificent, and excellent in flavour; and the climate of this district, though hot in the middle of the day, especially in summer, is always tempered by cool winds, for it must be remembered that the eastern plateau of the Transvaal stands not less than 5000 feet above the level of the sea. The diseases amongst cattle and men, which are so well known in the lower countries, are scarcely felt in the higher grounds.

Nothing is more easy than to lose one's way in these apparently endless plains. Although the whole country appears flat, yet in reality you keep ascending and descending gentle inclines, not monotonously as in the rolling prairies of America, which resemble huge waves, but at irregular distances. You sometimes see ponds of water where you least expect them, and occasionally on overtopping a gentle rise you may find yourself in face literally of thousands of game. The wildebeest, with his look of anger, his fierce eyes embowered in his thick and shadowy mane, snorts his surprise making circles, and whisking round and round, before he recedes out of range of your rifle.

Trees there are literally none, not even a bush.

The stump-eared pig was not uncommon in the valley, and the Korun were to be found in great numbers; but we only came across one zebra, who would not allow us to approach within reasonable distance. This species of game is rapidly becoming extinct on the prairies.

We now descended a tremendous hill by an almost perpendicular road to Broderick's at the rise of the Crocodile river. Here we met Mr. ——, brother of the Captain of the Commando, who was fined for retiring from the attack on Johannes' Kraal.

He was seeking his cattle, 300 head having been taken from him by the Kafirs in the neighbourhood. We had a drop of two feet into sprint, which tried the springs of the carriage; our Cape cart coming to grief, and turning right over into the middle of the stream. No one was injured, but it took us two hours to unpack the cart and repack the baggage, much of which was sadly injured. When again put up on its wheels, our old cart looked sadly disordered, its head was beaten in, it was covered with mud, and it had been some time under water; but it was not really injured by its rough treatment.

Here we met one of the farmers, who led a Commando against Secocoeni. He appeared a fine strong fellow, and a man who might naturally be selected; but the fact, I believe, was that he preferred seeing other people fight to fighting himself, and I believe that a good many others shared his views.

We were shown the process of tanning. A native red plant being steeped in water forms a strong astringent brine, said to be most effective, and to be quite as powerful as any bark for this purpose.

On our approach to Leydenburg we passed a small hotel, the only sign being the following words posted up on a square board:

"COME IN HERE AND HAVE YOUR DRINK,"

—a straightforward invitation, which few gold diggers, if they have any silver in their pockets, can refuse.

The country hereabouts is as pretty as a country can be which is devoid of trees; fine mountains rise on either hand, and lowering peaks in the distance, and streams flow in their stony beds. Much of it is as rocky as Connemara, as is generally the case in auriferous districts. While we were congratulating ourselves on our near approach to the centre city of the Gold Field region, a sudden crash snapped the perch of the carriage in two.

After an hour's detention we bound it up with the ever-valuable rim, and managed to reach the town of Leydenburg.

CHAPTER XXVI.

LEYDENBURG.

HERE we were received with great kindness and attention by Captain Clarke. He had just returned from an inspection of Johannes' Kraal, and had had a slight skirmish the day before with some natives, in which a princess had taken part. By firmness and judgment he had prevented a serious fight.

Leydenburg is situated in a large and fertile plain; the country round it is beautiful, and at some of the locations the finest land in the world is to be found. Wheat, considered to be nearly if not quite the best at the Paris Exhibition, was grown in this neighbourhood, and it is no wonder either that the farmers should be desirous of getting the land from the natives, or that the natives should wish to retain it.

Leydenburg is principally inhabited by Dutchmen, who possess very original opinions and stick to their old customs; they are particular upon points of religion. Not long since an altercation took place as to the unrighteousness of dancing, for which a party was tried by the synod, but on the trial an appeal was made to the court, and this appeal formed an important epoch in the history of the town.

The following was related to me by my aide-de-camp. Shortly before leaving Leydenburg, and while sitting sketching in front of the Paris Hotel, a man called Jack Sheppard offered him 10s. to make a portrait of a sailor called "Blue Skimmel," from his likeness to a singularly coloured horse.

This "Blue Skimmel" was as noted a character in the gold borders as was Jack Sheppard. Both had formed a part of the band of filibusters who fought under Von Schlickmann, and claimed credit for having stood beside Schlickmann when he was shot, although report said that everyone of his comrades had deserted him.

"Ah," said Jack Sheppard, "if your hanged Government had not stepped in we should have had a fine time of it, we intended to have helped ourselves, we did."

On the 30th of June we left Leydenburg at 9 A.M., having hired a waggon with twelve oxen and two Kafir drivers to carry our tents, cooking utensils, stores, and servants, at 1*l*. per day.

About five miles from Leydenburg we met Mr. Birch, a handsome gentleman with a foreign appearance and manner. He is the brother of Mr. Jullien, the great bandmaster, but has adopted the name of his mother, which was Birch. In conversation he admitted that he had taken a leading part in opposing our annexation of the Transvaal. He opposed it, he said, on patriotic grounds so long as the Republic existed, but now that the Proclamation was *un fait accompli*, and that the English ensign flew over the Government House at Pretoria, he would loyally support English rule.

He described the war, which had been carried on for about a year within a few miles of his own farm, as having been most ruinous to him, and he now looked for better times.

About seven miles further on we came to a beautiful glen called Spekboom, with a fine river running briskly through it. Here were some ruined houses, showing signs of having been destroyed by fire. They had been burned by the Kafirs in the war a few months previously, and in the woods, a few hundred yards from the river bank, were the remains of some bodies of the natives who had been shot in the engagement on that occasion. The Kafirs had driven the Boers from this house, and then used it as a hospital for their wounded; but they were in turn dislodged, which sealed the fate of the building.

We had great difficulty in getting our bullocks to face the opposite hill, but were assisted by two passing strangers, one of whom turned out to be of the name Reilly. He was another instance of steady honest conduct rewarded he was the son of a soldier in the Cape corps who had saved a little money. When wars were supposed to have become a thing of the past in South Africa, and his regiment was disbanded, he had found his way into the wilds of the Republic. After some hardships he had thriven, and his son was now the possessor of 10,000 acres of land joining the estate of Hortogh, where we had been shooting. In addition to this land he was the owner of 100 head of cattle, and some hundreds of sheep, horses, and waggons. His friend Mr. McLaughlin said that after he had made what he considered a tidy fortune, he had returned home to Ireland, where, as he expressed it, "he never saw the sun." When he had been there three months, he said, "This will never do for me, I am off again to South Africa." He felt himself more at home in the wild lands of the Dwasi, than in the city of Dublin.

A short distance to the north of "Spek Boom" a Boer farmer was said to have shot down one of his Kafir servants for the following reason:—It seems that the daughter of the Boer fell in love with a native, and after vainly beseeching her father to allow the marriage ran away with him. The father tracked them, and overtaking them, shot the young man, and ordered his daughter home with the remark, "Now that matter is completed, and we shall hear no more of it."

Towards the evening we reached Kruger's Port. A laager, or fortified post, had been formed about 500 yards distant from the house, which had been occupied during the last year by Mr. Glyn and his family and many of his neighbours, and from which he had had the mortification of seeing his house gutted by the Kafirs.

I examined this building, which had held out so long, and which evidenced the want of spirit and enterprise of the enemy. It was built without flank defences, and so placed as to be capable of approach by means of a ravine, which ran almost up to its walls.

The interior was divided into numerous small rooms, which had been crowded with the families of its defenders, who had brought their all into the camp, sacrificing their homesteads and farms.

This laager had been the abode of Mr. Glyn and his son and daughters for the eleven previous months, during the whole of which they had been continually exposed to an intermittent fire of musketry from the natives, and had been cooped up in little dark shanties, not larger and not nearly so well constructed as a pig-sty. Poor people! they must have been delighted when our annexation of the Transvaal brought security and a release from their troubles.

Some of their alarms were rather ludicrous, emanating from absurd sources. On one occasion a lady informed a police officer that certain Kafirs were hidden behind her kitchen in an outhouse, plotting mischief. The officer, understanding the Kafir language, went to listen, and discovered that the people were anxiously disputing as to which of their hens had laid the most eggs.

I met a Kafir who said, "Do you see that pony passing by? some three years since master exchanged me for that yellow cob."

Here I met some knob-nosed Kafirs. I had expected to have seen them with knobs like large apples or potatoes at the end of their noses, and I was somewhat disappointed to discover that, so far from this being the case, these natives were better formed and with more regular features than any I had yet seen in South Africa. On each side of their cheeks were rows of small pimples. These I was told had been produced by tying up the skin in little knots when the children were young, which had by no means an unpleasing effect.

These people are quiet and well-behaved, and considered to be valuable servants; they came from the north-east side of the Limpopo. They inhabit the country where the Ophir of King Solomon is supposed to have been, from whence wonderful accounts are transmitted at this day of the gold to be found in it. This territory is under the sway of Lo Bengula. Mr. Baines established a friendship with this chief, but when on the point of starting from Natal for his country, by permission of the king, he died. The 'Transvaal Argus' says:—

> From private sources I hear that the gold-fields in Mashona yield a splendid average of coarse gold and nuggets. Lo Bengula has forbidden any white man to enter the country without his special permission, and issued strict orders that no one is to dig or prospect. Repeated attempts have been made to gain the King's favour, and induce him to grant permission to explore the land, but with one result, in the sharply emphasized answer, "I refuse." The only one who could have successfully influenced him is now dead. Poor Baines! Not only have private individuals made application, but agents acting on behalf of companies. Some of these agents have not comported themselves at his capital in a manner calculated to excite respect, esteem, or confidence. Probably, if a well-accredited gentleman were entrusted with the mission, he might succeed in inducing Lo Bengula to open up the country to diggers and speculators.

A writer in the 'Diamond News' says:

> Lo Bengula appears to be a sad and merciless rascal; fleeces every white man that comes near him, and has turned the

Mashona country into a slaughter-house. He is desirous of keeping upon the best of terms with the British Government. He is doing his best by every artifice that he can devise to keep the white man out of his country. He knows full well that the Mashona country is the richest gold-field in South Africa, and he is afraid that if he permits the white man to go into that country he will lose his power over it. He does not like the intelligence that the British Government has annexed the Transvaal, because he thinks that that Government, being so close to him, will soon put an end to his incursions into the Mashona country, where he sends to slay and burn those who are too old to be made slaves of, and to kidnap all who are. He has always been determined to keep the Mashona gold-field sacred to himself. When permission was asked to go into the Mashona country, his first answer was, "There is no gold there." "Never mind that," said the applicant, "all I want is permission to go there." He then said, "If I tell you there is no meat in my pots, why will you not believe me? Why will you persist in having a look at them?" He was told Englishmen always liked to see new countries, and could sometimes see things which their owners could not see, but which it was good for the owner, as well as the prospector, should be discovered. He then said plainly, "I will not allow you to go into the country, for if I did I might as well give it you."

The chiefs of the Matabele have been renowned for being a savage set, but it is by no means impossible that the stories concerning Lo Bengula are very much exaggerated by those who are anxious to seek for gold. When two officers of the 32nd Regiment visited his country he received them with great attention, and they brought home the tusks of thirteen elephants. The knob-nosed Kafirs gave wonderful accounts of their native land in their imperfect style, telling us that minerals, and especially coffee, were so plentiful, and so pure that their knobkerries and their beads were generally made from it.

It is a very singular fact that the tenderness of meat, which depends among other things on the amount of time it has been kept, is greatly affected by electricity. The effect of a thunderstorm upon animal food is well known. It turns milk sour and meat bad. A moderate charge of electricity passed through freshly-killed meat is said to make it instantly fit for cooking. The same effect is produced at the Cape and elsewhere by placing it in contact with certain plants. In the Transvaal I have found that freshly-killed meat will become fit for eating in a few hours by being wrapped up in fig-leaves.

CHAPTER XXVII.

PILGRIMS' REST.

WE passed a night at Muller's Farm, a very fine estate, about ten miles this side of Pilgrims' Rest. There was an ugly story about some liquor which had been left during the war at a store near this.

Ill-natured persons said that it was poisoned and left as a temptation to the native rebels. I believe the truth to have been that the word poison which was written on the bottles was a hoax to prevent the contents being consumed by the Volunteers and Free Lances, who were crossing the country. The bottles are said to have been broken by a gentleman, who felt that some serious evil might result.

I was told that Van Muller was the owner of several farms at Pilgrims' Rest. He sold one for 25*l*. to a Mr. Strubos, who, on finding gold, sold it for 6240*l*.

Van Muller complained very much of the injury that was being done to him by the watercourses which were being dug across his lands in order to lead water to the gold diggings.

An enactment had been passed to include a certain area of country within the gold-bearing region, giving very extensive powers over the properties lying within it to certain appointed commissioners. Amongst these was the right to give sanction for watercourses to be dug to lead water to the mines. These furrows were cut along the hill sides, in some instances for miles, following carefully the curves of the mountain, and having regard to contour. They were frequently executed by self-taught engineers, and without theodolites or instruments, yet such was the exactness in gradual depression that the best instructed engineers could hardly have done better.

The proprietors of the lands have not the power of preventing these aqueducts being made; but a certain proportion of the charges for the right of digging is accorded to them, which gives them a very handsome remuneration, and I do not believe that Muller had, in reality, much cause of complaint.

The descent into the valley from the upper plateau is the most precipitous that I have yet witnessed for a wheeled carriage; indeed, no one who had not seen a waggon go down could believe it practicable.

We saw the mines of Pilgrims' Rest for hours before we reached them. The tents appeared like dots of white on the landscape. As we approached near the opposite side of the mountain it exactly represented an ant's nest, the busy workers creeping backwards and forwards in the golden sand.

We were kindly received by Mr. Bancroft, the most considerable merchant at the mines, and put up, much I am afraid to his own inconvenience.

Pilgrims' Rest is situated on a spur of the Drakensberg range, about 4000 feet above the sea, and not far from its eastern edge, where there is a steep descent into the lower country, which is little above the sea-level. It stands between two rivers, the "Crying" and the "Blyth" river. These are singular names, and have originated in the following circumstance:—On the first arrival of the pioneers, they left their families and went below the mountain to seek a new country. Not returning for a considerable time, the wives followed on their track; on reaching the edge of the mountain, however, they were afraid to descend, and set to crying, which gave the name to the river. Near to Mac-Mac, regaining courage, they tried to go down by another path, more towards the north. At the northern river they met their husbands returning, which made them happy, and the second river received the name of the "Blyth." It is there that the gold diggings called "Pilgrims' Rest" are situated. If at some future day an antiquary sets to investigating the names of these places, his task will be puzzling. No doubt there is not a village or hill in England the name of which has not originated from the doings of our forefathers. The men are forgotten, but the names of the places called after them, or after their exploits, remain, like fossils—marks of a state of society which has passed away for ever.

On the following morning, under the guidance of Mr. Gunn, the Commissioner, we were conducted for some miles through the diggings. They showed too clearly the arduous nature of the work, as well as its cruel uncertainty. The gold is found in hollow pockets, beneath the rocks, into which it has probably been washed down, from some high level, out of the interior of the mountain. But these pockets are not only covered over by the clayey soil, but by stupendous rocks and boulders, some of them far more than half the size of a moderately sized room.

To remove these, therefore, is an absolute necessity. How and by what means they are to be rolled away is the problem. The general method appeared to be, to dig a large hole below the rock, and then with levers and crowbars to cause the huge stone to roll into the newly excavated hollow. This completed, a careful search is made by digging down to the surface of the solid rock. The search is rewarded, generally indifferently, though occasionally magnificently.

At my visit Mr. Hoskyth was considered the most fortunate miner; he had arrived with a very small purse, but was said to be realising 300*l*. per week.

I never saw Kafirs work so hard as they did at these mines. Their wages appeared not at all extravagant for their labour; as they were rated at not more than twenty-five shillings per month, exclusive of their rations. The reason that their wages are low is, that immediately below the highlands on which the gold diggings are situated, there are countless numbers of natives of various races, so that the supply of labour is inexhaustible and continuous.

On the following morning, when we intended to have continued our journey to Spitskop, one of our horses had been let out of the stable and was not to be found. The linch-pin also, and the cover of the axle, had been removed, and the yokes of our oxen had been taken away. During the night we had heard a serenade by the diggers played upon tin pots, kettles, and banjos; and the boy who slept under our waggon said he saw the linch-pin being removed by this party, but he would not move lest he should be thrashed. I suspect that the linch-pin was removed at the instigation of the blacksmith, as he was the only person able to repair the damage, and seemed by no means surprised when informed of it. His charge for repairing it was 1*l*. 5*s*.

On leaving, Mr. Sheppeard insisted on presenting me with a specimen of gold, and on my firmly declining to accept it, he allowed me to purchase a beautiful specimen of virgin-ore of the weight of one ounce.

I then returned to Pretoria. In the interim, progress had been made in the cantonment, which evidenced the unremitting care of Colonel Montgomery. Watercourses had been cut, trees planted, a bathing house erected for the troops, wooden bedsteads made for the sick in large numbers, and a new hospital built. The houses had been partially covered in, and many other works had been carried out with zeal and energy.

I now used my best endeavours to complete the barracks for the soldiers of the 1-13th Regiment, in which the men gave immense assistance, both in levelling the ground, in making the bricks, in dressing the corner stones, in carpenter's work, and in preparing the thatching. It was now that the advantages of the workshops were most fully brought into light. No one who witnessed the handiwork of the 1-13th Regiment, from their Colonel downwards, would say that the British soldier is either idle or unskilful. If such an accusation ever had any truth in it, it was owing to the old want of system which encouraged idleness, rather than useful habits, which cannot fail, not only to be most valuable to the man himself and as a soldier, but to the community in general. In place of the soldier who used to return to his native village more ignorant of social requirements than when he left it on the day of his enlistment, a very large number of the army return, not only well acquainted with the three R's, but with confirmed habits of regularity and sobriety.

The officers set the very best example of industry. Indeed, they were obliged to work for themselves. I remember that on one occasion an officer of the commissariat was at work mending the leg of his table, which he finished very artistically. A master carpenter, who was passing by, asked him if he would work for him, saying, "I see you know your business; if you will chum along with me, I will give you 18s. a day and your grub."

An excellent canteen had also been established, not upon the old grog-drinking principle, but to supply the soldiers with every requisite article at a moderate price. I have heard the officers ridiculed for their knowledge of the business of a grocer. For my part, I think it highly creditable to them to have devoted their time, gratuitously, to the increase of the soldiers' comfort, and to the proper saving of the expenses of our army. I believe the invention of the canteen system is due to Lord Airey, and I believe, also, that it is the canteen which has given rise to the modern co-operative store, which has sprung from that source rather than from the celebrated efforts of the "Rochdale Pioneers."

Before finally quitting Pretoria, I desired to satisfy myself in regard to the position it was requisite to choose for the cavalry, and to decide which road should be adopted for military transport from Natal. With this object I again started south, proceeding this time through Heidelberg. The country bore the usual character, though more progress appeared to have been made. Heidelberg showed evident signs of improvement. Lying as it does on what is now the high road to the south, it will, no doubt, become a thriving town. We passed through it, but, missing the proper road, had to halt in the veldt.

One of our mules here became very ill, but he recovered, under the advice of a countryman, as the result of a singular operation. The animal was swelled out, probably by eating too much young grain. Our friend said, "I should stab him in the stomach;" and, taking a penknife, he gave the poor beast a blow driving the knife up to the handle, saying "This lets the wind out, I think he will soon recover." It had an excellent effect, the mule was relieved, and improved from that moment.

Two days afterwards we found ourselves again in Standerton. There I had directed an engineer officer and a medical officer to meet me, together with the officer commanding the cavalry, so that after hearing their opinions the situation of the new cavalry camp might be decided upon. It was most advisable that there should be as little delay as possible. The cold season was rapidly passing, and it was of the most material consequence that the men, and if possible the horses, should be secured before the hot and rainy season set in.

We succeeded in our selection of the site of the new cantonment, beyond my most sanguine expectation, and I trust no unforeseen circumstance has shown that its merits are not equal to our expectations.

My next duty was to establish the best road. For the purpose of examining the eastern one I struck across the country and followed it carefully up to Pretoria.

At Browne's farm the seams of coal lay very near the house, and were so productive as to induce me to give instructions that waggons and men should be sent over from Pretoria to procure coal.

Mr. Browne had given 150*l.* for his farm of 7300 acres about three years before. He seemed pleased that he had last year refused about ten times this amount, which was before the coal had been found.

My staff officers entered with delight into the sport of hog hunting, which in this country is quite equal, if it is not superior, to anything that can be enjoyed in India.

The wild boar of the Transvaal is different from that of India, or of Europe. It is a wiry, active, game animal, and smaller in size. It is called the Stump ear, from a curious bossy substance which grows near the eye.

It is found in the grass of the veldt, and generally near water. On being discovered it sets off at a tremendous pace, with its short tail erect in the air, and it requires a good horse to overtake it. It is savage when pressed, and will turn upon the horseman, and, as its tusks are quite equal in size and sharpness to the common boar, it will give most dangerous wounds.

My staff officers were unfortunately not provided with hog spears, and although they attempted, when they heard of these animals, to have rough substitutes forged, they found them useless, and were obliged to use their short carbines. I have no doubt that this will ere long be a favourite amusement in South Africa. It will be most useful for developing the attributes so useful in a soldier; eye, hand, a firm seat, courage and activity.

There is an interesting salt pan north of Pretoria. It is fully a mile across and from 300 to 400 feet deep. On descending to the margin, we found it consisted of brine, mixed with mud, which resembled ice covered with dirty snow. The pan was nearly circular. Some young native women were employed in picking up salt and putting it in baskets.

The right of conveying the salt from this lake had been sold annually for a very small sum by the late Government. Just before the annexation the pan was pawned for 400*l.*, under the condition that if it should not be redeemed within six months it should become the property of the lender. Fortunately, just before the expiration of the period named, the circumstance came to the knowledge of the admininistrator, who signed an order for the advance of the money, and saved the Government what may possibly within a year or two produce more than 500*l.* per annum.

The salt mine at Pretoria is more valuable on account of the high price which salt fetches in the Transvaal. I was told that—

	£	s.	d.
A ton of salt costs at Liverpool about	0	11	0
Its freight to Durban is	3	10	0
Carriage to Pretoria	20	0	0
Transvaal duty	3	10	0
Extras	1	10	0
Profit to trader	4	0	0
Total	£33	1	0

If this statement regarding salt is at all true, and I was assured that it was, my readers can easily understand why European goods are only to be bought in the country at a very high price.

CHAPTER XXVIII.

START FOR THE RETURN JOURNEY.

WE now bade farewell to Pretoria.

Shortly after leaving the city, we met parties of natives returning from the Diamond Fields towards Secocoeni's country. Every one of these men was armed with a rifle, the proceeds of their labours at the mines, and they were returning with it to their friends and their chief.

I examined some of these arms, and although they were not all of superior manufacture, they were not at all bad, and quite equalled those with which the 60th Rifles were armed in 1830. These very rifles are now being used against our troops in the north-east of the Transvaal.

About twenty miles from Pretoria is a remarkable mountain, much resembling Gibraltar in its appearance. Near it we came to a most fearful chasm in the road, over which we were fortunate enough to struggle, but where our mule cart came to grief.

Before reaching Brandt Vley our cart had again to be dragged out of a mud hole.

Here we met with a waggon with more than three or four tons of goods, all of which had to be unloaded and carried over the mud hole by hand, and reloaded on the other side. This enabled the waggon to get past the obstruction, showing clearly one of the reasons of the expense of land carriage, and why each article from the coast must, in addition to its original price, be charged at the rate of from 9d. to 10d. per lb. weight.

I had not sufficient time at my disposal to halt and examine the caves near Wolverman's, which are said to be very remarkable and extensive. The evening was getting dark, and we had to look out for a suitable spot where we could outspan and encamp for the night, and where we could find water and some fuel, as we had learned to be independent of everything else.

We passed no water for miles. When almost pitch dark we met a buggy, drawn by a pair of ponies, the only vehicle except ox-waggons which we had yet seen on the high road between the two capital towns of the Transvaal. This cart contained the post of the district, who gave us the pleasing information that for eighteen miles more we should meet neither with water nor fuel for man or beast. We therefore at once called a halt, outspanned for an hour, and proceeded again in the darkness. One of my orderlies held a lantern, and led the way, on my excellent shooting horse called Cape Town, giving notice of the pit-falls, mud holes, and other obstructions which lay in our path. The driver in the Cape cart was provided with a powerful railway whistle, so that he could give us notice when we got too far ahead of him, or of any difficulties which he might encounter.

After three hours of this somewhat dangerous travelling we received notice of a deep sprint or watercourse traversing the road. We selected a spot to cross, which appeared in the darkness to promise us success, but as we were on the point of emerging from the muddy obstruction, a heavy splash and bang was followed by the discovery that our pole was smashed into two pieces, and was dangling between the wheel-mule's legs.

Thus an outspan was now compulsory. Fortunately a violent barking of dogs at some distance told us that a farm was near. We sent there to purchase forage for our tired teams, but the Boer declared that he possessed nothing. We had no resource but to turn our eleven mules and ten horses adrift to stray at their own discretion. Hastily running up my little tent in the dark, I was glad enough to lie down on the ground, the rest of the men sleeping in and under the waggon and the cart. First, however, we were lucky enough to find sufficient fuel to cook a strong cup of coffee for all hands.

On waking on the morning of the 8th of August we found that horses and mules had disappeared, and as there was a heavy fog we had to wait till it cleared, when, after some careful spooring and some hours' delay, we regained our cattle, and inspanned.

With the returning light we found that two parties of Kafirs had rested in our immediate vicinity, one of which was proceeding to the Diamond Fields, the other returning. The contrast between those who composed the two parties was very marked.

Those going were a set of miserable half-starved wretches, with scarcely a rag to cover their nakedness, with no blankets, and shivering with the morning cold. Each of those returning was bearing his load of blankets. He had a good corduroy suit and a wide-awake hat, with jaunty feathers, and was so fat and so sleek-looking, that it was a pleasure to think that he could secure such satisfactory results from industry in the white man's service. Of course each carried a rifle.

A point in South African travel, which deserves a remark, is the almost certain immunity from camp pilferings. It is but rare that any robberies of horses take place. I speak, of course, of quiet times, when social disturbances are not abroad.

Natives may come near, but nothing is taken; property may be freely left about, yet none is "lifted." This will appear singular to any one who has led a travelling-camp life in India, as the first care on camping there is to inform the head of the neighbouring village that he is held responsible, in case any theft takes place; and as a small black mail is generally, as a necessity, both expected and paid.

When about fifteen miles from Potchefstrom we arrived at a fine farm called Wolverman's. The owner was very civil and agreeable. He told me that thirty-five years before, his father trekked from the colony and settled on this spot; that he brought with him four married children and seven unmarried, being accompanied by his servants, his stock, his waggons, and all his earthly goods; that the old man had died last year, being 85 years of age, and had left 160 children and grandchildren alive; and that he himself had now 16 children and 21 grandchildren alive, and the older ones were all doing well.

His estate measured about 30,000 acres of land, with a large farm-house and extensive offices, which had been erected by the industry of his father and himself. He said he would have no objection to trek further into the interior, and was ready to part with his estate for 5000*l.*, but as gold has since been reported to have been found in his neighbourhood, an alteration may have taken place in his views since last year.

The farm may be a great deal in excess of 30,000 acres, for I fancy that land is seldom carefully measured, the common method being for a horseman to gallop from landmark to landmark, calculating the size of the farm by the time of his doing so, and not by any accurate measurement. It is said that at Pretoria, some years since, a Government Commissioner measured more than sixty farms of 6000 acres each in one day. Each farm was rated at 3000 *morgen*, which is about equal to 6000 acres, but when really measured it was frequently found to be 9000, or even 12,000.

The measurement of one block of land, which was given out as 160,000 acres, when triangulated was proved to equal 240,000.

So far as I can judge, I think the Transvaal is as fine as any farming country in the world, and I have travelled in many lands.

It is eminently suited for the cultivation of cereals, as the ground is level. At present the progress of this truly magnificent country is retarded on account of its very sparse population. There is some difficulty, too, in getting out from

Europe. Moreover, the Government of the Transvaal has no land to give away, the greatest part having been already in the hands of Dutch farmers, who either do not occupy it or who cultivate only one-twentieth part of their holdings. It is said that the only plan to overcome this difficulty is a very serious one, and the only way to remove it would be by a heavy tax upon the unoccupied farms. The tax should be imposed so gradually that the owners would have time to get rid of their surplus. In this manner the Government might in time acquire some land which it could dispose of as I have indicated. The country is very rich in resources, the climate is excellent, and it is a pity that its advantages should not be developed by an enterprising and industrious population.

Fearing some such law, the great land owners are now most anxious to obtain settlers, and are ready to give them land on very advantageous terms.

Near to Wolverman's, an auriferous deposit has recently been discovered. I quote from a report concerning it.

The Cape Commercial Bank have lately sent home seven ounces of native gold that have been found at Blaauw bank, in this neighbourhood; if this exists to any considerable extent a great revolution in this neighbourhood must arise.

The life of the Wolverman's family, common to all people of their class, was very patriarchal. Twenty-four members of the circle sat down to their meals three times each day, the seniors towards the upper end of the board above the salt. All passing strangers who appeared respectable were welcome guests, and no remuneration was in general demanded even for the forage for their horses from the farm. Everything in the old-fashioned establishment forcibly reminded me of the description of the good old days of England.

At Wolverman's we met a disconsolate mason, returning to

his native town. After some years of labour in the Free State, during which he had saved a considerable sum, he had determined to try his luck once and for all at the Diamond Fields. He had purchased a claim, and worked it steadily for five weary months, assisted by half-a-dozen native labourers. During this time he had never found a single diamond. He had expended all his savings, and was now returning to begin life again. This is the fate of many, but the success of the few encourages the others, and there are those who, with no better prospects originally than this mason had, find themselves in a few years in such a state of prosperity as to enable them to return home with considerable fortunes, or purchase extensive properties in the colonies.

We met with very many curious names. A singular custom prevails amongst the Boers of calling their children after remarkable events which happened at the time of their birth, such as "Coronation," when the king or queen was crowned; "Expedition," on the occasion of a particular expedition against the natives; or after the name of some officer who has visited their farms, such as "Shepstone," "Clerke," or "Barkly," as this is the readiest means of reminding them of the dates of their birth.

CHAPTER XXIX.

POTCHEFSTROM.

We arrived at Potchefstrom about noon, and were met by the Landrost, who welcomed me most kindly to his city, and Chevalier Fossman, the Consul-General of Portugal, begged us to accept rooms at his house.

Chevalier Fossman has been in South Africa for more than twenty-five years. He is a man of great foresight and energy of character, and has had the sagacity to see the great position which this country is sure to fill in the world. By prudence and careful management he has become the possessor of an enormous and indeed princely property. Its extent in the aggregate is at least 800,000 acres or 1250 square miles, so that he is certainly the largest land owner in South Africa. Nor must it be imagined that this immense area consists of sandy deserts. His farms are all surveyed, all registered, and a printed description of each is in his office. With few exceptions, they consist of fine corn-growing lands, largely abounding in minerals—coal, iron, lead, silver, and gold.

A large proportion of his property is so situated as to be but little likely to suffer from the inroads of natives or from frontier disturbances.

The Chevalier said to me, "What I want is emigrants." He has seen many changes in his position since his arrival in the Transvaal. I understood him to be a Swede by birth. One of his earliest successful speculations is said to have been the bringing down a giraffe, which he had purchased in the Zoutspanberg for 22*l.* 10*s.*, through the desert Karoo to Cape Town. He made 200*l.* by showing the animal in the different towns he passed on his way, and he sold it for 170*l.* on his arrival.

He was very nearly as successful with a hippopotamus or sea-cow. His men had caught a fine specimen of this ferocious beast, for which he was to receive 500*l.*, but when he looked into the pit in which it had been confined, on the following morning, he found that the Kafirs had killed it during the night.

The immense area of country which he possesses has been obtained by purchase from the individuals who received it in government grants, no doubt frequently at little more than nominal prices. The Chevalier was using every endeavour to induce settlers to come to the country, and offering most advantageous conditions for his farms. He said he was willing to let them on the terms of receiving half produce, and that he would also lend the use of his ploughs and oxen, while at the termination of ten years or so the farm would become the property of the settler.

These terms appear to me most advantageous to emigrants, more especially when the excellence of the climate and the fertility of the soil are taken into account.

The tax, as I understood, upon each farm of 6000 acres is about 1*l.* 16*s.* per annum, or about 200*l.* a year for the 120 farms. Sorry as I should be to recommend anything that would be disagreeable to the Chevalier, I should like to see the unoccupied land more heavily taxed, which would not only be of immense advantage to the Transvaal and to federated South Africa, but would even prove a benefit to the land owners themselves.

I am now constantly asked the question as to whether I can recommend young men to emigrate to the Transvaal, and what a young man should do when he gets there. My answer is to ask: "Is your friend strictly sober? is he prudent, painstaking and methodical? is he possessed of a tolerably good constitution? and can he command from 500*l*. to 1000*l*.?"

In that case he will be welcomed in the new country, without much of an introduction, but he must be careful on his arrival not to involve himself in any speculation until he has learned something of the Dutch language and gained some insight into the people. Above everything he must be careful how he engages in farming operations before he has become well acquainted with the country. His character will be very soon known, and his services greedily sought; after which, time and his own sagacity will soon win for him a competence.

The drawback to intending emigrants to the Transvaal, and especially to those with families, is the great distance which they are compelled to travel before they can arrive at the field of action, and the consequent expense and loss of time involved. Facilities are now placed in their way by English companies.

It was reported in South Africa that the King of the Belgians was once desirous of making an arrangement with the Transvaal Republic for an exclusive emigration from Belgium to that country. There are no people who would meet with a more earnest welcome. Their industry and aptitude for all sorts of work are proverbial. The Belgians are excellent artisans, generally abstemious, and there can be no doubt of their success.

It was stated in the newspapers that Baron Silys de Fason advised President Burgers to put Sir T. Shepstone over the frontier into Natal, to prevent the organisation of Colonel Weatherley's volunteers, and to place their chief under arrest. He was convinced that Sir Theophilus would never make the annexation by force. This advice, I can understand, might have been politic, as he might have had hopes of making a better arrangement for his countrymen with the Republic than with the British Government. But the statement adds:

At the same time I discouraged the emigration of my countrymen to this country. For those reasons I was perhaps a "calamity to the Transvaal," but I preferred to study the interests of Belgium, and my conduct met the approval of the Government.

I cannot understand the Baron's views, for it is almost incredible that he can have supposed that the Republic would have been allowed to annex itself to Belgium.

I made an excursion to a neighbouring farm of 10,000 acres, which had lately been purchased by Captain Baillie, formerly an officer in the Blues. His occupation is horse-breeding. With this view he has imported some of the best thoroughbred stock procurable in England, and purchased from forty to fifty mares in the colony and the Free States. The greatest enemy that he has is the sickness to which horses in this portion of the Transvaal are so liable. I strongly advised him to purchase another estate near Standerton, where his stock could graze on the high veldt during the hot season in comparative immunity, and where, should he desire to change his own position temporarily, he would meet with many members of his former profession.

Captain Baillie had selected the Transvaal as his residence from the known excellence of climate for those who cannot bear the damp and cold winters of England.

At home he had never enjoyed a day's real health, whereas, both in the Free States and in the Transvaal, he had never known a day's sickness.

I next drove round the city. Great improvements were in

progress, and I was informed that property had doubled in value since the annexation.

Opposite to one store I observed many hundreds of pigs of lead, with the word "Bray" stamped upon them. I was told that they came from a lead mine not very distant from the city, a successful speculation of two young men who came into this country as engineers. I learned that they had purchased the farm on which the mine is for about 100*l*.; that the lead is very pure; that the silver which is extracted from it pays the expenses of working, and that the profit already accruing from it amounts to many thousands a year.

This lead does not find its market by leaving the Transvaal for the south, but is sold to traders on the Limpopo and the Zambesi for elephant shooting, and to the natives to supply the thousands of muskets which have been permitted to pass into their possession, from which many a bullet may yet find its billet in a British soldier's breast.

There was an amusing story regarding the Landrost. A happy couple came into Potchefstrom from the country to be "spliced." The bridegroom, having succeeded in obtaining the loan of a hat from one storekeeper, and a pair of boots from another, went with his young woman to the Landrost and had the matrimonial knot securely tied. The ceremony over, the Landrost found that the happy man had not the means to satisfy his demand for fees. His worship, therefore, refused to give the bride up, and detained her in court until the money should be forthcoming. The man's frantic endeavours to raise 15*s*. were heartrending, but he at last succeeded.

We now encamped near Mander's house. Mander is a pleasant old person, the owner of a fine, though not very extensive, farm, possessing some good pans of water. Finding the game plentiful, we determined to go in pursuit of them. We were well rewarded for so doing, for we brought home five blueback and two wildebeest. In the afternoon we came upon a fine pan of water, and as the neighbouring country was dry for many miles, all the game, wildebeest, blessbok, and springbok, had collected in thousands in its neighbourhood. Studying well the quarters from which the wind blew and circling round widely to windward (for in Africa the game always run up wind) we made sure that the entire flock would pass within a few hundred yards.

Alarmed by our appearance, yet obedient to the laws of their nature, the mass started, and for a considerable time the plain appeared literally alive with the countless numbers which defiled before us; hundreds and hundreds of wildebeests wildly dashing for their lives across the veldt, intermixed with thousands of blessbok and springbok. The pace was terrific, and the dust blinding, so as to render any certain aim impossible; but it was a magnificent sight, such as can seldom be seen but in the wide-spread plains of South Africa. The blessbok, and in fact all antelopes, are in their nature much like sheep, and religiously follow their leader, perfectly regardless or unconscious where he is conducting them. Mr. O——, who had a large tract of land in the east of the Free States, told me that upon one occasion he came across a very large herd of blessbok, which rushed towards a steep precipice, where, being hard pressed, the leader jumped over, and each of the animals successively followed. The descent was over the sheer face of the rock, and many perished below; the remainder, threading their way up a ravine, came again in sight of the tail of the herd, which was pressing wildly on the path they themselves had taken. Obedient, however, to their instinct, they followed on, and a second time leapt the precipice. This extraordinary movement continued for some time, many more being added each time to those who perished, and the result being that several waggon loads of dead deer were collected and skinned. The story may seem extraordinary to those who are not acquainted with the nature of the game on these plains; but it is by no means incredible by those who know the country.

On the following day we moved on to Bultfontein. Here, through the kind attention of Major Lanyon, the Administrator of Griqualand West, my mail reached me, as he had directed a policeman to convey it a distance of ninety-five miles across the veldt.

CHAPTER XXX.

THE TRANSVAAL, FARMING-SPORT.

The farmers of the Transvaal are excellent people, but children in the art of government. They complained of the war, and desired the remission of war-taxes. They complained that they were now bound to pay taxes, not at their own pleasure, but at regular periods, and that they were compelled to attend the courts of justice when summoned. Although most of them had far more land than they could manage, everybody desired more. To show how primitive these Boers are, I may narrate the following story:—

A schoolmaster was lately appointed in Zoutspanberg. One of his earliest lessons was to teach the children that the world turns on its own axis. He also endeavoured to make them understand the revolutions of the heavenly bodies. The children went home and were impertinent to their parents, and told them that the earth went round the sun. The elders of the district met and consulted regarding these new doctrines, and finally agreed to refer the subject to the minister, who requested the schoolmaster to explain. The schoolmaster said: "I teach them nothing but the movements of the heavenly bodies, and that the earth revolves round the sun. The minister answered, "Well, this may be true, no doubt, and what the earth does in Holland; but it would be more convenient at present if in the Zoutspanberg you would allow the sun still to go round the earth for a few years longer; we do not like sudden changes in such matters." The schoolmaster took the hint, and for the present the sun is allowed in Zoutspanberg to move as heretofore. The power of a minister of a parish is very great. A great deal depends upon him for the improvement and well-being of the town. Many a time it has been said to me when I observed that a town was flourishing, "Yes, we are fortunate in our minister;" and when it was falling backward it was, "Ah, all will alter when we get rid of our present minister."

To show the minister's influence over his parishioners, I will quote from a local paper a circumstance that occurred in the colony :—

This town is in a state of excitement at present, owing to the minister of the Dutch Reformed Church having refused to present a young lady to the congregation. The uncle of the girl thus details the circumstances in a letter of complaint to the minister. "Some months ago you confirmed my niece; last week you refused to present her, as a member of the church, a girl of unimpeachable character, before the congregation. Why? Because on Old Year's Night she danced in a private house with some young friends. The sin was so unpardonable in your sight that you at once went to my sister, the mother of the girl, a poor widow, and told her with much Christian charity and admonition that you could not 'present' her daughter, but that she would have to do penance three months for her sins, thus putting her under the ban of the church."

One evening I was resting in my tent while a knot of Kafirs were conversing outside. I heard the following remarks. A Kafir who had been partly educated at a Mission Station was expatiating upon the grandeur of the Queen, when he was answered by another, who said : "Why, friend, we are all well aware of the grandeur of her Majesty; not only is she the Queen of the Ocean, but her son is the Prince of Whales, ' Unconi' Yeamanina."

On the following morning a serious dispute as to the annexation of the Transvaal arose between two young Dutch farmers who accompanied us. From arguments they soon came to blows, and descending from their horses squared up in good English style. They had many rounds. The endeavours of the partisan of England were directed to knocking the wind out of his adversary with his fists, while the supporter of the late Republic attempted to effect a like result by planting blow after blow adroitly in the pit of his adversary's stomach with his right foot, causing him to gulp most strenuously. Fortunately his foot was only encased in a light shoe, of the untanned leather usually worn by the Boers.

I had now finished my military arrangements in the Transvaal, stationing the main body at Pretoria, and the mounted force at Standerton, and establishing an intermediate position at Newcastle between the Transvaal and Natal.

In case of disturbance or disaffection I saw that there were many military elements which could be called out in addition to her Majesty's troops, and that a considerable number of European gentlemen, upon whom every reliance could be placed, were very ready to give their assistance.

I proposed, in case of necessity, to form two separate forces from this civil element: one composed of young Dutch farmers, all excellent horsemen, well acquainted with the country and the natives, very hardy in their natures, men who, accustomed to privations, can resist the climate by night and the sun by day; and who, if led by British officers, would ere long, I feel convinced, emulate the Cossack, of whose attributes they possess so large a share.

The next would be a force raised from those from our parent island, who have come out to make their fortunes and failed, partly perhaps from their own recklessness and want of foresight, and partly through the force of circumstances.

These men are full of energy, dash and bravery, and though

very difficult to command, they would, under well-selected British officers of determination, prove most valuable.

I intended that both these corps should be mounted, and I have every reason to believe that my recommendations have been accepted, and that their services are proving most valuable.

There were excellent officers living in the Transvaal, who had proved themselves thoroughly capable, both in Europe and in India, such as Colonel Witherby and Sir Maurice Barlow, who, I am sure, would readily give their services to the Government if occasion required. Added to these, slender police forces of Europeans and native Zulus were already organised, which could readily be increased. They were commanded by a very superior officer of the Royal Artillery.

It is now proper that I should offer some remarks upon Shooting in the Transvaal. My military duties never permitted me to spend the time requisite to go in search of large game, such as the elephant, but with most other kinds I was very successful.

Although I had had great experience in other countries, I found that, like everything else, the art of hunting in South Africa requires to be learned. The points which it is requisite first to consider are, what description of shooting will satisfy the sportsman? what time has he at his disposal? and what amount of money does he propose to devote to his amusement?

To go to South Africa for the purpose of shooting pheasants and partridges, and such small game, would be ludicrous, though it exists, and is still found abundantly in the colony. Where it is common, the covert, however, is thick and impenetrable, causing great fatigue in its pursuit.

The shooting therefore in South Africa may be widely placed under three heads:

1st. The elephant, giraffe, and rhinoceros.

2nd. The buffalo, eland, hartebeest, sea-cow, zela.

3rd. The antelope, the gnu or wildebeest, the blessbuck, springbuck, and other small deer, such as the diker, the bluebuck, the bushbuck.

To enjoy elephant shooting, it is now requisite to devote to the sport a long period, at least eighteen months, and to make careful preparation for it. With this object I should recommend a waggon and oxen to be purchased, and the start to be made from Port Elizabeth. The waggon will cost about 140*l*., and sixteen oxen at least 160*l*. Two or three native servants should be engaged, and in addition a large supply of rifles, ammunition, and fowling-pieces or guns, as they are universally called in South Africa, should be taken from England, as presents for chiefs and headmen, and clothes and handkerchiefs and cheap ornaments for the women.

Some persons imagine that by laying in a trading stock their expenses will be covered, but I believe this to be a great mistake. Your party become traders or competitors with the merchants in the markets, and instead of commanding their assistance, you will naturally meet with hindrance, and the chiefs will not receive you with the same respect and cordiality as if you came to them as English gentlemen, travelling not for profit but for amusement.

It is quite true that two officers under my command, starting from King William's Town, travelled to Potchefstrom, and thence by Bangwangwallo into Lo Benguela's country, and having made great friends with this chief, were permitted by him to enter his elephant preserves. They were fortunate enough to kill fourteen elephants, the tusks of which were presented to them by the chief, so that their ivory nearly covered their expenses. But these officers went under very exceptional circumstances. They took with them letters from the High Commissioner in South Africa, and Lo Benguela, being anxious to court his favour, said at once that he would be delighted to obey the Governor's wishes, and give his servants what they desired. But the affair had somewhat of an awkward termination, for when the officers left, the chief wrote to his Excellency and said that he had fulfilled his desires, that his servants had met with some success, and he requested that *two pieces of cannon* might be sent him in return. This request was a very embarrassing one, as Lo Benguela's country borders on the Transvaal, and he might at any moment have been at war with us.

The Duke of Edinburgh killed elephants much nearer at hand, near the mouth of the Knysna river, between Mossel Bay and Port Elizabeth, but it was under exceptional circumstances. There are very dense and extensive forests in that locality reaching almost down to the sea, in which several herds of elephants are now to be found; but great care and circumspection were used to have the animals spoored and watched, and every possible arrangement was made to insure success.

There are herds of wild elephants within thirty miles of Port Elizabeth, on the line which the railroad has taken, and they have been reported as having committed some damage to the railroad, as the following extract from the 'Uitenhage Times' will show :

ELEPHANTS.—We ('Uitenhage Times') hear that a large troop of elephants have been seen near Grassridge. They have been doing a great deal of damage in the neighbourhood, and our informant states that the country, after they have crossed it, looks more like a well-used waggon-road than anything else. The elephants are said to be over one hundred strong; and the farmers are talking of organising a party to go in pursuit of them. Their haunts may be easily reached from Prentice Kraal, and we wonder that some of our celebrated rifle shots do not take advantage of the occasion to win an everlasting name for themselves.

Living as they do in comparative civilisation, these animals are far more wary and savage than those which are to be found farther from home.

No doubt other directions may be taken for elephant and rhinoceros, but the falls of the Zambesi appear to be the best country, and they can only be visited under the good auspices of the Chief of the Matabele, whose country lies between the Limpopo and the Zambesi rivers.

Some travellers have been exceedingly fortunate in gaining the good opinion and friendship of the potentates in the Matabele country. The success of one noted sportsman was owing to the fancy which was conceived for him by the chief's daughter, who, having great influence with her father, was able to obtain for him the permission which he coveted, of hunting at pleasure in the choicest part of his elephant grounds.

As regards the shooting in the neighbourhood of and on the Limpopo, Mr. Bulton, who is thoroughly acquainted with the country, recommended me to write to Mr. Cox, who, he said, would make arrangements with a Boer farmer, of the name of Barron Foister, who resides near Zoutspanberg. He is a famous hunter, and he goes every season—about the end of June—towards the borders of the Limpopo, into the forests, which abound with game, although not perhaps with the elephant and rhinoceros. By making timely plans with Barron Foister, there can be but little doubt that splendid sport would be obtained. Unfortunately, however, the whole of the country is at this moment in a very excited state, and the natives very well armed, so that it might prove hazardous to form shooting parties in these districts.

The third class of shooting is that which I had many opportunities of enjoying, both in the Free States and in the Transvaal, and to which in the course of my tours I have frequently alluded.

Although it is looked upon with disdain by the great

hunters of South Africa, I am not sure but that it affords more enjoyment than either of the former. One cause of its being despised by the regular huntsman, is that it affords no profit; but in my opinion the enjoyment of hard gallops over the plains after the game, and the pleasure of successfully stalking them, and bringing them down, repay any little hardship and privation which may be met with in its pursuit.

In the high veldt the wildebeest, the blessbuck, and the springbuck are almost the only antelopes which are now to be met with. These inhabit the open plains, as the blackbuck with its beautiful spiral horns does in India.

The eland, the koodoo, the zebra, and the hartebeest, which were largely to be found in the Free State in the days of Harris, have almost entirely disappeared.

There is also the stump-ear pig, which is now shot in large numbers, but which would afford us fine runs and as much sport with the hog-spear as any pig in India, with this advantage, that there is better galloping-ground on the high veldt in the Transvaal, where it is found, than is generally to be met with in the East Indies.

I may mention that in my opinion the best ground for this kind of hunting in the Transvaal is to be found in a tract of country on the Widge river, the Rheinoster river, and the Elephant river, about sixty miles to the east of Pretoria.

For these sports good horses are required; but as the winter months—June, July, August, and September—are the most agreeable to enjoy them, and the country is specially cool and free from horse sickness at that time, salted horses are scarcely required, and unsalted animals at about 30$l.$ each may readily be purchased in the Free States or in the Transvaal.

The sporting in the colony of the Cape of Good Hope itself, is of a different character. In the neighbourhood of Port Elizabeth, at the hospitable farm of Mr. Lovemore, at Bushy Park, near Kinblebosh, it is excellent; as well as in the Perie Bush, in the lower Amatotas, the great stronghold of Sandilli in the last war.

Bushbuck shooting may be had, but for this beaters driving the woods are required. Lower down in the colony, and in the neighbourhood of the Cape, the bluebuck, the diker, the reybuck, and steinbuck are commonly met with. They are generally killed by the Dutch farmers from their horses, and in this sport they are exceedingly expert. The country where they resort is excessively dry and parched, and the habits of these bucks are in accordance with it. I quote in regard to them some remarks by Commandant Bowker, a veteran sportsman, and a naturalist after whom many rare new species of insects have been named.

Wild bucks feed chiefly at night while the dew is falling, or during damp or wet days, and, I think, seldom or never drink water. The bushbuck, bluebuck, diker, reybuck, and steinbuck are found in spots on the coast, where fresh water is not obtainable. Having for many years taken an interest in the subject, and whenever an opportunity offered examined pools, I seldom, or never, found traces of any of the above-named bucks frequenting them for drinking. The question is an interesting one. Sheep, I have no doubt, if confined to a paddock, would soon follow the same course; feed during the night, and cool of the morning and evening, and rest during the heat of the day. There would be, however, one great difference. Wild as well as tame bucks prefer to grass the leaves of trees, bushes, or succulent plants, fruit, and roots (the bitter apple as well as the potato being great favourites with the diker). As I have stated, my notes apply to the coast line; but I have no doubt that the antelopes of the interior are much less dependent upon water than the sheep and cattle.

The above remarks will show that no sporting tour can be

made in South Africa, without devoting some little time to it, and that one cannot be carried out without some considerable amount of expense. For elephant shooting in the interior, eighteen months at least must be taken, and a first outlay of at least 1000*l.*, in waggons and horses, cattle, rifles, ammunition, presents to chiefs, &c., may be calculated on.

Once these are provided, the expense of living is little more than nominal, and the wages to the attendants are by no means large.

If good fortune attends the expedition, the prices on the sale of the above articles will equal their first cost; but oxen may die, waggons may break down, chiefs may be found difficult to deal with, and fever and disease may overtake the party. Success is probably as common as failure; but neither can be commanded, though the sportsmanlike qualities of those who undertake the adventure will have much to do with the result.

For shooting either below the High Veldt, or for milder work on the plains, the chief expense is that of horses and their forage, the last being exceedingly dear. The feed of each horse averages 3*s.* or 4*s.* a day. Otherwise, if luxuries are not a necessity, there is no great expense attendant on a tent life, and the freedom and health which are inseparable from it amply compensate for the small inconveniences which must be encountered.

Second-class shooting may be obtained by landing at Durban in Natal, and thence proceeding to the Gold Fields, where a waggon with oxen can be hired at about 1*l.* sterling per day, including the driver. Horses can be purchased in the eastern part of the Transvaal, at Utrecht, or in the neighbourhood of Newcastle, in Natal.

The safest and best time to start from the Gold Fields is the commencement of June. It is the healthiest and the coolest season in the year, and the dreaded fly is then least active.

At the present moment, an expedition towards the low

country, below the Gold Fields, would be difficult, and open to danger, as the country is disturbed by the war with Cetewayo, and towards the Limpopo by the attitude of Secocoeni and other chiefs on the north of Zoutspanberg.

But these things will pass over: and now that energetic steps are being taken to repress the great sale of arms and ammunition in the colony, and, if the report be true, that the Portuguese are repressing the trade from Delagoa Bay as much as possible, it is probable that large game shooting in this country will improve, rather than fall off, as was the case in India after the disarmament of the natives.

There is a good game country in the low lands of the east, towards Delagoa Bay, in the neighbourhood of the Limbouba Mountains, where the Tsetse fly abounds.

The Tsetse is very dangerous to cattle. Salted horses must be bought at great cost, or cheap and wretched ones purchased with the knowledge that they must be allowed to perish after having carried their master for a few days in pursuit of the game, or sporting must be carried on on foot, as it has often been with much success.

The Tsetse fly has been often described, and it is now beyond dispute that its bite is deadly to horses. It would appear to inhabit the low lands, in the neighbourhood of roads where neither horses, oxen, mules, nor dogs escape its bite.

On one of the Government maps the localities it inhabits are marked. These boundaries scarcely vary in the course of years, not so much as to alter the outline given. I insert a note which I took down from the lips of a hunter regarding this singular insect.

The Tsetse occupies districts, each of an area of six square miles, situated within well-known regions. It does not stick perpetually to define localities. The hunters inform themselves, by inquiries from the Kafirs, as to its present abode, and then take especial care to tether their horses during the day, a few yards beyond its limits. It is perfectly safe to pass through these limits during the night.

The hunters, therefore, take care to complete their march through the Tsetse location before the morning light. One bite will kill a dog, three any horse or ox. The fly is quite innocuous to wild game or goats. The bite is not more dangerous to a man than that of a musquito.

On a horse being bitten the first appearance is that the part assumes a soft pulpy feel, a yellow matter exuding from it. The horse soon sickens and dies, and even should he recover he seldom regains his former health or strength. The Tsetse fly is but a little bigger than a house fly, with a red striped body and stiff wings.

Mr. Wood, a very notable and experienced hunter on the Zambesi, possesses the power of being able to distinguish the position which the Tsetse fly is occupying by its humming noise, so that he precedes his waggon a few paces, and as soon as he hears the fly, changes the direction of his march.

It is said of Paul Kruger, that he had his waggons drawn by two natives, when he shot on the Limpopo.

Dr. Kirk, at Zanzibar, has been making investigations into the distribution of the Tsetse fly in Eastern Africa.

He finds that all along the road from the coast to Central Ugogo, the present limit of exploration, there are wide districts infested by it, but that there is some reason to hope that they are isolated and may be avoided when their exact limits have been clearly known and defined. Dr. Kirk reports, that the rule holds good everywhere, that where the fly is found large game are numerous; but he is of opinion that it by no means follows the game in their migrations, though it undoubtedly disappears when they are killed off. A curious circumstance is, that the natives appear to be well acquainted with the precise limits of the fly region, and are able to keep their cattle in safety quite close to it. No preventive or antidote has yet proved successful, and if ordinary beasts of burden are to be used to supersede the troublesome pagazi, the only way, according to Dr. Kirk, is to choose such a line of road as will entirely avoid the infested regions, or to cross them in a narrow part in the night time.

Having settled matters in the Transvaal, I prepared to return to Cape Town and started for Port Elizabeth.

At the Kabousie river, the railway from East London to Queenstown was rapidly progressing, but ere many weeks it was seriously interfered with by the war. These railroads are being carried out upon a departmental and not upon a contract system. The departmental system has the advantage of securing a vast amount of patronage. The contract system, under due supervision, would in all probability prove quicker and more economical. Small sub-contracts are made, and, if the following paragraph is correct, with very great profit to those who undertake them—

Not quite twelve months ago, a man walked up to a farmer's house, and after some little hesitation, asked for the loan of a 5*l*. note. In explanation, he told the farmer that he had an opportunity of taking a "small contract," and over and above the little money he had he wanted 5*l*. to enable him to enter upon it. The farmer advanced the money, and early in the succeeding month it was returned with many thanks. This incident led the farmer to invite him to spend the Sunday at his house; he did so, and they had some talk upon railway matters.

About a year afterwards the man announced his intention of going home. "How's that?" inquired the farmer, "I thought you had plenty of work." "So I have," replied the man, "but the fact is, I have saved a little money and intend to go home." "Well," observed the farmer, "you seem to be satisfied with a little, for it cannot be very much." "I don't know so much about that," retorted the mason, " in my part of the country, 1500*l.* is thought a good deal of." " Do you mean to say," inquired the farmer, "that you have made 1500*l.* since you have been on this line?" " I have not only done that," replied the man, " but I mean to say, that when you kindly lent me that 5*l.* I had only 15*l.* to my name." " But it's not twelve months ago," said the farmer. " It's nine months at the end of last month," continued the mason.

The farmer then became more inquisitive, and the man told him that when he made the contract he could hardly believe his own eyes and ears; that those above him must have been the greatest noodles under the sun not to know that he would make a pot of money by it; that had he been longer in the colony instead of a new comer, he would have made a great deal more.

As a good illustration of the wants of the natives, I may mention that the first goods train brought up spirits to King William's Town, and the first train down took away wool.

While I had been away, affairs in the colony had been growing more serious. The feeling of alarm had increased on the frontier, the armaments of the natives having raised their hopes. Our want of defence and the disorganisation of our arrangements had disquieted the colonists. I shall hereafter show in what respect the colonial forces were defective, and how the absurd jealousy which the Cape Government exhibited of Imperial control or advice had prevented these defects being remedied. These errors did not arise from want of warning. I had written letter after letter till I saw that it was useless. Article after article had appeared in the public prints. Speech after speech been made in the Assembly and in the provinces, and a Defence Commission had reported specially upon the subject.

While encamped on the Kabonsie, Mr. Charles Griffiths, the Resident of Basuto land, called at the camp on his way to King William's Town, having been sent by the Governor to take command of the Frontier police in consequence of the continued indisposition of the commandant of that force.

At this instant, Thomas, the post contractor, drove up. "General, the war cry has gone forth in Kreli's country; the Kafirs have risen." This was the first intimation of the war of 1877 and 1878.

I directed the mules to be inspanned, and arrived the same evening in King William's Town, having travelled from daylight to dark almost every day for eighty days together.

BOOK V.—THE SIXTH KAFIR WAR.

CHAPTER XXXI.

"THE FRONTIER SCARE."—WAR.

It was well for the interests of South Africa generally, that the Governor who arrived in the spring of 1877 was a man exactly fitted to undertake the difficult task in store for him, and able to dissipate the confusion into which the affairs of these provinces of the empire had drifted.

Sir Bartle Frere's career is too well known to the world for it to be necessary for me to allude to it. There can be no doubt that the appointment created universal confidence both at home and abroad.

At the time of my arrival in King William's Town on the 21st of September, Sir Bartle Frere had not returned from the Transkei.

He was engaged in judging the position of affairs for himself, more especially as regards Kreli, the head of the Galekas, and the Fingoes who were under our protection; and generally in forming his own judgment as to how far the information regarding the tranquillity of the country, which had been placed before him by his ministers, was a delusion or a reality.

I have already alluded to the general anxiety under which the eastern portion of the colony had laboured for the last two years, which was ridiculed by the ever wise Africander legislators as "the scare." Accompanied by expressions as insolent as they were ignorant, these insinuations gave rise to feelings of great indignation amongst the eastern farmers. Their intimate knowledge of the natives with whom they lived and held constant intercourse, gave them positive assurance that they were correct in their forecasts, and that troubles would soon arise.

I subjoin some extracts on this subject from local papers:

Utopians argue that the Kafir is too well contented with his lot, with the facility with which he can earn money to buy a gun or cows, which secure to him a wife or wives. To these men the Kafir is a quiet, harmless savage, easy to be reclaimed and to be Christianised, one who never dreams of war, provided always he be left alone to sleep away his life in his kraal, and be fed by the wives whom he has purchased with the white man's money.

We can prove that natives in the colony are now selling cows to procure guns, and I can state from a forty years' experience as a soldier in four wars, that when Kafirs sell their cows for weapons they mean something.

A native in this colony is busy buying ox-tails and drying them. He says they are wanted for war, and will be worn round the arms and legs, and that he gets a cow from a chief for every twenty-six tails he delivers. He adds that they have only been in demand during the last two or three months.

Among uninformed persons no regard would be given to such a circumstance as the purchase of ox-tails, but those who know these savages gave due weight to it. Many stories of the following kind were told, all of which had their meaning:

A native servant said to his master—

Have you heard about Kreli—he is *the* man; he has been put inside in a large hut, which was set on fire, and Kreli came out without a hair of his head touched. I am sorry for the women and children. They won't be hurt. We never kill women and children. I don't mean ours, I mean yours—so many women will be left widows, and children fatherless.

This story of Kreli and the hut was repeated by other native servants.

On the occasion of a banquet at Cape Town to Sir John Coode, the Prime Minister had taken the opportunity of severely commenting upon the borderers and the Press. He said—

> I am astonished and sorry that men on the frontier, who have taken up positions there and received land for nothing at all in consideration of their being called upon to defend the country, should be the first to be scared and run away at the moment of danger. (Loud cheers.) Let them come back and live in Cape Town if they do not like the frontier, and, let others take their place. But is it not absurd to see every stupid rumour and every drunken squabble magnified into a serious difficulty, and the Government called to act on it? I hope the Government will never do anything of the sort. (Cheers.) The Government will take care to keep its powder dry, and be ready for any emergency that may occur; and I am glad to think that not only his Excellency the Governor, but also the general and the military, all understand each other perfectly, and that if anything does occur we shall stand together and let the enemy see it, and they will regret the day that they entered into conflict with us. (Renewed applause.) I do not consider there is any occasion for alarm. I consider it as unjust to the native population. (Hear, hear.) If anything does occur on the frontier, those editors of

newspapers who scratch up everything they can, and to whom every bit of rumour is a godsend, will be to blame, for they just disclose to the enemy what he might do.

Editors of newspapers, for their own purposes, raise these scares, and disclose plans to the Kafirs by which they might sack the frontier and do the colony harm.

He then alluded to the period when he was a volunteer, in the war of 1846, and the services he had rendered at the front in his day, and said none were then scared by a few Kafirs. He severely rebuked the farmers who were living in the centre of this danger, and who did but warn the authorities of its existence and repeat their convictions of the necessity of making preparation against it. He justly offended those monitors of the public, the Press, who were advocating a recognition of the coming crisis, which he utterly ignored.

I quite concurred with the Prime Minister in his expressed opinion that there was a cordial understanding between the military and myself, but I frankly own that I could not understand the want of any due preparation on the frontier, or the disregard which was paid to the constant warnings which came from that quarter, and to which I had repeatedly called attention both officially and privately. The Ministry loudly proclaimed that there was no danger, that there never would be another Kafir war.

On the 22nd of September the Governor, in company with the Minister of Public Works, the Hon. J. X. Merriman, returned from the Transkei, and the command of the police force was placed in the hands of Commandant Griffiths. A fight on the borders between the Galekas and the Fingoes was then reported. The Kafirs could not bear to see those who had formerly been their servants now free and independent, and growing rich by their providence and industry, and the Galekas determined to assert their former superiority over them. A slight disagreement at a drinking-party ended in a serious quarrel, and a life was lost.

It was soon apparent that the ideas of the Galeka chief were not confined simply to avenging himself upon the Fingoes who had offended some of his tribe, but that he intended to drive them out of the country which had been in his own possession some years previously, and which he had forfeited in former wars with the British Government.

On the 26th of September the fight of Guadana was fought, the action was much criticised, and I was subsequently requested to give my views on it, as it was the first of this war. I insert a report concerning it.

THE BATTLE OF GUADANA,
The Commandant F. A. M. Police, Susize Camp.

SUSIZE CAMP,
October 28th, 1877.

Sir,—In accordance with your instructions, I have the honour to report that on the 26th ult. while returning to Idutywa reserve from the Ibeka camp, I was apprised of the fact that the Galekas had attacked the Fingoes on the Government reserve near the Guadana.

On receiving this information I continued my march along the main road, and when about two miles from the *Impulse*, opposite the Guadana, I observed the Galekas had crossed in numbers and attacked the Fingoes, and that an engagement was taking place between the two tribes.

In obedience to orders received (in the event of a battle) I proceeded to the scene of action in support of the Fingoes. Before taking any prominent part, I sent back to the *Impulse* to acquaint Mr. Ayliff (who was then in command of a large Fingo contingent) that the Galeka army had crossed into British territory. On the arrival of this gentleman with about 1000 Fingoes, I halted the gun and the men under my command, Mr. Ayliff, with his Fingoes, marching to the top of the Guadana hill.

In order to avoid surprise, I sent Sub-Inspector Hamilton to Mr. Ayliff to receive a report of the position of the Galeka army.

This officer returned with a request from Mr. Ayliff that I should march on with the gun and men, which I did. On arrival there, I found the Galeka army in three divisions at the foot of the hill. On our appearance the enemy made a move towards us. I immediately gave the order to the officer in command of the artillery (Sub-Inspector Cochrane) to open fire with the 7-pounder, which he did.

After the tenth round the gun became disabled, and on being reported to me, I gave the order "The gun will retire under Mr. Cochrane and the escort." This was immediately carried out, and the gun under Sub-Inspector Cochrane, and Sub-Inspector A. Maclean, with twenty-five men as gun escort, retired accordingly.

Before entering into action my men were extended in skirmishing order on the brow of the hill, the horses having been left out of sight, in hand, and in charge of the usual number of men. The Fingoes under Mr. Ayliff were placed on the left flank, between the gun and the Guadana forest, so as to command the bush. My men were placed on the right of the gun. When the Galekas came within rifle range I ordered the police to commence firing, and continuous independent firing was kept up for nearly two hours, which checked the enemy until the gun retired. When the Fingoes saw this they made a general retreat, running in among our horses and causing great confusion.

Finding that we were deserted by the Fingoes, and that by remaining on the ground any longer the lives of the whole European police would be sacrificed, I ordered the men to retire. The confusion by the Fingoes rushing about in all directions caused several of our horses to break loose, and through this unfortunate circumstance one officer and six men fell victims to the enemy.

The remainder of the men retired in order, and the gun was taken safely to the Idutywa.

The firing from the 7-pounder was most effective, and so was also that of the Sniders.

The estimated loss on the Galeka side was at least 200, besides wounded.

I may say that the Fingoes, when asked why they retreated so soon, replied that they had been watching the gun, and when they saw it move they thought it was time to leave the battle-field.

I cannot attach any blame to our men in the engagement; they stood their ground until the very last, fired steadily, and, were it not for the gun breaking down, I have no hesitation in asserting that the result would have been different.

Finding the gun and men were safe, I proceeded on to the Ibeka camp in company with Inspector J. Maclean and Sub-Inspector Hamilton, where I personally reported the engagement to you, and returned to the Idutywa reserve on the morning of the 27th September.

The Galeka army must have numbered about 5000. Our force consisted of 80 men (including gun escort and detachment) and about 1500 Fingoes.

I have, &c.,
E. B. CHALMERS,
Inspector Commanding No. 2 Troop, F.A.M.P.

Observations made by His Excellency General Sir Arthur Cunynghame, Commanding Forces, on the above report, by Inspector Chalmers, on the action fought at Guadana on the 26th September last.

To the Honourable Mr. Merriman, &c.

Sir,—Not having been placed in command of the colonial forces when this action was fought, I did not feel myself entitled to receive a report of it from Commandant Griffith. Had I been in command of the forces generally at that time I should have been most happy to have received it, and should have officially forwarded it to his Excellency the Governor, and should have published it with the rest.

On the 20th of October I very carefully examined the Guadana mountain. The field of battle, the position of the forces, the engagement in all particulars was explained very fully by one of the F. A. M. Police, who was present at the action.

The Fingoes were, I conceive, outflanked by the enemy. The gun was advanced to an excellent position until the trail broke. This, it appears, was colonial manufacture. It was well made, but had one defect, very excusable. This trail was colonial made, in consequence, as I am informed, of the proper Woolwich carriage having been lost in the *Windsor Castle*.

The gun could not and should not, in my opinion, have remained longer on the field of the engagement, and it was probably owing to the escort remaining too long, as well as to the unfortunate circumstance of their losing their horses, that those who were killed lost their lives.

I was told that nothing could exceed the bravery of Inspector Von Hohenau who fell, that in fact he lost his own life in his endeavour to carry off the field one of the men who had been wounded, and that while he was endeavouring to place this man on his own horse, he himself was shot through the body, and that he died like a British soldier.

I had the honour to assist in erecting a cairn to his memory. Its position commands Galekaland. So far from blame being attached to the police, if I may judge from the position as it was explained to me, and as I on careful survey found it—I consider credit is due to this force for the forward and excellent position they took up, the execution which they must have done to the enemy, until their gun was disabled, and the way in which they retained their position until they were compelled as mounted men outflanked by an enemy secured by thick wood to retire.

This is the decided conclusion that I arrive at after a careful examination of the ground, and full consideration of the subject.

A. CUNYNGHAME, *General*.

Van Hohenan appears to have behaved with great bravery. On the order to retire being given he, having (so it is said) assisted Evans into the saddle, was vaulting up behind, when he was shot in the hip, and both men rolled to the ground. The enemy were too close at hand for him to escape. A gentleman who witnessed the recovery of the bodies of the policemen who fell in the action, says:—" Evans had eighteen assegai wounds, mostly on the back. All the bodies were stripped, but Evans' coat was so full of holes that the natives left it. Sub-Inspector Van Hohenan had long boots on, and finding them difficult to get off, they severed the feet at the ankle-joint and took them away in the boots." One of the unfortunates was found scalped, a thing I believe unheard of in any previous Kafir war, and all the bodies were horribly mutilated. Perhaps the most revolting sight was a dog lying gorged by the side of his dead master, upon whose body it had been feeding from day to day. Galeka dogs were frequently seen eating dead Galekas. It is stated among the Galekas that whenever a commando of Kafirs took the field, a hare was invariably seen leading the army, and hence the disaster which always befel the natives. A doctor was consulted, who accused

Lindinxowa (Kreli's second son, and by far the best of them) of being a wizard, who sent the hare for the purpose of destroying the army. Lindinxowa was put to death for this.

There could now be very little doubt that the Kafirs meant war; and yet it was strongly denied in Cape Town. Men of influence were heard to say that the alarm was promoted by the officers of the Imperial Army, who were desirous of obtaining promotion and distinction. The real cause of the war was probably the pressure of population in the native locations. The Kafirs had multiplied till with their vagrant habits there was too little room for them. The war was known to the natives as "The Women's War," from the fact that it was mainly owing to the sex that the flagging interest amongst the men was maintained. As if by preconcerted action, the women taunted the younger men especially with having become the white man's slaves instead of warriors like their fathers.

CHAPTER XXXII.

STATE OF THE FORCES.

THE state of war was a fact. Let us now see what forces were available in the colony.

Her Majesty's troops on the frontier consisted of the greater portion of one regiment, the 1st Battalion 24th, but with no cavalry and no artillery. The horses of the infantry soldiers that I had selected for mounted service and those for the guns had been sold at the request of the ministry.

The frontier police probably numbered 1000 on paper. They were an excellent body of men, and many of their officers were intelligent, zealous, and enured to hardship, but their organisation was exceedingly defective. They were badly equipped for the field, and their system was so incomplete, and their arrangements so faulty, that it was difficult, nay impossible, to discover the whereabouts of a large portion of them. Indeed, the Minister for Public Works, acting as Minister of War, informed me that after more than a month's hard work he had failed to make out the locale of nearly 200 men out of a total of something over 1000. I do not speak at random, as the following extract from an official report of an inspection of a portion of the police, which was directed to be carried out by an officer of experience, will show:—

"Although due notice had been given of this inspection when Captain P—— arrived upon the parade-ground five minutes after the hour for which the muster had been ordered, he found that some of the men had still to be sent for, and others shouted for. Of one portion of the detachment, very few were provided with uniform, and many of them wore excessively uncleanly and disreputable clothes, and some of them were personally very dirty and unwholesome in appearance." Hardly any of the men knew how to discharge their weapons, and it could not be discovered that they had received any instruction. Certainly none had been received by the Danes and Germans in the detachment, for the men spoke nothing but their own language. Amongst the fifty-five men there were some nine or ten horses, of which one was sick and another was a two-year old. At Fort Murray, the training station, the barrack-room was found to be "strewed with débris of all kinds, old mattresses, rags, bits of board and branches of trees tied together to serve as beds."

Upon the receipt of this report, Sir Bartle Frere was moved to address a minute to his ministers in which he made pointed mention of the excellent quality of the men, the wanton neglect and needless hardships to which they were subjected, and the absence of well-qualified superior officers. "As far as I could see," says the Governor, "there were men in the ranks superior to many of the officers, both in natural capacity and in education and knowledge of their duty." No statement of pay and supply was procurable, and when at length some kind of return was shown to us, it proved, on examination, to be so flagrantly incorrect as to be nearly useless. Even such stores as an artillery seven-pounder could not be accurately traced on the head-quarter records. It was supposed to be at Foleni, and then at Ibeka. It finally turned up in a coachmaker's yard at King William's Town, where it had lain for months, and where it was accidentally discovered by the Hon. Mr. Merriman. His Excellency expressed a very natural fear that the Government had been misled by returns regularly rendered to Cape Town, in proper form, but not agreeing with facts.

And yet this was the only organised colonial force!

A large number of volunteers had enrolled themselves in the several towns in the colony; excellent material, fine strong athletic young men, but the term of their engagement allowed all service to be perfectly optional. They could attend parades or omit them at their pleasure, and if they consented to leave their towns on any expedition, no one had a right to object to their quitting the ranks and returning home at any moment they pleased.

As regards my own opinion of the personnel of these colonial forces, I quote from the words of the Governor—in which I entirely concur:—

"More than this, I was assured by both the late and the present Commander of the Forces that they would not wish for better troops for the kind of service we needed in this war, as far as material, equipment, and spirit went, than the volunteers you sent forward. All they required was order and regularity in calling them out, that they should be intelligently directed, and their wants attended to in the field, and that they should be exercised in the habit of acting, not independently, every man according to his own ideas, but in combination with others, and under the orders of a single commandant. These things do not come intuitively, some must be prescribed by law, some taught by practice; and I trust that another session of Parliament will not be allowed to pass without your providing for them. Let me add, as a practical point, that neither of the distinguished and experienced officers I have mentioned made any exception as regards their opinion of the goodness of your material. You need all arms in a country like this, and you have the means of furnishing all; but though the young colonist learns much of what is wanted in the course of the ordinary life of an active frontier farmer, teaching and training are required to make him capable of acting with others, and this your legislation and administration must give him."

The burgher farmers of the districts were able men. In their organisation they somewhat resembled our yeomanry, but the law did not require them to proceed beyond their own districts.

It was fortunate that there was a large number of Snider rifles stored in the frontier magazine, three thousand or more. On the interchange by the royal troops of the Snider for the Martini-Henry, I was directed to send all the former home.

Feeling sure that troubles must come, I recommended the Ministry to purchase them. They refused to do so. I still retained them, against my orders, and but for this fortunate circumstance the Colonial Government would have scarcely had a rifle on the frontier.

Such was the state of preparation of the colony to meet the attacks from the armed natives of the border states, and the armed rebels in the colony under Sandilli and other chiefs.

Every available man of the frontier police was sent over the Kei, and Commandant Griffiths, wisely recalling his forces from the Idutchwa reserve, concentrated them at Ibeka, a fine commanding position about fifteen miles to the west of the Guadana Mountain.

It is stated upon good authority that the natives do not believe in the power of the British to call up regiments from the vasty deep. The notion that prevails is that the troops so frequently passing nowadays are marched up overland, embarked at some port farther up the coast, landed again, and sent through once more, the obvious purpose being to magnify our real strength. Thus they were persuaded to think that we initiated the usual theatrical method of personating a considerable force.

I then wrote to the Governor that—

"Under the present circumstances I cannot but believe that the disunited commands are fraught with great danger, and that the proper person to exercise superior military authority in the area of disturbance is myself, and, such being my opinion, the responsibility which I consider should devolve upon me I am ready to accept. I consider that great danger is involved both to Imperial and Colonial interests, and that due military organisation should be established."

The same day the Governor replied that he concurred in the views I had expressed, and a few days afterwards a notice came out signed by the then Commissioner for Crown Land and Public Works, conferring upon me the command of the Colonial forces.

I at once pushed forward detachments of the 24th Regiment to the borders, to Konigha, Impetu, and Pullen's Farm.

The next information we received regarding Kreli and his Galekas was that he had attacked Ibeka with a large force.

The station was excellently defended, Commandant Griffiths, with his small force, completely routing the enemy. No doubt the attack was directed principally against the Fingoes, but Kreli is reported to have given orders to destroy those "dogs of Fingoes," and also to have said, "On your way sweep off those white tents on the hill, the sight of which disturbs me."

It now became my duty, as Commander of the Forces, to act in conjunction with the member of the Colonial Cabinet who represented the Ministry at King William's Town.

This post had been delegated to the Honourable Mr. Merriman. He was a man of active temperament, unbounded ambition, strong in faith in himself, not over-courteous in manner or conciliatory in disposition, most difficult to reason with, and he had set his face strenuously against the provision of any adequate defensive force, having declared in his place in the House of Assembly, "that he would rather see a Kafir war every ten years than that an increase in the frontier force should be made." Formerly strong in opposition, he had left his own party, in order to take office in this Ministry. I felt, therefore, that the task which I had accepted was no light one, more especially as I had so small a number of troops of the Imperial army to give weight to my representations.

The question now arose—

Should the Imperial troops be pressed forward over the Kei against the Galekas, or remain in the colony to defend the city of King William's Town, and other points of importance in the neighbourhood?

It was decided that it would be wise to defend the colony. In this I entirely concurred.

Efforts were then made to send all the burghers who could be brought together to assist Commandant Griffiths.

They came forward in considerable numbers, passing through King William's Town, or moving in a more direct line from Queen's Town to Ibeka.

It was difficult to obtain any correct idea of the number of these forces, but strenuous endeavours were made by me to place them upon some recognised system.

The next point was that of the commissariat, which is of vital importance to every army.

I strongly urged that this service should be entrusted to the officers of the Imperial Commissariat Department, who were ready to accept the grave responsibility of conducting its arrangements. I felt certain that, if the service was left in the hands of the colonists, it would break down.

Nothing could induce the ministers to listen to me. They were afraid of the expense which would be entailed upon them.

I represented that my officers were experienced in all its details, so that, though the Imperial Commissariat might be regarded as expensive, its administration was certain, and, in my opinion, any system they introduced would be equally costly.

The answer was given "that if the supplies cost double, the administration should not be placed in the hands of Imperial officers."

I then placed Commandant Griffiths in command over the Kei. It has been asserted that there was an arrangement that, although I was gazetted to the chief command, it was on the understanding I was not to exercise it. There is no truth whatever in that statement. No such understanding was ever entered into or even mentioned, nor would I have accepted the command with hands so fettered.

I felt that it would be unwise and, indeed, impossible for me to give Commandant Griffiths other than a wide discretion as to his movements. These I saw must depend on many points, his supplies, his ammunition, his reserves, over none of which had I any control whatever; and, moreover, I knew that the larger portion of the force with which he was undertaking these movements were in the field at their own discretion, to stay or leave at their pleasure. How unwise therefore would it have been to have hampered him with detailed rigid instructions!

I sent staff officers to the front, attaching them to his force, in order that they might become well acquainted with the country, in case (which I considered by no means improbable) the services of her Majesty's troops should eventually be required in Galeka land, and to acquaint me how things were proceeding, so that I might render every assistance in my power.

Being fearful of excesses by men not under perfect discipline, and smarting under the losses which had been occasioned to them in consequence of the continued robberies by the Kafirs I gave the following orders, which I have every reason to believe were obeyed with very rare exceptions both by her Majesty's and by the Colonial forces during the war.

General Order No. 13.

His Excellency, the General Commanding the Forces, is anxious to impress upon the troops generally that, in all cases where the ability of so doing exists, prisoners of war should be made, rather than that the enemy should, even in battle, be put to death without necessity.

By command of His Excellency, General Sir A. J. CUNYNGHAME, K.C.B., Commanding the Forces.

W. BELLAIRS, Colonel, Deputy Adjutant-General.

Commandant Griffiths was compelled to remain inactive until his supplies arrived, when his first advance was directed against the chief kraal, which he caused to be burnt.

Extract from Report of Commandant Griffiths.

"Although unable, from want of ammunition for native levies, to make a general and final forward movement into the Galeka country, I deemed it advisable, while waiting for the ammunition and stores to come up, to do what I could to inflict as heavy a blow as possible upon the enemy; and with this object I ordered an advance to be made yesterday from all our posts along the border, the different columns to converge on Kreli's 'Great Place,' which I determined to destroy.

"There was little or no resistance at the 'Great Place,' but at the springs on the Butterworth river, a considerable force of the enemy opposed the advance of the mounted burghers, but they were successfully overcome by Wainwright with the volunteers, in which service he was severely wounded."

The arrangements which Griffiths made were excellent, but he was compelled to return with his force to Ibeka. He could not prosecute his advance for want of supplies, and especially of ammunition.

This was by no means extraordinary. Anyone acquainted with war would confidently predict such a consequence of a Commissariat undertaken by persons ignorant of the subject.

I quote a few words of the many complaints in the public newspapers which met my eye at this time, and which, if they were true, as I firmly believe they were, at once exonerate Commandant Griffiths from not proceeding with his march as rapidly as he could have desired.

During the progress of the police from the Ibeka to the Bashee the greatest privations were endured, the principal evil being the smallness of the rations, which was the more acutely felt by the men owing to the hard work they had to perform. Affairs reached a climax at our camp, where, during three days of incessant rain, we were almost wholly without provisions, our sole food consisting of meat, without even a pinch of salt, and a few mealies given us by the Fingoes.

Shortly after this, at the place where we effected a junction with the Commandant, we were ordered to start, when the rations were two days overdue. On our refusal we were told to be careful what we were about; that it amounted to mutiny, &c.; but on the men remaining firm, Mr. Maclean spoke to the Commandant on the matter, and eventually we were served out with a handful of broken mouldy biscuit, some of the men, but not all, being fortunate enough to get a very small quantity of bad meal. This was declared to be all the provisions obtainable for us in the camp.

Later on, at a camp about twelve miles from the Willow, two days after rations were due, they were not only not served out, but we were ordered on the road, and proceeded as far as the Willow, but returned next morning owing to some mistake. When a patrol is warned, it is arranged so that we have to thrust hot and reeking meat into the saddle-bags, and take green coffee,* thus being deprived of our only luxury, and frequently having to throw away the meat; instead of being warned in time to dry the one, and grind (with two stones) the other.

The provisions are not weighed, but served out in pannikins, according to the judgment of the quartermasters.

By reason of the want of proper utensils, meal is mixed on a macintosh.

* Those who are acquainted with the Crimean War will remember the "green coffee."

CHAPTER XXXIII.

THE FIRST PART OF THE WAR — GRIFFITHS DRIVES THE GALEKAS OVER THE BASHEE.

AT this time Mapassa, a Galeka of consequence, left the tribe of Kreli and crossed the river Kei into the colony. He came over with a large number of followers. A fatal mistake was here made, in not disarming his people; but they were allowed to squat upon some pleasant lands with their cattle, and retain their muskets and their assegais.

The attitude of the native chiefs on the northern part of the frontier now became exceedingly doubtful. Umditchwa had been troublesome, and Umthonthlo had complaints. Extraordinary fetish rites were in some instances practised; the witch doctors occasionally promising success and sometimes failure. Curious stories like this were circulated:—

A trader reported that he had received reliable information that the two Kafir chiefs had recently held a consultation, the result being that they asked their witch doctors whether, in the event of their going to war against the white man, they would be successful. The witch doctors, after going through a round of incantations, ordered two oxen to be driven up to the kraal and skinned alive, one of the oxen being wholly black and the other wholly white. The barbarous sentence was carried out, and the poor animals were watched to see which would die first. The black ox lived twelve hours, the white ox nearly forty-eight hours; and consequently the two chiefs gave up all idea of war.

Map of KAFFERARIA

Griffiths advanced with all the forces at his command, consisting of about 500 frontier armed police, 1000 burghers, and probably 3000 or 4000 Fingoes; while a force consisting of about 3000 Tanbus, which Major Elliott had collected together, held a very excellent position near Fort Bowker, on the upper part of the Bashee river. The enemy retreated, making but a poor attempt to stand anywhere. They retreated along the sea-margin towards the Bashee mouth, driving their cattle and sending their women in advance into Bomvana land.

The Bomvanas under Moni were powerless to stop them, even if they had been willing. They gave shelter to their cattle, which, when claimed by the police, they declared to be their own property, although it was perfectly evident that they were not so.

Griffiths' force advanced with difficulty, resolutely overcoming all privations and inconveniences until they drove the enemy over the Umtata river into Guadiso's country.

The burghers by this time had come a long distance from their homes, and having captured a large amount of cattle, they made up their minds to return to their farms. Being entirely their own masters, and seeing but little chance of capturing more cattle, they could do so when they pleased. It was impossible to keep any of them; it was equally undesirable to keep the police alone in the Bomvana country. The Commandant, therefore, marched them back to Ibeka. The Fingoes were either dismissed to their homes (it has been said by direct orders from the Minister of War) or vanished.

Certain corps of infantry volunteers had before this been marched over the Kei to assist Commandant Griffiths in holding selected posts. They did not return immediately. Some were posted at Fort Bowker, another party at the Springs, and another at Toleni.

A complete defeat of Kreli's army was on all sides proclaimed.

I urged that the Bashee should be guarded to prevent

the return of the enemy; but I had no troops to send there, and Commandant Griffiths was unable to effect this object on account of the want of men.

The ministry did not appear to see the great importance of this point; but being sure that all difficulties were over, they proceeded to make allotments of the conquered country, proposing to give one part to Mapassa's people, and another to emigrant Germans, leaving but a scanty residue for the unfortunate Galekas.

I considered this to be a favourable moment for me to visit the Transkei, and on the 1st of November I left with my staff officers. We had sent on two light carts the evening before, we ourselves taking the railroad to the Kei station. We then mounted our horses, the weather being fearfully bad. Unfortunately the axle of one of the carts broke in consequence of the bad state of the roads, and as we were dependent upon them for tents and food, both for men and horse, we were delayed that day at Komgha.

Here I found that, prior to the arrival of her Majesty's troops, the clergyman and many of his parishioners had deserted their homes, and, taking their bedding into the church, had fortified it to the best of their ability, as they felt that no adequate protection for them existed in the town.

On the following morning we started early for the Kei river. I inspected the station at Pullen's Farm, which had been cleverly placed in a defensive state by the officer of the 24th in command.

We had not proceeded more than half a mile, when we came upon our baggage-cart lying on its side on the road. The driver, who was drunk, was sitting on a sack, and crying, while our traps of all kinds were strewed about in endless confusion.

The orderly said that old Abraham, being quite unable to manage the mules, had driven the cart into a deep hole, and upset it.

There was little damage done, except that some soup, which our cook had carefully placed in a jar, had been turned into my aide-de-camp's helmet.

Righting the cart, I placed my driver Mittons in it, and took my own spider-carriage with its four mules down the precipitous road.

The mules, as usual, were obstinate, and discarded all guiding, so that on a steep turn I was fairly jerked out. For one instant I was on the wheel, but grasping at the dashboard, I regained my position, and got all right to the river. The ford was not so deep as we had expected from the continued rains. A bridge was in course of erection; it was to be built on double concrete circular pillars encased with iron, at an estimated cost of 50,000*l.* It will be a noble work when completed, the length being over a quarter of a mile.

The engineer told us that singular things had occurred before the commencement of the war. The works were proceeding quietly when a Kafir woman passing by told the native workmen that the war-cry had sounded, and that they must go to the war. The men did not reply, but on the following morning every Kafir had vanished, and the war-cry loudly resounded over the hills.

We slept on the bank of the river, and on the following day reached Butterworth. In passing, I inspected the volunteers who were holding the position of Toleni.

The mission station at Butterworth looked peaceful and tranquil. Fingoes, as usual, were surrounding the grog-shop, and loitering on the grass with their bottles. We here saw some wounded Fingoes and Galekas, one of whom had been shot through the head, a portion of his brain having protruded from the skull. The man was reported as now getting on well and daily improving.

A strict guard was placed over the Galekas, not to prevent their leaving, but to prevent their being murdered by the wounded Fingoes, who were in the hospital with them, and who had been detected approaching one of them with a knife, to cut his throat.

On the morning of the 4th we entered Ibeka, and immediately afterwards set out on a twenty miles ride to visit the scene of the late battle of Guadana.

I have already alluded to this action, and to the opinion I gave concerning it. Guadana is otherwise called Mount Wodehouse. It was a singular fact that the first action in this war should occur at a mountain called after a Governor, who had trusted the word of Kreli "to live in peace," and had allowed him to return to the location on the borders of which the mountain is situated.

In our ride home, we came across a good many dead bodies of the Galekas, upon which the starving dogs were satiating themselves, as there were no means of burying them.

One body in particular, which had been partially covered with earth, the feet protruding from the soil, was said to be that of a chief from Bomvana land, and the blue coat that lay beside his body was a gift at his meeting with the Governor in September.

I did not desire to remain too long absent from King William's Town, as I was sceptical about the peaceful attitude of the Galekas. Accordingly, on the following morning, at early dawn, we mounted our horses to return. Before doing so, I was invited to inspect the head of the witch doctress, who had been killed at Ibeka, while leading on a body of Galeka warriors. She had been stabbed with an assegai by a Fingo. It was reported that no sooner did she fall than she was instantly surrounded by her friends, who proceeded to carry off her body.

This assured the Fingoes that she must be a person of consequence, and, rushing forward, they captured the body and cut the head off. She was said to be a daughter of Quito, the greatest witch doctor to the chief Kreli, who was one of the prime movers of the war. An ammunition-box full of lime was opened, which was emptied into a sack, and the head rolled out. It appeared very like a plaster-cast, as the lime adhered thickly to it.

The features and woolly hair were quite perfect. It was not a pleasing object, and one look was enough. Such was the end of this would-be enchantress, revered with trembling fear in life, in death a curiosity to the white stranger.

I quote from a Report concerning this woman,

who, as in the case of the cattle-slaughtering in 1856-7 appeared, professing to have seen visions of armed men, the ghosts of Hintza and other Galeka chiefs of old days, rising from the water and sending messages to call the tribes to arm.

It was said this prophetess or sorceress had told the Galekas that one of the messages from the spirits of their ancestors was a mandate to give up their old tactics of loose skirmishing, and to attack the enemy in heavy close columns, after the manner of the English soldiers; and that this was the cause of the departure of the Galekas from their usual system of fighting, and of their attacking our posts at Ibeka and elsewhere in masses.

It was also said that she had led the Galekas in their attack on Commandant Griffiths, and had been killed in its repulse; and various articles, rings, and charms have been handed round as relics of the Galeka prophetess.

I quote an illustration of the infatuation of these ignorant Kafirs from a letter which came from the northern frontier. Incredible as they may appear, I have little doubt of the accuracy of its statements.

A private letter from Saltpansberg mentions that one of Magato's chief men named Mashow, had, while on an elephant hunt,

Y

met a magician doctor, from whom, after much entreaty, he obtained a charm by which its possessor was rendered invulnerable to firearms; or when a bullet was smeared with it, it would be flattened against him on whom it was fired. Mashow bought a good quantity of this precious article, to the very great joy of Magato and his councillors. On the 13th of October this charm was to be tried. Magato and his council assembled. Mashow smeared a bullet well with the valuable ointment, and desired Magato to go and stand at a short distance, so that he (Mashow) might fire at him, and convince him that the bullet would have no effect. Magato was rather incredulous as to the power of this wonderful charm, and suggested that Mashow should be the target. Mashow quite readily complied, not only he, but several others; among them one of Magato's most dearly loved wives. Mashow indicated with his hand to his heart, and told Magato to fire there, as he was completely invulnerable. Magato fired. The result was that the bullet pierced Mashow's heart, and also mortally wounded Magato's wife in the abdomen; the arm of another Kafir was also broken, and he was dying when the letter was being written. That the people are very mad with the doctor who had deceived them may be readily imagined. It seems the fellow had humbugged Mashow by firing at him a charge of loose powder, and managing at the same time to project a flattened bullet against his body.

Thus ended the first episode in the war, and I returned to King William's Town.

CHAPTER XXXIV.

STUTTERHEIM.

If the Gaikas broke out I felt sure that they would make a point of occupying the Amatolas; I was therefore desirous of visiting Keiskama, so interesting from the recollections of the old war.

We started on the 29th of November. In the neighbourhood of King William's Town all appeared tranquil.

The men were generally naked, the women clothed in blankets, with curiously-worked petticoats. The manner in which these blankets were arranged displayed their dark polished forms to the best advantage.

We again passed the flats, on which that curious worm, the commitgee, commits such wonderful ravages. The face of the country for miles is fretted into holes. At ten we outspanned at a beautiful spot at the foot of the mountains called Bailey's Grave, the scene of the death of a brave man in the old war. Soon after we entered a wild pass, when we overtook a waggon full of arms for the use of the loyal Fingoes. Arrived at Keiskama, we visited Baron de Fyn, the Conservator of the Forests. This gentleman has long been a resident in this country. It is said that as a young man he held a high position at the Court of the Emperor of Austria, but that in consequence of a dispute with one of the Imperial Princes he left Europe, to which, I believe, he has never returned. He is a fine old man, most polished in his manners, which are altogether those of the old school.

We spent a very pleasant evening with the Baron, returning to our tents at a late hour. The following day the weather was beautiful, and the mountain scenery quite lovely.

We left again early in the morning, passing near the entrance of the Booma Pass, the well-remembered scene of some bloody Amatola strifes. The white tents of the police dotted the green sward at its entrance. On passing through the town of Alice we met the missionary in charge of the neighbouring station, who pressed us to visit it, and we were well rewarded for doing so. I was glad to see that he gave his pupils some practically instructive occupation. The tinsmith work carried on by the natives appeared to be successful. The singing of the girls was exceedingly beautiful, so much so as to induce me to suggest that it might be advisable to send the entire choir to England. Singularly enough, Mr. Taberer informed me that not only had such a scheme been already under consideration, but that an old lady of the name of Witcher had actually offered one thousand pounds to be permitted to carry it out, but that, as her death happened shortly after, the scheme had to be abandoned. Her case was an instance amongst many others of a hard life ending in prosperity. During the last war, a barrack was built at Keiskama, the ruins of which still stand in the neighbourhood of the town. The modern institution of the regimental canteen, now found so valuable, whereby the profits are used to cheapen the articles to the soldier, had not then been established. Mrs. Witcher attached herself to the army as a sutler, and supplied the wants of the troops for years. The result was that when she died about two years ago, she bequeathed, it is said, at least 60,000*l*. In case none of her relatives should be found, she divided that large sum between two of her young shopmen, who had shown her attention.

Whilst we were walking from the school-house, a snake passed in front of us, upon which Mr. Taberer at once set his foot—an imprudence for which he might have had to pay dearly, as it was declared to be very venomous.

The people in the neighbourhood of the mission are of mixed tribes, Kafirs and Fingoes, some of them very fanatical, and believing in demons and spirits.

Witch doctors are known to have great influence amongst them, and water-spirits are fully believed to exist. As an illustration of the dread and reverence with which the water-spirits are regarded, a native had fallen into the river some weeks before my visit, and although many men were near, no one would assist him, and he was allowed to be drowned. They thought the water-spirit had pulled him in, and that by giving him help they would offend that powerful being.

How difficult it must be for our magistrates and civil servants to deal with people who are subject to such infatuation.

Leaving the mission station, we skirted the base of the beautiful Amatola ranges, and reached the village of Stutterheim towards evening. The locations of Fingoes and Kafirs were intermingled—an advantageous plan, as the former are thus able to keep a watch over the latter.

Stutterheim is a pleasing little town. It was established by Germans of the legion who, after the Crimean War, volunteered to do service in South Africa, and was named after the commander, an adventurous elderly man, who raised the corps, and who is credited with having earned 70,000*l*. by so doing. On returning to Europe he is said to have gambled away this money. He lost a large sum one evening at Monaco, which he promised to pay immediately. On the following day he telegraphed to his banker in Paris for the requisite advance, but, not receiving a reply, and his spirit revolting at the thought of being considered a defaulter, he put a pistol to his head and shot himself.

Here I inspected a corps of Germans, fine old soldiers

of whom no one could doubt that they would render a good account of a large body of the enemy should they attack the town.

The district was placed under Commandant Schermbrücker, a very enterprising, indefatigable, and valuable officer, and one who, by his zeal and assiduity, rendered most excellent service in this war.

We encamped the same evening at a beautiful spot at the base of Frankport Hill. Great alarm pervaded the entire settlement, not so much from a fear of the actual power of the Gaikas in the intermediate vicinity, as from the want of preparation, defence, and organisation. On the following morning we returned to King William's Town.

This and other military inspection tours that I made on the frontier enabled me to see a great deal of the families of emigrants on the different properties: and it is with a feeling of pride, as an Englishman, that I can bear witness to the courage which they displayed in remaining in their homes when surrounded by so much danger.

CHAPTER XXXV.

FURTHER SPREAD OF DISAFFECTION—THE FIGHT AT UMZITZANI.

THE state of things over the Kei and the chances of rebellion in the colony had now to be anxiously considered.

The Governor, long inured to dangers of war and rebellion, was determined to act upon the principles of constitutional government. He was desirous of giving every possible consideration to the Ministry, who had been chosen by the voice of the colony. The Ministry were, however, infatuated. They had pledged themselves that there was no danger to the colony, and that there would be no rebellion, and they steadily adhered to their words, and refused to make proper defensive preparations though the danger was so imminent.

Seeing the danger in which the colony stood, and feeling how little I could do with the slender forces under my command, I advised the Secretary of State at home that two regiments should be sent out. But as the necessity for this measure had not yet become apparent the despatch of troops was delayed till later.

In the face of the difficulties then pending on the Eastern Question, it was naturally considered to be the duty of a wealthy colony with a responsible government to provide for its own defence. I also strongly recommended that a battery of field artillery should be sent out for service in the Cape Colony, in Natal, or the Transvaal, as might be required.

I had no field artillery under guns at my command, none but garrison gunners, with a detachment of about a dozen drivers at Natal. Two regiments and the artillery were eventually sent from home. I made a point of inspecting the Volunteers and the Burgher Corps coming from Galeka land.

A fine body of Mounted Rangers, called Bowker's Rovers, marched into King William's Town; and in conversation with their second officer I said that I supposed that now the colony would be tranquil. His answer was, " Don't you believe it, General; we are on the eve of a rising of the tribes within the colony." I was much struck with this opinion given by a man who knew the frontier well.

I now deemed it advisable to visit the posts at which my troops were located on the north of King William's Town, at Fort Cunynghame, at Cathcart, and on the Thomas river. Should the Gaikas rise, these would be points of much significance, as it was through this line that they were sure to break, unless prevented, in order to gain the Amatolas. On my return, I recommended that a chain of mounted burghers should be so posted as to patrol this line in force.

As I represented, my infantry could hold the towns, but as they were more than twenty miles asunder, it was impossible for them to prevent the rebels from regaining the mountains.

The War Minister ridiculed the idea that any difficulties could arise should the enemy gain their fastnesses. He said that so large a number of Fingoes were now established near them, that the Kafirs would be driven out in two days. With this opinion the Governor was far from satisfied, and the present Prime Minister, Mr. Sprigg, who was fully alive to the danger, thought that preparation should be made to meet it; using the following strong expressions:—

The border was never in such a deplorable state in any period of its history. Turn where you will, we see nothing but a mass of savagedom in incipient rebellion, and the Government without a force. On the other hand we see large tracts of country abandoned by their inhabitants because the country was overrun by thieves, who set law and order at defiance, and laughed to scorn the threats of the Government, knowing they had no force.

Then again we have had a series of ruinous scares, causing ruin and misery on all sides, and which has culminated in war and bloodshed with one tribe, and a threatened general uprising of the other. And why? Because this obstinate and wicked Ministry would not be encumbered with the maintenance of a force. Have not this Ministry been warned time after time of the danger threatening the border? and have they not been implored by petition after petition, prayer after prayer, to put the country into a state of defence, and have not these petitions been wilfully ignored? and have we not been taunted with cowardice when imploring this Government to put this country into a state of defence? and was it not published and announced, that peace was on the border, and that property was never at any time so secure, whilst the suffering farmers were driven to destruction by the wholesale robberies and unbearable insolence of lawless Kafirs?

Information was given that in the Gaika division shops were being broken open. The following are extracts from some of the many newspaper articles which daily appeared:

All the traders have trecked out of Kafir land, mostly leaving everything behind. This Gray Town is a poor place to stand a brush in, but I suppose we shall go into the fort if anything does turn up. My opinion is that there will be war between us and the Gaikas.

And, again—

There is undoubtedly much excitement throughout Kaffraria.

People who have the facilities for doing so are hastening to those centres of population which promise security to life, and stock is being removed to the Orange Free State. Traders and clergymen are on the move, and the injury done to the colony is incalculable.

If there was any sign of action on the part of the Government there might be some quietude, but when the country is at the mercy of a drunken savage (Sandilli), whose war whistle would at a moment turn peaceful isolated localities into scenes of massacre, there is no wonder that people feel unprotected, and are inclined to form themselves into associations for mutual protection. Prompt action is all that is required.

Very great anxiety now pervaded the colony. Both at King William's Town and Grahamstown public meetings were held for the object of petitioning the Governor to assemble Parliament at any convenient town on the frontier.

At King William's Town, Mr. Walker moved the following resolution:—

That this Meeting deems it necessary that, whilst immediate and prompt measures are required for suppressing the existing disturbances, the Government shall be armed with the necessary power to enforce Burgher duty, and requests his Excellency the Governor to call a special session of Parliament, to be held in some town in the Eastern Province, for the purpose of passing a Burgher law.

In a spirited speech he expressed his conviction "that the Government had never realised the gravity of the situation," and warmly attacked the line of conduct they had pursued. Captain Webster seconded the resolution. Mr. Walker also said, "The Government would, in the end, meet with the retribution they deserved, as being personally responsible for the blood that had been shed. For the robberies committed, for the houses that had been burnt, and for the losses that had fallen upon the farmer, each one of those five men was before Almighty God personally responsible."

The resolution, which it should have been stated was also supported by Mr. Geard, was then put, and all but unanimously carried amidst cheers.

These extracts will show the feeling that prevailed on the eastern frontier.

Towards the end of November, the danger of having permitted Mapasso, the Galeka, with a large following, to remain within the colony armed was fully recognised, and it was settled that he should be disarmed.

I saw that there would be difficulty in putting this into execution; and that if the attempt were not successful, no end of mischief would ensue. I offered in consequence to accept the entire responsibility of this ticklish operation. The acting Minister of War told me that it was a question of police, and vested in the hands of the civil Government.

Very great mismanagement was shown. McKinnon, a warrior chief, defying those that were sent to disarm him, made his way with his followers to the Gaikas, and, like a firebrand, set the whole location on flame. The attempt at disarmament was in my opinion carried out so feebly as to court resistance; and McKinnon's flight was the natural result of the way in which the civil police mismanaged the affair. Being appealed to in extremity I formed a small force, which I placed under Colonel Walker, so as to protect the frontier from invasion, otherwise the rebels could in a few hours have burned the railway station at the Kei Road, and even threatened King William's Town. The Minister for Native Affairs then met Sandilli, from whom he could get but little satisfaction, beyond the remark, "Beware. You tread on a snake; he will turn, and bite you."

At this time the Kafirs were selling their sheep and their poultry at nominal prices, and purchasing blankets, tinder-boxes, and butchers' knives by the thousand.

The country was very excited. Cattle-lifting had reached such an extent as to bid fair to ruin every farmer.

The farmers held meetings, and formed Vigilance Committees. They loudly proclaimed that they would not be ruined, and that they would take matters into their own hands.

Commandant Griffiths now reported that the Galekas, Kreli's forces, were recrossing the Bashee in large numbers, and advancing again into the locations which he had cleared, and that he had not a sufficient force to repel them. I requested him to state what further force he required, when he named about 500 mounted men, and as many infantry. The answer displeased the War Minister so much that he suggested the recall and supercession of the Commandant.

But it was impossible that such a step could be taken after the Commandant had been recommended, and most deservedly recommended, for distinction?

A report was now received from the Transkei, of an action which had been fought near Holland's Farm. It appeared that a body of infantry volunteers, accompanied by two cannon, under a most able officer, Captain Bayly, late Adjutant of the 9th Regiment, were returning across Galeka land towards the colony (their services having been dispensed with), when they were attacked at Umzitzani.

The defence of the position they took up did them the greatest credit, and fully bore out the opinion which had been always expressed concerning them, that, when well commanded (as they here were by Captain Bayly), they would be successful.

The following is an account of this action, written by an eye-witness :—

We left Ibeka at four P.M. on Saturday, 1st, intending to camp for the night at the Residency.

We did not get on the road till about nine o'clock. Steady marching for a couple of miles brought us opposite the spot where Kreli's and Sigcau's kraals stood not long since, and just here we were wakened out of our "March at easy style." A couple of policemen galloped up and brought an order from Inspector Bourne to press on as the Galekas were out in force, and had attacked him. Captain Bayly, Lieutenant Stigant, and Lieutenant Wells, with the Grahams' Town Artillery, went off at a trot, and we stepped out as hard as we could. We marched as fast as we could for a couple of hours, and at last arrived at a place called "Holland's Shop," a name which requires no explanation, the embers and burnt iron marking where a shop once stood. We found that the police had been fired on, and one of their horses shot in the shoulder. The Galekas could be seen on a ridge opposite to us. Below us was a deep kloof, leading to the Buora Kuga river. As far as I could judge, the police and Graham's Town Artillery were sent round to the opposite side to drive the enemy down the kloof to us, we marching down the ridge on our side to meet them as they came through. But we did not get a chance at them then, as they were too far off for us to use our rifles. The Cape Town Artillery sent three or four shells right among them, one being a splendid shot. On the other side the Grahams' Town Artillery and police had some hot work. The enemy retired down the hill as our men advanced, but several were shot by the police. A little way down the artillery sent a round of canister into a bush with murderous effect. The enemy swarmed out on the other side, and came on to the ridge, as if determined to fight. After the artillery had driven the niggers out of the bush on to the ridge, they came on, between 200 and 300 in number. There were only 15 police, and 11 artillery; so you may guess what fearful odds were against our men. In fact the majority of the police at once mounted and galloped off as hard as their horses could go. Inspector Bourne, with a couple of sergeants, fought gallantly to keep the enemy in check, but, unfortunately, three dismounted policemen who had lost their horses were right in the line of fire of the gun, so Lieutenant Wells could not use the canister with which his gun was loaded. He waited until the enemy was not more than seventy-five yards away, coming on, shouting like demons, and pouring volleys along the ridge, and then reluctantly ordered the charge to be withdrawn, and the men to retire. Inspector Bourne managed to bring one of the dismounted men up to the gun, and another was brought up by the artillery; but the third, a young fellow named Wesley, was caught, and assegaied. He fought hard for life, and three or four of the enemy who were stabbing him fell over his body to the rifles of the police and artillery as they retired. The artillery horses brought the gun up the hill at a gallop, although two extra men were on the gun.

As the day wore on, numerous parties of the enemy were seen on both our right and our left, and a few showed themselves on the ridge in front of the camp. For perhaps ten minutes the men were excited, and many fired at random. Not for long, however; they soon settled down to steady work, reserving their fire until they had covered a foe. But for quite an hour and a half there was one incessant rattle of musketry, and it is little less than a miracle that any of us escaped. And the danger was as great from the rear as to the front for being hemmed in; bullets fired at one flank passed over to the other. Not till after eight o'clock did the enemy's fire slacken, and a chance was given us to breathe. As long as the enemy peppered away so long they were peppered in return. Now and then they tried a cheer, but we beat them hollow at that amusement. For nearly a couple of hours the bullets went whistling past, or dropped around us like hail. We, lying on the ground, were to some extent safe, but the officers, walking up and down the line, directing us, supplying ammunition, and giving orders, were especial marks, and yet no one was hit. It seems truly wonderful that they escaped. Soon after eight o'clock the enemy's fire began to slacken, but it was continued at intervals until after nine o'clock. Every now and then the enemy would come up the kloof and give us a volley, but we had our rifles ready to return the compliment, and did so with such effect that they got tired of it at last, and all was still.

Of the enemy's loss we have had no opportunity of judging. Both guns and sniders played fearful havoc. Down the kloof on the right thirty bodies have been counted. On the hill and round the ridge the number of bodies is still larger. It may be accepted that the Galekas lost seventy-five dead and over two hundred wounded. All the wounded were carried off, with one exception, and he was at the point of death when discovered. Some of those killed were men of importance, judging from their ornaments.

So ends my story of the battle of Umzitzani, fought on Sunday, December 2nd, 1877. It has shown all that the war is not over, and that we may expect hard fighting yet.

The fight at Umzitzani caused no small anxiety on the frontier. It was now quite clear that the Galekas had returned, and in large numbers. Certain information was received that, leaving their valuable property, their young women, and their cattle over the Bashee, the fighting men had again retaken the field, unencumbered. Now it was that the Ministry began to see upon what a slender reed they had relied, and how mistaken they had been.

The acting Minister of War desired to bring the Burgher Corps again to the front, but it was reported that he had so irritated the commandants by his hasty and uncourteous manners, that they would not answer to his call.

I then made propositions to the Government, which I felt sure the Burghers would accept, that if they brought their horses, I would arm, clothe, and ration both man and horse, and supply them with transport and ammunition.

So great was the jealousy of the influence that this would give to our British officers, that the Minister declined my offer, stating that it would interfere with his own arrangements, and that the Burghers were not willing to serve under her Majesty's officers. This opinion the War Minister conveyed to his Excellency. The incorrectness of it has been subsequently proved beyond all doubt, as the following extract from a speech of an influential person will illustrate.

Again, Gentlemen, I was repeatedly assured, on very high authority, that there was an invincible repugnance on the part of the volunteers to be commanded by officers of her Majesty's forces. That the fact of the command in the field being vested in the General commanding her Majesty's Forces, was sufficient to deter men from volunteering from service. I took the liberty of doubting from my own experience whether any feeling of the kind existed, and I can only say that during all the time I was on the Frontier I saw nothing of it, and that both the late and the present General commanding the forces assured me they had seen and experienced nothing of any such feeling, and that on the contrary they always found all volunteers and Burghers, whencesoever they came, and whatever might be the race from which they sprung, most ready and willing to serve under them, and to stand shoulder to shoulder alongside her Majesty's troops in the field and only too eager to do their full share of the fighting.

It was impossible that the Governor could see an army of savages collecting on the border of the colony threatening any day to overrun it without taking the most strenuous measures in his power to disperse and destroy them. He saw that this could not be accomplished by the neglected defensive forces of the colony, and despite the chances of a rebellion within our frontier, he requested me to use my utmost endeavours to collect together the best force I could, and march them over the Kei. This was on the 6th of December.

CHAPTER XXXVI.

MARCH OF THE BRITISH TROOPS OVER THE KEI.

My first act was to order every available man of the 88th Regiment, then in Cape Town, to the front.

I mounted about fifty men of the 24th Regiment for cavalry service. Arms were placed in the hands of every non-combatant of the forces in King William's Town, and the band of the 24th was instructed in the gun exercise. A 7-pounder (weighing 150 lbs.) was placed under their charge. The rapidity with which they learnt this exercise was amazing. After ten days' instruction, they were able to load and come into action in *fifteen seconds;* but there was no duty whatever which the 24th Regiment could not be found equal to. I at once purchased horses for four 7-lb. guns, and formed a small force of artillery. There were scarcely sufficient troops to defend the city in King William's Town, the 24th Regiment being divided between seven or eight small stations in the district. There were no stores for a march, no transport, no mounted men, no regular artillerymen, and the civil Government could not or would not supplement any of these requisites.

The War Minister urged the advance of her Majesty's troops even without these essentials. "Push over the Kei," said he, "with a few Scotch carts; cross by the nearest route the Chickaba."

I should indeed have ill performed my duty to her Majesty or to the colony, if I had sent 200 men (all that could possibly be brought together) wildly, without transport, ammunition, or guns, into a dense bush, across a river running through stupendous ravines, under the conditions recommended, "with a few Scotch carts," and over a drift which afterwards proved impracticable.

But the fact was that this Minister knew that by his faulty arrangements he had gone well nigh to ruin the colony, and therefore only thought of saving his own credit at the expense of everyone around him.

With the utmost expedition the detachments were concentrated by forced marches, verging towards the Komgha. I at once informed his Excellency the Governor that the supply and transport for all the force, whether imperial or colonial, over the Kei, must be placed under the management of British officers, to which he assented. Under that admirable officer, Deputy-Commander General Strickland, ably seconded by Assistant-Commissary Warneford, the commissariat then worked wonders impossible of accomplishment by any but well instructed and efficient officers. They collected supplies and transport in spite of incredible difficulties.

I purchased as much powder and lead as I could procure in King William's Town, and despatched it to the front. I had to depend for the escort of all these supplies upon my own military force.

The supplies across the Kei had been so completely neglected, that I discovered, after much difficulty, that they consisted of only a week's food for the men and horses of the frontier force, and only three charges of powder and one bullet per man for the native allies.

I greatly appreciated the zeal and intelligence of Colonel Glyn, whom I directed to take command in the Transkei, and of all his officers.

The Minister kept urging that I should dash the first few soldiers that could be got over the Kei against the enemy.

Faithful to what I knew to be my military duty, I would not consent to such folly, or bring what I believed likely to be inevitable disgrace on her Majesty's troops. I was determined to make a certainty of success, and the result, as I will show, entirely proved the wisdom of the course I took.

One consideration of great importance had to be taken into account, the possible flooding of the Kei river. Should this occur before supplies had been got over, the force could not exist, and we were in the very season in which a flood might be expected. In the year 1874, forty waggons had actually been detained at the drift for three months, owing to the impassable condition of the river.

In eighteen days my force was ready, sufficient provision made for the defence of the positions which were to be evacuated by troops, and garrisoned by volunteers, and enough supplies prepared to justify an advance.

The vicious system of a double commissariat, which eventually caused so large an outlay and expenditure, now became apparent. A competition in the market was set up between the Colonial and Imperial purchasers.

The greater part of my small force was assembled near Ibeka by the 22nd and 23rd, the artillery arriving on the evening of the 25th. The three columns marched at 5 A.M. on the 26th, and I am happy to say that during the time they remained in the Transkei there was no waiting for rations, and no delay for ammunition.

The Governor sanctioned my raising a corps of cavalry and two corps of infantry. I placed the first under command of Lieutenant Carrington; the infantry under Major Pulleine. The zeal and success of these officers were of great service.

His Excellency had requested the Commodore to bring up H.M.S. *Active*, and a naval brigade was formed. This most valuable adjunct was marched to the Komgha, where I directed one-half of it, with its rockets and gun, to cross the

Kei. The other half was posted at the Komgha and Fort Cunyinghame, an arrangement which proved most valuable, especially when Sandilli and the Gaikas broke into open rebellion.

The difficulties I had to surmount were considerable. By far the greatest was to discover the number and situation of the Volunteer Corps, for they were constantly being moved by order of the Minister of War, who did not inform me of their whereabouts.

The continued support and assistance which the Governor rendered me was invaluable, and I felt deeply grateful for it. His own exertions were such as could only be understood by those who knew what he had accomplished during the Indian Mutiny, when in the Council of the Viceroy of India.

On the 21st of December I left King William's Town to join the forces in the Transkei, passing by Deadman's Gulley, Hangman's Bush, and Murderer's Kop (a gloomy list of prominent points). I arrived that evening at the Komgha.

On the following morning at six, when starting for the river, I was informed that Kiva, a noted warrior of the Galekas, had crossed the Kei with a large force, and that he was but a few miles in my front.

All the cavalry and mounted men that I had were but a few orderlies, and not more than eight mounted police could be assembled.

With this force my aide-de-camp and Major Moore advanced to the frontier between the Komgha and the river. My principal source of anxiety was for the two guns which had preceded me on the previous evening, and would by this time be exactly in the line of march of Kiva's force. No cavalry escort could be procured for them, as I did not possess any. Fortunately, Lieut. Kell, 88th Regiment, the intelligent officer to whom, in default of a regular artillery man, I had entrusted the command, had heard of the advance and remained at Pullen's farm to wait for orders.

The few police under Major Moore came up with the rear of Kiva's force just as they were entering Murderer's Kop, but could do little more than watch their movements. Thus this dangerous character had crossed into the colony, as he could not have done had a sufficient force of mounted burghers been stationed in the positions I had indicated long before.

On the morning of the 23rd, having ascertained that the way was clear for the guns, I crossed at right angles to the path which Kiva had taken on the previous day, and we thus passed through the ravine and over the river, arriving at Foleni on the 24th. On Christmas Day we pushed on to Ibeka, where I established my headquarters.

CHAPTER XXXVII.

ATTACKS BY THE KAFIRS UPON THE MAILS BETWEEN THE
CIS- AND TRANS-KEI.

On the 25th we ate our Christmas dinner with the 24th Regiment. That evening the guns arrived. Next day at daybreak the columns started; the centre under Colonel Glyn, the right from the springs, under Major Hopton, the left under Captain Upcher, to each of whom was allotted a part of the artillery, the mounted police, and the Naval brigade, with about 1000 Fingoes all told, the latter being chiefly attached to the centre division.

Exactly the same measures were carried out as on the previous occasion under Commandant Griffiths, sweeping the enemy from west to east, first by the Manubee forest, then along the coast to the Bashee. The ravines, mountains, and rivers, presented the same difficulties, but with the assistance of a pontoon the movement was completed within a few days. A great many cattle were captured, more than 1000 head by Colonel Glyn's column, and 500 by Captain Upcher. H.M.S. *Active*, under Commodore Sullivan, moved along the coast as the troops advanced, and communicated with them at the mouth of the Bashee.

Under sanction of the High Commissioner I offered 500 head of cattle, or 100*l.*, for the capture of Kreli, not dead or alive, but to be delivered in safety into camp. This reward continued to be offered to the end of the war, but, to the honour of the Galekas be it said, that although they were in such a starving state as *to be actually eating the bark of the trees*, no traitor was found base enough to betray him. It reminds one of the days of the Pretender, when a reward of 30,000*l.* could not induce a Highlander to betray his prince.

A few small engagements took place, but none of any consequence. A policeman carrying despatches was shot, and many farms on the borders were burned. I used my best endeavours at Ibeka to discover if the enemy were collecting in any particular direction. One of my greatest difficulties was in the intelligence department, which appeared to have been sadly neglected, for although handsome allowances had been paid for the service to native policemen, they appeared either unable or unwilling to afford me such advantages as an officer in command has a right to expect.

On the 29th of December, telegraphic news arrived, that the Gaikas, who occupied the country in our rear, had at length risen in rebellion, and that our mails to the colony had been seized. In fact, our communications were entirely cut off, and no force existed to keep them open. No waggon passed for three weeks, and had we not been well supplied beforehand the consequences might have been very serious.

On the 29th and 30th December, small bodies of troops sent to clear the road for the postal service were attacked by the enemy, whom they signally defeated. Brevet-Major Moore, 88th Regiment, reported that on the 29th of December, he left the Komgha camp with a patrol of thirty-two noncommissioned officers and men of the frontier armed and mounted police under Sub-Inspector Mitchell, in the direction of Draaibosch, near which place the postriders, carrying the mails to Kei Road, had been fired on and forced to return. His report goes on to say :—

About four miles from Komgha I turned off the road to the

right, and advanced cautiously, with patrols thrown out to
the top of a neighbouring hill, on the further slope of which,
among large boulders, were posted a number of Kafirs with
guns and assegais. I was with the advanced party, and called
upon the Kafirs nearest to me to lay down their arms. In
reply, a shot was fired at us by a man thirty or forty yards
off, and others quickly followed. The troop having come up
presently, I ordered the men to dismount, and half to
skirmish. The Kafirs, about 100 in number, then began to
run down the slope towards the Kabousie, followed for a
short distance by our skirmishers. We then mounted, and
took up a commanding position about a mile nearer the
Draaibosch, from which we could see another party of Kafirs
coming from the direction of the Kabousie, with the intention apparently, of getting round our left. Having again
dismounted and commenced skirmishing, the enemy retired
in haste towards the river. We then turned away sharp to
the left, towards Draaibosch, in order to gain a detachment
of 40 men, 88th Regiment, under Lieutenant Wool, who
were escorting ammunition waggons to Komgha. About two
miles from the ruins of Macdonald's canteen, our right patrol
came upon a body of about 300 Kafirs, who were advancing
in our direction; the troop was ordered to dismount to
receive them, but after firing a few shots retired. The
Kafirs followed up, and having overtaken one man, Private
Glesse, who was dismounted, killed him with assegais, despite
the efforts of a few to rescue him. I grieve to say that we
were unable to recover the body.

Major Moore again wrote under date December 31:—

I left Komgha yesterday at 11 A.M. with forty men of the
88th Regiment under Captain Acklom, and twenty-one frontier
armed mounted police, for the purpose of escorting the mail
from the Transkei past Draaibosch. When we approached

Savage's Shop, six miles from Komgha, large bodies of Kafirs were seen mustered about a mile to our right, *i.e.* north. Fearing an attack, I selected a good defensive position on the crown of a hill, about half a mile beyond Savage's Shop, and close to the road. We were not kept long in suspense as to the enemy's intention, for by the time our arrangements were completed about 600 footmen and 50 mounted men (the latter took no part in the action) were seen advancing rapidly and in perfect order. At about 500 yards we opened fire, upon which the bullocks ran off with our ammunition-cart to our rear. The enemy continued to advance, and detached large bodies to both flanks, chiefly to our right, some men also getting to our rear, into whose hands the ammunition-cart fell. The fight lasted from 2.15 to 3.45 P.M., bodies of the enemy being within assegai range; but very few assegais were thrown, nearly all the Kafirs opposed to us being armed with guns and rifles. Our ammunition, of which the troops carried forty rounds, beginning to fall short, matters were becoming critical, and we were obliged to have recourse to frequent bayonet charges, before which the enemy always gave way. We were careful to keep fast hold of the hill top, and the Kafirs at length began to retire from all sides, leisurely making their way in the direction from which they came. The Connaught Rangers, boys though they are—not one of them had ever seen an enemy before—and some of the frontier armed mountain police, behaved admirably well; they repelled attack after attack from large bodies advancing in every direction, charging with a cheer when called on, and held final possession of the well-contested hill-top. Their fire, however, was very mild, to which may be attributed the small number of the enemy accounted for.

Major Moore was severely wounded with an assegai as

he was standing over the body of a disabled policeman, but notwithstanding this he still continued his command.

All accounts concur in stating that the action was a most spirited affair. The onslaught of the Kafirs, personally led by Dhimba and Mackinnon, was repeated with desperate persistence, and nothing but coolness and prudence could have saved the handful of men from being hemmed in and cut to pieces. All were loud in the praises of Major Moore, whose gallantry was no less conspicuous than his careful manipulation of the men under his command.

The Connaught Rangers are said to have displayed great readiness and pluck, but the police themselves reluctantly admit that these qualities were rather the exception than the rule among their own force. It is, however, but fair to them to say that some of them were as young as, and less instructed than, the Connaught Rangers. In the beginning of January Mr. R. G. Tainton, Mr. J. H. Tainton, and Mr. W. C. Brown were murdered at Berlin, about eleven miles from King William's Town. These gentlemen were imprudently placed in the power of the Kafirs, and this tragic result was the consequence.

The sad story told by the Fingo orderly of Mr. R. G. Tainton is as follows:—

I was near the river when I heard a school Kafir woman cry, "Look! they are being surrounded," and I saw a number of armed natives gathering in the bushes; running up I saw three gentlemen go into the hut and get their guns and ammunition, and I got mine also. The enemy were then quite close to us, and advanced menacingly upon our party. We were told not to shoot, and Mr. R. G. Tainton advanced towards the Kafirs, who were then about fifty yards off, saying, "Do not fire; we are not here to fight; go back," and other words to this effect. I think that they quieted a little; they were right round us, and one of the police madly fired his rifle off (this, however, is not corroborated by the others), and it was at once answered with a volley from the Kafirs. Some twenty of the men of our party then bolted without firing a shot, and the Kafirs cried: "See, they are leaving their great chiefs;" but the rest of us fired. I saw Mr. R. G. Tainton shoot a Kafir in the neck, who fell dead; but, as he was in the act of putting another cartridge in his gun, a Kafir shot him from behind, striking him in the groin; he did not fall, but slowly sank stoopingly over the gun, and several Kafirs rushed in stabbing him with assegais in the back of the head and neck, thus killing him. Mr. John Tainton, on seeing his brother fall, ran to his assistance, shooting one of the murderers, who was within a few inches of the muzzle of his gun, but before he could reload he was also stabbed to death. Mr. Brown was also surrounded by these remorseless savages, and after bringing down one or two of the enemy, he too was assegaied in a similar manner. Seeing my masters were killed, I dived away into a bush, injuring my leg in doing so. I heard the Kafirs kill a policeman in a kloof, who asked loudly for mercy. I then got away as quickly as I could; some of the horses we managed to catch and bring away, but guns and many other things we had fell into the hands of our enemies. I consider that we let them get too close before firing, but Mr. Tainton was anxious not to fight. The headman evidently agreed to settle the matter, because he wanted to gain time to make an attack on us. They gave the war cry as they advanced upon us.

This circumstance created a great sensation on the eastern frontier. The Gaikas then began to throw off all semblance of respect for authority.

I visited my camp in the east of Galeka land, and in conjunction with Captain Nixon, the senior officer of the Royal Engineers, selected suitable positions for erecting posts. I also visited the "Idulchwa" reserve, where a large force of Tambookies was stationed under Major Elliott. These natives were in charge of their chief Gangeleswe. During the war he had done good service to the Government. This, however, was not so much to be wondered at, as he was a bitter foe of Kreli's.

It will be remembered that I described how of their quarrel began. It originated in Gangeleswe's ill-treatment of his wife, Kreli's daughter. When the Galeka chief subsequently became a fugitive and a hunted outcast in his own country, and when his family was starving, his daughter was persuaded again to seek an asylum in Tembu land. Gangeleswe had made continual endeavours to effect her return to him, not at all on account of any repentance for his former conduct, or from any affectionate feelings towards her, but for the following reason. The ceremony of circumcision is a positive obligation in his tribe. By native custom or law this rite can not be undergone except in the presence of the mother, should she be alive, so that nothing could exceed his delight in recovering her in whose presence alone this ceremony could be legally performed upon his sons. Not long after her arrival at the chief's kraal, fresh quarrels arose, and this "great wife" caused him to be summoned to appear before a Council of Indunas or Elders. She accused him of beating her eight different times, thrice with knobkerries and five times with his hand; she showed the marks of his blows, and she complained that he had not properly furnished her house. The first accusation, he replied, was not true, he had only beaten her four times; and in regard to the furniture she was fastidious. He asked, had he not presented her with a mat and a calabash, and given her two cows, and what more could she desire? He added that the chastisement which he had given her was justified by her continued use of improper and insulting language to him. On being requested to give further explanation, he said that she persisted in using words in her conversation with him that commenced with a syllable in his name, instead of using a paraphrase to express her thoughts.

On the war breaking out, he attached himself, like a trembling cur, to the heels of Major Elliott, fearful lest he should be murdered if he remained at home. He had about 3000 followers, who, however, were great cowards, and very inferior to the Fingoes or Galekas.

On my return, and shortly before reaching Ibeka, I overtook a party of Kafir women who were carrying beer in wooden vessels to serve the camp. This was for the refreshment of the natives employed with the transport. It resembled weak pig-wash, as nearly as I am able to describe it, dark fatty substances floating through the mess. Notwithstanding its uninviting appearance, I had the curiosity to try the sour, horrid mixture; but it was some hours before I could get rid of its acid and revolting taste. This beer had been brought from the kraal of one Smith Possa. He is said to be the grandchild of a French woman, who escaped with several other ladies from the wreck of a vessel bound from India to Europe. The crew were murdered, and the women divided as wives amongst the adjacent chiefs.

CHAPTER XXXVIII.

THE OPERATIONS OF THE BRITISH TROOPS IN THE TRANSKEI.

It is now time to return to the doings of the columns which had been sent out to scour the country. I had retained the volunteers to guard stores at Ibeka, regretting that I could not employ them in the field. They frequently requested to be sent home; but as I left it entirely optional to them to stay or go, it was fortunate for me that they remained, as our stores of food and ammunition would otherwise have been placed in some danger, my force at Ibeka consisting without them of less than a hundred men, while thousands of the enemy were within ten miles of my camp.

We received information that a large body of Galekas had doubled back, and were concentrating near the Kei, with a force of the Gaikas, who had come over from Sandilli's location. Upon this I sent an express to Colonel Glyn, who was then at the mouth of the Bashee, directing him to march at once, and with the utmost celerity, to Ibeka. Losing not a moment, he obeyed my orders, arriving on the third day by forced marches, sailors, soldiers, and police being equally delighted with the chance of meeting the enemy who had so often eluded them.

Colonel Glyn's operations had been most successful. He had driven the natives before him, attacking them whenever they made the slightest stand, and never ceasing his marches till called away to obey my orders.

Early on the morning of the 13th the troops marched to

join the Quintana column, which was now under command of Major Owen, 88th Regiment, Major Hepton having been selected for special service on the other side of the Kei. Scarcely had Colonel Glyn reached his camp when my aide-de-camp, Lieutenant Coghill, galloped up with intelligence from me of an intended attack by the enemy. Resuming his march with all speed, he joined the troops in advance, and finally united with Major Owen's column. Thus the forces which were so widely apart two days before were rapidly concentrated.

When Major Owen's camp at Nyumaxa was reached, large bodies of the enemy were reported gathering on the neighbouring heights. Captain Robinson, R.A., and seventy Frontier Army Mounted Police, with two 7-pounder guns, were left to protect the camp, and the order to advance and attack was given, Colonel Glyn taking command of both columns, Major Owen commanding his own, which was the first line of attack, and Captain Upcher the second.

The Fingoes, 200 in number, under Captain Veldtman, had preceded the advance, and disposed themselves so as to co-operate in the attack. On reaching the brow of the hill the enemy were perceived in large numbers. On the columns getting in sight the Kafirs advanced.

The first line consisted of one company 24th Regiment on the right, and an equal number of the 88th Regiment on the left. In the centre were the guns, under Lieutenant Kell, and one rocket party of blue-jackets, under Lieutenant Cochrane, and another with the men of the 24th Regiment, under Lieutenant Maine, R.E.

Inspector Bourne's troop of police were in rear, commanding a deep kloof to protect the left flank; Inspector Chalmers on the right, to watch another dangerous kloof; and Captain Upcher's party, consisting of the 24th Regiment, and marines, under Lieutenant Dowding, in reserve.

The country was an undulating plain, with rugged country in

the foreground, and deep-wooded kloofs on either hand. The ground in the immediate front of the position fell away into a small valley, covered by long grass, stones, and tangled brushwood, well adapted for skirmishing.

At 4.30 the first shot was fired by Lieutenant Maine's rocket-party into the masses of the enemy, who were swarming on the face of the opposite hills. The first was a little high, but the second was most effective, three men falling. The Kafirs, who were unaccustomed to such fireworks, dispersed, taking to the kloofs on either flank. Almost directly small-arm firing was commenced by Inspector Bourne's troop, and the action became general.

The troops broke into skirmishing order, and advanced. The 88th, gallantly led by Major Owen, rushed forward with a cheer, and opened a hot fire on the Kafirs, who were creeping up the kloofs, taking advantage of the long grass and broken ground in front of the position. The 88th being hotly engaged, and four of the men having fallen, three of them severely wounded, Colonel Glyn reinforced them by the mounted men of the 24th Regiment, who, leaving their horses on the brow, dashed down in skirmishing order, led by Lieutenant Clements, and forced the enemy to evacuate their positions. The Kafirs having now come up in great force, Colonel Glyn sent for the reserve. Captain Upcher brought his men up at the double, and, breaking into skirmishing order, outflanked the enemy on their right, and opened a galling fire. This, after a short time, forced the enemy back, and they retired sullenly, returning the fire of the troops. On the right the troops were equally successful, forcing the enemy back with loss, and driving them into the kloofs, which, unfortunately for them, were already occupied by Captain Veldtman's Fingoes, who attacked them and did great execution. During the action the kloofs and wooded krantzes were shelled by the two 7-pounder guns under Lieutenant Kell, 88th Regiment, and searched by the rockets of the two parties detached for that service, both of whom did great damage to the enemy. By about 5.15 the Kafirs were in full retreat.

They were pursued from bush to bush, and driven from the various strongholds where they attempted to make a stand. By 6 o'clock, as evening was drawing on, Colonel Glyn gave the order to cease the pursuit, and, recalling his men, marched back to camp. Thus ended the action of Nyumaxa, the enemy losing fifty-four counted dead on the field; and from the reports of the number of wounded brought in on the following day, and the subsequent discovery of many more bodies in the kloofs and woods, we may fairly conjecture that a salutary lesson was administered to him.

It has since been stated that four chiefs were killed in this engagement.

On many of the bodies of the dead Kafirs were found passes certifying that they were loyal subjects.

The soldiers of the 24th Regiment were much elated at the first chance they had of meeting the enemy, and the more so, as the action was fought on the anniversary of the battle of Chillianwallah, in which their regiment had so greatly distinguished itself twenty years before. After that battle the lifeless bodies of thirteen officers of the regiment were stretched on the mess-table.

At no time had the power of the Martini-Henry rifle been more conspicuously shown; indeed, it was perhaps the first occasion when it had been fairly used by the soldiers of the British army.

Several instances of the long range of this weapon were recorded. All of them, however, were eclipsed at the Waterkloof, when the Sergeant Instructor of Musketry of the 90th Light Infantry killed a Kafir, by deliberate aim, at 1800 yards' distance—a little over a mile! He also shot a small bird (a parrot) in a tree at 200 yards' range. Near

Baillie's Grave, one of the enemy made himself defiantly conspicuous to a party of the 2nd-24th Regiment. Several shots were fired at him, which caused the fellow gradually to increase his distance. At slightly over a thousand yards the native appeared to consider himself safe, but an officer came upon the scene, and at his first shot the whooping and dancing Kafir received a fatal bullet between his shoulders.

The small 7- and 9-pounder guns, as well as the rockets, gave our troops a great advantage.

Kreli was known to have become possessed of a small cannon, which was buried somewhere near his "Great Place." When at Ibeka I endeavoured to procure it, but was not successful. He is said to have prized it greatly, as the "mother of muskets," though I am sure he did not himself believe in such a fable.

On the 8th of January a cypher message was received from Captain Wardell, commanding a detachment of the 24th Regiment at Impetu, conveyed by a native who had succeeded in eluding the enemy, giving information that his post was completely surrounded and cut off. Whilst inflicting loss on the enemy, he had succeeded in beating them off without greater loss than that of the commissariat oxen attached to the post. The message ran as follows:

> Our communications are cut off. We are surrounded on all sides by Kafirs, who are destroying everything. Spencer is here with his men from Port Buffalo, all except party at Fort Linsingen. I do not see my way to relieving them at present. The enemy being so strong between us in the Chichaba, it will be as much as we can do to hold our own here. Spencer's camp was attacked last night; it adjoined our redoubt. Enemy driven off. No loss to us. Expect same will occur often in some form, as they appear so very determined. In broad daylight yesterday they carried off

about one hundred of our commissariat oxen. The Chichaba is full of Kafirs, under five chiefs. We want ammunition to complete our reserve, and also Sniders for volunteers. I should like a field-piece, also some rockets; our position being so very open and exposed. We have supplies for about ten days. Ten families in "laager" here. Have seventy women and children, who passed night in ditch of our fort; no other place of safety; also our horses. Maclean has not returned. We are obliged to be under arms all night lately. Can you send me any sand-bags?

On the following morning, the 7th, Lieutenant-Colonel Lambert left Komgha with a force of three 7-pounders, 467 infantry, 86 horse, and 250 Fingo levies. No enemy was encountered. Reaching Impetu, distant eighteen miles from Komgha, it was found that the seventeen men shut up in Fort Linsingen had been relieved from their critical position with assistance rendered by Mapassa, the Galeka Chief, who had sought our protection at the commencement of this campaign, and whose tribe was located on the Galeka side of the Kei. The men had been thus enabled to fall back, though with much difficulty, on Impetu, being attacked on their way, and the Impetu garrison marching to their assistance. Many farmers, with their families, friendly natives, and over one hundred women and children, had taken refuge in the small ditch around the camp; and these, with a long train of waggons, 310 head of cattle, and 2349 sheep, accompanied the troops on their return to Komgha, materially lengthening the march.

CHAPTER XXXIX.

USE OF THE TELEGRAPH IN THE WAR.

I HAD arranged by telegram a few days previously with my Adjutant-General, Colonel Bellairs, who was commanding at King William's Town, a general advance from both sides of the Kei river, on the Chichaba, a dense and very extensive forest, on either side of the Kei river, commencing near the junction of the Butterworth river, and extending towards the sea.

Before the commencement of the war, the Colonial Government had most wisely commenced paying attention to the general telegraphic communication of the colony; and most fortunately Mr. Severight, an active, intelligent, and well-instructed gentleman, had been out to superintend them.

His exertions were never relaxed in placing our telegraphic communications in order, and thus we held communication early in the war with almost every position in which troops were located. It may naturally be asked, how it was that the Kafirs, moving with impunity over large tracts of country traversed by these wires, did not destroy them?

The only answer is, that they looked upon them as English witchcraft. They dreaded them, they prayed even to them at night, they made incantations around the tall posts and mysterious wires, invoking their kindness and leniency. This treating with deference the gods of an enemy is a very peculiar trait of savage feeling. They thought that these wires were hurtful to them in some mysterious way, but they dared not destroy them, and their happy infatuation preserved to us one of the greatest advantages.

By the liberal use of the telegraph I was enabled to make the Governor acquainted with every move on the Transkei, and was informed of many military circumstances relating to my force, and was able to converse with my Deputy-Adjutant-General at pleasure. Thus the arrangements which were made for the attack upon the Chichaba were perfect even to the smallest details. At some of the minor stations rather singular mistakes were occasionally made. For instance: a telegram came from an officer, who was zealous in correct detail, asking for certain "rules and regulations;" but as supplies for the troops were in the mind of every one, the clerk read it, "Send us mules and vegetables." The mules arrived and were most acceptable, for the guns, and the potatoes were far more useful to the troops than any code of regulations could have been.

It was very important that a native Fingo force should be collected for the attack upon Chichaba, which can be traversed only with great difficulty by English soldiers alone. The Fingoes spy out the enemy, and firmly rely upon the English when they have occasion to retreat. They perform most excellent service, and evince much bravery, quite equal to either the Gaikas or the Galekas, or any other tribes who have become famous as warriors.

In making my preparations, on calling for bodies of these men from the magistrates in Fingoland, what was my disappointment to find that the Colonial Minister of War had already desired those that had arms to march in another direction, and join a column of the force which he had collected in the neighbourhood of Queenstown. They had taken with them the arms and ammunition which I had issued to them from the small stores in my possession, for the very purpose for which I now required their services.

This caused me great difficulties, as the arrangements for our movement were of a peculiarly complicated character.

After great exertions I managed, however, to collect about one-third of the number which I desired.

I had only two small corps of Burgher Cavalry attached to my troops, of about twenty-five men each. They were farmers whose properties lay immediately in the vicinity of the Komgha, and who did not desire to be far distant from their homes. My cavalry force under that excellent officer, Carrington, was now, however, attaining some sort of organisation, and did good service in keeping open my communications.

A short time prior to the attack upon Chichaba Captain Boyes was killed in the bush, his death being occasioned by his penetrating with too small a force into the dense forest.

Captain von Leiningen, a brave and excellent officer, very nearly shared the same fate. He met some Kafir women. After they had passed it came into his mind to tell them to join another party of women, who had passed shortly before, and had said they were moving off. He rode back with two of his men, and after searching for a while found the party. Whilst he was speaking with them, two women came up panting and dripping with sweat—one drawing nearer and nearer to his horse. When he followed the looks of her eyes he saw a great number of Kafirs creeping up towards him in the long grass. His party had only time to fire off their guns and retreat.

The troops for the attack of the Chichaba left Komgha on the 14th of January, the right column under the command of Colonel Lambert, and the left in charge of Major Moore, both officers of the 80th Regiment. The total strength of each comprised about 200 white troops, including police and volunteers, and in addition to these about 1000 Fingoes assisted in the attack. Impetu was reached on the 15th, and here the force was strengthened by Captain Brabant, in command of the

East London volunteers, who had already had a brush with the enemy, and had captured 3000 head of cattle and several thousand sheep. On learning that large herds of cattle had been seen in the valley, Colonel Lambert at once sent his men forward to attempt a capture, and they returned to camp towards dusk in possession of nearly 4000 head. The Kafirs in that particular locality were not in great force, and made little or no resistance. On the following morning an attack was made on a long deep ravine, filled with Kafirs and cattle. The natives here showed a bold front, but only for a short time, as they fell back after a brief engagement with a loss of forty men. Owing to the impracticable nature of the ground it was impossible to follow up this success with such speed as would have enabled our force to overtake the enemy. However, 4000 more cattle were captured, and the Kafirs completely driven out of the valley by the very effective shell and rocket firing. Our attacking force numbered not more than 500 Europeans and 1000 Fingoes. The enemy was strongly posted over an area of perhaps twenty square miles of most difficult country. From the representations of prisoners and other natives, it would appear that he was greatly surprised at the ease with which the white man drove him from his stronghold, and that the rockets passed his comprehension altogether. The only cavalry was that of Captain Brabant, who had consented to join the expedition for two days' service. When the cattle were driven out of the forest these mounted men were on the watch, ten miles in advance of the force, and they at once pounced upon 4000 head, not, however, without receiving some shots from Captain McClean's Fingoes, who were in the act of capturing them from the Transkei side, and to whom was due the credit of driving them from the bush.

The column on the western side of the Kei then returned to the Komgha, ready for any attack which it might be considered advantageous for them to make upon Kreli. They had captured more than 10,000 head of cattle and 500 sheep, and as the greatest proof of victory in South Africa is the capture of cattle, these successes were very satisfactory.

The column under Colonel Glyn had some further skirmishes on the east bank of the Kei, in a very difficult and intricate country.

A calamity as great as war itself was now threatening us. There was but little doubt that a period of famine was fast approaching. At this season of the year the hillsides are usually covered with rich green grass; this year, however, the long-continued drought parched and withered every blade, and the country was red instead of green. Every streamlet was dried up, and the rivers stood still in their beds. Then, again, when the farmers should have been ploughing and sowing, they were called away to protect their lands and their lives.

From a military point of view, the advantage of this extraordinary drought was twofold. The miserable Kafirs were perishing with hunger, which caused numbers to deliver themselves, with their arms, up to the Government. As there were no floods, the communications with Galekaland were never interrupted.

The Minister of War now devised a species of troops called "special constables," in order that they might be free of the control either of the Governor as commander-in-chief, or of any of the British officers. They were in reality a burgher mounted corps, drawn from the various towns on the eastern side of the colony, even as far off as Cradock. He kept this force under his own control, and, for a long time, its numbers were not known either to the Governor or to myself. We shall see in the sequel that the patience of the Governor was eventually exhausted.

A man may be ever so clever and energetic, but if he is ignorant of a business, and too proud to learn, he cannot be expected to succeed.

The first command was delegated to an officer whom I have every reason to believe to have been energetic and zealous, and whose services I should have most gratefully received.

On the 16th, Commandant Frost, at the head of a troop of Tarkastadt burghers, engaged a large body of the enemy near the junction of the Kei and Kabousie rivers. Some very hard fighting ensued, but the enemy was completely routed, and more than 100 bodies were counted on the field after the action. On our side one man was killed and several severely wounded.

Commandant Frost's supplies being insufficient, he appeared at my storehouse at the Komgha with nothing for man or horse. My commissary very properly supplied his force with sufficient sustenance for the time, but it was utterly impossible for him to make adequate provision for the troops if he was to be subject to such uncertain demands upon his stores.

Towards the end of January I received information from King William's Town that the War Minister had converted his special constables into a by no means small force; that they probably numbered 7000 or more Europeans; that by his orders military movements on a large scale were being carried out in the north; that reports were received by him, ignoring the proper channel through which this military information is invariably given; and that, slighting the position of his Excellency the Governor, he had published his despatches in the *Gazette* by his own authority and with his own signature alone.

Moreover, as appointments could not be valid without the authority of the Governor, or the persons appointed draw their pay without it, so without his Excellency's sanction he had gone so far as to publish their names in the *Gazette* as "by authority."

Commandant Griffiths was gazetted under a title unknown in England or her Majesty's colonies as "Commandant-General," thus openly disregarding all constitutional precedent and law, so that the Colonial War Minister assumed a position which was justly described in some of the newspapers as that of "military dictator."

A report was extant that an expedition against a chief in the Tambookie location named Gougobella was actually going on, but the Governor could give me no information on the subject.

His Excellency has said—

Two important movements—Frost's and Brabant's—were in contemplation, both under the exclusive direction of Mr. Merriman, who gave us what information we possess on the subject. The information, however, we have regarding both is so vague and defective, that useful co-operation is almost impossible, and does not seem to be desired, as no apparent attempt is made to supply defects of mounted and native levies, which must be supplied if the detachments of her Majesty's troops are to be actively utilised, and Frost's operations are, I believe, proceeding under defective conditions of co-operation, which I have warned you, I think, likely to lead to disaster; though, of course, they may succeed.

It appeared to me a kind of raid which was to be deprecated, especially at this moment, and one more likely to drive natives into rebellion than to avert it.

But troops had now assembled at Queenstown, and the farmers that composed these forces were naturally irritated at the losses which they had sustained in cattle; and as there was no control from supreme authority, military movements were carried on by the commandants and civil magistrates.

The remarks upon this expedition by the *Northern Post* were as follows:—

It must be confessed that either Mr. Merriman, the War Minister, or Mr. Hemming, the President Magistrate of

Queenstown, who led the expedition against Gongobella, or whoever else was responsible for it, was, apparently, particularly anxious to take up the first excuse for fighting. It was touch and go, whether the expedition against Gongobella was enough to stir up the whole of the Tambookie tribe, and it certainly endangered the district of Wodehouse and Dordrecht in a manner most needless and reckless. Gongobella was a British subject, residing within the jurisdiction of our courts of law, and if he had committed any act against the laws of the colony, there were proper methods of procedure; but it is not tolerable that any resident magistrate should be given carte-blanche to lead a warlike expedition against any person who has not successfully obeyed his command to capture and deliver up wrong doers, or who, under a false impression, has taken suitable measures to repel an anticipated attack. In all that Gongobella did, there is nothing to indicate any disloyalty against Government, and it is the purest tyranny of might to crush him to pieces on the first paltry excuse. Without caring to commit ourselves to an opinion detrimental to Mr. Hemming's motives, or the motives of any one, it does seem very much as if it was regarded as convenient by the Queenstown people to take advantage of the presence of a large number of Albert Burghers and some Alwial North Volunteers, in order to stamp out a petty chief who had given occasion for uneasiness. We are in the Cape Colony, and, therefore, we may not expect that any official will be called to account for any arbitrary and illegal steps that he may have been guilty of as against any native chief. Was the urgency of the occasion so great that a warlike expedition should be fitted out against a people up to then loyal and peaceful, and who had already furnished a considerable contingent of men against the coast tribes? From whom came the authority to Mr. Hemming to attack a section of the Great Tambookie tribe before they had committed a single act of disloyalty against Government? The expedition may have been carried out smartly, and with very little loss to the European forces engaged in it. But where is the justification for the expedition at all? Unless answered satisfactorily, the rectification of wrongs should lead to the summary fall of some person or persons whom an inquiry can alone disclose as being responsible for what appears to be an unjustifiable wrong.

A copy of my letter on the same subject, written a short time previously, is to be found in the Colonial Blue Book.

The immediate command of the troops in the Cis-Kei had now been placed in the hands of the Deputy-Adjutant-General, Colonel Bellairs, a trustworthy officer of experience, who reported to me as follows:—

King William's Town, February 1st, 1878.

In my despatch of the 14th ultimo I had the honour to report to your Excellency that the enemy had collected in two main bodies on the eastern frontier—the one in the Kabousie-Kei country, and the other in the Chichaba valley. The successful operations carried out in this latter resulting in the complete dispersion of the enemy, and capture of enormous herds of their cattle, have been already made known to your Excellency by my report of the 23rd ultimo.

It had been my intention to have caused the columns engaged in these operations to have afterwards swept through the Kei valley to Mordenaar's kop, thence acting with columns moving from the Bolo and down the Kabousie, to have hemmed in the enemy in the Kabousie-Kei country. This plan was however frustrated in part through the action taken by the Colonial Government in withholding the native levies and mounted corps then coming up (upon which I had depended), and forming columns to act under their own inspiration.

These Colonial forces, amounting to about 600 Europeans and 1600 Fingoes, were placed under the immediate command of Commandant Frost. They moved from Fort Cunynghame and the Bolo drift on the 14th ultimo, and would appear to have subsequently formed a junction at Lugilo mission station, thence skirting the rugged Kabousie-Kei country, to have crossed the Kabousie river, and passed through the Gaika location, which had already been patrolled by the troops under my command, arriving at Komgha on the 18th. This last movement was caused no doubt by defective commissariat arrangements, but having obtained supplies from our commissariat department, and ammunition for his men, Commandant Frost retraced his steps, and proceeded north towards the Thomas river, where he is said to have again fallen in with the enemy in some force.

From the published reports of this expedition it would seem that upwards of 8000 head of cattle, and as many sheep, were captured with little resistance from the enemy. About 100 Kafirs are stated to have fallen, with slight loss on the Colonial side.

Satisfactory as in some respects these operations were, yet I am of opinion that they might have been rendered more final had the forces been combined under military direction in properly organised columns, with efficient arrangements for supplies, and a common plan of action.

It may be reasonably surmised that the fact of the Gaikas having been able to push their way past the Colonial forces towards the north may not have been without its influence on the reported rising of the emigrant Tambookies and others.

I desire to point out that the condition of the Gaika women and children has become most deplorable. Left by the rebels to shift for themselves, their habitations burnt, their mealpits destroyed, their cattle captured, and a drought all over the land, they are reported to me during the past fortnight

as frequently passing outposts in gangs twenty to fifty strong, pathetically replying when questioned, " We have no food and are going in search of work." Wherever our patrols go they seem to meet with these helpless creatures.
Humanity requires that they should be immediately cared for. Deserted by the rebels, it might perhaps be considered good policy to remove them to the interior of the colony, so that the children might be brought up among loyal natives.

I immediately placed these humane suggestions before the Colonial Government.

The Colonial forces were at this time supplied with the Snider rifle, and the Imperial with the Martini-Henry. It would appear that one small Colonial corps had obtained the Martini, but no provision had been made by the Minister of War for ammunition.

CHAPTER XL.

DISMISSAL OF THE MINISTRY.

THE native locations within the colony being now in rebellion, I thought it necessary to return to King William's Town, which I reached in the first week of February. I placed the command of the troops in the Transkei again in the hands of Colonel Glyn and recrossed the river.

At the beginning of February the Diamond Field Volunteer Cavalry reached King William's Town. They were under the command of Captain Warren of the Royal Engineers with the local rank of Colonel from Griqualand.

These were fine young men, and a very valuable adjunct, as I still had not burgher cavalry to keep open my communications with the Transkei, and my convoys were always liable to be cut off. This corps was well horsed but insufficiently armed, the agreement to furnish them with carbines by the civil government not being acted up to until they talked of returning home. Unless faith in every respect is kept, how can we expect men to undertake such arduous and self-sacrificing duties? This corps performed excellent service in the colony. They were raised by his Excellency Colonel Lanyon, and subsequently marched under his command against Gasiborne and the rebels in the north.

I have always had a high opinion of the volunteers themselves, and am certain that if they had only been placed under military command their services would have been far more valuable than they were. I do not altogether agree with the observations which Mr. Frost is reported to have made on the 16th of May in the House of Assembly :—

> Most of these heroes served from love of cattle, and not from love of their country. Now that the enemy's cattle have all been appropriated the spirit of volunteering is dying out.

Affairs within the colony were now in considerable confusion. The Fingoes, our allies, were guilty of great outrages upon the unfortunate Gaikas. They went about in bands, intercepting the women and plundering them, and if they found a man in a woman's dress, they made very short work of him with assegais.

On all sides difficulties seemed to be on the increase. A war unfinished on the Kei, a rebellion in the colony, of which the proportions could not be ascertained, but reaching to our doors, a rising in Pondoland, and insults heaped upon the Government by the paramount chief Umgaikela. An outbreak in the East Griqualand location at Kokstadt; the Transvaal continually threatened by Secocoeni; and Cetewayo, King of the Zulus, actually in arms on the border of Natal, driving away the settlers, and erecting his forts upon the Boer locations.

Alarming letters were received by the Lieutenant-Governor of the Transvaal from the extreme eastern frontier by every post, and a force was then at Utrecht, protecting our borders, while the small number of Imperial troops at Pretoria were detaching men to Middleburg, and the Boers were holding seditious meetings even in the capital.

There were risings on the borders of Griqualand West, the Baralongs and the Batlapins taking the field.

About this time Mr. Molteno arrived at King William's Town. I do not propose to enter into details of what happened to him there. It is enough to say that he showed such contempt for the authority of the Governor, and enunciated such

2 B

extraordinary views of constitutional government, that the Governor was obliged to request him and his government to resign. His opinion may be summed up by saying that in his mind the Governor and the Queen were ciphers, whose only duty was to give a formal assent to the doings of himself and of his war minister, Mr. Merriman.

He refused to resign, and the Governor dismissed him. It is not within the scope of this book to criticise his conduct. They are a part of the history of the colony; but, with regard to Mr. Merriman, with whom circumstances brought me into closer contact, I may say a few words. I do not desire to impugn his private character—that is no business of mine. It is only with regard to his public acts that I have a right to make these observations. He was a man of talent and energy, but his thirst for power almost amounted to a mania. Most efficient as a Commissioner of Public Works, he was totally incompetent to conduct the Colonial War Department. His ignorance of military matters was only surpassed by the obstinacy of his determination not to learn the principles of war. The vote of credit which the Cape Colony gave to the Government that succeeded that of which he was a member, has marked the public judgment upon his acts; for all the skill in debate he showed in his speech in the House of Assembly, and all his ready ingenuity in casting the blame due to himself upon others, were not sufficient to save his party.

When the question of the expenses of this war comes to be considered by Parliament at home, I must say that I hope that the British taxpayer, burdened as he must naturally be by all the important enterprises he has now in hand, will refuse to any considerable extent to defray the cost of a war which the late Cape Government brought upon the colony. I am sorry for the colony, and especially for the most unjustly abused settlers on the frontier and in the east; but it seems only fair that they should suffer for the misdeeds of their own cabinet.

The following observations by the British Secretary of State for War sum up this subject in a few words:

. . . Besides, there is the increased expenditure required for the additional men sent to the Cape. I hope this sum will be repaid by the Cape Colony; but I am bound to say that is a colony which is not very satisfactory in regard to these repayments, and I think it is time for the House to take into consideration this question as to the sending out of troops to a colony like the Cape, which is really able to pay a great deal. I say this more especially as we have seen from the newspapers what has occurred there, and that the attempt has been made to separate the colonial forces from the regular troops, thus giving the Commander-in-Chief all the responsibility, with none of the control, of the colonial forces. That is a state of things which it would be degrading to the country to submit to (hear, hear); and therefore I think we should only be doing our duty in withdrawing our troops from the frontier of that colony and employing them for the original purposes for which they were sent there—namely, in taking care of Simon's Bay and the neighbouring coast. Natal, of course, is in different circumstances. I do not mince matters; I think the Cape colonists ought to pay, as they are able to do, something of this expenditure (hear, hear), and I am sure that they will never organise any military force for themselves if we undertake to fight for them and pay also.

CHAPTER XLI.

THE FIGHT AT QUINTANA.

ON the 7th of February Kreli gathered his strength for one last attempt. Colonel Glyn, it will be remembered, had been left in command of the troops in the Transkei. I had, with the advice of Captain Nixon, R.E., selected Quintana as a position for a defensive post, and shelter-trenches had been constructed there. It was known that Kreli and Sandilli were close by, but it was uncertain whether they would attack our head position at Ibeka or the post at Quintana. Finally intelligence was received that the Kafirs intended to attack Quintana. Due preparation was therefore made to receive them. The troops under Captain Upcher were stationed at the now partly completed post which stands on a spur, round the foot of which runs a small stream. The infantry was formed into a square, with a gun at each corner, and the waggons collected into a laager close by. Kreli, with his Galekas, advanced from the south; and Sandilli, with the Gaikas, from the north-west. Captains Rainsforth and Carrington were ordered to advance and fire, and then make a feigned retreat. This they did, and the Kafirs approached within range. Then followed an engagement, with the cannon and rifles on our side and with muskets on the part of the Kafirs.

In about twenty minutes the Kaffirs discovered that we were too strong for them, and broke, when they were pursued

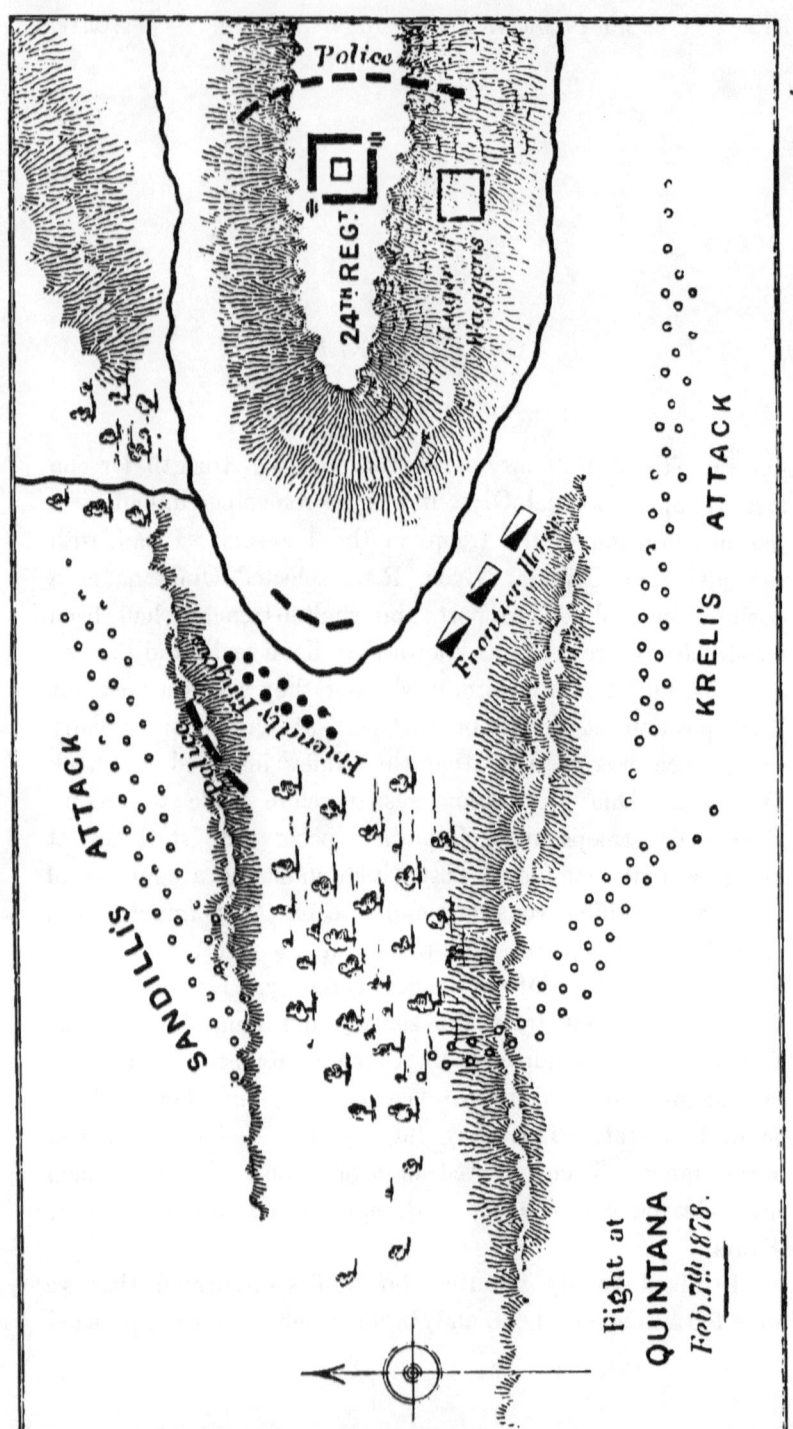

by the police, the Fingoe levies, and by one of the pieces of artillery. It is impossible to say how many were killed. At first it was thought the number was about 200, but subsequently it turned out to be much larger, as numbers of bodies were discovered hidden in the kloofs and bushes. The loss on our side was insignificant.

From this defeat neither the Gaikas nor Galekas recovered. They never again showed themselves in bodies in the field, but only haunted the bushes and kloofs in small bands, whence it was necessary to hunt them out like animals. Several painful sights were often to be seen on these occasions. Women with infants were shot, and found dead and dying. But in these wars the women take a considerable part; they form the Kafir commissariat; they venture into the towns in peaceable guise and purchase stores; they follow the army both with food and ammunition. It is thus unavoidable that they should be occasionally killed.

On one occasion a woman came forward leading a band of warriors. She had wisps of straw in her ears, a charm which she believed rendered not only her but her party invulnerable. In ignorance of her sex a private of police took aim at her and shot her dead, upon which the natives ran away.

It was after this battle that I most regretted that no sufficient force of cavalry had been placed under my orders. If I had had a larger force of mounted men I am certain that the Kafirs would never have succeeded in getting into the Amatola Mountains, from which both myself and my successor had some trouble in dislodging them. When fighting against savages so swift-footed as these, it is indispensable, in my opinion, to be well provided with mounted men, so that they can be at once launched against the enemy before the happy moment for doing so has passed away.

Under the new Ministry my duties became light compared to what they were before. The divided command, which had been productive of such confusion, was abolished, and both troops and commissariat, of all kinds, were placed in military hands. To show what a beneficial effect the stoppage of competition in the market between the British and Colonial Commissariat officers had upon prices, I quote, on the authority of the Deputy-Commissary-General, the contract prices of the Colonial and Imperial Commissariat respectively:—

		Colonial	Imperial
Oats per 100 lbs.	.	25s.	20s.
Mealies „	.	30s.	20s.
Forage „	.	25s.	18s.
Meal „	.	55s.	41s.
Flour „	.	32s.	21s. 6d.

The 90th Regiment and a field battery now arrived from England, a welcome addition to our forces. Tini Makomo, who, as I mentioned before, had been allowed to settle in that most dangerous position, the Waterkloof, having shown signs of disaffection, we had to drive him out.

This was the end, my last act, in South Africa. Having by seniority attained the rank of full General, I had become of too high rank to retain my command, according to the rules of the service. It had, however, been intimated to me that it was intended to leave me at the Cape to complete the period of a Lieutenant-General's command. At the latter end of February, however, I was informed that this would not be carried out, and the reason alleged was that there was "a want of cordiality between me and the Colonial Ministry." I have endeavoured to enable the reader to judge how far this want of cordiality came from my side. I will now let Sir Bartle Frere give his opinion upon the question:

My experience, says Sir Bartle Frere, did not induce me to expect from him (Mr. Merriman) consistency or calm judgment, or the power of conciliating cordial co-operation from men of diverse views and opinions. He never concealed his contempt for every form of skilled or trained military experience, while his own rash impetuosity imperilled and repeatedly threw away chances of more complete success. His attempt to substitute an amateur commissariat for the trained officers of the department seemed to me an expensive failure, whilst his headstrong disregard of the sound military opinions given to him were, I believe, the proximate causes of the disastrous spread of civil war in the colony [despatch of May 21, No. 87, Colonial Blue Book C. 2079; 1878, page 211]. Instead of cordially communicating and co-operating with the Governor and military authorities, we were, as it were, in a quarantine, cut off from anything like free and unrestrained communication, and I found that Mr. Merriman was actively engaged in arranging military operations in the Gaika location and to the north of it, whilst the Governor and military authorities were kept in the dark as to what he was doing, and its object [*ibid.* page 91].

It was a great comfort to me to have received, up to the moment of my leaving South Africa, the approval of my superiors, and their concurrence in my military views. On my departure, Sir Bartle Frere was pleased to use expressions to me which I naturally do not quote here, nor should I have alluded to the subject had not Mr. Merriman, after failing in his attack on the Governor, made ungenerous remarks about myself when I was far away and unable to answer his assertions.

Thus ended my stay in this interesting country. I have travelled over every part of it, and received great kindness from the hospitable colonists; and although I met with difficulties at the hands of the late Government, I can only say that my relations have always been most pleasant with the officials and the colonists in general. I wish them every success. May Heaven grant them a happy issue out of the difficulties which still beset them, and favour and protect and smile upon the future of the colony!

THE END.

VOYAGES AND TRAVELS.

OUR FUTURE HIGHWAY TO INDIA. By Commander CAMERON, R.N. With Illustrations and Map. 2 vols. Crown 8vo. 21s.

MAROCCO AND THE GREAT ATLAS; a Journal of a Tour in. By Sir J. D. HOOKER, K.C.S.I., C.B., F.R.S., and JOHN BALL, F.R.S. With Appendices, including a Sketch of the Geology of Marocco, by G. MAW, F.L.S., F.G.S. With Maps and Illustrations. 8vo. Cloth extra. 21s.

A YEAR'S HOUSEKEEPING IN SOUTH AFRICA. By Lady BARKER. Illustrated. Cheaper Edition. Crown 8vo. 6s.

NOTES BY A NATURALIST ON THE "CHALLENGER." Being an Account of various Observations made during the Voyage of H.M.S. *Challenger* Round the World in 1872-76. By H. N. MOSELEY, F.R.S., Member of the Scientific Staff of the *Challenger*. In 8vo. With Maps, Coloured Plates, and Woodcuts. Price 21s.

LOG-LETTERS FROM THE "CHALLENGER." By Lord GEORGE CAMPBELL. With Map. New and Cheaper Edition. Crown 8vo. 6s.

WATERTON'S WANDERINGS IN SOUTH AMERICA. Edited, with Biographical Introduction and Index, by the Rev. J. G. WOOD. New and Cheaper Edition. With 100 Illustrations. Crown 8vo. 6s.

DUTCH GUIANA. By W. G. PALGRAVE, Author of "Travels in Central and Eastern Arabia." 8vo. 9s.

CENTRAL AND EASTERN ARABIA: a Personal Narrative of a Year's Journey through. By W. GIFFORD PALGRAVE. Sixth Edition. With Map, &c. Crown 8vo. 6s.

GREATER BRITAIN. By Sir CHARLES DILKE, M.P. A Record of Travel in English-speaking Countries (America, Australia, India) during 1866-7. Sixth Edition. Illustrated. Crown 8vo. 6s.

THE MALAY ARCHIPELAGO; the Land of the Oran-Utan and the Bird of Paradise. A Narrative of Travel, with Studies of Man and Nature. By ALFRED RUSSEL WALLACE. Sixth Edition. With Maps and numerous Illustrations. Crown 8vo. 7s. 6d.

TRANSCAUCASIA AND ARARAT. Notes of a Vacation Tour in the Autumn of 1876. By JAMES BRYCE. With an Illustration and Map. Third Edition. Crown 8vo. 9s.

MY CIRCULAR NOTES. Extracts from Journals, Letters sent Home, &c., written while travelling Westward round the World. By J. F. CAMPBELL. Illustrated. Crown 8vo. 6s.

SPORT AND WORK ON THE NEPAUL FRONTIER; or, Twelve Years' Sporting Reminiscences of an Indigo Planter. By "MAORI." With Illustrations. 8vo. 14s.

NORTHWARD HO! By Captain ALBERT H. MARKHAM, R.N., Author of "The Great Frozen Sea," &c. Including a Narrative of Captain Phipps's Expedition, by a Midshipman. With Illustrations. Crown 8vo. 10s. 6d.

MACMILLAN AND CO., LONDON.

VOYAGES AND TRAVELS.

BY SIR SAMUEL W. BAKER, F.R.S.:—

ISMAILÏA: a Narrative of the Expedition to Central Africa for the Suppression of the Slave Trade, organised by Ismail, Khedive of Egypt. With Portraits, Maps, and numerous Illustrations. New and Cheaper Edition. Crown 8vo. 6s.

THE ALBERT N'YANZA, GREAT BASIN OF THE NILE, AND EXPLORATION OF THE NILE SOURCES. Fourth Edition. Maps and Illustrations. Crown 8vo. 6s.

THE NILE TRIBUTARIES OF ABYSSINIA AND THE SWORD HUNTERS OF THE HAMRAN ARABS. With Maps and Illustrations. Fifth Edition. Crown 8vo. 6s.

CYPRUS AS I SAW IT IN 1879. With Frontispiece. 8vo. 14s.

NORDENSKIOLD'S ARCTIC VOYAGES, 1858-79. 8vo. With Maps and numerous Illustrations. 16s.

MARGARY'S JOURNEY FROM SHANGHAE TO BHAMO, AND BACK TO MANWYNE. Edited from his Journals and Letters, with a brief Biographical Preface, a Concluding Chapter by Sir RUTHERFORD ALCOCK, K.C.B., a Steel Portrait engraved by C. H. JEENS, and Route Map. 8vo. 10s. 6d.

MANDALAY TO MOMIEN: a Narrative of the two Expeditions to Western China of 1868 to 1875, under Colonel E. B. Sladen and Colonel Horace Browne. By JOHN ANDERSON, M.D. Edin., F.R.S.E., Medical and Scientific Officer to the Expedition. With numerous Illustrations and Maps. 8vo. 21s.

AT LAST: a Christmas in the West Indies. By CHARLES KINGSLEY. Sixth Edition. With Maps and numerous Illustrations. Crown 8vo. 6s.

A RAMBLE ROUND THE WORLD, 1871. By M. le Baron DE HUBNER, formerly Ambassador and Minister. Translated by Lady HERBERT. New and Cheaper Edition. With numerous Illustrations. Crown 8vo. 6s.

CHINA: a History of the Laws, Manners, and Customs of the People. By the Ven. J. H. GRAY, Archdeacon of Hong Kong. Second Edition. With 150 Illustrations by Chinese Artists. 2 vols. 8vo. 32s.

FOURTEEN MONTHS IN CANTON. By Mrs. GRAY. With Illustrations. Crown 8vo. 9s.

PERU: Incidents of Travel and Exploration in the Land of the Incas. By E. G. SQUIER, M.A., F.S.A., late U.S. Commissioner to Peru. Second Edition. With 300 Illustrations. 8vo. 21s.

A RIDE IN EGYPT, from SIOOT TO LUXOR, in 1879; with Notes on the Present State and Ancient History of the Nile Valley, and some account of the various ways of making the Voyage Out and Home. By the Rev. W. J. LOFTIE. With Illustrations. Crown 8vo. 10s. 6d.

TELEGRAPH AND TRAVEL. A Narrative of the Formation and Development of Telegraphic Communication between England and India, under the Orders of Her Majesty's Government, with Incidental Notices of the Countries traversed by the Lines. By Colonel Sir FREDERIC GOLDSMID, C.B., K.C.S.I., late Director of the Government Indo-European Telegraph. With numerous Illustrations and Maps. 8vo. 21s.

MACMILLAN AND CO., LONDON.

BEDFORD STREET, STRAND, LONDON, W.C.
August, 1879.

MACMILLAN & CO.'S CATALOGUE of Works in the Departments of History, Biography, Travels, Critical and Literary Essays, Politics, Political and Social Economy, Law, etc.; and Works connected with Language.

HISTORY, BIOGRAPHY, TRAVELS, &c.

Albemarle.—FIFTY YEARS OF MY LIFE. By GEORGE THOMAS, Earl of Albemarle. With Steel Portrait of the first Earl of Albemarle, engraved by JEENS. Third and Cheaper Edition. Crown 8vo. 7s. 6d.

"*The book is one of the most amusing of its class. . . . These reminiscences have the charm and flavour of personal experience, and they bring us into direct contact with the persons they describe.*"—EDINBURGH REVIEW.

Anderson.—MANDALAY TO MOMIEN; a Narrative of the Two Expeditions to Western China, of 1868 and 1875, under Colonel E. B. Sladen and Colonel Horace Browne. By Dr. ANDERSON, F.R.S.E., Medical and Scientific Officer to the Expeditions. With numerous Maps and Illustrations. 8vo. 21s.

"*A handsome, well-timed, entertaining, and instructive volume.*"—ACADEMY.

"*A pleasant, useful, carefully-written, and important work.*"—ATHENÆUM.

Appleton.—Works by T. G. APPLETON :—
A NILE JOURNAL. Illustrated by EUGENE BENSON. Crown 8vo. 6s.
SYRIAN SUNSHINE. Crown 8vo. 6s.

Arnold.—ESSAYS IN CRITICISM. By MATTHEW ARNOLD. New Edition, Revised and Enlarged. Crown 8vo. 9s.

Atkinson.—AN ART TOUR TO NORTHERN CAPITALS OF EUROPE, including Descriptions of the Towns, the Museums, and other Art Treasures of Copenhagen, Christiania, Stockholm,

Abo, Helsingfors, Wiborg, St. Petersburg, Moscow, and Kief. By J. BEAVINGTON ATKINSON. 8vo. 12s.

"*Although the main purpose of the book is strictly kept in view, and we never forget for long that we are travelling with a student and connoisseur, Mr. Atkinson gives variety to his narrative by glimpses of scenery and brief allusions to history and manners which are always welcome when they occur, and are never wordy or overdone. We have seldom met with a book in which what is principal and what is accessory have been kept in better proportion to each other.*"—SATURDAY REVIEW.

Bailey.—THE SUCCESSION TO THE ENGLISH CROWN. A Historical Sketch. By A. BAILEY, M.A., Barrister-at-Law. Crown 8vo. 7s. 6d.

Baker (Sir Samuel W.)—Works by Sir SAMUEL BAKER, Pacha, M.A., F.R.G.S.:—

ISMAILIA: A Narrative of the Expedition to Central Africa for the Suppression of the Slave Trade, organised by Ismail, Khedive of Egypt. With Portraits, Map, and fifty full-page Illustrations by ZWECKER and DURAND. New and Cheaper Edition. With New Preface. Crown 8vo. 6s.

"*A book which will be read with very great interest.*"—TIMES. "*Well written and full of remarkable adventures.*"—PALL MALL GAZETTE. "*Adds another thrilling chapter to the history of African adventure.*"—DAILY NEWS. "*Reads more like a romance . . . . incomparably more entertaining than books of African travel usually are.*"—MORNING POST.

THE ALBERT N'YANZA Great Basin of the Nile, and Exploration of the Nile Sources. Fifth Edition. Maps and Illustrations. Crown 8vo. 6s.

"*Charmingly written;*" says the SPECTATOR, "*full, as might be expected, of incident, and free from that wearisome reiteration of useless facts which is the drawback to almost all books of African travel.*"

THE NILE TRIBUTARIES OF ABYSSINIA, and the Sword Hunters of the Hamran Arabs. With Maps and Illustrations. Sixth Edition. Crown 8vo. 6s.

The TIMES *says:* "*It adds much to our information respecting Egyptian Abyssinia and the different races that spread over it. It contains, moreover, some notable instances of English daring and enterprising skill; it abounds in animated tales of exploits dear to the heart of the British sportsman; and it will attract even the least studious reader, as the author tells a story well, and can describe nature with uncommon power.*"

Bancroft.—THE HISTORY OF THE UNITED STATES OF AMERICA, FROM THE DISCOVERY OF THE CONTINENT. By GEORGE BANCROFT. New and thoroughly Revised Edition. Six Vols. Crown 8vo. 54s.

HISTORY, BIOGRAPHY, TRAVELS, ETC.   3

Barker (Lady).—Works by LADY BARKER :—
A YEAR'S HOUSEKEEPING IN SOUTH AFRICA. With Illustrations. New and Cheaper Edition. Crown 8vo. 6s.
"*We have to thank Lady Barker for a very amusing book, over which we have spent many a delightful hour, and of which we will not take leave without alluding to the ineffably droll illustrations which add so very much to the enjoyment of her clear and sparkling descriptions.*"—MORNING POST.

Beesly.—STORIES FROM THE HISTORY OF ROME. By Mrs. BEESLY. Extra fcap. 8vo. 2s. 6d.
"*A little book for which every cultivated and intelligent mother will be grateful for.*"—EXAMINER.

Bismarck—IN THE FRANCO-GERMAN WAR. An Authorized Translation from the German of Dr. MORITZ BUSCH. Two Vols. Crown 8vo. 18s.
The TIMES *says* :—"*The publication of Bismarck's after-dinner talk, whether discreet or not, will be of priceless biographical value, and Englishmen, at least, will not be disposed to quarrel with Dr. Busch for giving a picture as true to life as Boswell's 'Johnson' of the foremost practical genius that Germany has produced since Frederick the Great.*"

Blackburne.—BIOGRAPHY OF THE RIGHT HON. FRANCIS BLACKBURNE, Late Lord Chancellor of Ireland. Chiefly in connexion with his Public and Political Career. By his Son, EDWARD BLACKBURNE, Q.C. With Portrait Engraved by JEENS. 8vo. 12s.

Blanford (W. T.)—GEOLOGY AND ZOOLOGY OF ABYSSINIA. By W. T. BLANFORD. 8vo. 21s.

Brontë.—CHARLOTTE BRONTË. A Monograph. By T. WEMYSS REID. With Illustrations. Third Edition. Crown 8vo. 6s.
Mr. Reid's little volume, which is based largely on letters, hitherto unpublished, from Charlotte Brontë to her school-fellow and life-long friend, Miss Ellen Nussey, is meant to be a companion, and not a rival, to Mrs. Gaskell's well-known "Life." To speak of the advantage of making biography autobiographical by the liberal use of correspondence has she was by nature (as Mr. Reid puts it) "a happy and high-spirited girl, and that even to the very last she had the faculty of overcoming her sorrows by means of that steadfast courage which was her most precious possession, and to which she was indebted for her successive victories over trials and disappointments of no ordinary character."
The book is illustrated by a Portrait of the Rev. Patrick Brontë, several Views of Haworth and its neighbourhood, and a facsimile of one of the most characteristic of Charlotte's letters.

A 2

Brooke.—THE RAJA OF SARAWAK: an Account of Sir James Brooke, K.C.B., LL.D. Given chiefly through Letters or Journals. By GERTRUDE L. JACOB. With Portrait and Maps. Two Vols. 8vo. 25s.

"*They who read Miss Jacob's book—and all should read it: all who are under the delusion that in our time there is no scope for heroism, and no place for romantic adventure, and no place for enterprise and ambition —will see how incident is crowded upon incident, and struggle upon struggle, till in the very abundance of materials that come to her hand the authoress can scarcely stop to give sufficient distinctness to her wonderful narrative.*"—ACADEMY.

Brooke.—RECOLLECTIONS OF THE IRISH CHURCH. By RICHARD S. BROOKE, D.D., late Rector of Wyton, Hunts. Crown 8vo. 4s. 6d.

Bryce.—Works by JAMES BRYCE, D.C.L., Regius Professor of Civil Law, Oxford :—

THE HOLY ROMAN EMPIRE. Sixth Edition, Revised and Enlarged. Crown 8vo. 7s. 6d.

"*It exactly supplies a want: it affords a key to much which men read of in their books as isolated facts, but of which they have hitherto had no connected exposition set before them.*"—SATURDAY REVIEW.

TRANSCAUCASIA AND ARARAT: being Notes of a Vacation Tour in the Autumn of 1876. With an Illustration and Map. Third Edition. Crown 8vo. 9s.

"*Mr. Bryce has written a lively and at the same time an instructive description of the tour he made last year in and about the Caucasus. When well-informed a jurist travels into regions seldom visited, and even walks up a mountain so rarely scaled as Ararat, he is justified in thinking that the impressions he brings home are worthy of being communicated to the world at large, especially when a terrible war is casting a lurid glow over the countries he has lately surveyed.*"—ATHENÆUM.

Burgoyne.—POLITICAL AND MILITARY EPISODES DURING THE FIRST HALF OF THE REIGN OF GEORGE III. Derived from the Life and Correspondence of the Right Hon. J. Burgoyne, Lieut.-General in his Majesty's Army, and M.P. for Preston. By E. B. DE FONBLANQUE. With Portrait, Heliotype Plate, and Maps. 8vo. 16s.

Burke.—EDMUND BURKE, a Historical Study. By JOHN MORLEY, B.A., Oxon. Crown 8vo. 7s. 6d.

"*The style is terse and incisive, and brilliant with epigram and point. Its sustained power of reasoning, its wide sweep of observation and reflection, its elevated ethical and social tone, stamp it as a work of high excellence.*"—SATURDAY REVIEW.

HISTORY, BIOGRAPHY, TRAVELS, ETC.   5

Burrows.—WORTHIES OF ALL SOULS: Four Centuries of English History. Illustrated from the College Archives. By MONTAGU BURROWS, Chichele Professor of Modern History at Oxford, Fellow of All Souls. 8vo. 14s.
"*A most amusing as well as a most instructive book.*—GUARDIAN.

Campbell.—LOG-LETTERS FROM THE "CHALLENGER." By LORD GEORGE CAMPBELL. With Map. Fifth and cheaper Edition. Crown 8vo. 6s.
"*A delightful book, which we heartily commend to the general reader.*" —SATURDAY REVIEW.
"*We do not hesitate to say that anything so fresh, so picturesque, so generally delightful, as these log-letters has not appeared among books of travel for a long time.*"—EXAMINER.
"*A more lively and amusing record of travel we have not had the fortune to read for some time. The whole book is pervaded by a spirit of life, animation, and fun.*"—STANDARD.

Campbell.—MY CIRCULAR NOTES: Extracts from Journals; Letters sent Home; Geological and other Notes, written while Travelling Westwards round the World, from July 6th, 1874, to July 6th, 1875. By J. F. CAMPBELL, Author of "Frost and Fire." Cheaper Issue. Crown 8vo. 6s.
"*We have read numbers of books of travel, but we can call to mind few that have given us more genuine pleasure than this. A more agreeable style of narrative than his it is hardly possible to conceive. We seem to be accompanying him in his trip round the world, so life-like is his description of the countries he visited.*"—LAND AND WATER.

Campbell.—TURKS AND GREEKS. Notes of a recent Excursion. By the Hon. DUDLEY CAMPBELL, M.A. With Coloured Map. Crown 8vo. 3s. 6d.

Carstares.—WILLIAM CARSTARES: a Character and Career of the Revolutionary Epoch (1649—1715). By ROBERT STORY, Minister of Rosneath. 8vo. 12s.

Chatterton: A BIOGRAPHICAL STUDY. By DANIEL WILSON, LL.D., Professor of History and English Literature in University College, Toronto. Crown 8vo. 6s. 6d.

Chatterton: A STORY OF THE YEAR 1770. By Professor MASSON, LL.D. Crown 8vo. 5s.

Clark.—MEMORIALS FROM JOURNALS AND LETTERS OF SAMUEL CLARK, M.A., formerly Principal of the National Society's Training College, Battersea. Edited with Introduction by his WIFE. With Portrait. Crown 8vo. 7s. 6d.

Combe.—THE LIFE OF GEORGE COMBE, Author of "The Constitution of Man." By CHARLES GIBBON. With Three Portraits engraved by JEENS. Two Vols. 8vo. 32s.

"*A graphic and interesting account of the long life and indefatigable labours of a very remarkable man.*"—SCOTSMAN.

Cooper.—ATHENÆ CANTABRIGIENSES. By CHARLES HENRY COOPER, F.S.A., and THOMPSON COOPER, F.S.A. Vol. I. 8vo., 1500—85, 18s.; Vol. II., 1586—1609, 18s.

Correggio.—ANTONIO ALLEGRI DA CORREGGIO. From the German of Dr. JULIUS MEYER, Director of the Royal Gallery, Berlin. Edited, with an Introduction, by Mrs. HEATON. Containing Twenty Woodbury-type Illustrations. Royal 8vo. Cloth elegant. 31s. 6d.

Cox (G. V.)—RECOLLECTIONS OF OXFORD. By G. V. Cox, M.A., New College, late Esquire Bedel and Coroner in the University of Oxford. *Cheaper Edition.* Crown 8vo. 6s.

Cunynghame (Sir A. T.)—MY COMMAND IN SOUTH AFRICA, 1874—78. Comprising Experiences of Travel in the Colonies of South Africa and the Independent States. By Sir ARTHUR THURLOW CUNYNGHAME, G.C.B., then Lieutenant-Governor and Commander of the Forces in South Africa. Third Edition. 8vo. 12s. 6d.

The TIMES *says* :—"*It is a volume of great interest,* . . . . *full of incidents which vividly illustrate the condition of the Colonies and the character and habits of the natives.* . . . . *It contains valuable illustrations of Cape warfare, and at the present moment it cannot fail to command wide-spread attention.*"

"**Daily News.**"—THE DAILY NEWS' CORRESPONDENCE of the War between Germany and France, 1870—1. Edited with Notes and Comments. New Edition. Complete in One Volume. With Maps and Plans. Crown 8vo. 6s.

THE DAILY NEWS' CORRESPONDENCE of the War between Russia and Turkey, to the fall of Kars. Including the letters of Mr. Archibald Forbes, Mr. J. E. McGahan, and other Special Correspondents in Europe and Asia. Second Edition, enlarged. Cheaper Edition. Crown 8vo. 6s.

FROM THE FALL OF KARS TO THE CONCLUSION OF PEACE. Cheaper Edition. Crown 8vo. 6s.

Davidson.—THE LIFE OF A SCOTTISH PROBATIONER; being a Memoir of Thomas Davidson, with his Poems and Letters. By JAMES BROWN, Minister of St. James's Street Church, Paisley. Second Edition, revised and enlarged, with Portrait. Crown 8vo. 7s. 6d.

HISTORY, BIOGRAPHY, TRAVELS, ETC. 7

Deas.—THE RIVER CLYDE. An Historical Description of the Rise and Progress of the Harbour of Glasgow, and of the Improvement of the River from Glasgow to Port Glasgow. By J. DEAS, M. Inst. C.E. 8vo. 10s. 6d.

Denison.—A HISTORY OF CAVALRY FROM THE EARLIEST TIMES. With Lessons for the Future. By Lieut.-Col. GEORGE DENISON, Commanding the Governor-General's Body Guard, Canada, Author of "Modern Cavalry." With Maps and Plans. 8vo. 18s.

Dilke.—GREATER BRITAIN. A Record of Travel in English-speaking Countries during 1866-7. (America, Australia, India.) By Sir CHARLES WENTWORTH DILKE, M.P. Sixth Edition. Crown 8vo. 6s.
"*Many of the subjects discussed in these pages*," says the DAILY NEWS, "*are of the widest interest, and such as no man who cares for the future of his race and of the world can afford to treat with indifference.*"

Doyle.—HISTORY OF AMERICA. By J. A. DOYLE. With Maps. 18mo. 4s. 6d.
"*Mr. Doyle's style is clear and simple, his facts are accurately stated, and his book is meritoriously free from prejudice on questions where partisanship runs high amongst us.*"—SATURDAY REVIEW.

Drummond of Hawthornden: THE STORY OF HIS LIFE AND WRITINGS. By PROFESSOR MASSON. With Portrait and Vignette engraved by C. H. JEENS. Crown 8vo. 10s. 6d.

Duff.—Works by M. E. GRANT-DUFF, M.P., late Under Secretary of State for India :—
NOTES OF AN INDIAN JOURNEY. With Map. 8vo. 10s. 6d.
"*These notes are full of pleasant remarks and illustrations, borrowed from every kind of source.*"—SATURDAY REVIEW.

MISCELLANIES POLITICAL AND LITERARY. 8vo. 10s. 6d.

Eadie.—LIFE OF JOHN EADIE, D.D., LL.D. By JAMES BROWN, D.D., Author of "The Life of a Scottish Probationer." With Portrait. Second Edition. Crown 8vo. 7s. 6d.
"*An ably written and characteristic biography.*"—TIMES.

Elliott.—LIFE OF HENRY VENN ELLIOTT, of Brighton. By JOSIAH BATEMAN, M.A. With Portrait, engraved by JEENS. Extra fcap. 8vo. Third and Cheaper Edition. 6s.

Elze.—ESSAYS ON SHAKESPEARE. By Dr. KARL ELZE. Translated with the Author's sanction by L. DORA SCHMITZ. 8vo. 12s.
"*A more desirable contribution to criticism has not recently been made.*" —ATHENÆUM.

English Men of Letters. Edited by JOHN MORLEY. A Series of Short Books to tell people what is best worth knowing as to the Life, Character, and Works of some of the great English Writers. In crown 8vo. Price 2s. 6d. each.

I. DR. JOHNSON. By LESLIE STEPHEN.
"*The new series opens well with Mr. Leslie Stephen's sketch of Dr. Johnson. It could hardly have been done better; and it will convey to the readers for whom it is intended a juster estimate of Johnson than either of the two essays of Lord Macaulay.*"—PALL MALL GAZETTE.

II. SIR WALTER SCOTT. By R. H. HUTTON.
"*The tone of the volume is excellent throughout.*"—ATHENÆUM.
"*We could not wish for a more suggestive introduction to Scott and his poems and novels.*"—EXAMINER.

III. GIBBON. By J. C. MORISON.
"*As a clear, thoughtful, and attractive record of the life and works of the greatest among the world's historians, it deserves the highest praise.*"—EXAMINER.

IV. SHELLEY. By J. A. SYMONDS.
"*The lovers of this great poet are to be congratulated on having at their command so fresh, clear, and intelligent a presentment of the subject, written by a man of adequate and wide culture.*"—ATHENÆUM.

V. HUME. By Professor HUXLEY.
"*It may fairly be said that no one now living could have expounded Hume with more sympathy or with equal perspicuity.*"—ATHENÆUM.

VI. GOLDSMITH. By WILLIAM BLACK.
"*Mr. Black brings a fine sympathy and taste to bear in his criticism of Goldsmith's writings as well as in his sketch of the incidents of his life.*" ATHENÆUM.

VII. DEFOE. By W. MINTO.
"*Mr. Minto's book is careful and accurate in all that is stated, and faithful in all that it suggests. It will repay reading more than once.*" —ATHENÆUM.

VIII. BURNS. By Principal SHAIRP, Professor of Poetry in the University of Oxford.
"*It is impossible to desire fairer criticism than Principal Shairp's on Burns's poetry . . . . . None of the series has given a truer estimate either of character or of genius than this little volume . . . . and all who read it will be thoroughly grateful to the author for this monument to the genius of Scotland's greatest poet.*"—SPECTATOR.

IX. SPENSER. By the Very Rev. the DEAN OF ST. PAUL'S.
"*Dr. Church is master of his subject, and writes always with good taste.*"—ACADEMY.

X. THACKERAY. By ANTHONY TROLLOPE.
"*Mr. Trollope's sketch is excellently adapted to fufil the purpose of the series in which it appears.*"—ATHENÆUM.

HISTORY, BIOGRAPHY, TRAVELS, ETC. 9

English Men of Letters.—*continued.*
BURKE. By JOHN MORLEY.
MILTON. By MARK PATTISON. } [*Nearly ready.*
Others in preparation.

Eton College, History of. By H. C. MAXWELL LYTE, M.A. With numerous Illustrations by Professor DELAMOTTE, Coloured Plates, and a Steel Portrait of the Founder, engraved by C. H. JEENS. New and cheaper Issue, with Corrections. Medium 8vo. Cloth elegant. 21*s*.

"*Hitherto no account of the College, with all its associations, has appeared which can compare either in completeness or in interest with this. ... It is indeed a book worthy of the ancient renown of King Henry's College.*"—DAILY NEWS.

" *We are at length presented with a work on England's greatest public school, worthy of the subject of which it treats. ... A really valuable and authentic history of Eton College.*"—GUARDIAN.

European History, Narrated in a Series of Historical Selections from the best Authorities. Edited and arranged by E. M. SEWELL and C. M. YONGE. First Series, crown 8vo. 6*s.*; Second Series, 1088-1228, crown 8vo. 6*s.* Third Edition.

" *We know of scarcely anything,*" says the GUARDIAN, *of this volume,* "*which is so likely to raise to a higher level the average standard of English education.*"

Faraday.—MICHAEL FARADAY. By J. H. GLADSTONE, Ph.D., F.R.S. Second Edition, with Portrait engraved by JEENS from a photograph by J. WATKINS. Crown 8vo. 4*s.* 6*d.*
PORTRAIT. Artist's Proof. 5*s.*

Forbes.—LIFE AND LETTERS OF JAMES DAVID FORBES, F.R.S., late Principal of the United College in the University of St. Andrews. By J. C. SHAIRP, LL.D., Principal of the United College in the University of St. Andrews; P. G. TAIT, M.A., Professor of Natural Philosophy in the University of Edinburgh; and A. ADAMS-REILLY, F.R.G.S. 8vo. with Portraits, Map, and Illustrations, 16*s.*

Freeman.—Works by EDWARD A. FREEMAN, D.C.L., LL.D. :—
HISTORICAL ESSAYS. Third Edition. 8vo. 10*s.* 6*d.*
CONTENTS :—*I. " The Mythical and Romantic Elements in Early English History;" II. "The Continuity of English History;" III. "The Relations between the Crowns of England and Scotland;" IV. "St. Thomas of Canterbury and his Biographers;" V. " The Reign of Edward the Third;" VI. " The Holy Roman Empire;" VII. " The Franks and the Gauls;" VIII. "The Early Sieges of Paris;" IX. " Frederick the First, King of Italy;" X. "The Emperor Frederick the Second;" XI. "Charles the Bold;" XII. " Presidential Government.*

Freeman—*continued*.

A SECOND SERIES OF HISTORICAL ESSAYS. 8vo. 10s. 6d.
The principal Essays are:—"*Ancient Greece and Mediæval Italy:*" "*Mr. Gladstone's Homer and the Homeric Ages:*" "*The Historians of Athens:*" "*The Athenian Democracy:*" "*Alexander the Great:*" "*Greece during the Macedonian Period:*" "*Mommsen's History of Rome:*" "*Lucius Cornelius Sulla:*" "*The Flavian Cæsars.*"

HISTORICAL ESSAYS. Third Series. [*In the press*.

COMPARATIVE POLITICS.—Lectures at the Royal Institution. To which is added the "Unity of History," the Rede Lecture at Cambridge, 1872. 8vo. 14s.

THE HISTORY AND CONQUESTS OF THE SARACENS. Six Lectures. Third Edition, with New Preface. Crown 8vo. 3s. 6d.

HISTORICAL AND ARCHITECTURAL SKETCHES: chiefly Italian. With Illustrations by the Author. Crown 8vo. 10s. 6d.
"*Mr. Freeman may here be said to give us a series of 'notes on the spot' in illustration of the intimate relations of History and Architecture, and this is done in so masterly a manner—there is so much freshness, so much knowledge so admirably condensed, that we are almost tempted to say that we prefer these sketches to his more elaborate studies.*"—NONCONFORMIST.

HISTORY OF FEDERAL GOVERNMENT, from the Foundation of the Achaian League to the Disruption of the United States. Vol. I. General Introduction. History of the Greek Federations. 8vo. 21s.

OLD ENGLISH HISTORY. With *Five Coloured Maps*. Fourth Edition. Extra fcap. 8vo., half-bound. 6s.
"*The book indeed is full of instruction and interest to students of all ages, and he must be a well-informed man indeed who will not rise from its perusal with clearer and more accurate ideas of a too much neglected portion of English history.*"—SPECTATOR.

HISTORY OF THE CATHEDRAL CHURCH OF WELLS, as illustrating the History of the Cathedral Churches of the Old Foundation. Crown 8vo. 3s. 6d.
"*The history assumes in Mr. Freeman's hands a significance, and, we may add, a practical value as suggestive of what a cathedral ought to be, which make it well worthy of mention.*"—SPECTATOR.

THE GROWTH OF THE ENGLISH CONSTITUTION FROM THE EARLIEST TIMES. Crown 8vo. 5s. Third Edition, revised.

Freeman—*continued.*
GENERAL SKETCH OF EUROPEAN HISTORY. Being Vol. I. of a Historical Course for Schools edited by E. A. FREEMAN. New Edition, enlarged with Maps, Chronological Table, Index, &c. 18mo. 3s. 6d.

"*It supplies the great want of a good foundation for historical teaching. The scheme is an excellent one, and this instalment has been accepted in a way that promises much for the volumes that are yet to appear.*"—EDUCATIONAL TIMES.

THE OTTOMAN POWER IN EUROPE : its Nature, its Growth, and its Decline. With Three Coloured Maps. Crown 8vo. 7s. 6d.

Galileo.—THE PRIVATE LIFE OF GALILEO. Compiled principally from his Correspondence and that of his eldest daughter, Sister Maria Celeste, Nun in the Franciscan Convent of S. Matthew in Arcetri. With Portrait. Crown 8vo. 7s. 6d.

Geddes.—THE PROBLEM OF THE HOMERIC POEMS. By W. D. GEDDES, LL.D., Professor of Greek in the University of Aberdeen. 8vo. 14s.

Gladstone—Works by the Right Hon. W. E. GLADSTONE, M.P. :—
JUVENTUS MUNDI. The Gods and Men of the Heroic Age. Crown 8vo. cloth. With Map. 10s. 6d. Second Edition.

"*Seldom,*" says the ATHENÆUM, "*out of the great poems themselves, have these Divinities looked so majestic and respectable. To read these brilliant details is like standing on the Olympian threshold and gazing at the ineffable brightness within.*"

HOMERIC SYNCHRONISM. An inquiry into the Time and Place of Homer. Crown 8vo. 6s.

"*It is impossible not to admire the immense range of thought and inquiry which the author has displayed.*"—BRITISH QUARTERLY REVIEW.

Goethe and Mendelssohn (1821—1831). Translated from the German of Dr. KARL MENDELSSOHN, Son of the Composer, by M. E. VON GLEHN. From the Private Diaries and Home Letters of Mendelssohn, with Poems and Letters of Goethe never before printed. Also with two New and Original Portraits, Facsimiles, and Appendix of Twenty Letters hitherto unpublished. Crown 8vo. 5s. Second Edition, enlarged.

"*. . . Every page is full of interest, not merely to the musician, but to the general reader. The book is a very charming one, on a topic of deep and lasting interest.*"—STANDARD.

Goldsmid.—TELEGRAPH AND TRAVEL. A Narrative of the Formation and Development of Telegraphic Communication between England and India, under the orders of Her Majesty's Government, with incidental Notices of the Countries traversed by the Lines. By Colonel Sir FREDERIC GOLDSMID, C.B., K.C.S.I., late Director of the Government Indo-European Telegraph. With numerous Illustrations and Maps. 8vo. 21s.

"*The merit of the work is a total absence of exaggeration, which does not, however, preclude a vividness and vigour of style not always characteristic of similar narratives.*"—STANDARD.

Gordon.—LAST LETTERS FROM EGYPT, to which are added Letters from the Cape. By LADY DUFF GORDON. With a Memoir by her Daughter, Mrs. ROSS, and Portrait engraved by JEENS. Second Edition. Crown 8vo. 9s.

"*The intending tourist who wishes to acquaint himself with the country he is about to visit, stands embarrassed amidst the riches presented for his choice, and in the end probably rests contented with the sober usefulness of Murray. He will not, however, if he is well advised, grudge a place in his portmanteau to this book.*"—TIMES.

Gray.—CHINA. A History of the Laws, Manners, and Customs of the People. By the VENERABLE JOHN HENRY GRAY. LL.D., Archdeacon of Hong Kong, formerly H.B.M. Consular Chaplain at Canton. Edited by W. Gow Gregor. With 150 Full-page Illustrations, being Facsimiles of Drawings by a Chinese Artist. 2 Vols. Demy 8vo. 32s.

"*Its pages contain the most truthful and vivid picture of Chinese life which has ever been published.*"—ATHENÆUM.

"*The only elaborate and valuable book we have had for many years treating generally of the people of the Celestial Empire.*"—ACADEMY.

Green.—Works by JOHN RICHARD GREEN :—

HISTORY OF THE ENGLISH PEOPLE. Vol. I.—Early England—Foreign Kings—The Charter—The Parliament. With 8 Coloured Maps. 8vo. 16s. Vol. II.—The Monarchy, 1461—1540 ; the Restoration, 1540—1603. 8vo. 16s. Vol. III. —Puritan England, 1603—1660 ; the Revolution, 1660—1688. With 4 Maps. 8vo. 16s. [*Vol. IV. in the press.*

"*Mr. Green has done a work which probably no one but himself could have done. He has read and assimilated the results of all the labours of students during the last half century in the field of English history, and has given them a fresh meaning by his own independent study. He has fused together by the force of sympathetic imagination all that he has so collected, and has given us a vivid and forcible sketch of the march of English history. His book, both in its aims and its accomplishments, rises far beyond any of a similar kind, and it will give the colouring to the popular view to English history for some time to come.*"—EXAMINER.

Green.—*continued.*

A SHORT HISTORY OF THE ENGLISH PEOPLE. With Coloured Maps, Genealogical Tables, and Chronological Annals. Crown 8vo. 8s. 6d. Sixty-first Thousand.
"*To say that Mr. Green's book is better than those which have preceded it, would be to convey a very inadequate impression of its merits. It stands alone as the one general history of the country, for the sake of which all others, if young and old are wise, will be speedily and surely set aside.*"

STRAY STUDIES FROM ENGLAND AND ITALY. Crown 8vo. 8s. 6d. Containing: Lambeth and the Archbishops—The Florence of Dante—Venice and Rome—Early History of Oxford—The District Visitor—Capri—Hotels in the Clouds—Sketches in Sunshine, &c.
"*One and all of the papers are eminently readable.*"—ATHENÆUM.

Guest.—LECTURES ON THE HISTORY OF ENGLAND. By M. J. GUEST. With Maps. Crown 8vo. 6s.

Hamerton.—Works by P. G. HAMERTON:—

THE INTELLECTUAL LIFE. With a Portrait of Leonardo da Vinci, etched by LEOPOLD FLAMENG. Second Edition. Crown 8vo. 10s. 6d.
"*We have read the whole book with great pleasure, and we can recommend it strongly to all who can appreciate grave reflections on a very important subject, excellently illustrated from the resources of a mind stored with much reading and much keen observation of real life.*"—SATURDAY REVIEW.

THOUGHTS ABOUT ART. New Edition, revised, with an Introduction. Crown 8vo. 8s. 6d.
"*A manual of sound and thorough criticism on art.*"—STANDARD.

Hill.—THE RECORDER OF BIRMINGHAM. A Memoir of Matthew Davenport Hill, with Selections from his Correspondence. By his Daughters ROSAMOND and FLORENCE DAVENPORT-HILL. With Portrait engraved by C. H. JEENS. 8vo. 16s.

Hill.—WHAT WE SAW IN AUSTRALIA. By ROSAMOND and FLORENCE HILL. Crown 8vo. 10s. 6d.
"*May be recommended as an interesting and truthful picture of the condition of those lands which are so distant and yet so much like home.*"—SATURDAY REVIEW.

Hodgson.—MEMOIR OF REV. FRANCIS HODGSON, B.D., Scholar, Poet, and Divine. By his Son, the Rev. JAMES T. HODGSON, M.A. Containing numerous Letters from Lord Byron and others. With Portrait engraved by JEENS. Two Vols. Crown 8vo. 18s.

"*A book that has added so much of a healthy nature to our knowledge of Byron, and that contains so rich a store of delightful correspondence.*"—ATHENÆUM.

Hole.—A GENEALOGICAL STEMMA OF THE KINGS OF ENGLAND AND FRANCE. By the Rev. C. HOLE, M.A., Trinity College, Cambridge. On Sheet, 1s.

A BRIEF BIOGRAPHICAL DICTIONARY. Compiled and Arranged by the Rev. CHARLES HOLE, M.A. Second Edition. 18mo. 4s. 6d.

Hooker and Ball.—MAROCCO AND THE GREAT ATLAS: Journal of a Tour in. By Sir JOSEPH D. HOOKER, K.C.S.I., C.B., F.R.S., &c., and JOHN BALL, F.R.S. With an Appendix, including a Sketch of the Geology of Marocco, by G. MAW, F.L.S., F.G.S. With Illustrations and Map. 8vo. 21s.

Hozier (H. M.)—Works by CAPTAIN HENRY M. HOZIER, late Assistant Military Secretary to Lord Napier of Magdala :—

THE SEVEN WEEKS' WAR; Its Antecedents and Incidents. *New and Cheaper Edition.* With New Preface, Maps, and Plans. Crown 8vo. 6s.

"*All that Mr. Hozier saw of the great events of the war—and he saw a large share of them—he describes in clear and vivid language.*"—SATURDAY REVIEW.

THE INVASIONS OF ENGLAND : a History of the Past, with Lessons for the Future. Two Vols. 8vo. 28s.

The PALL MALL GAZETTE says :—"*As to all invasions executed, or deliberately projected but not carried out, from the landing of Julius Cæsar to the raising of the Boulogne camp, Captain Hozier furnishes copious and most interesting particulars.*"

Hübner.—A RAMBLE ROUND THE WORLD IN 1871. By M. LE BARON HÜBNER, formerly Ambassador and Minister. Translated by LADY HERBERT. New and Cheaper Edition. With numerous Illustrations. Crown 8vo. 6s.

"*It is difficult to do ample justice to this pleasant narrative of travel . . . . it does not contain a single dull paragraph.*"—MORNING POST.

Hughes.—Works by THOMAS HUGHES, Q.C., Author of "Tom Brown's School Days."

ALFRED THE GREAT. New Edition. Crown 8vo. 6s.

HISTORY, BIOGRAPHY, TRAVELS, ETC.   15

Hughes.—*continued.*

MEMOIR OF A BROTHER. With Portrait of GEORGE HUGHES, after WATTS. Engraved by JEENS. Crown 8vo. 5s. Sixth Edition.

"*The boy who can read this book without deriving from it some additional impulse towards honourable, manly, and independent conduct, has no good stuff in him.*"—DAILY NEWS.

Hunt.—HISTORY OF ITALY. By the Rev. W. HUNT, M.A. Being the Fourth Volume of the Historical Course for Schools. Edited by EDWARD A. FREEMAN, D.C.L. 18mo. 3s.

"*Mr. Hunt gives us a most compact but very readable little book, containing in small compass a very complete outline of a complicated and perplexing subject. It is a book which may be safely recommended to others besides schoolboys.*"—JOHN BULL.

Irving.—THE ANNALS OF OUR TIME. A Diurnal of Events, Social and Political, Home and Foreign, from the Accession of Queen Victoria to the Peace of Versailles. By JOSEPH IRVING. *Fourth Edition.* 8vo. half-bound. 16s.

ANNALS OF OUR TIME. Supplement. From Feb. 28, 1871, to March 19, 1874. 8vo. 4s. 6d.

ANNALS OF OUR TIME. Second Supplement. From March, 1874, to the Occupation of Cyprus. 8vo. 4s. 6d.

"*We have before us a trusty and ready guide to the events of the past thirty years, available equally for the statesman, the politician, the public writer, and the general reader.*"—TIMES.

James.—Works by HENRY JAMES, Jun. FRENCH POETS AND NOVELISTS. Crown 8vo. 8s. 6d.

CONTENTS :—*Alfred de Musset; Théophile Gautier; Baudelaire; Honoré de Balzac; George Sand; The Two Ampères; Turgenieff, &c.*

Johnson's Lives of the Poets.—The Six Chief Lives—Milton, Dryden, Swift, Addison, Pope, Gray. With Macaulay's "Life of Johnson." Edited, with Preface, by MATTHEW ARNOLD. Crown 8vo. 6s.

Killen.—ECCLESIASTICAL HISTORY OF IRELAND, from the Earliest Date to the Present Time. By W. D. KILLEN, D.D., President of Assembly's College, Belfast, and Professor of Ecclesiastical History. Two Vols. 8vo. 25s.

"*Those who have the leisure will do well to read these two volumes. They are full of interest, and are the result of great research. . . . We have no hesitation in recommending the work to all who wish to improve their acquaintance with Irish history.*"—SPECTATOR.

16   *MACMILLAN'S CATALOGUE OF WORKS IN*

Kingsley (Charles).—Works by the Rev. CHARLES KINGSLEY, M.A., Rector of Eversley and Canon of Westminster. (For other Works by the same Author, *see* THEOLOGICAL and BELLES LETTRES Catalogues.)

ON THE ANCIEN RÉGIME as it existed on the Continent before the FRENCH REVOLUTION. Three Lectures delivered at the Royal Institution. Crown 8vo. 6s.

AT LAST: A CHRISTMAS in the WEST INDIES. With nearly Fifty Illustrations. Fifth Edition. Crown 8vo. 6s.
Mr. Kingsley's dream of forty years was at last fulfilled, when he started on a Christmas expedition to the West Indies, for the purpose of becoming personally acquainted with the scenes which he has so vividly described in " Westward Ho!" These two volumes are the journal of his voyage. Records of natural history, sketches of tropical landscape, chapters on education, views of society, all find their place. " We can only say that Mr. Kingsley's account of a 'Christmas in the West Indies' is in every way worthy to be classed among his happiest productions."—STANDARD.

THE ROMAN AND THE TEUTON. A Series of Lectures delivered before the University of Cambridge. New and Cheaper Edition, with Preface by Professor MAX MÜLLER. Crown 8vo. 6s.

PLAYS AND PURITANS, and other Historical Essays. With Portrait of Sir WALTER RALEIGH. New Edition. Crown 8vo. 6s.
In addition to the Essay mentioned in the title, this volume contains other two—one on " Sir Walter Raleigh and his Time," and one on Froude's " History of England."

Kingsley (Henry).—TALES OF OLD TRAVEL. Re-narrated by HENRY KINGSLEY, F.R.G.S. With *Eight Illustrations* by HUARD. Fifth Edition. Crown 8vo. 5s.
" We know no better book for those who want knowledge or seek to refresh it. As for the 'sensational,' most novels are tame compared with these narratives."—ATHENÆUM.

Lang.—CYPRUS: Its History, its Present Resources and Future Prospects. By R. HAMILTON LANG, late H.M. Consul for the Island of Cyprus. With Two Illustrations and Four Maps. 8vo. 14s.
" The fair and impartial account of her past and present to be found in these pages has an undoubted claim on the attention of all intelligent readers."—MORNING POST.

Laocoon.—Translated from the Text of Lessing, with Preface and Notes by the Right Hon. SIR ROBERT J. PHILLIMORE, D.C.L. With Photographs. 8vo. 12s.

HISTORY, BIOGRAPHY, TRAVELS, ETC. 17

Leonardo da Vinci and his Works.—Consisting of a Life of Leonardo Da Vinci, by MRS. CHARLES W. HEATON, Author of "Albrecht Dürer of Nürnberg," &c., an Essay on his Scientific and Literary Works by CHARLES CHRISTOPHER BLACK, M.A., and an account of his more important Paintings and Drawings. Illustrated with Permanent Photographs. Royal 8vo, cloth, extra gilt. 31s. 6d.

"*A beautiful volume, both without and within. Messrs. Macmillan are conspicuous among publishers for the choice binding and printing of their books, and this is got up in their best style. . . . No English publication that we know of has so thoroughly and attractively collected together all that is known of Leonardo.*"—TIMES.

Liechtenstein.—HOLLAND HOUSE. By Princess MARIE LIECHTENSTEIN. With Five Steel Engravings by C. H. JEENS, after Paintings by WATTS and other celebrated Artists, and numerous Illustrations drawn by Professor P. H. DELAMOTTE, and engraved on Wood by J. D. COOPER, W. PALMER, and JEWITT & Co. Third and Cheaper Edition. Medium 8vo. cloth elegant. 16s.

Also, an Edition containing, in addition to the above, about 40 Illustrations by the Woodbury-type process, and India Proofs of the Steel Engravings. Two vols. medium 4to. half morocco elegant. 4l. 4s.

"*When every strictly just exception shall have been taken, she may be conscientiously congratulated by the most scrupulous critic on the production of a useful, agreeable, beautifully-illustrated, and attractive book.*"—TIMES. "*It would take up more room than we can spare to enumerate all the interesting suggestions and notes which are to be found in these volumes. . . . . The woodcuts are admirable, and some of the autographs are very interesting.*"—PALL MALL GAZETTE.

Lloyd.—THE AGE OF PERICLES. A History of the Arts and Politics of Greece from the Persian to the Peloponnesian War. By W. WATKISS LLOYD. Two Vols. 8vo. 21s.

"*No such account of Greek art of the best period has yet been brought together in an English work. . . . Mr. Lloyd has produced a book of unusual excellence and interest.*"—PALL MALL GAZETTE.

Macarthur.—HISTORY OF SCOTLAND, By MARGARET MACARTHUR. Being the Third Volume of the Historical Course for Schools, Edited by EDWARD A. FREEMAN, D.C.L. Second Edition. 18mo. 2s.

"*It is an excellent summary, unimpeachable as to facts, and putting them in the clearest and most impartial light attainable.*"—GUARDIAN.
"*No previous History of Scotland of the same bulk is anything like so trustworthy, or deserves to be so extensively used as a text-book.*"—GLOBE.

B

18 MACMILLAN'S CATALOGUE OF WORKS IN

Macmillan (Rev. Hugh).—For other Works by same Author, see THEOLOGICAL and SCIENTIFIC CATALOGUES.

HOLIDAYS ON HIGH LANDS; or, Rambles and Incidents in search of Alpine Plants. Second Edition, revised and enlarged. Globe 8vo. cloth. 6s.

"*Botanical knowledge is blended with a love of nature, a pious enthusiasm, and a rich felicity of diction not to be met with in any works of kindred character, if we except those of Hugh Miller.*"—TELEGRAPH.
"*Mr. Macmillan's glowing pictures of Scandinavian scenery.*"—SATURDAY REVIEW.

Macready.—MACREADY'S REMINISCENCES AND SELECTIONS FROM HIS DIARIES AND LETTERS. Edited by Sir F. POLLOCK, Bart., one of his Executors. With Four Portraits engraved by JEENS. New and Cheaper Edition. Crown 8vo. 7s. 6d.

"*As a careful and for the most part just estimate of the stage during a very brilliant period, the attraction of these volumes can scarcely be surpassed. . . . . Readers who have no special interest in theatrical matters, but enjoy miscellaneous gossip, will be allured from page to page, attracted by famil'ar names and by observations upon popular actors and authors.*"—SPECTATOR.

Mahaffy.—Works by the Rev. J. P. MAHAFFY, M.A., Fellow of Trinity College, Dublin :—

SOCIAL LIFE IN GREECE FROM HOMER TO MENANDER. Third Edition, revised and enlarged, with a new chapter on Greek Art. Crown 8vo. 9s.

"*It should be in the hands of all who desire thoroughly to understand and to enjoy Greek literature, and to get an intelligent idea of the old Greek life, political, social, and religious.*"—GUARDIAN.

RAMBLES AND STUDIES IN GREECE. With Illustrations. Crown 8vo. 10s. 6d. New and enlarged Edition, with Map and Illustrations

"*A singularly instructive and agreeable volume.*"—ATHENÆUM.

"Maori."—SPORT AND WORK ON THE NEPAUL FRONTIER; or, Twelve Years' Sporting Reminiscences of an Indigo Planter. By "MAORI." With Illustrations. 8vo. 14s.

Margary.—THE JOURNEY OF AUGUSTUS RAYMOND MARGARY FROM SHANGHAE TO BHAMO AND BACK TO MANWYNE. From his Journals and Letters, with a brief Biographical Preface, a concluding chapter by Sir RUTHERFORD ALCOCK, K.C.B., and a Steel Portrait engraved by JEENS, and Map. 8vo. 10s. 6d.

"*There is a manliness, a cheerful spirit, an inherent vigour which was never overcome by sickness or debility, a tact which conquered the*

HISTORY, BIOGRAPHY, TRAVELS, ETC. 19

prejudices of a strange and suspicious population, a quiet self-reliance, always combined with deep religious feeling, unalloyed by either priggishness, cant, or superstition, that ought to commend this volume to readers sitting quietly at home who feel any pride in the high estimation accorded to men of their race at Yarkand or at Khiva, in the heart of Africa, or on the shores of Lake Seri-kul."—SATURDAY REVIEW.

Markham.—NORTHWARD HO! By Captain ALBERT H. MARKHAM, R.N., Author of "The Great Frozen Sea," &c. Including a Narrative of Captain Phipps's Expedition, by a Midshipman. With Illustrations. Crown 8vo. 10s. 6d.

Martin.—THE HISTORY OF LLOYD'S, AND OF MARINE INSURANCE IN GREAT BRITAIN. With an Appendix containing Statistics relating to Marine Insurance. By FREDERICK MARTIN, Author of "The Statesman's Year Book." 8vo. 14s.

Martineau.—BIOGRAPHICAL SKETCHES, 1852—1875. By HARRIET MARTINEAU. With Additional Sketches, and Autobiographical Sketch. Fifth Edition. Crown 8vo. 6s.
"*Miss Martineau's large literary powers and her fine intellectual training make these little sketches more instructive, and constitute them more genuinely works of art, than many more ambitious and diffuse biographies.*"—FORTNIGHTLY REVIEW.

Masson (David).—For other Works by same Author, *see* PHILOSOPHICAL and BELLES LETTRES CATALOGUES.

CHATTERTON: A Story of the Year 1770. By DAVID MASSON, LL.D., Professor of Rhetoric and English Literature in the University of Edinburgh. Crown 8vo. 5s.

THE THREE DEVILS: Luther's, Goethe's, and Milton's; and other Essays. Crown 8vo. 5s.

WORDSWORTH, SHELLEY, AND KEATS; and other Essays. Crown 8vo. 5s.

Mathews.—LIFE OF CHARLES J. MATHEWS, Chiefly Autobiographical. With Selections from his Correspondence and Speeches. Edited by CHARLES DICKENS.
"*The book is a charming one from first to last, and Mr. Dickens deserves a full measure of credit for the care and discrimination he has exercised in the business of editing.*"—GLOBE.

Maurice.—THE FRIENDSHIP OF BOOKS; AND OTHER LECTURES. By the REV. F. D. MAURICE. Edited with Preface, by THOMAS HUGHES, Q.C. Crown 8vo. 10s. 6d.
"*The high, pure, sympathetic, and truly charitable nature of Mr. Maurice is delightfully visible throughout these lectures, which are excellently adapted to spread a love of literature amongst the people.*"—DAILY NEWS.

Mayor (J. E. B.)—WORKS edited by JOHN E. B. MAYOR, M.A., Kennedy Professor of Latin at Cambridge :—
CAMBRIDGE IN THE SEVENTEENTH CENTURY. Part II. Autobiography of Matthew Robinson. Fcap. 8vo. 5s. 6d.
LIFE OF BISHOP BEDELL. By his SON. Fcap. 8vo. 3s. 6d.

Melbourne.—MEMOIRS OF THE RT. HON. WILLIAM, SECOND VISCOUNT MELBOURNE. By W. M. TORRENS, M.P. With Portrait after Sir. T. Lawrence. Second Edition. 2 Vols. 8vo. 32s.

"*As might be expected, he has produced a book which will command and reward attention. It contains a great deal of valuable matter and a great deal of animated, elegant writing.*"—QUARTERLY REVIEW.

Mendelssohn.—LETTERS AND RECOLLECTIONS. By FERDINAND HILLER. Translated by M. E. VON GLEHN. With Portrait from a Drawing by KARL MÜLLER, never before published. Second Edition. Crown 8vo. 7s. 6d.

"*This is a very interesting addition to our knowledge of the great German composer. It reveals him to us under a new light, as the warm-hearted comrade, the musician whose soul was in his work, and the home-loving, domestic man.*"—STANDARD.

Merewether.—BY SEA AND BY LAND. Being a Trip through Egypt, India, Ceylon, Australia, New Zealand, and America—all Round the World. By HENRY ALWORTH MEREWETHER, one of Her Majesty's Counsel. Crown 8vo. 8s. 6d.

Michael Angelo Buonarotti; Sculptor, Painter, Architect. The Story of his Life and Labours. By C. C. BLACK, M.A. Illustrated by 20 Permanent Photographs. Royal 8vo. cloth elegant, 31s. 6d.

"*The story of Michael Angelo's life remains interesting whatever be the manner of telling it, and supported as it is by this beautiful series of photographs, the volume must take rank among the most splendid of Christmas books, fitted to serve and to outlive the season.*"—PALL MALL GAZETTE.

Michelet.—A SUMMARY OF MODERN HISTORY. Translated from the French of M. MICHELET, and continued to the present time by M. C. M. SIMPSON. Globe 8vo. 4s. 6d.

Milton.—LIFE OF JOHN MILTON. Narrated in connection with the Political, Ecclesiastical, and Literary History of his Time. By DAVID MASSON, M.A., LL.D., Professor of Rhetoric and English Literature in the University of Edinburgh. With Portraits. Vol. I. 18s. Vol. II., 1638—1643. 8vo. 16s. Vol. III. 1643—1649. 8vo. 18s. Vols. IV. and V. 1649—1660. 32s. Vol. VI. in the press.

This work is not only a Biography, but also a continuous Political, Ecclesiastical, and Literary History of England through Milton's whole time.

HISTORY, BIOGRAPHY, TRAVELS, ETC. 21

Mitford (A. B.)—TALES OF OLD JAPAN. By A. B. MITFORD, Second Secretary to the British Legation in Japan. With upwards of 30 Illustrations, drawn and cut on Wood by Japanese Artists. New and Cheaper Edition. Crown 8vo. 6s.

"*These very original volumes will always be interesting as memorials of a most exceptional society, while regarded simply as tales, they are sparkling, sensational, and dramatic, and the originality of their idea and the quaintness of their language give them a most captivating piquancy. The illustrations are extremely interesting, and for the curious in such matters have a special and particular value.*"—PALL MALL GAZETTE.

Monteiro.—ANGOLA AND THE RIVER CONGO. By JOACHIM MONTEIRO. With numerous Illustrations from Sketches taken on the spot, and a Map. Two Vols. crown 8vo. 21s.

"*Gives the first detailed account of a part of tropical Africa which is little known to Englishmen. . . . The remarks on the geography and zoology of the country and the manners and customs of the various races inhabiting it, are extremely curious and interesting.*"—SATURDAY REVIEW. "*Full of valuable information and much picturesque description.*" PALL MALL GAZETTE.

Morison.—THE LIFE AND TIMES OF SAINT BERNARD, Abbot of Clairvaux. By JAMES COTTER MORISON, M.A. New Edition. Crown 8vo. 6s.

Moseley.—NOTES BY A NATURALIST ON THE *CHALLENGER*: being an Account of various Observations made during the Voyage of H.M.S. *Challenger*, Round the World, in 1872-76. By H. N. MOSELEY, F.R.S., Member of the Scientific Staff of the *Challenger*. 8vo. with Maps, Coloured Plates, and Woodcuts. 21s.

Murray.—ROUND ABOUT FRANCE. By E. C. GRENVILLE MURRAY. Crown 8vo. 7s. 6d.

"*These short essays are a perfect mine of information as to the present condition and future prospects of political parties in France. . . . It is at once extremely interesting and exceptionally instructive on a subject on which few English people are well informed.*"—SCOTSMAN.

Napier.—MACVEY NAPIER'S SELECTED CORRESPONDENCE. Edited by his Son, MACVEY NAPIER. 8vo. 14s.

"*This exceedingly interesting work. . . . Mr. Napier has certainly been well advised in admitting the general public to the knowledge of a volume which is hardly to be surpassed in point of interest among recent publications.*"—EXAMINER.

22 MACMILLAN'S CATALOGUE OF WORKS IN

Napoleon.—THE HISTORY OF NAPOLEON I. By P.
LANFREY. A Translation with the sanction of the Author. Vols.
I. II. and III. 8vo. price 12s. each. [*Vol. IV. in the press.*
The PALL MALL GAZETTE *says it is "one of the most striking pieces of historical composition of which France has to boast," and the* SATURDAY REVIEW *calls it "an excellent translation of a work on every ground deserving to be translated. It is unquestionably and immeasurably the best that has been produced. It is in fact the only work to which we can turn for an accurate and trustworthy narrative of that extraordinary career. . . . The book is the best and indeed the only trustworthy history of Napoleon which has been written."*

Nichol.—TABLES OF EUROPEAN LITERATURE AND HISTORY, A.D. 200—1876. By J. NICHOL, LL.D., Professor of English Language and Literature, Glasgow. 4to. 6s. 6d.
TABLES OF ANCIENT LITERATURE AND HISTORY, B.C. 1500—A.D. 200. By the same Author. 4to. 4s. 6d.

Oliphant (Mrs.).—THE MAKERS OF FLORENCE: Dante Giotto, Savonarola, and their City. By Mrs. OLIPHANT. With numerous Illustrations from drawings by Professor DELAMOTTE, and portrait of Savonarola, engraved by JEENS. Second Edition. Medium 8vo. Cloth extra. 21s.
"*Mrs. Oliphant has made a beautiful addition to the mass of literature already piled round the records of the Tuscan capital.*"—TIMES.
"*We are grateful to Mrs. Oliphant for her eloquent and beautiful sketches of Dante, Fra Angelico, and Savonarola. They are picturesque, full of life, and rich in detail, and they are charmingly illustrated by the art of the engraver.*"—SPECTATOR.

Oliphant.—THE DUKE AND THE SCHOLAR; and other Essays. By T. L. KINGTON OLIPHANT. 8vo. 7s. 6d.
"*This volume contains one of the most beautiful biographical essays we have seen since Macaulay's days.*"—STANDARD.

Otte.—SCANDINAVIAN HISTORY. By E. C. OTTÉ. With Maps. Extra fcap. 8vo. 6s.
"*We have peculiar pleasure in recommending this intelligent résumé of Northern history as a book essential to every Englishman who interests himself in Scandinavia.*"—SPECTATOR.

Owens College Essays and Addresses.—By PROFESSORS AND LECTURERS OF OWENS COLLEGE, MANCHESTER. Published in Commemoration of the Opening of the New College Buildings, October 7th, 1873. 8vo. 14s.

Palgrave (R. F. D.)—THE HOUSE OF COMMONS; Illustrations of its History and Practice. By REGINALD F. D. PALGRAVE, Clerk Assistant of the House of Commons. New and Revised Edition. Crown 8vo. 2s. 6d.

Palgrave (Sir F.)—HISTORY OF NORMANDY AND OF ENGLAND. By Sir FRANCIS PALGRAVE, Deputy Keeper of Her Majesty's Public Records. Completing the History to the Death of William Rufus. 4 Vols. 8vo. 4*l*. 4*s*.

Palgrave (W. G.)—A NARRATIVE OF A YEAR'S JOURNEY THROUGH CENTRAL AND EASTERN ARABIA, 1862-3. By WILLIAM GIFFORD PALGRAVE, late of the Eighth Regiment Bombay N. I. Sixth Edition. With Maps, Plans, and Portrait of Author, engraved on steel by Jeens. Crown 8vo. 6*s*.

"*He has not only written one of the best books on the Arabs and one of the best books on Arabia, but he has done so in a manner that must command the respect no less than the admiration of his fellow-countrymen.*"—FORTNIGHTLY REVIEW.

ESSAYS ON EASTERN QUESTIONS. By W. GIFFORD PALGRAVE. 8vo. 10*s*. 6*d*.

"*These essays are full of anecdote and interest. The book is decidedly a valuable addition to the stock of literature on which men must base their opinion of the difficult social and political problems suggested by the designs of Russia, the capacity of Mahometans for sovereignty, and the good government and retention of India.*"—SATURDAY REVIEW.

DUTCH GUIANA. With Maps and Plans. 8vo. 9*s*.

"*His pages are nearly exhaustive as far as facts and statistics go, while they are lightened by graphic social sketches as well as sparkling descriptions of scenery.*"—SATURDAY REVIEW.

Patteson.—LIFE AND LETTERS OF JOHN COLERIDGE PATTESON, D.D., Missionary Bishop of the Melanesian Islands. By CHARLOTTE M. YONGE, Author of "The Heir of Redclyffe." With Portraits after RICHMOND and from Photograph, engraved by JEENS. With Map. Fifth Edition. Two Vols. Crown 8vo. 12*s*.

"*Miss Yonge's work is in one respect a model biography. It is made up almost entirely of Patteson's own letters. Aware that he had left his home once and for all, his correspondence took the form of a diary, and as we read on we come to know the man, and to love him almost as if we had seen him.*"—ATHENÆUM. "*Such a life, with its grand lessons of unselfishness, is a blessing and an honour to the age in which it is lived; the biography cannot be studied without pleasure and profit, and indeed we should think little of the man who did not rise from the study of it better and wiser. Neither the Church nor the nation which produces such sons need ever despair of its future.*"—SATURDAY REVIEW.

Pauli.—PICTURES OF OLD ENGLAND. By Dr. REINHOLD PAULI. Translated, with the approval of the Author, by E. C. OTTE. Cheaper Edition. Crown 8vo. 6*s*.

Payne.—A HISTORY OF EUROPEAN COLONIES. By E. J. PAYNE, M.A. With Maps. 18mo. 4s. 6d.

The TIMES *says:—" We have seldom met with a historian capable of forming a more comprehensive, far-seeing, and unprejudiced estimate of events and peoples, and we can commend this little work as one certain to prove of the highest interest to all thoughtful readers."*

Persia.—EASTERN PERSIA. An Account of the Journeys of the Persian Boundary Commission, 1870-1-2.—Vol. I. The Geography, with Narratives by Majors ST. JOHN, LOVETT, and EUAN SMITH, and an Introduction by Major-General Sir FREDERIC GOLDSMID, C.B., K.C.S.I., British Commissioner and Arbitrator. With Maps and Illustrations.—Vol. II. The Zoology and Geology. By W. T. BLANFORD, A.R.S.M., F.R.S. With Coloured Illustrations. Two Vols. 8vo. 42s.

*"The volumes largely increase our store of information about countries with which Englishmen ought to be familiar. . . . . They throw into the shade all that hitherto has appeared in our tongue respecting the local features of Persia, its scenery, its resources, even its social condition. They contain also abundant evidence of English endurance, daring, and spirit."—*TIMES.

Prichard.—THE ADMINISTRATION OF INDIA. From 1859 to 1868. The First Ten Years of Administration under the Crown. By I. T. PRICHARD, Barrister-at-Law. Two Vols. Demy 8vo. With Map. 21s.

Raphael.—RAPHAEL OF URBINO AND HIS FATHER GIOVANNI SANTI. By J. D. PASSAVANT, formerly Director of the Museum at Frankfort. With Twenty Permanent Photographs. Royal 8vo. Handsomely bound. 31s. 6d.

The SATURDAY REVIEW *says of them, " We have seen not a few elegant specimens of Mr. Woodbury's new process, but we have seen none that equal these."*

Reynolds.—SIR JOSHUA REYNOLDS AS A PORTRAIT PAINTER. AN ESSAY. By J. CHURTON COLLINS, B.A. Balliol College, Oxford. Illustrated by a Series of Portraits of distinguished Beauties of the Court of George III.; reproduced in Autotype from Proof Impressions of the celebrated Engravings, by VALENTINE GREEN, THOMAS WATSON, F. R. SMITH, E. FISHER, and others. Folio half-morocco. £5 5s.

Rogers (James E. Thorold).—HISTORICAL GLEANINGS: A Series of Sketches. Montague, Walpole, Adam Smith, Cobbett. By Prof. ROGERS. Crown 8vo. 4s. 6d. Second Series. Wiklif, Laud, Wilkes, and Horne Tooke. Crown 8vo. 6s.

HISTORY, BIOGRAPHY, TRAVELS, ETC. 25

Routledge.—CHAPTERS IN THE HISTORY OF POPULAR PROGRESS IN ENGLAND, chiefly in Relation to the Freedom of the Press and Trial by Jury, 1660—1820. With application to later years. By J. ROUTLEDGE. 8vo. 16s.

"*The volume abounds in facts and information, almost always useful and often curious.*"—TIMES.

Rumford.—COUNT RUMFORD'S COMPLETE WORKS, with Memoir, and Notices of his Daughter. By GEORGE ELLIS. Five Vols. 8vo. 4l. 14s. 6d.

Seeley (Professor).—LECTURES AND ESSAYS. By J. R. SEELEY, M.A. Professor of Modern History in the University of Cambridge. 8vo. 10s. 6d.

CONTENTS:—*Roman Imperialism*: 1. *The Great Roman Revolution*; 2. *The Proximate Cause of the Fall of the Roman Empire*; *The Later Empire.* — *Milton's Political Opinions* — *Milton's Poetry* — *Elementary Principles in Art* — *Liberal Education in Universities* — *English in Schools* — *The Church as a Teacher of Morality* — *The Teaching of Politics: an Inaugural Lecture delivered at Cambridge.*

Shelburne.—LIFE OF WILLIAM, EARL OF SHELBURNE, AFTERWARDS FIRST MARQUIS OF LANSDOWNE. With Extracts from his Papers and Correspondence. By Lord EDMOND FITZMAURICE. In Three Vols. 8vo. Vol. I. 1737—1766, 12s. ; Vol. II. 1766—1776, 12s. ; Vol. III. 1776—1805. 16s.

"*Lord Edmond Fitzmaurice has succeeded in placing before us a wealth of new matter, which, while casting valuable and much-needed light on several obscure passages in the political history of a hundred years ago, has enabled us for the first time to form a clear and consistent idea of his ancestor.*"—SPECTATOR.

Sime.—HISTORY OF GERMANY. By JAMES SIME, M.A. 18mo. 3s. Being Vol. V. of the Historical Course for Schools Edited by EDWARD A. FREEMAN, D.C.L.

"*This is a remarkably clear and impressive History of Germany. Its great events are wisely kept as central figures, and the smaller events are carefully kept not only subordinate and subservient, but most skilfully woven into the texture of the historical tapestry presented to the eye.*"— STANDARD.

Squier.—PERU: INCIDENTS OF TRAVEL AND EX- PLORATION IN THE LAND OF THE INCAS. By E. G. SQUIER, M.A., F.S.A., late U.S. Commissioner to Peru. With 300 Illustrations. Second Edition. 8vo. 21s.

The TIMES *says*:—"*No more solid and trustworthy contribution has been made to an accurate knowledge of what are among the most wonderful ruins in the world. The work is really what its title implies. While of the greatest importance as a contribution to Peruvian archæology, it is also a thoroughly entertaining and instructive narrative of travel. Not the least important feature must be considered the numerous well executed illustrations.*"

Strangford.—EGYPTIAN SHRINES AND SYRIAN SEPULCHRES, including a Visit to Palmyra. By EMILY A. BEAUFORT (Viscountess Strangford), Author of "The Eastern Shores of the Adriatic." New Edition. Crown 8vo. 7s. 6d.

Tait.—AN ANALYSIS OF ENGLISH HISTORY, based upon Green's "Short History of the English People." By C. W. A. TAIT, M.A., Assistant Master, Clifton College. Crown 8vo. 3s. 6d.

Thomas.—THE LIFE OF JOHN THOMAS, Surgeon of the "Earl of Oxford" East Indiaman, and First Baptist Missionary to Bengal. By C. B. LEWIS, Baptist Missionary. 8vo. 10s. 6d.

Thompson.—HISTORY OF ENGLAND. By EDITH THOMPSON. Being Vol. II. of the Historical Course for Schools, Edited by EDWARD A. FREEMAN, D.C.L. New Edition, revised and enlarged, with Maps. 18mo. 2s. 6d.
"*Freedom from prejudice, simplicity of style, and accuracy of statement, are the characteristics of this volume. It is a trustworthy text-book, and likely to be generally serviceable in schools.*"—PALL MALL GAZETTE.
"*In its great accuracy and correctness of detail it stands far ahead of the general run of school manuals. Its arrangement, too, is clear, and its style simple and straightforward.*"—SATURDAY REVIEW.

Todhunter.—THE CONFLICT OF STUDIES; AND OTHER ESSAYS ON SUBJECTS CONNECTED WITH EDUCATION. By ISAAC TODHUNTER, M.A., F.R.S., late Fellow and Principal Mathematical Lecturer of St. John's College, Cambridge. 8vo. 10s. 6d.
CONTENTS:—*I. The Conflict of Studies. II. Competitive Examinations. III. Private Study of Mathematics. IV. Academical Reform. V. Elementary Geometry. VI. The Mathematical Tripos.*

Trench (Archbishop).—For other Works by the same Author, see THEOLOGICAL and BELLES LETTRES CATALOGUES, and page 30 of this Catalogue.
GUSTAVUS ADOLPHUS IN GERMANY, and other Lectures on the Thirty Years' War. Second Edition, revised and enlarged. Fcap. 8vo. 4s.
PLUTARCH, HIS LIFE, HIS LIVES, AND HIS MORALS. Five Lectures. Second Edition, enlarged. Fcap. 8vo. 3s. 6d.
LECTURES ON MEDIEVAL CHURCH HISTORY. Being the substance of Lectures delivered in Queen's College, London. Second Edition, revised. 8vo. 12s.

Trench (Maria).—THE LIFE OF ST. TERESA. By MARIA TRENCH. With Portrait engraved by JEENS. Crown 8vo, cloth extra. 8s. 6d.
"*A book of rare interest.*"—JOHN BULL.

Trench (Mrs. R.)—REMAINS OF THE LATE MRS. RICHARD TRENCH. Being Selections from her Journals, Letters, and other Papers. Edited by ARCHBISHOP TRENCH. New and Cheaper Issue, with Portrait. 8vo. 6s.

Trollope.—A HISTORY OF THE COMMONWEALTH OF FLORENCE FROM THE EARLIEST INDEPENDENCE OF THE COMMUNE TO THE FALL OF THE REPUBLIC IN 1831. By T. ADOLPHUS TROLLOPE. 4 Vols. 8vo. Half morocco. 21s.

Uppingham by the Sea.—A NARRATIVE OF THE YEAR AT BORTH. By J. H. S. Crown 8vo. 3s. 6d.

Victor Emmanuel II., First King of Italy.—HIS LIFE. By G. S. GODKIN. 2 vols., crown 8vo. 16s.
"*An extremely clear and interesting history of one of the most important changes of later times.*"—EXAMINER.

Wallace.—THE MALAY ARCHIPELAGO: the Land of the Orang Utan and the Bird of Paradise. By ALFRED RUSSEL WALLACE. A Narrative of Travel with Studies of Man and Nature. With Maps and numerous Illustrations. Sixth Edition. Crown 8vo. 7s. 6d.
"*The result is a vivid picture of tropical life, which may be read with unflagging interest, and a sufficient account of his scientific conclusions to stimulate our appetite without wearying us by detail. In short, we may safely say that we have never read a more agreeable book of its kind.*"—SATURDAY REVIEW.

Ward.—A HISTORY OF ENGLISH DRAMATIC LITERATURE TO THE DEATH OF QUEEN ANNE. By A. W. WARD, M.A., Professor of History and English Literature in Owens College, Manchester. Two Vols. 8vo. 32s.
"*As full of interest as of information. To students of dramatic literature invaluable, and may be equally recommended to readers for mere pastime.*"—PALL MALL GAZETTE.

Ward (J.)—EXPERIENCES OF A DIPLOMATIST. Being recollections of Germany founded on Diaries kept during the years 1840—1870. By JOHN WARD, C.B., late H.M. Minister-Resident to the Hanse Towns. 8vo. 10s. 6d.

Waterton (C.)—WANDERINGS IN SOUTH AMERICA, THE NORTH-WEST OF THE UNITED STATES, AND THE ANTILLES IN 1812, 1816, 1820, and 1824. With Original Instructions for the perfect Preservation of Birds, etc., for Cabinets of Natural History. By CHARLES WATERTON. New Edition, edited with Biographical Introduction and Explanatory Index by the Rev. J. G. WOOD, M.A. With 100 Illustrations. 8vo. Cloth elegant. 21s.

Wedgwood.—JOHN WESLEY AND THE EVANGELICAL REACTION of the Eighteenth Century. By JULIA WEDGWOOD. Crown 8vo. 8s. 6d.

Whewell.—WILLIAM WHEWELL, D.D., late Master of Trinity College, Cambridge. An Account of his Writings, with Selections from his Literary and Scientific Correspondence. By I. TODHUNTER, M.A., F.R.S. Two Vols. 8vo. 25s.

White.—THE NATURAL HISTORY AND ANTIQUITIES OF SELBORNE. By GILBERT WHITE. Edited, with Memoir and Notes, by FRANK BUCKLAND, A Chapter on Antiquities by LORD SELBORNE, Map, &c., and numerous Illustrations by P. H. DELAMOTTE. Royal 8vo. Cloth, extra gilt. Cheaper Issue. 21s.

Also a Large Paper Edition, containing, in addition to the above, upwards of Thirty Woodburytype Illustrations from Drawings by Prof. DELAMOTTE. Two Vols. 4to. Half morocco, elegant. 4l. 4s.

"*Mr. Delamotte's charming illustrations are a worthy decoration of so dainty a book. They bring Selborne before us, and really help us to understand why White's love for his native place never grew cold.*"—TIMES.

Wilson.—A MEMOIR OF GEORGE WILSON, M.D., F.R.S.E., Regius Professor of Technology in the University of Edinburgh. By his SISTER. New Edition. Crown 8vo. 6s.

Wilson (Daniel, LL.D.)—Works by DANIEL WILSON, LL.D., Professor of History and English Literature in University College, Toronto :—

PREHISTORIC ANNALS OF SCOTLAND. New Edition, with numerous Illustrations. Two Vols. demy 8vo. 36s.

"*One of the most interesting, learned, and elegant works we have seen for a long time.*"—WESTMINSTER REVIEW.

PREHISTORIC MAN : Researches into the Origin of Civilization in the Old and New World. New Edition, revised and enlarged throughout, with numerous Illustrations and two Coloured Plates. Two Vols. 8vo. 36s.

"*A valuable work pleasantly written and well worthy of attention both by students and general readers.*"—ACADEMY.

CHATTERTON : A Biographical Study. By DANIEL WILSON, LL.D., Professor of History and English Literature in University College, Toronto. Crown 8vo. 6s. 6d.

HISTORY, BIOGRAPHY, TRAVELS, ETC.

Wyatt (Sir M. Digby).—FINE ART: a Sketch of its History, Theory, Practice, and application to Industry. A Course of Lectures delivered before the University of Cambridge. By Sir M. DIGBY WYATT, M.A. Slade Professor of Fine Art. Cheaper Issue. 8vo. 5s.

"*An excellent handbook for the student of art.*"—GRAPHIC. "*The book abounds in valuable matter, and will therefore be read with pleasure and profit by lovers of art.*"—DAILY NEWS.

Yonge (Charlotte M.)—Works by CHARLOTTE M. YONGE, Author of "The Heir of Redclyffe," &c., &c. :—

A PARALLEL HISTORY OF FRANCE AND ENGLAND: consisting of Outlines and Dates. Oblong 4to. 3s. 6d.

CAMEOS FROM ENGLISH HISTORY. From Rollo to Edward II. Extra fcap. 8vo. Third Edition. 5s.

SECOND SERIES, THE WARS IN FRANCE. Extra fcap. 8vo. Third Edition. 5s.

THIRD SERIES, THE WARS OF THE ROSES. Extra fcap. 8vo. 5s.

"*Instead of dry details,*" says the NONCONFORMIST, "*we have living pictures, faithful, vivid, and striking.*"

FOURTH SERIES. [*Nearly ready.*

HISTORY OF FRANCE. Maps. 18mo. 3s. 6d.
[*Historical Course for Schools.*

POLITICS, POLITICAL AND SOCIAL ECONOMY, LAW, AND KINDRED SUBJECTS.

Anglo-Saxon Law.—ESSAYS IN. Contents: Law Courts—Land and Family Laws and Legal Procedure generally. With Select cases. Medium 8vo. 18s.

Arnold.—THE ROMAN SYSTEM OF PROVINCIAL ADMINISTRATION TO THE ACCESSION OF CONSTANTINE THE GREAT. Being the Arnold Prize Essay for 1879. By W. T. Arnold, B.A. Crown 8vo. 6s.

Ball.—THE STUDENT'S GUIDE TO THE BAR. By WALTER W. BALL, M.A., of the Inner Temple, Barrister-at-Law. Crown 8vo. 2s. 6d.
"*The student will here find a clear statement of the several steps by which the degree of barrister is obtained, and also useful advice about the advantages of a prolonged course of 'reading. in Chambers.'*"—ACADEMY.

Bernard.—FOUR LECTURES ON SUBJECTS CONNECTED WITH DIPLOMACY. By MONTAGUE BERNARD, M.A., Chichele Professor of International Law and Diplomacy, Oxford. 8vo. 9s.
"*Singularly interesting lectures, so able, clear, and attractive.*"—SPECTATOR.

Bright (John, M.P.)—Works by the Right Hon. JOHN BRIGHT, M.P.
SPEECHES ON QUESTIONS OF PUBLIC POLICY. Edited by Professor THOROLD ROGERS. Author's Popular Edition. Globe 8vo. 3s. 6d.
"*Mr. Bright's speeches will always deserve to be studied, as an apprenticeship to popular and parliamentary oratory; they will form materials for the history of our time, and many brilliant passages, perhaps some entire speeches, will really become a part of the living literature of England.*"—DAILY NEWS.
LIBRARY EDITION. Two Vols. 8vo. With Portrait. 25s.
PUBLIC ADDRESSES. Edited by J. THOROLD ROGERS. 8vo. 14s.

Bucknill.—HABITUAL DRUNKENNESS AND INSANE DRUNKARDS. By J. C. BUCKNILL, M.D., F.R.S., late Lord Chancellor's Visitor of Lunatics. Crown 8vo. 2s. 6d.

WORKS IN POLITICS, ETC. 31

Cairnes.—Works by J. E. CAIRNES, M.A., Emeritus Professor of Political Economy in University College, London.

ESSAYS IN POLITICAL ECONOMY, THEORETICAL and APPLIED. By J. E. CAIRNES, M.A., Professor of Political Economy in University College, London. 8vo. 10s. 6d.

POLITICAL ESSAYS. 8vo. 10s. 6d.

SOME LEADING PRINCIPLES OF POLITICAL ECONOMY NEWLY EXPOUNDED. 8vo. 14s.

CONTENTS :—*Part I. Value. Part II. Labour and Capital. Part III. International Trade.*

"*A work which is perhaps the most valuable contribution to the science made since the publication, a quarter of a century since, of Mr. Mill's 'Principles of Political Economy.'*"—DAILY NEWS.

THE CHARACTER AND LOGICAL METHOD OF POLITICAL ECONOMY. New Edition, enlarged. 8vo. 7s. 6d.

"*These lectures are admirably fitted to correct the slipshod generalizations which pass current as the science of Political Economy.*"—TIMES.

Clarke.—EARLY ROMAN LAW. THE REGAL PERIOD. By E. C. CLARKE, M.A., of Lincoln's Inn, Barrister-at-Law, Lecturer in Law and Regius Professor of Civil Law at Cambridge. Crown 8vo. 5s.

Cobden (Richard).—SPEECHES ON QUESTIONS OF PUBLIC POLICY. By RICHARD COBDEN. Edited by the Right Hon. John Bright, M.P., and J. E. Thorold Rogers. Popular Edition. 8vo. 3s. 6d.

Fawcett.—Works by HENRY FAWCETT, M.A., M.P., Fellow of Trinity Hall, and Professor of Political Economy in the University of Cambridge :—

THE ECONOMIC POSITION OF THE BRITISH LABOURER. Extra fcap. 8vo. 5s.

MANUAL OF POLITICAL ECONOMY. Fifth Edition, with New Chapters on the Depreciation of Silver, etc. Crown 8vo. 12s.

The DAILY NEWS *says:* "*It forms one of the best introductions to the principles of the science, and to its practical applications in the problems of modern, and especially of English, government and society.*"

PAUPERISM : ITS CAUSES AND REMEDIES. Crown 8vo. 5s. 6d.

The ATHENÆUM *calls the work* "*a repertory of interesting and well digested information.*"

SPEECHES ON SOME CURRENT POLITICAL QUESTIONS. 8vo. 10s. 6d.

"*They will help to educate, not perhaps, parties, but the educators of parties.*"—DAILY NEWS.

Fawcett.—*continued.*
ESSAYS ON POLITICAL AND SOCIAL SUBJECTS. By PROFESSOR FAWCETT, M.P., and MILLICENT GARRETT FAWCETT. 8vo. 10s. 6d.

"*They will all repay the perusal of the thinking reader.*"—DAILY NEWS.

FREE TRADE AND PROTECTION: an Inquiry into the Causes which have retarded the general adoption of Free Trade since its introduction into England. Third Edition. 8vo. 7s. 6d.

"*No greater service can be rendered to the cause of Free Trade than a clear explanation of the principles on which Free Trade rests. Professor Fawcett has done this in the volume before us with all his habitual clearness of thought and expression.*"—ECONOMIST.

Fawcett (Mrs.)—Works by MILLICENT GARRETT FAWCETT.
POLITICAL ECONOMY FOR BEGINNERS. WITH QUESTIONS. New Edition. 18mo. 2s. 6d.

The DAILY NEWS *calls it "clear, compact, and comprehensive;" and the* SPECTATOR *says, "Mrs. Fawcett's treatise is perfectly suited to its purpose."*

TALES IN POLITICAL ECONOMY. Crown 8vo. 3s.

"*The idea is a good one, and it is quite wonderful what a mass of economic teaching the author manages to compress into a small space... The true doctrines of International Trade, Currency, and the ratio between Production and Population, are set before us and illustrated in a masterly manner.*"—ATHENÆUM.

Freeman (E. A.), M.A., D.C.L.—COMPARATIVE POLITICS. Lectures at the Royal Institution, to which is added "The Unity of History," being the Rede Lecture delivered at Cambridge in 1872. 8vo. 14s.

"*We find in Mr. Freeman's new volume the same sound, careful, comprehensive qualities which have long ago raised him to so high a place amongst historical writers. For historical discipline, then, as well as historical information, Mr. Freeman's book is full of value.*"—PALL MALL GAZETTE.

Goschen.—REPORTS AND SPEECHES ON LOCAL TAXATION. By GEORGE J. GOSCHEN, M.P. Royal 8vo. 5s.

"*The volume contains a vast mass of information of the highest value.*" —ATHENÆUM.

Guide to the Unprotected, in Every Day Matters Relating to Property and Income. By a BANKER'S DAUGHTER. Fourth Edition, Revised. Extra fcap. 8vo. 3s. 6d.

"*Many an unprotected female will bless the head which planned and the hand which compiled this admirable little manual. . . . This book was very much wanted, and it could not have been better done.*"— MORNING STAR.

Hamilton.—MONEY AND VALUE: an Inquiry into the Means and Ends of Economic Production, with an Appendix on the Depreciation of Silver and Indian Currency. By ROWLAND HAMILTON. 8vo. 12s.

"*The subject is here dealt with in a luminous style, and by presenting it from a new point of view in connection with the nature and functions of money, a genuine service has been rendered to commercial science.*"—BRITISH QUARTERLY REVIEW.

Harwood.—DISESTABLISHMENT: a Defence of the Principle of a National Church. By GEORGE HARWOOD, M.A. 8vo. 12s.

Hill.—Works by OCTAVIA HILL :—

HOMES OF THE LONDON POOR. Extra fcap. 8vo. 3s. 6d.
"*She is clear, practical, and definite.*"—GLOBE.

OUR COMMON LAND; and other Short Essays. Extra fcap. 8vo. 3s. 6d.

CONTENTS:—*Our Common Land. District Visiting. A More Excellent Way of Charity. A Word on Good Citizenship. Open Spaces. Effectual Charity. The Future of our Commons.*

Historicus.—LETTERS ON SOME QUESTIONS OF INTERNATIONAL LAW. Reprinted from the *Times*, with considerable Additions. 8vo. 7s. 6d. Also, ADDITIONAL LETTERS. 8vo. 2s. 6d.

Holland.—THE TREATY RELATIONS OF RUSSIA AND TURKEY FROM 1774 TO 1853. A Lecture delivered at Oxford, April 1877. By T. E. HOLLAND, D.C.L., Professor of International Law and Diplomacy, Oxford. Crown 8vo. 2s.

Hughes (Thos.)—THE OLD CHURCH: WHAT SHALL WE DO WITH IT? By THOMAS HUGHES, Q.C. Crown 8vo. 6s.

Jevons.—Works by W. STANLEY JEVONS, M.A., Professor of Political Economy in University College, London. (For other Works by the same Author, *see* EDUCATIONAL and PHILOSOPHICAL CATALOGUES.)

THE COAL QUESTION: An Inquiry Concerning the Progress of the Nation, and the Probable Exhaustion of our Coal Mines. Second Edition, revised. 8vo. 10s. 6d.

Jevons.—*continued.*

THE THEORY OF POLITICAL ECONOMY. Second Edition, revised, with new Preface and Appendices. 8vo. 10s. 6d.

"*Professor Jevons has done invaluable service by courageously claiming political economy to be strictly a branch of Applied Mathematics.*" —WESTMINSTER REVIEW.

PRIMER OF POLITICAL ECONOMY. 18mo. 1s.

Laveleye.— PRIMITIVE PROPERTY. By EMILE DE LAVELEYE. Translated by G. R. L. MARRIOTT, LL.B., with an Introduction by T. E. CLIFFE LESLIE, LL.B. 8vo. 12s.

"*It is almost impossible to over-estimate the value of the well-digested knowledge which it contains; it is one of the most learned books that have been contributed to the historical department of the literature of economic science.*"—ATHENÆUM.

Leading Cases done into English. By an APPRENTICE OF LINCOLN'S INN. Third Edition. Crown 8vo. 2s. 6d.

"*Here is a rare treat for the lovers of quaint conceits, who in reading this charming little book will find enjoyment in the varied metre and graphic language in which the several tales are told, no less than in the accurate and pithy rendering of some of our most familiar 'Leading Cases.'*"—SATURDAY REVIEW.

Lubbock.—ADDRESSES, POLITICAL AND EDUCATIONAL. By Sir JOHN LUBBOCK, Bart., M.P., &c., &c. 8vo, pp. 209. 8s. 6d.

The ten speeches given are (1) on the Imperial Policy of Great Britain, (2) on the Bank Act of 1844, (3) on the Present System of Public School Education, 1876, (4) on the Present System of Elementary Education, (5) on the Income Tax, (6) on the National Debt, (7) on the Declaration of Paris, (8) on Marine Insurances, (9) on the Preservation of Ancient Monuments, and (10) on Egypt.

Macdonell.—THE LAND QUESTION, WITH SPECIAL REFERENCE TO ENGLAND AND SCOTLAND. By JOHN MACDONELL, Barrister-at-Law. 8vo. 10s. 6d.

Martin.—THE STATESMAN'S YEAR-BOOK: A Statistical and Historical Annual of the States of the Civilized World, for the year 1879. By FREDERICK MARTIN. Sixteenth Annual Publication. Revised after Official Returns. Crown 8vo. 10s. 6d.

The Statesman's Year-Book is the only work in the English language which furnishes a clear and concise account of the actual condition of all the States of Europe, the civilized countries of America, Asia, and

Africa, and the British Colonies and Dependencies in all parts of the world. The new issue of the work has been revised and corrected, on the basis of official reports received direct from the heads of the leading Governments of the world, in reply to letters sent to them by the Editor. Through the valuable assistance thus given, it has been possible to collect an amount of information, political, statistical, and commercial, of the latest date, and of unimpeachable trustworthiness, such as no publication of the same kind has ever been able to furnish. "As indispensable as Bradshaw."—TIMES.

Monahan.—THE METHOD OF LAW: an Essay on the Statement and Arrangement of the Legal Standard of Conduct. By J. H. MONAHAN, Q.C. Crown 8vo. 6s.
"Will be found valuable by careful law students who have felt the importance of gaining clear ideas regarding the relations between the parts of the complex organism they have to study."—BRITISH QUARTERLY REVIEW.

Paterson.—THE LIBERTY OF THE SUBJECT AND THE LAWS OF ENGLAND RELATING TO THE SECURITY OF THE PERSON. Commentaries on. By JAMES PATERSON, M.A., Barrister at Law, sometime Commissioner for English and Irish Fisheries, etc. Cheaper issue. Two Vols. Crown 8vo. 21s.
"Two or three hours' dipping into these volumes, not to say reading them through, will give legislators and stump orators a knowledge of the liberty of a citizen of their country, in its principles, its fulness, and its modification, such as they probably in nine cases out of ten never had before."
—SCOTSMAN.

Phillimore.—PRIVATE LAW AMONG THE ROMANS, from the Pandects. By JOHN GEORGE PHILLIMORE, Q.C. 8vo. 16s.

Rogers.—COBDEN AND POLITICAL OPINION. By J. E. THOROLD ROGERS. 8vo. 10s. 6d.
"Will be found most useful by politicians of every school, as it forms a sort of handbook to Cobden's teaching."—ATHENÆUM.

Stephen (C. E.)—THE SERVICE OF THE POOR; Being an Inquiry into the Reasons for and against the Establishment of Religious Sisterhoods for Charitable Purposes. By CAROLINE EMILIA STEPHEN. Crown 8vo. 6s. 6d.
"The ablest advocate of a better line of work in this direction that we have ever seen."—EXAMINER.

Stephen.—Works by Sir JAMES F. STEPHEN, K.C.S.I., Q.C.
A DIGEST OF THE LAW OF EVIDENCE. Third Ed with New Preface. Crown 8vo. 6s.

Stephen.—*continued.*

A DIGEST OF THE CRIMINAL LAW. (Crimes and Punishments.) 8vo. 16s.

"We feel sure that any person of ordinary intelligence who had never looked into a law-book in his life might, by a few days' careful study of this volume, obtain a more accurate understanding of the criminal law, a more perfect conception of its different bearings a more thorough and intelligent insight into its snares and pitfalls, than an ordinary practitioner can boast of after years of study of the ordinary textbooks and practical experience of the Courts unassisted by any competent guide."—SATURDAY REVIEW.

A GENERAL VIEW OF THE CRIMINAL LAW OF ENGLAND. Two Vols. Crown 8vo. [*New edition in the press.*

Stubbs.—VILLAGE POLITICS. Addresses and Sermons on the Labour Question. By C. W. STUBBS, M.A., Vicar of Granborough, Bucks. Extra fcap. 8vo. 3s. 6d.

Thornton.—Works by W. T. THORNTON, C.B., Secretary for Public Works in the India Office :—

ON LABOUR : Its Wrongful Claims and Rightful Dues ; Its Actual Present and Possible Future. Second Edition, revised, 8vo. 14s.

A PLEA FOR PEASANT PROPRIETORS : With the Outlines of a Plan for their Establishment in Ireland. New Edition, revised. Crown 8vo. 7s. 6d.

INDIAN PUBLIC WORKS AND COGNATE INDIAN TOPICS. With Map of Indian Railways. Crown 8vo. 8s. 6d.

Walker.—Works by F. A. WALKER, M.A., Ph.D., Professor of Political Economy and History, Yale College :—

THE WAGES QUESTION. A Treatise on Wages and the Wages Class. 8vo. 14s.

MONEY. 8vo. 16s.

"It is painstaking, laborious, and states the question in a clear and very intelligible form. . . . The volume possesses a great value as a sort of encyclopædia of knowledge on the subject."—ECONOMIST.

Work about the Five Dials. With an Introductory Note by THOMAS CARLYLE. Crown 8vo. 6s.

"A book which abounds with wise and practical suggestions."—PALL MALL GAZETTE.

WORKS CONNECTED WITH THE SCIENCE OR THE HISTORY OF LANGUAGE.

Abbott.—A SHAKESPERIAN GRAMMAR: An Attempt to illustrate some of the Differences between Elizabethan and Modern English. By the Rev. E. A. ABBOTT, D.D., Head Master of the City of London School. New and Enlarged Edition. Extra fcap. 8vo. 6s.

"*Valuable not only as an aid to the critical study of Shakespeare, but as tending to familiarize the reader with Elizabethan English in general.*"—ATHENÆUM.

Besant.—STUDIES IN EARLY FRENCH POETRY. By WALTER BESANT, M.A. Crown 8vo. 8s. 6d.

Breymann.—A FRENCH GRAMMAR BASED ON PHILOLOGICAL PRINCIPLES. By HERMANN BREYMANN, Ph.D., Professor of Philology in the University of Munich late Lecturer on French Language and Literature at Owens College, Manchester. Extra fcap. 8vo. 4s. 6d.

"*We dismiss the work with every feeling of satisfaction. It cannot fail to be taken into use by all schools which endeavour to make the study of French a means towards the higher culture.*"—EDUCATIONAL TIMES.

Ellis.—PRACTICAL HINTS ON THE QUANTITATIVE PRONUNCIATION OF LATIN, FOR THE USE OF CLASSICAL TEACHERS AND LINGUISTS. By A. J. ELLIS, B.A., F.R.S., &c. Extra fcap. 8vo. 4s. 6d.

Fleay.—A SHAKESPEARE MANUAL. By the Rev. F. G. FLEAY, M.A., Head Master of Skipton Grammar School. Extra fcap. 8vo. 4s. 6d.

Goodwin.—SYNTAX OF THE GREEK MOODS AND TENSES. By W. W. GOODWIN, Professor of Greek Literature in Harvard University. New Edition. Crown 8vo. 6s. 6d.

Hadley.—ESSAYS PHILOLOGICAL AND CRITICAL. Selected from the Papers of JAMES HADLEY, LL.D., Professor of Greek in Yale College, &c. 8vo. 16s.

Hales.—LONGER ENGLISH POEMS. With Notes, Philological and Explanatory, and an Introduction on the Teaching of English. Chiefly for use in Schools. Edited by J. W. HALES, M.A., Professor of English Literature at King's College, London, &c. &c. Fifth Edition. Extra fcap. 8vo. 4s. 6d.

Helfenstein (James).—A COMPARATIVE GRAMMAR OF THE TEUTONIC LANGUAGES : Being at the same time a Historical Grammar of the English Language, and comprising Gothic, Anglo-Saxon, Early English, Modern English, Icelandic (Old Norse), Danish, Swedish, Old High German, Middle High German, Modern German, Old Saxon, Old Frisian, and Dutch. By JAMES HELFENSTEIN, Ph.D. 8vo. 18s.

Masson (Gustave).—A COMPENDIOUS DICTIONARY OF THE FRENCH LANGUAGE (French-English and English-French). Followed by a List of the Principal Diverging Derivations, and preceded by Chronological and Historical Tables. By GUSTAVE MASSON, Assistant-Master and Librarian, Harrow School. Fourth Edition. Crown 8vo. Half-bound. 6s.

"*A book which any student, whatever may be the degree of his advancement in the language, would do well to have on the table close at hand while he is reading."*—SATURDAY REVIEW.

Mayor.—A BIBLIOGRAPHICAL CLUE TO LATIN LITERATURE. Edited after Dr. E. HUBNER. With large Additions by JOHN E. B. MAYOR, M.A., Professor of Latin in the University of Cambridge. Crown 8vo. 6s. 6d.

"*An extremely useful volume that should be in the hands of all scholars."*—ATHENÆUM.

Morris.—Works by the Rev. RICHARD MORRIS, LL.D., Member of the Council of the Philol. Soc., Lecturer on English Language and Literature in King's College School. Editor of "Specimens of Early English," etc., etc. :—

HISTORICAL OUTLINES OF ENGLISH ACCIDENCE, comprising Chapters on the History and Development of the Language, and on Word-formation. Sixth Edition. Fcap. 8vo. 6s.

ELEMENTARY LESSONS IN HISTORICAL ENGLISH GRAMMAR, containing Accidence and Word-formation. Third Edition. 18mo. 2s. 6d.

Oliphant.—THE OLD AND MIDDLE ENGLISH. By T. L. KINGTON OLIPHANT, M.A., of Balliol College, Oxford. A New Edition, revised and greatly enlarged, of "The Sources of Standard English." Extra fcap. 8vo. 9s.

"*Mr. Oliphant's book is, to our mind, one of the ablest and most scholarly contributions to our standard English we have seen for many years."*—SCHOOL BOARD CHRONICLE. "*The book comes nearer to a history of the English language than anything we have seen since such a history could be written, without confusion and contradictions."*—SATURDAY REVIEW.

Peile (John, M.A.)—AN INTRODUCTION TO GREEK AND LATIN ETYMOLOGY. By JOHN PEILE, M.A., Fellow and Tutor of Christ's College, Cambridge. Third and revised Edition. Crown 8vo. 10s. 6d.

"*The book may be accepted as a very valuable contribution to the science of language.*"—SATURDAY REVIEW.

Philology.—THE JOURNAL OF SACRED AND CLASSICAL PHILOLOGY. Four Vols. 8vo. 12s. 6d. each.

THE JOURNAL OF PHILOLOGY. New Series. Edited by JOHN E. B. MAYOR, M.A., and W. ALDIS WRIGHT, M.A. 4s. 6d. (Half-yearly.)

Roby (H. J.)—A GRAMMAR OF THE LATIN LANGUAGE, FROM PLAUTUS TO SUETONIUS. By HENRY JOHN ROBY, M.A., late Fellow of St. John's College, Cambridge. In Two Parts. Second Edition. Part I. containing:—Book I. Sounds. Book II. Inflexions. Book III. Word Formation. Appendices. Crown 8vo. 8s. 6d. Part II.—Syntax, Prepositions, &c. Crown 8vo. 10s. 6d.

"*The book is marked by the clear and practical insight of a master in his art. It is a book which would do honour to any country.*"—ATHENÆUM. "*Brings before the student in a methodical form the best results of modern philology bearing on the Latin language.*"—SCOTSMAN.

Schmidt.—THE RYTHMIC AND METRIC OF THE CLASSICAL LANGUAGES. To which are added, the Lyric Parts of the "Medea" of Euripides and the "Antigone" of Sophocles; with Rhythmical Scheme and Commentary. By Dr. J. H. SCHMIDT. Translated from the German by J. W. WHITE, D.D. 8vo. 10s. 6d.

Taylor.—Works by the Rev. ISAAC TAYLOR, M.A.:—

ETRUSCAN RESEARCHES. With Woodcuts. 8vo. 14s.

The TIMES *says:*—"*The learning and industry displayed in this volume deserve the most cordial recognition. The ultimate verdict of science we shall not attempt to anticipate; but we can safely say this, that it is a learned book which the unlearned can enjoy, and that in the descriptions of the tomb-builders, as well as in the marvellous coincidences and unexpected analogies brought together by the author, readers of every grade may take delight as well as philosophers and scholars.*"

WORDS AND PLACES; or, Etymological Illustrations of History, Ethnology, and Geography. By the Rev. ISAAC TAYLOR. Third Edition, revised and compressed. With Maps. Globe 8vo. 6s.

GREEKS AND GOTHS: a Study on the Runes. 8vo. 9s.

Trench.—Works by R. CHENEVIX TRENCH, D.D., Archbishop of Dublin. (For other Works by the same Author, *see* THEOLOGICAL CATALOGUE.)

SYNONYMS OF THE NEW TESTAMENT. Eighth Edition, enlarged. 8vo, cloth. 12s.

"*He is,*" *the* ATHENÆUM *says,* "*a guide in this department of knowledge to whom his readers may entrust themselves with confidence.*"

ON THE STUDY OF WORDS. Lectures Addressed (originally) to the Pupils at the Diocesan Training School, Winchester. Seventeenth Edition, enlarged. Fcap. 8vo. 5s.

ENGLISH PAST AND PRESENT. Tenth Edition, revised and improved. Fcap. 8vo. 5s.

A SELECT GLOSSARY OF ENGLISH WORDS USED FORMERLY IN SENSES DIFFERENT FROM THEIR PRESENT. Fourth Edition, enlarged. Fcap. 8vo. 4s.

Whitney.—A COMPENDIOUS GERMAN GRAMMAR. By W. D. WHITNEY, Professor of Sanskrit and Instructor in Modern Languages in Yale College. Crown 8vo. 6s.

"*After careful examination we are inclined to pronounce it the best grammar of modern language we have ever seen.*"—SCOTSMAN.

Whitney and Edgren.—A COMPENDIOUS GERMAN AND ENGLISH DICTIONARY, with Notation of Correspondences and Brief Etymologies. By Professor W. D. WHITNEY, assisted by A. H. EDGREN. Crown 8vo. 7s. 6d.

The GERMAN-ENGLISH Part may be had separately. Price 5s.

Yonge.—HISTORY OF CHRISTIAN NAMES. By CHARLOTTE M. YONGE, Author of "The Heir of Redclyffe." Cheaper Edition. Two Vols. Crown 8vo. 12s.

R. CLAY, SONS, AND TAYLOR, PRINTERS, LONDON.

www.ingramcontent.com/pod-product-compliance
Lightning Source LLC
Chambersburg PA
CBHW022138300426
44115CB00006B/241